D0151831

AFRICAN AMERICANS IN
SCIENCE, MATH, AND INVENTION

A TO Z
OF AFRICAN AMERICANS

AFRICAN AMERICANS IN SCIENCE, MATH, AND INVENTION

Ray Spangenburg and Kit Moser

Facts On File, Inc.

Note on Photos

Many of the illustrations and photographs used in this book are old, historical images. The quality of the prints is not always up to current standards, as in some cases the originals are from old or poor quality negatives or are damaged. The content of the illustrations, however, made their inclusion important despite problems in reproduction.

African Americans in Science, Math, and Invention

Copyright © 2003 by Ray Spangenburg and Kit Moser

All rights reserved. No part of this book may be reproduced or utilized in any form or by any means, electronic or mechanical, including photocopying, recording, or by any information storage or retrieval systems, without permission in writing from the publisher. For information contact:

Facts On File, Inc.
132 West 31st Street
New York NY 10001

Library of Congress Cataloging-in-Publication Data

    Spangenburg, Ray, 1939–
    African Americans in science, math, and invention / by Ray Spangenburg
      and Kit Moser.
        p. cm.
    Includes bibliographical references and indexes.
    ISBN 0-8160-4806-1
    1. African American scientists—Biography. 2. African American
    scientists—Directories. I. Moser, Diane, 1944– II. Title.
    Q141 .S6285 2003
    509.2'273—dc21   2002008763

Facts On File books are available at special discounts when purchased in bulk quantities for businesses, associations, institutions, or sales promotions. Please call our Special Sales Department in New York at (212) 967-8800 or (800) 322-8755.

You can find Facts On File on the World Wide Web at http://www.factsonfile.com

Text design by Joan M. Toro
Cover design by Nora Wertz

Printed in the United States of America

VB Hermitage 10 9 8 7 6 5 4 3 2 1

This book is printed on acid-free paper.

⁓

In appreciation of African Americans of the past and present
who have blazed trails for future generations
and have expanded human knowledge
in science, math, and invention
despite great and unjust obstacles

⁓

Contents

PRESTON RIDGE LIBRARY
COLLIN COLLEGE
FRISCO, TX 75035

LIST OF ENTRIES

Jemison, Mae Carol
Johnson, Katherine G.
Jones, Eleanor Green Dawley
Jones, Frederick McKinney
Julian, Percy Lavon
Just, Ernest Everett
King, James, Jr.
King, Reatha Belle Clark
Kittrell, Flemmie Pansy
Knox, William Jacob, Jr.
Kornegay, Wade M.
Kountz, Samuel Lee, Jr.
Langford, George Malcolm
Latimer, Lewis Howard
Lawson, James Raymond
Leevy, Carroll Moton
Leffall, LaSalle D., Jr.
Lewis, Harold Ralph
Lewis, Julian Herman
Lloyd, Ruth Smith
Logan, Joseph Granville, Jr.
Lu Valle, James Ellis
Macklin, John W.
Maloney, Arnold Hamilton

Massey, Walter Eugene
Massie, Samuel Proctor
Matzeliger, Jan
Mayes, Vivienne Lucille
    Malone
McAfee, Walter Samuel
McBay, Henry Ransom Cecil
McCoy, Elijah
McKinney, Roscoe Lewis
McNair, Ronald Erwin
Mickens, Ronald Elbert
Milligan, Dolphus Edward
Mishoe, Luna Isaac
Mitchell, James Winfield
Morgan, Garrett Augustus
Murray, Sandra
Nabrit, Samuel Milton
Okikiolu, Kathleen Adebola
Owens, Joan Murrell
Parker, John P.
Peery, Benjamin Franklin
Person, Waverly
Quarterman, Lloyd Albert
Rillieux, Norbert

Roberts, Louis Wright
Rouse, Carl Albert
Russell, Edwin Roberts
Shaw, Earl D.
Slaughter, John Brooks
Taylor, Welton Ivan
Temple, Lewis, Sr.
Tolbert, Margaret Ellen Mayo
Turner, Charles Henry
Tyson, Neil de Grasse
Walker, Arthur Bertram
    Cuthbert, II
Walker, Sarah Breedlove
    McWilliams
Washington, Warren Morton
West, Harold Dadford
Wilkins, J. Ernest, Jr.
Williams, Daniel Hale
Woods, Geraldine Pittman
Woods, Granville T.
Wright, Jane Cooke
Wright, Louis Tompkins
Young, Roger Arliner

ACKNOWLEDGMENTS

We would like to express our appreciation to the scientists, mathematicians, and inventors who helped us by reading entries for accuracy, sending material and photographs, and in some cases discussing their work by phone or e-mail. We would also like to thank the Sacramento Public Library system and its librarians for the helpful online and on-site services they provided, as well as the library at California State University at Sacramento. A big thank-you goes to Seth Pauley at Facts On File, whose encouragement and extraordinary energy helped keep things moving along. Thanks also to Laura Shauger, who ably took up the baton. And special appreciation to Nicole Bowen, our editor at Facts On File, who suggested this project and, as always, provided helpful insights along the way.

AUTHORS' NOTE

How can one possibly decide which scientists, mathematicians, and inventors to include in a biographical dictionary such as this one? We have tried to use sound criteria—but we certainly will have made some decisions that others would question. Today, there is much exciting work being done by African Americans who have taken up the batons of those who pioneered in science, mathematics, and invention.

But in this work, space is an obvious limitation. As a result, to all those whose work deserves to be included here, please accept our apologies.

In putting together our table of contents, we sought to include African Americans who have made significant contributions as scientists, mathematicians, or inventors, including:

- Recipients of honors and awards for their work, such as National Science Foundation Awards, induction into the National Inventors Hall of Fame, etc.

- Authors of respected research, scientific publications; patent holders
- Those who have achieved prominent positions as a result of achievements as scientist/mathematician/inventor, including prominent scientists and mathematicians in government
- Recognized figures in science or math education
- African-American "firsts," such as the first African American to receive a Ph.D. in physics, etc.
- Diversity: As much as possible, a balanced representation of women; geographical balance, including representatives from Canada; and balance among the disciplines
- Respected scientists who are still in midcareer

More and more talented individuals are swelling these ranks, and tomorrow, another, bigger, better book will need to be written.

INTRODUCTION

Curiosity and the quest for knowledge stand among the most priceless gifts humanity has inherited down through the ages. The human mind brims with questions and thirsts for answers. Since the earliest humans looked toward the nighttime skies and wondered about the heavens' mysteries, people have sought to know. From the bright, shimmering lights in the skies to the deep darkness that surrounded them; from the causes of rain and snow to the origins of drought; from the flowering of life to the reasons for death—people have always tried to find methods for understanding and explaining.

Arguably the most productive method ever developed by humankind is the scientist's set of tools—including the scientific method, experimentation, collection of data, analysis, and comparison. Many people see this process as a continuing accretion of knowledge carefully and systematically won, with each new piece of knowledge having an impact on what was known before.

Perhaps the purest, most abstract method for describing the world is mathematics, that ultimate tool for quantifying, using numbers and formulas to reflect the vast complexities of the universe. And the most practical and applied side of science is the product of invention, that insightful blend of creativity with the uncanny vision of an inventor and engineer.

This is a book not of questions, but of questioners, in particular those who have used the methods of science, mathematics, and invention. It is about people who love the excitement of each step progressing toward a solution, men and women who know the joy of finding an answer they can prove, the pleasure of applying discipline that produces results, and the satisfaction of attaining success in their fields.

It is also in particular about a people, men and women, whose contributions to science are little known or recognized: African-American scientists, inventors, and mathematicians. It is about people such as inventor Norbert Rillieux, who automated the process of refining sugarcane into sugar; Ernest Everett Just, who studied the development and growth of animal egg cells; Arthur Bertram Cuthbert Walker, Jr., who gained fame as a solar physicist and X-ray astronomer; mathematician Fern Hunt, who explores the complexities of chaos theory; and psychophysiologist Patricia Suzanne Cowings, who has developed a system for physiological training that helps astronauts combat space sickness.

This book is not a statistical study by any means, but out of the effort to provide a balanced representation from every generation an interesting picture begins to take shape. Only one scientist—Benjamin Banneker—emerged who was born in the 18th century, early in America's history. Banneker was surrounded by African Americans who were enslaved, although he was free. He inherited a small farm, but he did not have the benefit of formal education. In the evening hours, though, his thirsty curiosity prompted him to soak up all he could about astronomy and to publish useful almanacs that sold well. His prominence and achievement caused even the president of the United States, Thomas Jefferson, to reconsider some of his short-sighted assumptions about African-American potential.

Inventors, especially, dominated among those born in the first half of the 19th century—including Lewis Temple, Sr., and his harpoon, Norbert Rillieux and his innovations in sugar production, and Elijah McCoy and his improved oil dispersion method for railroad locomotives. In fact, all eight of those born before 1850 and profiled in this book were inventors. Because of a series of unjust laws, most were banned from holding patents on their inventions and had to sell their rights to entrepreneurs to make any money from the fruit of their own genius. Yet, invention in their time was one way to make money that was more lucrative than most, and few other options were open to a slave (before 1865) or former slave who wanted to use his or her brain gainfully.

Things began to change for those born in the 1850s. Edward Alexander Bouchet was a slave, but he was freed as a young man and became the first African American to earn a Ph.D. at Harvard University—at a time when only a handful of people in the entire country received doctorates at any university, let alone such a demanding institution. Jan Matzeliger was from Surinam, a Dutch colony in South America, and came to the United States to seek his fortune. He was a talented inventor, but he had to sell his rights (because he, too, could not hold a patent). Granville T. Woods was another inventor, and Daniel Hale Williams, who was born free, was a prominent physician, the first to perform a successful heart surgery.

For African Americans born during the Civil War or just afterward, during the carpetbagger days, being black was a huge hardship.

Many of those profiled in this book—including George Washington Carver and Madame C. J. Walker—had to overcome many challenges and had to live much of their lives by their wits.

From those born in the 1880s on, though, a new group emerges. Ernest Everett Just became a biologist, respected by his white colleagues for his substantial research. Louis Tompkins Wright became the first African-American physician to serve on the staff of a New York hospital and was an early pioneer in cancer research. Percy Lavon Julian was a research chemist who synthesized a low-cost cortisone and other synthetic drugs. It was a time when African Americans continued to face prejudice, though. Slavery was still recent in the nation's experience. Opportunities for blacks were limited. So, those who found loopholes in the system that allowed them to make substantial contributions often did not receive the credit they deserved. Just was never able to obtain the grant money that he needed for his research in the United States. The school where he taught, Howard University, did not have the level of prestige required for attracting the grant money he needed. Yet he could not obtain a position at one of the big research universities because they would not offer a faculty position to an African American. Some African-American scientists, including Rillieux and Just, grew disgusted and unhappy with this stigma, and they spent much of their time in Europe instead, where fewer people cared what color one's skin was.

The scientific fields grew more attractive in years that followed, though. Only six scientists profiled in this book were born between 1905 and 1909. That number had more than doubled 20 years later, to 14 between 1925 and 1929, and the numbers swelled to 18 prominent scientists, mathematicians, and inventors born in the five-year period 1930 to 1934.

These were years when money was scarce everywhere in the country—the years of the

Great Depression. In story after story young men and women decided that their best asset was their brain. Parents trying to scratch a living for their family from share-crop farming in the leached southern soils encouraged their sons and their daughters to get an education, use their brains, and get out of the desperate poverty they had been subjected to. Southern laws still called for segregation of public schools and most schools would not admit black students. Most of the historically black colleges and universities did not yet offer graduate programs, and some state schools offered to pay tuition and some living expenses for African-American students who would go north to study. Mentors on the faculties at those schools knew, however, that scholarships were available for promising students so, ironically, the southern laws that would not admit black students to some of the more or less mediocre all-white southern state colleges and universities ended up sending them where they could get a much better education. It was an exciting opportunity but a lonely one. Often only one black student or a small group would be studying at a northern school such as Rensselaer or the University of Chicago at one time. These future scientists and mathematicians—and also those born over the next 20 years—were the trailblazers. They are the ones who broke the color barriers, who attended classes but were often ignored or stigmatized socially. They often were sent to live in crowded conditions with African-American families off campus because blacks were not allowed in dormitories. They are the ones who began the process of blending in. They were the Rosa Parkses for the sciences. Amid all this adversity, they earned their master's degrees and their doctorates. They completed their doctoral research and defended their dissertations. They earned faculty positions or jobs in industry. They all did something special with their lives. And they prevailed for all to see.

Today, many African-American scientists hold prominent management, research, and teaching positions. Mark Dean's prominence as an inventor became firmly established when he earned three key patents on the original International Business Machines (IBM) Personal Computer chip. He sums up his view of the 21st century's opportunities for African Americans with his favorite comment, "There may be obstacles, but there are no limits." For his work with parallel computing, Philip Emeagwali was recognized by then President Bill Clinton as "one of the great minds of the Information Age." Jewell Plummer Cobb became president of California State University at Fullerton. Fitzgerald Burton Bramwell headed the University of Kentucky. Margaret E. M. Tolbert became director of the United States Department of Energy's New Brunswick Laboratory. Astrophysicist Neil de Grasse Tyson directed the Hayden Planetarium at the American Museum of Natural History in New York City. These men and women, among others, have all broken barriers to provide leadership at major institutions, taking positions that were out of reach for African Americans in the first half of the 20th century. Progress has been real though slow.

The lives of these trailblazers demonstrate what one can achieve with powerful determination, talent teamed with intelligence, and an absolute unwillingness to give up. Many of these men and women have given their dedicated support, including much time, energy, and expense to excellence in education for African-American children and young adults at every level of education. George Washington Carver began this tradition with a lifetime of mentoring—substantially helping everyone around him that he could. Many scientists, mathematicians, and inventors today have focused especially on encouraging the pursuit of math, science, and technology careers. They have given hours of time to mentoring, speaking tours, and summer seminars and after-school programs to guide the next generation in making more informed future career choices. Many also extend their support to students who form part of any group—including Hispanic students and women—that remains underrepresented in the sciences, mathematics, and invention.

By looking at the lives and works of these men and women, readers can understand more fully that science, mathematics, and invention are universal human endeavors that belong not to one nation, one race, or one gender—but to all people everywhere.

A

Alcorn, George Edward, Jr.
(1940–) *physicist, inventor*

George Edward Alcorn, Jr., has achieved distinction as an inventor, administrator, and teacher. Recognized for invention of several patented and commonly used semiconductor devices, he was named Inventor of the Year in 1984 by the National Aeronautics and Space Administration (NASA) and NASA's Goddard Space Flight Center (GSFC) for his invention of an improved imaging X-ray spectrometer and methods for producing it.

George Edward Alcorn, Jr., was born on March 22, 1940, just after the Great Depression and less than two years before the United States entered World War II. He was one of two sons born to George Alcorn, Sr., and Arletta Dixon Alcorn. George Sr. was a car mechanic and was keenly aware of the difference a good education would make for the two boys. He made many sacrifices to pave the way for George and his younger brother, Charles, to achieve that dream—a dream that was realized by both sons. Charles would later become a research physicist.

On graduation from high school, George E. Alcorn received a four-year scholarship to Occidental College in Los Angeles. There, while earning eight letters in football and baseball, he obtained a B.A. in physics with honors, which

he received in 1962. The following year, he completed a master's degree in nuclear physics at Howard University. During the intervening summers, he worked for North American Rockwell in the space division calculating trajectories and orbital mechanics for rockets and missiles, including the *Titan I* and *II*, *Saturn IV* (for the Apollo space program), and the *Nova*. He obtained a NASA grant to fund his research on negative ion formation from 1965 to 1967, and he completed his Ph.D. in atomic and molecular physics at Howard University in 1967. In 1969, he married Marie DaVillier, and they have one son, who was born in 1979.

During the 12 years following the completion of his studies, Alcorn worked for Philco-Ford, Perker-Elmer, and IBM. In 1973, he was selected to teach at Howard University as IBM Visiting Professor in Electrical Engineering. Alcorn has also taught electrical engineering as a full professor at the University of the District of Columbia.

Alcorn joined NASA in 1978, where he invented an imaging X-ray spectrometer that made use of thermomigration of aluminum, earning a patent for this instrument in 1984. X-ray spectrometry provides highly useful analytical data for a wide range of scientific and technical applications—and it is especially useful in space science for obtaining information about remote solar system and stellar objects, including the study of the Sun. Alcorn also devised a way to use laser drilling to improve production efficiency for his X-ray spectrometer.

In 1984, Alcorn also embarked on an administration and management phase of his career, assuming the position of deputy project manager for advanced development of new technologies for use on the International Space Station. He became manager for advanced programs at NASA/GSFC in 1990, and in 1992, he became chief of the Office of Commercial Programs for the Goddard Space Flight Center. In this position he facilitated "spin-off" applications for technologies developed at Goddard—including commercial uses. This aspect of the space program requires innovative insights into ways space technology and uses of the space program can benefit Earth-bound industries, small businesses, and other activities.

Holder of more than 25 patents, Alcorn pioneered in development of plasma etching, processes for fabricating plasma semiconductor devices, and computer modeling for several types of etched structures. His work has included adaptation of chemical ionization mass spectrometers for the detection of amino acids, as well as other methods for detecting life on other planets. He has done classified work on missiles as well as extensive work developing instruments for use in space.

Alcorn has also been active in mentoring inner-city middle-school-age youngsters through a program he founded called Saturday Academy. Through the Meyerhoff Foundation, he has encouraged African-American men to pursue careers in science and engineering. In 1994, he was honored by Howard University as a Black Achiever in Science and Technology. As of late 2002, Alcorn continues to serve as chief of the Office of Commercial Programs at GSFC.

Further Reading

Great Lakes Patent and Trademark Center, African-American Inventors Database. Available online. URL: www.detroit.lib.mi.us/glptc/aaid/. Updated 2002.

Kaiser, Mark J. "George Edward Alcorn," *Notable Black American Scientists*, Kristine Krapp, ed. Detroit: Gale Research, 1999, 2–3.

"Spectrometer: Willard Bennett–George Edward Alcorn," Inventors. Information provided by the Department of Energy. Available online. URL: http://inventors.About.com/library/inventors/blbennett.htm. Downloaded on November 1, 2002.

Amos, Harold
(1919–   ) *microbiologist, immunologist*

Focusing his research on nutrition, enzyme synthesis, and the effects of hormones, Harold Amos is best known for his discovery that starvation profoundly increases glucose uptake activity in primary cells. He is also widely recognized for his energetic and effective encouragement of minority students entering biomedical research and medicine as well as his contributions to health research and related fields.

Born in Pennsauken, New Jersey, on September 7, 1919, Harold Amos spent his early years on a farm. By the time he reached age 22, he had left the rural regions of the Garden State behind and had completed a bachelor of science degree from Springfield College in Massachusetts. World War II interrupted young Amos's plans for a career in science, though. Pressed into military duty by the draft, he spent the next five years in the army. After the war, he made up for lost time, earning his master's degree from Harvard by 1947.

Over the next five years he worked with J. Howard Mueller, chair of bacteriology and immunology at Harvard Medical School, on research relating to the treatment of purified herpes virus particles. He hoped to find a treatment that would lower the virus's ability to infect chick eggs in which embryos had formed. His dissertation, entitled "Study of the Factors

Contributing to the Loss of Infectivity of Herpes Simplex Virus," centered on this line of research. By 1952 he completed his Ph.D. at Harvard. A two-year Fulbright Fellowship enabled him to continue his research in postdoctoral studies at the Louis Pasteur Institute in Paris.

While pursuing his doctorate, Amos had begun teaching at Springfield College in 1947, and after his studies in Paris he joined the faculty at Harvard Medical School as an instructor in bacteriology and immunology. He became a full professor in 1969, and in 1975 he was awarded the prestigious Presley Professorship. He served twice as chair of the Department of Microbiology and Molecular Genetics, and he served as associate dean for Basic Sciences. He also served on the National Cancer Advisory Board, to which he was appointed in 1971 by President Richard Nixon.

During his career, Amos's research centered on areas of nutrition, enzyme synthesis, and hormonal effects. In 1989, the Harvard medical institution's newsletter *Focus* noted, "Perhaps his most influential discovery was the profound effect of starvation to increase glucose uptake activity in primary cells." Amos found that when cells are deprived of glucose, the glucose uptake rate may increase by as much as five to 15 times.

Amos received numerous awards throughout his career. In 1951, he was selected as a Fulbright scholar. Howard University Hospital chose Amos in 1989 to receive the first $50,000 Dr. Charles R. Drew World Medical Prize for his "significant lifetime contributions to public health, health research, or the delivery of health care." The prize is awarded once yearly to two persons of color—one from the United States and another from a developing nation. The 1989 competition included a field of 87 candidates from 31 countries.

In 1995, Amos received the Public Welfare Medal, awarded by the National Academy of Sciences "[f]or his tremendous success, for over

Microbiologist Harold Amos found that starvation greatly increases glucose uptake activity in primary cells—one of a series of discoveries he made regarding the relationships of normal cells and cancer cells to glucose uptake. *(Bettmann/Corbis)*

25 years in encouraging and facilitating the entry and advancement of underrepresented minorities into careers in medicine and biomedical research." He is a fellow of the American Academy of Sciences. In 1991, he was elected by the American Association for the Advancement of Science (AAAS) and he is a member of the Institute of Medicine.

Harold Amos retired in 1989 from his position as Harvard Medical School's Maude and Lillian Presley Professor of Microbiology and Molecular Genetics. Never married, Amos remained in Boston following his retirement.

Further Reading

Hightower, Marvin. "11 to Receive Honorary Degrees," *The Harvard Gazette* (June 6, 1996), The Harvard Gazette Archives, 1998. Available online. URL: http://www.news.harvard.edu/gazette/1996/06.06/11ToReceiveHono.html. Downloaded on April 12, 2002.

Sammons, Vivian Ovelton. *Blacks in Science and Medicine.* New York: Hemisphere Publishing, 1990.

Wellford, Alison. "Harold Amos," *Notable Black American Scientists,* Kristine Krapp, ed. Detroit: Gale Research, 1999, 10–11.

Anderson, Gloria Long

(1938–) *chemist*

Named in 1983 by *Atlanta Magazine* as one of the best and brightest scientists in Atlanta, Georgia, Gloria Anderson has distinguished herself both as a chemist and science educator. In 1972, she received a presidential appointment to serve a six-year term as board member of the Corporation for Public Broadcasting (CPB), and during that time she also served two years as vice chair.

Born November 5, 1938, to Charley Long and Elsie Lee Foggie, Gloria Long began her life in Altheimer, Arkansas. By the time she entered college at the Arkansas Agricultural, Mechanical, and Normal College (which later became the University of Arkansas at Pine Bluff), Gloria Long had already begun to gain recognition for her abilities, receiving a Rockefeller Fellowship for the years 1956 to 1958. She graduated in 1958 with a bachelor of science degree summa cum laude.

Two years later she and Leonard Sinclair Anderson married. Though later divorced, the Andersons have one son, Gerald. Gloria Anderson continued her education, completing her M.S. degree at Atlanta University in 1961 and

her Ph.D. in organic chemistry at the University of Chicago in 1968.

In the meantime, Anderson had already begun her teaching career, which would become one of her many strengths. She started as an instructor of chemistry at South Carolina State College in Orangeburg for a year, then taught at Morehouse College in Atlanta for two years, followed by teaching and research assistantships during her years at the University of Chicago.

Anderson's dissertation and research interests centered on aspects of fluorine-19, an isotope of fluorine. (That is, a form of fluorine having the same atomic number and similar chemical behavior but having a different mass, causing it to have a plus or minus charge.) Anderson's research on fluorine-19 focused primarily on this isotope's uses in nuclear magnetic resonance (NMR), a phenomenon that occurs when a static magnetic field surrounds the nuclei of certain atoms and then a second, oscillating magnetic field is introduced. NMR spectroscopy is very useful in analyzing the structure of complex organic molecules and it has benefited research in many fields, ranging from chemistry and biochemistry to biophysics and solid-state physics. NMR takes place only with atoms that have a property called "spin"— and some atoms have spin, while the atoms of other substances do not. Fluorine-19 is particularly well suited for NMR, and this imaging technique using fluorine-19 has proved highly useful in exploring many subjects from human metabolism to drug development.

After completion of her doctorate, Anderson pursued her teaching interests by joining the faculty at Morris Brown College in Atlanta in 1968 as an associate professor in chemistry and chair of the chemistry department. She was named Fuller E. Callaway professor of chemistry in 1973, remaining chair of the department. From 1984 to 1989, she served as dean of academic affairs, returning in 1990 to her position as Callaway professor of chemistry.

During most of those years, however, Anderson continued her research in fluorine-19 chemistry and related areas of pharmaceutical development. For research facilities and funding, Anderson turned to government and independent research agencies, such as the Atlanta University Center Research Committee, the National Institutes of Health, the National Science Foundation, and the Office of Naval Research. Her studies, financed by research grants, included research on amantadines, a type of pharmaceutical used in prevention of viral infection. As a United Negro Fund Distinguished Scholar in 1985, she researched possibilities for synthesizing antiviral drugs. She also studied the synthesis of solid propellants for rockets for the Air Force Office of Scientific Research. In 1990, she became a research consultant for BioSPECS of The Hague, Netherlands.

Anderson has been honored with many awards for her teaching contributions at Morris Brown, including recognition in 1976 as an outstanding teacher, a Teacher of the Year award in 1983, and election to the Faculty/Staff Hall of Fame at the college. She also received an Alumni All-Star Excellence Award in 1987 from the University of Arkansas at Pine Bluff, where she began her college studies.

In 1972, President Richard Nixon appointed Anderson to the board of the Corporation for Public Broadcasting (the CPB), a private nonprofit corporation created by Congress in 1967 to serve and fund the more than 1,000 local public radio and television stations across the country. To an already daunting workload Anderson added committee responsibilities for the CPB that included serving as chair on Minority Training, Minorities and Women, and Human Resources. She also served as vice chair for the last two years of her six-year board term, from 1977 to 1979.

Highly valued for her scientific expertise and judgment, as of August 2001, Anderson continued to serve as a member of the Advisory Committee for Pharmaceutical Science in the Office of Pharmaceutical Science of the Food and Drug Administration (FDA). In this capacity she and the other members of the committee are responsible for offering advice on scientific and technical issues concerning the safety and effectiveness of human generic drugs, as well as on other products for which the FDA has regulatory responsibility; making

Gloria Long Anderson's research has centered on the chemistry of fluorine-19 and synthesis of antiviral drugs. *(AP/Wide World Photos)*

appropriate recommendations to the FDA Commissioner; and reviewing FDA-sponsored biomedical research programs.

Further Reading

"Advisory Committee for Pharmaceutical Science," U.S. Food and Drug Administration Center for Drug Evaluation and Research. Available online. URL: http://www.fda.gov/cder/OPS/OPS_AdvisoryComm.htm. Updated on August 9, 2001.

"Atlanta's Best and Brightest Scientists," *Atlanta Magazine* (April 1983).

Proffitt, Pamela. *Notable Women Scientists.* Detroit: Gale Group, 2000, 13–14.

B

Bacon-Bercey, June
(1932–) *meteorologist*

In 1972, June Bacon-Bercey became the first woman to earn the American Meteorological Society's Seal of Approval for television and radio meteorology. She was a weather forecaster in New York at the time and later became internationally recognized as an expert on meteorology and aviation.

June Bacon-Bercey was born in Wichita, Kansas, on October 23, 1932. As she later recalled, from the time of her childhood, she always wanted a career in science. She earned a bachelor's degree with honors in 1954 and a master's degree the following year, both in mathematics and meteorology from the University of California at Los Angeles (UCLA).

By 1956, she had found employment in her field, working for the United States Weather Bureau in Washington, D.C., where she gained her first exposure to weather forecasting and chartmaking over the next six years. From 1962 to 1974, she worked for the Sperry Rand Corporation. By then, her experience in meteorology earned her a position as a network-wide weather forecaster for television's National Broadcasting Company (NBC). Concurrently, she handled the duties of news correspondent and morning talk-show moderator for NBC stations in New York and Buffalo.

In 1975, Bacon-Bercey returned to the National Weather Service, where she served as a weathercaster and broadcaster until 1979, when she completed a master's in public administration degree. That same year, she accepted a position as public affairs specialist at the National Oceanic and Atmospheric Agency (NOAA) and later as chief of television services until 1982, when she moved to California. As a trainer for the National Weather Service, she trained weather forecasters for the state until 1990, when she left that position to begin development of educational programs for children and young adults who show an interest in science.

Always active in scientific organizations in her field, Bacon-Bercey served on the American Geophysical Union committee on Women and Minorities in Atmospheric Sciences and was a founding member of the American Meteorological Society's Board on Women and Minorities, established in 1975. Bacon-Bercey also has established a scholarship, administered by the American Geophysical Union in Washington, D.C., to encourage women to pursue graduate degrees in the atmospheric sciences.

Further Reading

"American Meteorological Society's Board on Women and Minorities," American Meteorological Society. Available online. URL: http://www.amsbwm.org/alumnimembers.html. Updated in 2000.

"Founding Members of the American Meteorological Society's Board on Women and Minorities," American Meteorological Society. Available online. URL: http://www.amsbwm.org/foundingmembers.html. Downloaded on April 10, 2002.

Viets, Pat. "NOAA Supporting Conference in Atmospheric Sciences at Howard University," NOAA Press Release, NOAA 2000-305. Available online. URL: http://www.publicaffairs.noaa.gov/releases2000/mar00/noaa00r305.html. Posted on March 15, 2000.

Banneker, Benjamin

(1731–1806) *mathematician, astronomer*

In 1791, at the age of 60, Benjamin Banneker served as scientific assistant to chief surveyor Andrew Ellicott during the survey made to establish the site for the newly formed republic's capital city. He also calculated and wrote the scientific contents of several almanacs published under his name.

Banneker, born in Maryland on November 9, 1731, was fortunate enough to be born free at a time when most African Americans labored in slavery. Both his father and grandfather were former slaves. His grandmother, Molly Welsh, worked as an indentured servant in Maryland. Once free of her obligation, she managed to rent and later buy a tobacco farm, which she worked with the help of two African-American slaves. Her husband was Bannka, a man who had previously worked for her as a slave and said to be the son of an African chieftain. The couple continued to work the farm and raised a family. Benjamin was her only grandson, one of four children of Molly and Bannka's daughter Mary, and Robert, a former slave from Guinea who had gained his freedom.

As a boy, Banneker learned to read and write from his grandmother. He had an agile mind that learned quickly and retained information accurately. His grandmother later arranged for the bright youngster to attend a nearby one-room school, where two other black children and a handful of white children learned together from a Quaker schoolmaster. A classmate, Jacob Hall, later recalled about Banneker that "all his delight was to dive into his books."

Banneker's formal schooling lasted only a short time, though. Soon he was needed even in the winter months to help with the time-consuming chores on his parents' tobacco farm. During the spring, summer, and fall the whole family was completely absorbed by tobacco cultivation every day from sunrise to sunset.

When he was a young man of 22, Banneker first gained fame for his construction of a timepiece, a wooden chiming clock—in an age when timepieces were uncommon in his part of the country. In fact, he had seen only two instruments for keeping time, a sundial and a pocket watch. He borrowed a watch, took it apart, and studied its mechanics. From the drawings he made, he calculated the necessary increase in size and the number of teeth for the gears. He carved the wheels and mechanical works from hard-grained wood, adding a few necessary parts of iron or brass, a dial, and a casing. To his neighbors, the achievement was remarkable, and it became a legend in the valley where he lived.

From the time of his father's death in 1759 until his mother's death some 20 years later, Banneker supported his mother, with whom he lived. (His sisters had all married.) His farming and responsibilities left little time for science, but he became well known as a man of learning, sought by his neighbors to make calculations for them or write letters—since few of them could read or write. Those who knew him described him as a man of dignity—gentlemanly, quiet, and modest, yet proud.

In the early 1770s, a remarkably industrious and ambitious family came to Banneker's neighborhood. The Ellicott brothers built a mill on the Patapsco River, just a mile from Banneker's house. They established a general store as well, which soon became a meeting place where nearby farmers gathered for discussion and conversation. Banneker visited there often and became known for his cogent contributions to the talk. He also soon became friends with one of the younger Ellicotts—George—who was 29 years younger than Banneker but shared the older man's interest in science and math. Through George, Banneker became fascinated with astronomy. Ellicott had astronomy texts and instruments, including a telescope and a celestial globe, some of which he loaned to Banneker. Ellicott also knew surveying and probably loaned Banneker texts on that subject, too. George Ellicott became an important link between Banneker and the outside world—the kind of link he had never had before.

Encouraged by Ellicott, Banneker completed the astronomical calculations in 1790 for a 1791 almanac. Almanacs were best-sellers for local printers. They were calendars—but they were also filled with much additional information, both useful and interesting. For rural households, they often provided the only available reading material, so they often contained essays, poetry, aphorisms, and stories. More important, they provided planting and harvesting dates, weather forecasts, calculations of ephemerides (tables providing coordinates of celestial bodies at particular times), and eclipse predictions. Farmers and other rural residents relied on this information, which was usually supplied by someone skilled in calculations and, often, self-taught in astronomy.

This was a formidable undertaking, requiring detailed observations and calculations. Ban-

Benjamin Banneker published a widely read yearly almanac between 1792 and 1802. This image appeared on the frontispiece of *Benjamin Banneker's Pennsylvania, Delaware, Maryland and Virginia Almanac*, 1795. *(The Maryland Historical Society, Baltimore, Maryland)*

neker based his calculations on observations recorded in his astronomical journals. They provide a detailed record of the steps he followed, where he made mistakes—and how he corrected them. After completion of the ephemerides, Banneker checked and rechecked them. Finally, he bundled up his manuscript and sent it to the first of three printers in Baltimore. Turned down by the first, he submitted his work to the second and the third. The final printer, Hayes and Company, declined after considerable hesitation. By then, the year 1791 had arrived, and it was too late.

However, in that same year, Banneker became involved in what he called his greatest life adventure—the land survey for the national capital, the region now known as the District of Columbia. President George Washington had chosen the site, the commissioners had been appointed, and a survey had to be conducted to define the area, a tract of land 10 miles square, located on the Potomac River. George Ellicott's cousin, Andrew Ellicott, a distinguished professional surveyor, was a natural choice for the job. Andrew consulted with Thomas Jefferson, then secretary of state, who approved the choice of Banneker as his scientific assistant. Banneker accepted, delighted at the opportunity to use Andrew Ellicott's astronomical instruments, probably the best in the country.

Once in the field, Ellicott put Banneker in charge of most observations in the observatory tent and the astronomical clock, a precision timepiece that was key to the operation. It was extremely sensitive to changes in temperature, jolts, or disturbances of any kind. Banneker checked its rate for accuracy by making careful observations of the sun at regular intervals. The crew worked seven days a week, and Banneker's tasks required him to make astronomical observations throughout the night, debrief Ellicott when he arrived in the morning, and then sleep intermittently, awakening several times throughout the day to check the rate of the observatory clock. At age 60, Banneker found the schedule to be hard on him physically, especially because of the damp and cold, but he remained on the job until the square of the "Federal Territory" had been laid out. He then returned to his farm in April 1791.

Returning to his astronomical observations, Banneker prepared a series of almanacs for which he again calculated the ephemerides. When he approached printers for the 1792 edition, he met with more success than before. After consulting with George Ellicott, he also sought the help of George's brother Elias in Philadelphia, in hope of obtaining a separate printing there. Elias saw

Banneker's almanac as an opportunity to further the antislavery cause—by clearly disproving a popular belief that African Americans were inferior in intellect.

Banneker was unhappy that his work was gaining recognition because he was African American and not because of the accuracy and competency of his calculations, which he considered a misplaced emphasis on his race rather than his achievements. However, he was eager to have the almanac published.

His success—beginning much of his study as late as 58 years of age—celebrates his industrious and inquiring quest for knowledge, unhampered by the many obstacles that stood in his way. His story serves as a reminder that thirst for knowledge can enrich maturity as well as youth, and his experience shows an early and solid example of someone who longed to know and let nothing stand in the way of his learning.

Benjamin Banneker was 74 when he died Sunday, October 25, 1806. In 1980, the United States Postal Service released a commemorative stamp in Banneker's honor. Today, a marker stands in his honor near Oella, Maryland.

Further Reading

Banneker, Benjamin. *Copy of a Letter from Benjamin Banneker to the Secretary of State, with His Answer.* Philadelphia: Printed and Sold by Daniel Lawrence . . ., 1792.

Bedini, Silvio A. *The Life of Benjamin Banneker: The First African-American Man of Science,* 2nd ed. Baltimore: Maryland Historical Society, 1999.

Litwin, Laura Baskes. *Benjamin Banneker, Astronomer and Mathematician* (African-American Biographies). Berkeley Heights, N.J.: Enslow Publishers, 1999.

Tyson, Martha Ellicott. *A Sketch of the Life of Benjamin Banneker; From Notes Taken in 1836.* Read by J. S. Norris, before the Maryland Historical Society, October 5th, 1854. [Baltimore]: Printed by J. D. Toy, [1854].

Barnes, Robert Percy
(1898–1990) *organic chemist*

In 1933, Robert Percy Barnes became the first black student to receive a Ph.D. in chemistry from Harvard University. He also served on the National Science Foundation's first National Science Board. He published some 40 papers in scientific journals during the course of his career.

Robert Percy Barnes was born on February 26, 1898, in Washington D.C., the son of Reverend William Humphrey Barnes and Mary Jane Thomas Barnes. A member of the class of 1921 at Amherst College in Amherst, Massachusetts, he received his bachelor's degree that year, earning membership in the Phi Beta Kappa honor society for his high scholastic achievement. Working as an instructor in chemistry at the college the following year, he became the first African American appointed to the Amherst faculty.

The following year Howard University in Washington, D.C., offered him his first full-time faculty teaching position. Over the coming years, he coordinated teaching at Howard with his continuing graduate studies at Harvard University, in part funded by a General Education Board fellowship from 1928 to 1931. He obtained his master's degree (1931) and doctorate (1933), both in chemistry from Harvard.

President Harry S. Truman appointed Barnes in 1950 to the first National Science Board of the National Science Foundation. The board, made up of 24 respected scientists, established policy guidelines for science education and scientific research. Barnes held this position for eight years, retiring from Howard University in 1967. He died in Washington, D.C. on March 18, 1990.

Further Reading
"Barnes, Robert Percy," Amherst College Biographical Record. Available online. URL: www.amherst.edu/~rjyanco/genealogy/acbiorecord/index/byname/ b/barnes.html. Posted August 29, 2000.

Petrusso, A. "Robert Percy Barnes," *Notable Black American Scientists*, Kristine Krapp, ed. Detroit: Gale Research, 1999.

Barnes, William Harry
(1887–1945) *surgeon, inventor*

An innovative ear, nose, and throat specialist, William Harry Barnes invented the hypophyscope, a device to assist surgical access to the pituitary gland. He was the first African American to become a board-certified otolaryngologist and he served as chief otolaryngologist at Frederick Douglass Hospital in Philadelphia.

William Harry Barnes was born in Philadelphia, Pennsylvania, on April 4, 1887, and remained a lifelong resident of that city. Growing up poor, unable even to afford trolley fare, Barnes walked the 10 miles to school daily—and he became determined to find a way out of the poverty he lived in. Scoffed at by family and friends for his plans for becoming a doctor, he remained committed to his vision. He graduated from high school in 1908, spent the summer preparing for the University of Pennsylvania Medical School scholarship exam, took it, and became the first black ever to win the scholarship. He completed his M.D. degree in 1912, interning the following year at Douglass and Mercy Hospitals. He specialized in ear, nose, and throat (ENT) and became assistant otolaryngologist at Douglass Hospital in 1913 and an acting assistant surgeon for the U.S. Public Health Service in 1918.

By 1921, Barnes was ready to pursue postgraduate studies in ENT treatment and surgery for which he returned to the University of Pennsylvania. Dissatisfied with the level of training available there, in 1924 he traveled to France for a year of more advanced studies at the University of Paris and the University of Bordeaux. He also studied with Dr. Chevalier Jackson, a respected Philadelphia ENT specialist, who taught Barnes methods in bronchoscopy for examination of the bronchial tubes. By 1931, he had received an appointment to the faculty of Howard University Medical School, where he taught bronchoscopy for 32 years, commuting from Philadelphia.

Though Barnes became a nationally respected ENT specialist—admired by his colleagues for his diagnostic and surgical expertise—his invention of the hypophyscope made him famous. This instrument enables a surgeon to see the pituitary gland through the sphenoid sinus (cavity behind the eyes). He also devised other surgical techniques and created an effective system for keeping medical records.

In 1935, Barnes served as president of the National Medical Association, a professional association of African-American physicians, dedicated to the health concerns of African Americans. He also helped found the Society for the Promotion of Negro Specialists in Medicine. His other professional affiliations included the American Medical Association and the American Laryngological Association.

After suffering a spinal injury in 1943 that left him paralyzed, William Harry Barnes died of bronchial pneumonia on January 15, 1945. He was 58. He is remembered for his expertise; his dedication to his profession as a clinician, diagnostician, and surgeon; and his insightful innovations.

Further Reading

Kaufman, Martin, Stuart Galishoff, and Joseph Savitt. Eds. *Dictionary of American Medical Biography*. Westport, Conn.: Greenwood Press, 1984, 37–38.

McMurray, Emily, ed. *Notable Twentieth Century Scientists*. Detroit: Gale Research, 1995, 114–115.

Sammons, Vivian Ovelton. *Blacks in Science and Medicine*. New York: Hemisphere Publishing, 1990, 20–21.

"William Henry Barnes, MD," Early African Americans in Otolaryngology. American Academy of Otolaryngology. Available online. URL: www.entnet.org/museum/eaao4b.html. Updated in 2000.

Beard, Andrew Jackson
(1849–1921) *inventor*

A prolific inventor, Andrew Jackson Beard is best known for his invention of a device that automatically coupled railroad cars.

Andrew Jackson Beard was born a slave in Eastlake, Alabama, in 1849. He was freed at the age of 15 and spent the next few years of his life farming. During this time he also began to experiment with various inventions.

Although he never attended school, Beard was gifted with a quick mind and a keen eye for finding solutions to problems. In 1872, after an unprofitable farm season, he turned his attention to mill-wrighting. While working in a flour mill in Hardwicks, Alabama, he watched the operations of mills at work. Having learned the workings of mills from his observations, he built his own flour mill shortly afterward, which he operated successfully.

While working his mill, Beard continued to turn his agile mind toward inventing. His first patent, for a new plow design, was awarded in 1881. He sold the patent for $4,000 in 1884 and returned for a while to farming. In 1887, he was awarded a second plow patent, which he sold for $5,200. Using the money from his inventions and farming ventures, he invested in real estate as an entry into the real estate business, while continuing to think of new problems to which he could turn his mind.

Although he had no training in engines or metalwork, Beard had also kept a keen eye on the problems of the new railroad industry. In 1882 he obtained a patent for his design for a new rotary steam engine.

In an interview with the *Cleveland Gazette* in 1890, he said, " . . . I have another thing in view, a coupling machine. I propose to couple cars irrespective of height. This has been a great difficulty with railroads." Coupling, or attaching, railroad cars together was a dangerous business for railroad workers. The only way the cars could be locked together was with a large metal pin that the workers had to drop into place precisely as the cars crashed together. Any slight miscalculation and a worker could lose his fingers, hands, or arms in the crush of machinery.

Beard's solution, which he patented in 1897, was both simple and elegant, using two horizontal "jaws," one on each car, which locked automatically upon joining. It was the first automatic coupling device used on railroads in America. Beard sold the patent that same year for the then gigantic sum of $50,000.

Little is known about the last years of Andrew J. Beard's life. He died in 1921.

Further Reading

"Andrew Beard: Making the Railways Safer," Inventors Museum, 1999. Available online. URL: http://www.inventorsmuseum.com/abeard.htm. Downloaded on August 1, 2002.

James, Portia P. *The Real McCoy: African-American Inventors and Innovation, 1619–1930.* Washington, D.C.: Smithsonian Institution, 1989.

Moore, Patrick, "Andrew Jackson Beard," *Notable Black American Scientists.* Kristine Krapp, ed. Detroit: Gale Research, 1990, 21–22.

Sullivan, Otha Richard. *African American Inventors.* Black Stars series, Jim Haskins, ed. New York: John Wiley & Sons, 1998.

Bharucha-Reid, Albert Turner
(Albert Turner Reid)
(1927–1985) *mathematician*

A. T. Bharucha-Reid was one of the most prolifically published mathematicians in the world. Recognized widely for his work in areas of mathematics, statistics, and physics, he taught and lectured internationally, and his work has appeared in many translations, including Russian. Particularly intrigued by probability theory, Bharucha-Reid produced work that had consequences for many disciplines, including biology, physics, engineering, economics, and mathematics.

Named Albert Turner Reid by his parents, Bharucha-Reid was born to William Thaddeus Reid and Mae Elaine Beamon Reid on November 13, 1927, in Hampton, Virginia. He did his undergraduate studies in biology and math at Iowa State University, completing his bachelor's degree in 1949. He continued his studies at the University of Chicago during the years of 1950 to 1953, focusing on mathematics, mathematical biology, probability, and statistics, and by the age of 26, he had already published eight articles, primarily in the field of mathematical biology. Reid served as a research assistant in mathematical biology during his years at the University of Chicago, and a research associateship in mathematical statistics at New York's Columbia University enabled him to pursue his studies in probability and statistics there during the following academic year. In 1954, Reid married Rodab Phiroze Bharucha and hyphenated his name thereafter. The couple subsequently had two sons.

In 1955–56, Bharucha-Reid held a position as assistant research statistician at the University of California at Berkeley, moving on to the University of Oregon, where he was an instructor of mathematics for two years. He then traveled to Poland for a year, where he had a fellowship at the Mathematical Institute at the Polish Academy of Sciences in 1958–59, returning to the University of Oregon as assistant professor of mathematics the following academic year. He continued to travel, obtaining visiting professorships worldwide, from India to Wayne State University in Detroit, and from Madison, Wisconsin, to Poland. In 1965, he became full professor of mathematics at Wayne State University in 1965, and in 1970, he was selected to serve as dean of the School of Arts and Sciences. In 1981, Bharucha-Reid accepted a position of professor of mathematics at the Georgia Institute of Technology in Atlanta. In 1983, he was appointed distinguished professor of mathematics at Atlanta University.

Bharucha-Reid's first book was published in 1960, and in subsequent years he published more than 70 papers. He also wrote a total of six published books in fields ranging from algebra to mathematical biology, and from statistics to topology. Much of his interest centered on probability theory, including stochastic processes and Markov chains (named after Russian mathematician Andrei Markov). A stochastic process is a sequence of random variables, often describing the evolution of a phenomenon over time. A Markov chain is a type of stochastic process that exhibits the principle that the probability of an event is dependent only on the outcome of the last previous event.

A. T. Bharucha-Reid died on February 26, 1985. He was 57. The National Association of Mathematicians has established a lecture series in his honor.

Further Reading

Garcia-Johnson, R. "Albert Turner Bharucha-Reid," *Notable Black American Scientists.* Kristine Krapp, ed. Detroit: Gale Research, 1990, 24–25.

Mickens, Ronald E. "Albert Turner Bharucha-Reid" *Physics Today* (December 1985): 92.

Newell, Virginia K., et al., eds. *Black Mathematicians and Their Works.* Ardmore, Pa.: Dorrance & Company, 1980, 277–278.

Blackwell, David Harold

(1919–) *mathematician*

David Blackwell is one of the most prolific and widely published African-American mathematicians of all time. His work is respected worldwide for its clarity and rigor, and he has made major contributions in numerous areas of theoretical statistics, including work in Bayesian statistical analysis, information theory, game theory, and dynamic programming. Blackwell has also made his mark as a distinguished teacher.

Born on April 24, 1919, in Centralia, Illinois, David Harold Blackwell is the son of Grover Blackwell, who worked for the Illinois Central Railroad, and Mabel Johnson Blackwell. He loved mathematical problems even as a child, and he was fascinated with games such as checkers—and the possibility that being the first to make a move might provide a potentially unbeatable advantage. In high school, Blackwell delighted in the challenging problems posed by the mathematics club adviser—enjoying his first publication when one of his answers came out in the *School Science and Mathematics* journal.

After graduating from high school at 16, Blackwell completed his A.B. degree at the University of Illinois at Champaign-Urbana in 1938 and his A.M. the same year. He earned his Ph.D. from the same institution in 1941. His dissertation explored Markov chains, an aspect of probability theory that is named after the Russian mathematician Andrei Markov. Markov chains exhibit the principle that the probability of an event is dependent only on the outcome of the previous event. In the year following completion of his doctorate, he received a Rosenwald Fellowship to attend the Institute for Advanced Study in Princeton, New Jersey.

Initially, Blackwell had planned to teach elementary school, but by the time he was working on his master's degree, he began to recognize that college-level teaching would challenge him far more productively. During his early years, he constantly sought a challenging environment, moving from school to school. From 1942 to 1943, he was instructor at Southern University at Baton Rouge, Louisiana, moving to Clark College in Atlanta, Georgia for the 1943–44 academic year. As assistant professor, he then joined the faculty at Howard University, the most prestigious black university in the country. He distinguished himself as a teacher there for 10 years, from 1944 to 1954, publishing some 20 articles during that time. During the years 1948 to 1950, he spent summers working at the RAND Corporation in Santa Monica, California. There he became especially interested in game theory, using statistical analysis to explore the viability of various decision-making options in a given situation. In 1954, he joined the faculty at the University of California at Berkeley as a full professor in mathematics and served as chair of the department of statistics from 1957 to 1961.

In recognition of his significant body of work, in 1979 the Operations Research Society of America and the Institute of Management Science awarded Blackwell with the prestigious von Neumann Prize. That honor could be topped only by the R. A. Fisher Award given by the Committee of Presidents of Statistical Societies, which Blackwell received in 1986.

Blackwell has received honorary doctorates from several institutions, including Harvard University, the University of Illinois, Michigan State University, Southern Illinois University, Howard University, and the National University of Lesotho, in southern Africa. In 1965, his prominence in his field was honored when he was elected to membership in the National Academy of Sciences.

Although he retired from UC Berkeley in 1989, as of 2002, David Blackwell remains active as a respected and productive scholar.

Further Reading

A Century of Mathematics in America, vol. 3. Providence, R.I.: American Mathematical Society, 1989, 589–615.

"David Harold Blackwell," The Mathematical Association of America. Available online. URL: http://www.maa.org/summa/archive/blackwl.htm. Downloaded on April 7, 2002.

David Blackwell gained worldwide recognition for his prodigious and rigorous publications in the field of theoretical statistics. He became professor emeritus of statistics at the University of California, Berkeley in 1989. *(UC Berkeley)*

"David Harold Blackwell," School of Mathematics and Statistics, University of St. Andrews, Scotland. Available online. URL:http://www-gap.dcs.st-and.ac.uk/~history/Mathematicians/Blackwell.html.

Henderson, Ashyia N., ed. *Who's Who Among African Americans,* 14th ed. Detroit: Gale Group, 2001, 103.

Blair, Henry
(ca. 1804–1860) *inventor*

Henry Blair was the first African American to be designated as black in the official records of the United States Patent Office.

Unfortunately little record remains of Henry Blair's personal life. He was born about 1804 or 1807, and he was apparently a farmer who used his ingenuity to devise two products that would be useful to himself—and to other farmers—in planting and harvesting crops.

His first patent was granted October 14, 1834, for a seed planter. This device looked something like a wheelbarrow, with a compartment to hold seed and rakers behind to cover the seed. Its purpose was to allow farmers to plant corn more efficiently.

Blair obtained his second patent two years later, on August 31, 1836, for a cotton planter, which had a similar purpose. The seed bin on the cotton planter dispensed seed in a checkerboard pattern using a two-section valve that was triggered by a trip wire. The checkerboard planting pattern improved weed control.

Notation was made in the patent record that the inventor was a "colored man," although generally, no indication of race is included in patent records. It is unclear whether Blair was a slave or free. At the time Blair's patents were granted, United States patent law allowed patents to be granted to both free men and slaves. In 1857, the patent law was challenged by a slave owner who patented a slave's invention in his own name, claiming he owned all the fruits of the slave's labor. In 1858, the law was changed, stipulating that slaves were not citizens and could not therefore hold patents. Later, in 1871, after the Civil War, the U.S. government changed the patent law again. The revised law granted all American men (though not women) the right to patent their inventions, regardless of race.

Blair was not, however, the first African American to receive a patent, since records exist indicating that Thomas Jennings holds that honor, having received a patent in 1821 for "dry scouring of clothes." The patent record contains no mention that he was black, although that fact is known from other records.

Henry Blair died in 1860.

Further Reading

"Blair, Henry", Great Lakes Patent and Trademark Center African-American Inventors Database. Available online. URL: http://www.detroit.lib.mi.us/glptc/aaid/index.asp?Inventor=Blair%2C+Henry&Invention=. Downloaded on February 01, 2001.

James, Portia P. *The Real McCoy.* Washington, D.C.: Smithsonian Institution Press, 1989.

Sammons, Vivian Ovelton. *Blacks in Science and Medicine.* New York: Hemisphere Publishing, 1990.

Bluford, Guion Stewart, Jr.
(Guy Bluford)
(1942–) *engineer, astronaut*

To become an astronaut is arguably the most glamorous career path a scientist can choose, and Guion "Guy" Bluford, who made history as the first African American to fly in space, unquestionably holds an honored position in United States history. The launch of the space shuttle *Challenger* on August 30, 1983, was a momentous occasion, not only for Bluford, but also for the African-American community. The U.S. space agency, the National Aeronautics and Space Administration (NASA), invited some 250 black educators and professionals to witness the liftoff from Kennedy Space Center in Florida. In the words of NASA aerospace engineer and administrator ISAAC THOMAS GILLAM IV, "It was one of the high points of my life to . . . watch that launch."

Guion Stewart Bluford, Jr., was born in Philadelphia, Pennsylvania, on November 22, 1942. His parents both had enjoyed a good education and valued achievement—his mother taught school and his father was an inventor and a mechanical engineer. As a boy, Bluford built model airplanes, had a high interest in math and science, and set out to become an aerospace engineer.

By the time he was 22, Bluford had achieved the first step in that dream, graduating in 1964 from Pennsylvania State University with a bachelor's degree in aerospace engineering. While in college, he had enrolled in the Air Force Reserve Officer Training Corps (ROTC) and after graduation, he trained to become a pilot at Williams Air Force Base in Arizona. He served combat duty as a pilot during the Vietnam War, flying 144 combat missions. After working as a flight instructor at Sheppard Air Force Base in Texas, he became a career air force aerospace engineer in 1974, when he obtained his M.S. degree with distinction in aerospace engineering from the Air Force Institute of Technology at Wright-Patterson Air Force Base in Ohio. While continuing his studies at the Institute of Technology, he worked at the U.S. Air Force Flight Dynamics Laboratory, where he was deputy for advanced concepts with the aeromechanics division, later becoming branch chief of the aerodynamics and airframe branch. In 1978, Bluford completed his Ph.D. in aerospace engineering, carrying a minor in laser physics, and that same year, he received acceptance into NASA's astronaut program. He was one of only 35 applicants accepted from a field of 10,000.

Unquestionably the most exciting moment in Bluford's career came five years later, when *Challenger* lifted off from the launch pad at Kennedy Space Center in Florida. For the first 26 years of the U.S. human presence in space, no African American was included in the astronaut corps. Not until the moment of *Challenger*'s liftoff in August 1983 did that precedent change—forever. The spectacular nighttime launch caused the dark Florida skies to flash with the incredible brightness of the solid rocket ignition and the shuttle's main engines. Bluford was the first, but others would follow. In fact, Bluford was one of three African Americans in the astronaut corps at the time of his flight. The other two, who would soon also take their first voyages into space, were RONALD ERWIN MC-NAIR and FREDERICK DREW GREGORY. Another group of three would soon also be in the wings.

Bluford spent 15 months in training for his first trip into space. During the mission, he served as mission specialist, helping to launch a $45 million communications and weather information satellite to serve India. He also helped conduct experiments studying the effects of microgravity (the greatly reduced presence of gravity in orbit) on living cells. The crew also made medical measurements to contribute to understanding the biophysiological effects of space flight on human beings.

On September 5, 1983, *Challenger* landed safely at Edwards Air Force Base in California. In the coming 10 years, Bluford would fly three

Guion "Guy" Bluford was the first African American in space. *(Photo by NASA)*

PRESTON RIDGE CAMPUS

more missions—one more time aboard *Challenger*, in October 1985, and aboard the orbiter *Discovery* in April 1991 and December 1992. During his years as an astronaut, he logged 688 hours in space during his four shuttle missions. He also completed a master's of business administration at the University of Houston, Clear Lake, in 1987.

Bluford retired from the United States Air Force in 1993, also leaving NASA and Houston to join NYMA, Inc., an engineering and software firm. There, he accepted the position of vice president and general manager of the Engineering Services Division, located in Brook Park, Ohio. NYMA later became part of Federal Data Corporation (FDC), which then became part of Northrop Grumman. As of 2002, Bluford was vice president, Microgravity R & D and Operations, Logicon Operations and Services, for Logicon, Inc., a Northrop Grumman company with headquarters in Herndon, Virginia.

Bluford received many honors from the Air Force, NASA, and other organizations for his achievements and the trail he blazed. They include the 1991 Black Engineer of the Year Award, the Ebony Black Achievement Award and the NAACP Image Award in 1983, Pennsylvania's Distinguished Service Medal in 1984, the NASA Exceptional Service Medal, and honorary doctorate degrees from numerous universities. Bluford also recognized the symbolic importance of his 1983 space shuttle mission, remarking, "From a black perspective, my flight on the shuttle represented another step forward. Opportunities do exist for black youngsters if they work hard and strive to take advantage of those opportunities."

Further Reading

"Astronaut Bio: Guion S. Bluford, Jr.," Biographical Data, NASA: Lyndon B. Johnson Space Center. Available online. URL: http://www.jsc.nasa.gov/Bios/htmlbios/bluford-gs.html. Updated in January 1996.

Burns, Khephra, and William Miles. *Black Stars in Orbit: NASA's African American Astronauts.* San Diego, Calif.: Harcourt Brace, 1995.

"This Week in Black History: August 30, 1983," *Jet*, September 6, 1999, 19.

Bolden, Charles Frank, Jr. (Charlie Bolden)
(1946–   )   *astronaut*

Charles Bolden made four spaceflights aboard the space shuttle, two as pilot and two as commander, logging 680 hours in space. Through his work onboard the space shuttle, he contributed to the fields of astronomy, astrophysics, the study of Earth's atmosphere and climate, materials processing, and others. He has also served in significant policy-making administrative positions within the National Aeronautics and Space Administration (NASA). A man of vision, Bolden once remarked: "People always ask me, 'What are we going to discover?' I don't know. I don't have any idea. If I knew, we wouldn't need to go. That's one of the exciting parts about spaceflight, just the prospect of what's going to come out that you never even dreamed of before."

Born in Columbia, South Carolina, on August 19, 1946, Charles Frank Bolden, Jr., grew up during the intense years of the Civil Rights movement. Both his parents—Charles F. Bolden, Sr., and Ethel M. Bolden—and his teachers encouraged his curiosity, though, and his dream of becoming a pilot. "It was not a time for black kids growing up in Columbia to have those thoughts," he later remarked, "but I never gave up on the thought of flying." Bolden married Alexis (Jackie) Walker, also of Columbia, South Carolina. They have a son, Anthony Che, born in 1971, and a daughter, Kelly, born in 1976.

Following completion of his B.S. degree from the United States Naval Academy in 1968, Bolden received a commission as second lieutenant in the U.S. Marine Corps. After flight training, he became designated as a naval aviator in 1970. From 1972 to 1973, during the Vietnam War, he flew more than 100 combat missions in Southeast Asia.

In 1977, Bolden received his M.S. in systems management from the University of Southern California. Bolden was also a test pilot, completing his training at the U.S. Naval Test Pilot School at Patuxent River, Maryland, in June 1979. In all, he logged more than 6,000 hours of flying time.

Bolden was selected by NASA as an astronaut candidate in 1980 and he entered the astronaut corps in August of the following year. He became the second African American to pilot a space shuttle (FREDERICK DREW GREGORY was the first) with the launch of STS-61C, the space shuttle *Columbia* on January 12, 1986. The crew deployed the SATCOM KU satellite from the shuttle's cargo bay and conducted experiments in astrophysics and materials processing. Columbia made a night landing at Edwards Air Force Base in California. It was the last successful shuttle flight before the tragic *Challenger* accident that would take the life of African-American astronaut RONALD ERWIN MCNAIR.

On April 24, 1990, Bolden piloted the space shuttle *Discovery* for his second mission, STS-31. During this landmark scientific five-day mission, Bolden and the crew deployed the *Hubble Space Telescope*, the orbiting telescope that has since served to revolutionize astrophysicists' view of the universe, its size, and its beginnings. From the record-setting orbit of 400 miles above Earth, Bolden and the crew also conducted Earth observations using two IMAX cameras—one from within the cabin and the other from the shuttle's cargo bay.

Shuttle mission STS-45 launched on March 24, 1992, with Charles Bolden as commander of the seven-member crew aboard the space shuttle *Atlantis*, ultimately responsible for the safety of the crew and the accomplishment of the mis-

sion. This spaceflight conducted the first *Spacelab* mission dedicated to NASA's Mission to Planet Earth, which focused on conducting studies of Earth's environment, including atmosphere, oceans, landforms, and biosphere. The crew conducted the 12 experiments carried by a cargo system known as ATLAS-1 (Atmospheric Laboratory for Applications and Science). These experiments involved making an enormous number of precise measurements that substantially advanced the database of information about the chemical and physical nature of Earth's climate and atmosphere.

Bolden made his fourth and final space mission as commander of STS-60 aboard the space shuttle *Discovery*. It was the first U.S. mission to include a Russian cosmonaut, Sergei K. Krikalev, among its crew, a landmark beginning to coordinated efforts in space between the two countries. Launched February 3, 1994, the mission carried the Space Habitation Module-2 (SPACEHAB module) science activities.

Bolden also served at NASA in numerous ground-based technical and administrative capacities, including the position of assistant deputy administrator, NASA Headquarters. In these capacities and during spaceflight, he contributed to the scientific legacy of NASA's human spaceflight program.

In June 1994, Bolden resigned from NASA to return to active duty in the U.S. Marine Corps as assistant wing commander of the 3rd Marine Aircraft Wing, stationed in Miramar, California. He became deputy commanding general of the Pacific Marine Forces from 1997 to 1998 and of Marine Forces in Japan from 1998 to 2000, serving briefly during Desert Storm in 1998 as commanding general in support of operations in Kuwait. In August 2000, he received a promotion to commanding general of the Third Marine Aircraft Wing. Among the 11,000 marines under his command some played a key part in military operations against the Taliban and al-Qaeda forces in the war on terrorism in

As one of the first African-American astronauts, Charles F. "Charlie" Bolden, Jr., flew four Space Shuttle missions, piloting the historic 1990 flight that deployed the Hubble Space Telescope, one of the most important astronomical tools of the following decade. *(Photo by NASA)*

Afghanistan following the September 11, 2001 terrorist attacks on the United States.

Concluding 34 years of service, Major General Charles F. Bolden, Jr., retired from the U.S. Marine Corps in August 2002. He received a certificate of appreciation from President George W. Bush and a Distinguished Service Medal for "exceptionally meritorious service to the Government of the United States in a duty of great responsibility."

For his courage, expertise, and leadership, Charles F. Bolden, Jr., has also received numerous other awards and honors, including honorary doctorates from the University of South Carolina (1984), Winthrop College (1986), and Johnson C. Smith University (1990); and the NASA Outstanding Leadership Medal (1991) and three NASA Exceptional Service Medals (1988, 1989, and 1991).

Charles Bolden not only achieved his goal of becoming a pilot, but he also piloted and commanded the Space Shuttle and has served in key positions of leadership in both the Marine Corps and NASA. Bolden points out that in the early days of NASA's space program, blacks were conspicuously absent, but on the other hand, blacks also did not apply for positions. As a pioneer African American in NASA's astronaut program, Bolden encourages young people to apply, as he did, for positions that may seem beyond their reach.

Further Reading

Burns, Khephra, and William Miles. *Black Stars in Orbit: NASA's African-American Astronauts.* 1st ed. San Diego: Harcourt Brace, 1995.

Carreau, Mark. "Marine general, ex-astronaut nominated as top NASA aide," *Houston Chronicle,* 1/31/02. Available online. URL: http://www.chron.com/cs/CDA/story.hts/space/1235489. (Cached file: 2/24/02).

"Charles Bolden, Astronaut," South Carolina African American History Online. Available online. URL: http://www.scafam-hist.org/search_detail.asp?FeatureMonth=1&FeatureYear=1990. Posted on January 1, 1990.

"Charles F. Bolden, Jr." Biographical Data, Lyndon B. Johnson Space Center. Available online. URL: http://www.jsc.nasa.gov/Bios/htmlbios/bolden-cf.html. Posted in June 1997.

Hawley, Eileen. "Release: J02-12. Former Astronaut Charles F. Bolden to Return to NASA," NASA News. Available online. URL: http://www.jsc.nasa.gov/pao/media/rel/2002/J02-12.html. Posted on February 01, 2002.

"Official Biography for Charles F. Bolden Jr." U.S. Marine Corps. Available online. URL: http://www.

usmc.mil/genbios2.nsf/biographies/81BE83E8 9B03DDC88525680B000CC9F0? opendocument. Posted on December 15, 2002.

Platoff, Annie. "Charles F. Bolden, Jr. (Colonel, U.S. Marine Corps): Former Astronaut," NASA JSC Special Events, JSC Celebrates Black History Month. Available online. URL: http://www.jsc. nasa.gov/pao/black_history/blackhistory.html. Posted on February 23, 1996.

Wellford, Alison. "Charles F. Bolden, Jr." *Notable Black American Scientists.* Kristine Krapp, ed. Detroit: Gale Research, 1990, 32–34.

Bouchet, Edward Alexander

(1852–1918) *physicist*

Edward Alexander Bouchet was the first African American to earn a Ph.D. in the United States—the sixth person, regardless of ethnic background, to receive a doctorate in physics in the Western Hemisphere. He was also the first African American to graduate from Yale College (now Yale University).

Edward Bouchet was born on September 15, 1852, in New Haven, Connecticut. His father, William Frances Bouchet, was born into slavery and had arrived in New Haven as the personal valet of John B. Robertson of Charleston, South Carolina, a wealthy student at Yale College. After obtaining his freedom, William Bouchet went to work as a janitor at the university. Bouchet's mother, the former Susan Cooley, may also have worked on campus, laundering students' clothes.

The youngest and the only boy in a family of four children, Bouchet attended New Haven High School from 1866 to 1868, transferring to Hopkins Grammar School, a school that prepared boys for entrance at Yale College, in 1868. He graduated highest in his class at Hopkins in 1870.

Entering Yale College in 1870, Bouchet obtained his B.A. in 1874. A brilliant student, Bouchet was nominated to Phi Beta Kappa in 1874, but because the Yale chapter of Phi Beta Kappa had been deactivated he was not officially elected until the chapter's reactivation in 1884.

Bouchet received his Ph.D. in physics from Yale in 1876 with a dissertation titled *Measuring Refractive Indices.* He was the first African American to obtain a Ph.D. from an American college or university. Despite his degree Bouchet was unable to find a position at any college, university, or research facility. In 1876, he accepted a teaching position at the Institute for Colored Youths in Philadelphia, Pennsylvania. The school had no library and no research facilities for Bouchet, but it did have a reputation for high academic standards. He remained there for 26 years, until—amid the controversy over academic versus vocational education that raged at the time between W. E. B. Du Bois and GEORGE WASHINGTON CARVER—the school closed its college preparatory program to become a vocational and teacher-training school and relocated to Cheney, Pennsylvania. It later became Cheney State College.

Bouchet left the Institute in 1902 to teach science for a short time at Summer High School in St. Louis, Missouri. The following year, he left Summer as well as teaching to become business manager at Provident Hospital in St. Louis and then for two years he served as U.S. Inspector of Customs for the Louisiana Purchase Exposition.

Bouchet returned to his career in education in 1905 as director of academics at St. Paul's Normal and Industrial School in Lawrenceville, Virginia. Three years later, he took a position as principal of Lincoln High School in Galipolis, Ohio.

Bouchet received his first and only opportunity to teach at a college level with his appointment to the faculty of Bishop College in Marshal, Texas, in 1913. Ill health forced him to retire only three years later, in 1916.

Edward Alexander Bouchet died in New Haven, Connecticut, on October 18, 1918. For many years, no headstone marked his burial site, until Yale University placed a marker commemorating him in 1998. His was a story of a man with a fine mind never given the chance to explore his full potential. The loss was society's as well as Bouchet's.

In memory of Bouchet, Yale University has also established the Edward A. Bouchet Undergraduate Fellowship Program, a competitive program designed to encourage Asian-American, African-American, Latino, and Native American students at Yale to pursue doctoral degrees and careers in academia.

Further Reading

"Edward Alexander Bouchet: Physicist," Faces of Science: African Americans in the Sciences. Available online. URL: http://www.princeton.edu/~mcbrown/display/bouchet.html. Posted on June 4, 2000.

Mickens, Ronald E., ed. *Edward Bouchet: The First African-American Doctorate*. River Edge, N.J.: World Scientific Publishing Co., 2002.

Reinstein, Gila. "10/09/98: Belated Honors to Yale's First Black Alumnus," Yale News Release. Available online. URL: http://www.yale.edu/opa/newsr/98-10-09-01.all.html. Posted on October 9, 1998.

"Tombstone pays belated tribute to achievements of first black Ph.D.," Yale Bulletin & Calendar, 27:8. Available online. URL: http://www.yale.edu/opa/ybc/v27.n8.news.04html. Downloaded on February 22, 2002.

Williams, Scott. "Edward Alexander Bouchet," Physicists of the African Diaspora. Available online. URL: http://www.math.buffalo.edu/mad/physics/bouchet_edward_alexander.html. Posted in June 2001.

Edward A. Bouchet earned a Ph.D. in physics from Yale College in 1876, becoming the first African American to receive a doctorate in the United States. *(Yale University)*

Boykin, Otis Frank

(1920–1982) *inventor, electronics engineer*

Otis Boykin invented a type of electronic resistor that became commonly used in both guided missiles and computers. Thanks to his inventiveness, production costs for radios and televisions lowered. In all, he invented a total of some 26 electronic devices, also including a thief-proof cash register and a chemical air filter. He also invented an electronic regulating device for the first heart pacemaker—perhaps his most important invention of all.

On August 29, 1920, in Dallas, Texas, Walter Benjamin Boykin and his wife Sarah Boykin became the parents of a son, Otis Frank. As a young man, Otis Boykin attended Fisk University, in Nashville, Tennessee, where he earned his bachelor's degree in 1941. After graduation Boykin took a position at Majestic Radio & TV Corporation in Chicago, which he left in 1944 to become a research engineer with P. J. Nilson Research Labs of Oak Park, Illinois. He returned to school at the Illinois Institute of Technology from 1946 to 1947, while working for Nilson

Labs. Leaving Nilson after five years, from 1949 to 1964, Boykin worked for a variety of firms in Illinois and Indiana, always gaining new experience in radio technology and related fields. Beginning in 1964, he became an independent consultant to numerous electronics firms in the United States and Europe.

Early in Boykin's career, he invented a type of resistor used in computers, radios, television sets, and many other electronic devices. He succeeded in lowering the cost of producing electronic controls for radio and television, which enhanced the cost effectiveness of producing these devices for both military and commercial uses.

Boykin also invented a resistor used in guided missiles, as well as a type of small-component thick-film resistors for computers, a cash register that resisted burgling, and a chemical air filter.

The Boykin invention that touched more lives more deeply than any other, though, was his improvement on the regulating device for the cardiac pacemaker. Since a pacemaker's purpose is to maintain a regular heartbeat by "setting the pace" through the use of electrical pulses, the regulating device holds a prime importance.

At age 61, Boykin died of heart failure in Chicago, Illinois, in 1982—perhaps an ironic ending for the life of a man who improved the cardiac pacemaker. His legacy of innovation, independence, and ingenuity remains, however. As of 2002, many Boykin inventions continue to be used in products used worldwide.

Further Reading

"African-American Inventors Database," Great Lakes Patent and Trademark Center. Available online. URL: http://www.detroit.lib.mi.us/glptc/aaid/index.asp. Downloaded on February 5, 2002.

Sammons, Vivian Ovelton. *Blacks in Science and Medicine.* New York: Hemisphere Publishing, 1990, 34.

U.S. Department of Energy. *Black Contributors to Science and Energy Technology.* DOE/OPA-0035. Washington, D.C.: Office of Public Affairs, 1979, 20.

Bradley, Benjamin
(ca. 1830–unknown) *inventor*

Benjamin Bradley invented a steam engine for powering a small boat, or cutter, for carrying provisions for a "sloop of war." However, U.S. law at the time prevented Bradley from obtaining a patent on his invention. He did, however, attain his freedom in exchange for proceeds from his work.

Historical records have not retained much information about Benjamin Bradley's personal life. Bradley was born into slavery and lived in Annapolis, Maryland, for some or possibly all of his life. His date of birth is not recorded, although estimates place his birth in the year 1830. No one knows in what year he died. Reliable correspondence does exist, though, describing the following piece of history.

Owned by a man living in Annapolis, Maryland, Bradley was working in an Annapolis printing shop when he was about 16. Already manifesting both singular mechanical ability and ingenuity, he used what were probably scraps of material lying about the shop—a piece of a gun barrel, some pewter, pieces of round steel, and a few other materials—to fashion a working model of a steam engine.

Shortly thereafter, Bradley's master found him a position at the Naval Academy in Annapolis as a helper in the department of natural and experimental philosophy, where physics, chemistry, and other sciences were taught. Surrounded by sailors, Bradley saw an opportunity to turn his invention to profit and sold his steam engine model to a midshipman at the Academy. Bradley's master allowed him to keep $5 (today about $20) each month for himself. To this amount, Bradley added the proceeds from the sale of his model so he could build a full-scale engine able to drive a cutter, or small boat, at the rate of 16 nautical miles per hour.

The Naval Academy professor for whom Bradley set up laboratory demonstration experiments remarked on Bradley's intelligence and aptitude for the work. The professor is said to have noted, "he looks for *the law* by which things act."

Ultimately, Bradley succeeded in buying his freedom through proceeds from his inventions and his work for hire, even though U.S. law prevented him from patenting his steam engine.

Further Reading

Haskins, James. *Outward Dreams: Black Inventors and Their Inventions.* New York: Walker, 1991, 24ff.

Bragg, Robert Henry
(1919–) *physicist*

During his career as a researcher and educator in materials science and mineral engineering, Robert Henry Bragg has become a nationally recognized expert in materials science and the use of X-ray techniques to study the structure and electrical properties of carbon and other substances.

Robert Henry Bragg was born in Jacksonville, Florida, on August 11, 1919. His father, also named Robert Henry Bragg, became an organizer for the longshoremen's union in Mobile, Alabama. When he was 9, Bragg's parents separated, and his mother, Lilly Camille McFarland Bragg, became a seamstress to support her family. Young Robert Bragg went to Chicago in 1933 to live with an uncle, a plumbing contractor who urged his young nephew to capitalize on his technical aptitude. The encouragement took.

After graduation from high school in 1937, Bragg attended Woodrow Wilson Junior College. He enrolled in an Army Signal Corps training program for defense plant workers that was taught at the Illinois Institute of Technology (IIT). However, the U.S. entry into World War II was clearly approaching, and Bragg joined the army in 1942, earning the rank of second lieutenant. His orders took him to combat zones in both New Guinea and the Philippines, and he received two military decorations for his service there. After the war he returned to IIT to continue exploring radar and electronics concepts that he had worked with during his earlier training and military duty. However, he soon switched to physics because he wanted to delve deeper into why things work the way they do—not just how they work. He completed his bachelor's degree at IIT in 1949 and went on to earn a master's degree in physics in 1951, also at IIT.

Bragg worked at the Portland Cement Association of Skokie, Illinois, for several years, using X-ray crystallography to detect chemical compounds present in samples he was studying. However, he soon returned to IIT to soak up more knowledge. There, he completed his Ph.D. in physics in 1960, with a dissertation on X-ray crystallography—delving deeper into the uses of this powerful methodology. X-ray crystallography not only enables scientists to determine the presence of particular substances but it also allows them to examine the very structure and arrangement of individual atoms within the molecules of a substance.

While completing his doctorate, Bragg worked from 1959 to 1961 as a senior physicist at the Research Institute at IIT. Then he began a long association, from 1961 to 1981, with Lockheed Missile and Space Company's Palo Alto Research Laboratory in the San Francisco Bay Area. Lockheed was currently working on heat shields for spacecraft that would need protection while reentering the atmosphere from space. This kind of protection is required by all reentry modules, such as the Apollo command module, at the time, or more recently, the space shuttle. The characteristics of carbon make this substance an ideal material for heat shields. It is not heavy, it absorbs heat well, and it can hold up under extremely high temperatures. Bragg used X-ray crystallography to study the structure and reactions of carbon at the atomic and molecular level.

During his years at Lockheed, Bragg also joined the faculty of the University of California at Berkeley in 1969 as professor of materials science and mineral engineering, retiring in 1987. He also served as chair of the department from 1978 to 1981. Bragg had a concurrent appointment during the same period as principal investigator for the Materials and Molecular Division at nearby Lawrence Berkeley National Laboratory, which is affiliated with the university.

Bragg has served in many capacities as a scientific adviser in Washington, D.C., including work as a program director for the Department of Energy in the Division of Materials Science from 1981 to 1982. He has also consulted for the Naval Research Laboratory, the National Institute of Standards and Technology, and the National Science Foundation. In 1992 and 1993, he worked in Nigeria as a Fulbright scholar.

Bragg has received numerous professional honors, including election in 1995 as a Fellow of the National Society of Black Physicists. It is an award he values highly.

Further Reading

Heppenheimer, T. A. "Robert Henry Bragg," *Notable Black American Scientists*. Kristine Krapp, ed. Detroit: Gale Research, 1990, 40–41.

Sammons, Vivian Ovelton. *Blacks in Science and Medicine*. New York: Hemisphere Publishing, 1990, 179.

Bramwell, Fitzgerald Burton (Jerry Bramwell)
(1945–) *chemist, educator*

A dedicated science educator, Fitzgerald Burton Bramwell has served as a beacon of direction for graduate university research in chemistry, the sciences, and the humanities for more than 30 years. Through his research, he has also made contributions to chemistry, including the development of superconductors and organic fungicides.

Fitzgerald Burton Bramwell was born on May 16, 1945, in Brooklyn, New York. Jerry, as he was known, was the son of Lula Burton Bramwell, one of the first women in New York City to become a high school principal, and Fitzgerald Bramwell, who held a degree in chemical engineering from Cooper Union College in New York (1934) at a time when few African Americans had obtained engineering degrees. Encouraged by his parents and other members of his family, Jerry excelled in school. His parents sent him at age 13 to Phillips Academy, a respected college preparatory school in Andover, Massachusetts, where he laid the groundwork to become a research chemist.

Bramwell enrolled at Columbia University in 1962, where he earned his bachelor's degree in 1966. That spring, he spent three months in Delft in the Netherlands doing advanced research under a scholarship from the Royal Dutch Shell Corporation. The following year, Bramwell completed a M.S. in chemistry at the University of Michigan, Ann Arbor, and received his Ph.D. in chemistry, also from the University of Michigan, in 1970.

Bramwell's research for both his master's and doctorate degrees examined the ability of light to quickly transform the structure and reactivity of certain carbon-based molecules. In his experiments, Bramwell cooled the molecules to extremely cold temperatures, just a few degrees above absolute zero (–273 degrees Celsius or –460 degrees Fahrenheit). He was able to use electron spin resonance spectroscopy to study the greatly slowed molecular changes as they took place. His interest focused on corranulene and paracyclophanes, which are particularly light-sensitive carbon-based compounds.

Bramwell began his career as a research chemist at ESSO Research and Engineering Company, studying the electrical properties of petroleum products. However, he soon moved on from industrial employment to the challenges

PRESTON RIDGE LIBRARY
COLLIN COLLEGE
FRISCO, TX 75035

Fitzgerald Burton "Jerry" Bramwell is the author of more than 250 publications and invited presentations in the field of organotin chemistry, organic superconductors, and applications of electron spin resonance spectroscopy. As vice president of the University of Kentucky, he made numerous advancements in the university's standing as a science research center. *(Photo by Lee P. Thomas, courtesy of Fitzgerald B. Bramwell)*

lege students of chemistry, first published in 1978 and revised in 1990. By making the study of science a positive experience Bramwell hopes to attract more students, including minority students, to science as a profession.

Bramwell continued to pursue his research as well, exploring the development of carbon-based superconductors (materials that conduct electricity almost completely without resistance when cooled to very low temperatures). He is the author of more than 250 abstracts, papers and invited presentations in the field of organotin chemistry, organic superconductors, and applications of electron spin resonance spectroscopy. He serves as a consultant in research and technology transfer to universities, states, scientific organizations, the National Science Foundation, and the National Institutes of Health. More recently, he has worked on the development of new carbon-based molecules known as organotins. These organic molecules when combined with tin atoms are useful as fungicides.

In 1995, Bramwell accepted the post of vice president, research and graduate studies, at the University of Kentucky (UK). In this position, among his accomplishments were advancing the University of Kentucky national research ranking from 47th to 32nd among public research institutions; leading the graduate school in meeting desegregation guideline goals, becoming the first major University of Kentucky academic unit ever to achieve this goal; nearly tripling university patent and royalty income; nearly doubling income from grants and contracts; ensuring the employment of more than 5,000 Kentuckians in scientific research related positions; facilitating more than 20 high technology start-up companies; establishing numerous research centers, institutes, and agreements, including an agreement for UK researchers in molecular biology to use the powerful X rays of the Advanced Photon Source facilities at Argonne National Laboratory in Chicago for the study of molecular

of academia, accepting a position on the faculty of Brooklyn College, part of the City University of New York (CUNY). In 1971, he was promoted to the graduate faculty at CUNY, with promotion to full professor by 1988. In 1989, he served as acting dean for research and graduate studies and was confirmed as dean in 1990.

Always committed to effective science education, Bramwell and his colleagues developed laboratory and textbook materials for use by col-

structures. Bramwell continued as vice president of the university until July 2001, when he returned to teaching.

Further Reading

Kessler, James H., J. S. Kidd, Renee A. Kidd, and Katherine A. Morin. *Distinguished African American Scientists of the 20th Century*. Phoenix, Ariz.: Oryx Press, 1996, 60–62.

McArthur, Maureen. "UK Researchers will have Access to Argonne Facility," UK Chandler Medical Center News. Available online. URL: http://www.mc.uky.edu/mcpr/news/1999/march/argonne.htm. Updated on October 25, 1999.

Branson, Herman Russell

(1914–1995) *physicist, chemist, educator*

Herman Branson did significant work in biochemistry in collaboration with chemist Linus Pauling, helping to define the structure of proteins. He headed the physics department at Howard University for 27 years and developed programs for both an undergraduate major and graduate studies in physics. He also served as president for both Central State University and Lincoln University.

Born in Pocahontas, Virginia, on August 14, 1914, Herman Branson and his family later moved to Washington, D.C., where he became valedictorian of his graduating class at Dunbar High School in 1932. After attending Pittsburgh University for two years, he completed his bachelor's degree at Virginia State College at Petersburg, graduating summa cum laude in 1936.

Three years later, in 1939, he earned a Ph.D. in physics from the University of Cincinnati, where he became the first African American to earn that distinction. His dissertation had three parts: a description of his research results, "The Differential Action of Soft X-Rays on Tubifex;" a practical description, "The Construction and Operation of an X-Ray Intensity Measuring Device;" and a theoretical section, "On the Quantization of Mass."

He accepted a position teaching mathematics and physics for two years at Dillard University in New Orleans, Louisiana. In 1941, he became assistant professor of physics and chemistry at Howard University in Washington, D.C. He became head of the physics department that same year, a position he held until 1968. He was promoted to full professor in 1944.

During the 1948–49 academic year, Branson accepted a research grant as a National Research Council Senior Fellow to work with Linus Pauling at the California Institute of Technology. He contributed to research that led to dramatically new understanding of the helical structure of proteins. This discovery had broad implications for the fields of biology and biochemistry, as well as diseases caused by aberrations in protein structure. Sickle cell anemia is one such disease.

Branson left Howard in 1968 to serve as president at Central State University in Wilberforce, Ohio. He remained for two years, before accepting the role of president at Pennsylvania's Lincoln University, the first U.S. college founded for black students. He remained there until his retirement in 1985, at the age of 71. After his retirement, he returned to Howard, where he continued his lifetime work of encouraging students to become scientists.

Herman Branson died on June 7, 1995, in Washington, D.C.

Further Reading

Kessler, James H., J. S. Kidd, Renee A. Kidd, and Katherine A. Morin. *Distinguished African American Scientists of the 20th Century*. Phoenix, Ariz.: Oryx Press, 1996.

"Lincoln University's Prexy Branson Ends 15-Year Term," *Jet*, April 22, 1985, 32.

Obituary. *New York Times (Late New York Edition)*. (June 13, 1995), B7.

Obituary. *New York Times Biographical Service*, 26 (June 1995), 864.

Bromery, Randolph Wilson
(Bill Bromery)
(1926–) *geologist, geophysicist*

Randolph Wilson Bromery pioneered the study of geophysical structures from the air. He has made a mark as an educator and provided administrative guidance as president or acting president at several colleges and universities. He has also headed several geoscience and geophysical firms, as well as serving as president of the Geological Society of America.

On January 18, 1926, "Bill" Bromery was born in Cumberland, Maryland, to Lawrence E. Bromery, a talented jazz musician, and Edith E. Bromery. He spent his childhood years in Cumberland, where the Bromerys, their four children, and two grandparents lived together in a small house. By the time Bill was four, the Great Depression had begun to take its toll on the family's finances, his father lost his main employment as a restaurant manager, and the family relied on his father's income from playing trumpet in a jazz quintet and janitorial work. Bill's mother and grandmother also ran a catering service, and Bill's grandmother was a hairdresser. His grandfather was a Pullman porter.

During World War II, Bromery served in the U.S. Air Force as a member of the Tuskegee Airmen. After the war, he took correspondence courses, studied at the University of Michigan and at Howard University. He earned his B.S. degree in 1957 at Howard University in Washington, D.C., and obtained his M.S. degree in 1962 from American University, also in Washington, D.C. In 1968, he received his Ph.D. in geology from Johns Hopkins University, in Baltimore, Maryland.

From 1948 to 1967, Bromery held a position as exploration geophysicist with the U.S. Geological Survey, becoming professor of geophysics and department chair at the University of Massachusetts at Amherst in 1968. In 1970, he became vice chancellor and was promoted to chancellor in 1971, a position he held for eight years, after which he returned to teaching.

Bromery subsequently became acting president of Westfield State College from 1988 to 1990. He also held the position of president of the Geological Society of America in 1989 and headed the board in 1992. He became president of Springfield College in 1993.

Further Reading

Garcia-Johnson, R. "Randolph Wilson Bromery," *Notable Black American Scientists*, Kristine Krapp, ed. Detroit: Gale Research, 1999, 43–45.

Kessler, James H., J. S. Kidd, Renee A. Kidd, and Katherine A. Morin. *Distinguished African American Scientists of the 20th Century*. Phoenix, Ariz.: Oryx Press, 1996, 22–27.

Who's Who Among African Americans, 13th ed. Detroit: Gale Group, 2000.

Brooks, Carolyn Branch
(1946–) *microbiologist, educator*

As a microbiologist, Carolyn Branch Brooks has made productive contributions to the study of molecular biology and environmental microbiology, with an emphasis on crop production improvement through microbiology, including genetic engineering and selective breeding of plants. An outstanding and supportive mentor, she also has received accolades for her high level of commitment to teaching.

Carolyn Branch grew up in a well-to-do African-American neighborhood in Richmond, Virginia. She was born on July 8, 1946, the second daughter of Shirley Booker Branch and Charles Walker Branch. She and her sister lived with their parents and great-grandparents. When her parents moved across town in the 1950s, Carolyn continued to attend her former school in north Richmond, traveling to school daily on a public bus. At a time when schools, public transportation, and many other facilities were segregated by law in Richmond, she unknowingly broke the law every day by sitting at the front of the bus—but no one ever reprimanded her so she did not recognize her own unconscious activism until civil rights demonstrations in Richmond made her aware of it.

As a youngster and as a teenager, Carolyn excelled at sports and was an avid student. She became interested in microbiology when she met a microbiologist through a summer program designed to encourage young African Americans to pursue careers in science. However, while her mother encouraged her to pursue her ambitions, her father thought spending money on college was impractical, since she did not need a college degree to get a job that paid well. The controversy became a moot point, however, when Carolyn received scholarship offers from six different colleges.

Branch decided in favor of Tuskegee University in Tuskegee, Alabama. Science was a respected discipline at Tuskegee, possibly thanks to the legacy of GEORGE WASHINGTON CARVER. At Tuskegee, she met Henry Brooks, an education major, and the two married at the conclusion of Branch's second year at the university. Encouraged by faculty and her husband, she combined raising a family with earning her degree, which she received in 1968. She went on to complete her master's degree in 1971, by which time she had two sons and a daughter.

Brooks received a scholarship to Ohio State University, in Columbus, Ohio, where she completed her doctorate in microbiology in 1977. There, her dissertation research explored how macrophages help the human immune system destroy invading malaria parasites in the bloodstream.

Moving to Kentucky after completing her Ph.D., she worked on a community health nutrition study at Kentucky State University in Frankfort. Working with elderly patients, she tried to find a method for tracking key trace mineral nutrients in their diets without relying on oral reports. She observed a correlation between trace minerals in patients' hair and the amount of the same trace mineral nutrients in their diets, indicating that hair analysis might prove useful. However, she also noticed that the level of intake for other nutrients did not correlate with hair analysis results. From this she concluded that hair analysis at best has very limited usefulness as an indicator of diet.

In 1981, Brooks joined the faculty at the University of Maryland Eastern Shore (UMES), a land-grant, historically black college founded in 1886. By 1994, she had become dean of the School of Agriculture and Natural Sciences and director of 1890 research (research programs funded by land-grant legislation passed in 1890). There, much of her research has emphasized agricultural crop improvement that can be gained by encouragement of nitrogen-fixing soil bacteria and their relationship with plants, in particular legumes (such as peas and beans). As of early 2002, Brooks had added the position of executive assistant to the president and chief of staff to her other duties.

She traveled to Africa to augment her studies, visiting Togo and Senegal in West Africa in 1984 and 1985 and Cameroon, West Africa, in 1988. She helped local scientists increase food crops in both regions. Her research during her first visit helped improve food production through the study of the nitrogen-fixing microbes present in an African groundnut.

In 1988, Brooks was one of several African-American educators honored in a White House ceremony celebrating their "exemplary achievements as educators, researchers and role models." In 1990, she received the Outstanding Educator Award from the Maryland Association for Higher Education.

Further Reading

Fontes, David E. "Carolyn Branch Brooks," *Notable Black American Scientists.* Kristine Krapp, ed. Detroit: Gale Research, 1990, 45.

Kessler, James H., J. S. Kidd, Renee A. Kidd, and Katherine A. Morin. *Distinguished African American Scientists of the 20th Century*. Phoenix, Ariz.: Oryx Press, 1996.

Brown, Russell Wilfred
(1905–1986) *microbiologist*

Best known for his work with polio vaccine at Tuskegee University, Russell Wilfred Brown was also recognized by his colleagues as a meticulous and thorough researcher in microbiology. In 1951, Brown was selected to lead a research group at Tuskegee that developed a strain of cells for use in development of a polio vaccine.

Russell Wilfred Brown was born on January 17, 1905, in the small town of Gray, located in Terrebonne Parish in southeastern Louisiana. He obtained his B.S. degree in 1926 from Howard University in Washington, D.C., after which he enrolled for graduate studies at the University of Chicago without completing a degree there. He taught biology for a year in 1930 at Rust College in Mississippi, and he then returned to his graduate studies at Iowa State University, receiving a master's degree in 1932.

Again interspersing his teaching with his graduate studies, Brown received an appointment to the faculty of Langston University in Oklahoma as assistant professor of bacteriology. He completed his doctorate at Iowa State in 1936.

In that year, Brown began a long and productive association with Tuskegee Institute (now Tuskegee University), joining the faculty as instructor. Taking a brief hiatus in 1943 to work at Iowa State as a research assistant, he returned to Tuskegee later that year with an appointment as professor of bacteriology. In 1944, the Institute placed Brown in charge of the Carver Research Foundation, which he headed until 1951. (The Carver Research Foundation was founded in 1938 by GEORGE WASHINGTON CARVER with $30,000 of his own savings to continue his work after his death.) Though Brown went on to an interesting research project, he continued to serve on the foundation's board until his retirement.

In 1951, Brown was asked to head a research team at Tuskegee that was to develop a strain of cells for use in experimentation, development, and testing of potential polio vaccines. Part of the challenge was not only to produce cultures in large quantities but also to find and test methods for keeping them safe from temperature changes and other damaging environments during storage and shipping to the laboratories that would use them. The volume was impressive—some 600,000 cultures were shipped by the Tuskegee group to polio research laboratories nationwide between 1953 and 1955. One of the colleagues Brown involved in this project was JAMES HENRY MERIWETHER HENDERSON, a research associate and professor of biology at Tuskegee, with whom Brown later coauthored a paper about the project for the *Journal of the History of Medicine and Allied Sciences*.

Brown spent the 1956–57 academic year in postgraduate studies at Yale, but he returned to Tuskegee, where he became vice president and dean in 1962. Brown retired in 1970. The following year, the board of directors of the University of Nevada honored Brown with a one-year appointment as Distinguished Professor of Microbiology at the University of Nevada School of Medical Sciences. He received an honorary doctorate from Tuskegee that same year.

Russell Wilfred Brown died on July 29, 1986.

Further Reading
Brown, Russell W., and James H. M. Henderson. "The Mass Production of HeLa Cells at Tuskegee Institute, 1953–55." *Journal of the History of Medicine and Allied Sciences* 38, no. 4 (1938): 415–431.

Sammons, Vivian O. *Blacks in Science and Medicine*. Hemisphere Publishing, 1990.

Browne, Marjorie Lee
(1914–1979) *mathematician*

In 1949, along with EVELYN BOYD GRANVILLE, Marjorie Lee Browne became one of the first African-American women to earn a Ph.D. in mathematics. Browne taught mathematics at North Carolina Central University (NCCU) for 30 years and took a strong hand in obtaining funding and computer equipment for her department and her students.

Marjorie Lee was born in Memphis, Tennessee, on September 9, 1914. Her mother, Mary Taylor Lee, died when Marjorie was still an infant, but her father, Lawrence Johnson Lee, took an interest in his children's growth and learning. A postal clerk for the railroad, he had attended college classes for two years, which was quite unusual in both black and white communities in 1914. He loved mathematics, was good at mental calculations, and passed on his enthusiasm to his children. He also had a good, steady job, which combined with loans and Marjorie's own employment to help make a private high school and a college education possible for Marjorie, even in the depression years of the 1930s.

As a young woman, Marjorie Lee excelled at her studies, music, and tennis (earning the title of Memphis city women's tennis singles champion as a teenager). She went to public schools at the elementary level but attended LeMoyne High School, a private school. After graduation in 1931, she enrolled for her undergraduate studies at Howard University in Washington, D.C., where she graduated cum laude in 1935.

After a short stint teaching physics and mathematics at Gilbert Academy in New Orleans, she entered graduate school at the University of Michigan at Ann Arbor, where she earned her master's degree in mathematics in 1939. For several years she taught during the school year as a faculty member at Wiley College, located in Marshall, Texas. Then she spent summers in Michigan working on her doctorate.

Her life became a little less split in 1947, when she became a teaching fellow at the University of Michigan. She received her doctorate in mathematics in 1949—shortly after Evelyn Boyd Granville received hers from Yale University in New Haven, Connecticut.

That year, Browne joined the mathematics faculty at North Carolina Central University (NCCU), where she taught for 30 years. Browne was committed to improving secondary school education in mathematics and through her efforts, NCCU received a National Science Foundation grant to establish a series of summer institutes for teachers. NCCU was the first primarily black university to receive such a grant from the NSF. Browne directed many of these seminars and she also wrote four instructional textbooks for the seminars: *Sets, Logic, and Mathematical Thought* (1957), *Introduction to Linear Algebra* (1959), *Elementary Matrix Algebra* (1969), and *Algebraic Structures* (1974). She also wrote a brief article on classical groups, which was published by *American Mathematical Monthly* in 1955.

Browne also spearheaded a proposal to IBM that brought the school a $60,000 grant for establishing the school's first computer laboratory, which she helped install and set up in 1960 to 1961. She also lined up a Shell Grant for the school's mathematics students, providing awards to outstanding students over a 10-year period.

Browne had several opportunities during her career to extend her postgraduate studies. In the 1952–53 school year, she held a Ford Foundation fellowship that enabled her to study combinatorial topology at Cambridge University in England, also giving her a chance to travel throughout Europe. Five years later, during 1958–59, she studied numerical analysis and computing at the University of California at Los Angeles under a National Science Foundation Faculty Fellowship. She took advantage of that location to extend her travels to Mexico. In 1965–66, she obtained a fellowship to pursue the study of differential topology at Columbia University in New York. In 1975, Browne was honored by the North Carolina Council of Teachers of Mathematics with the first award of the W. W. Rankin Memorial Award for Excellence in Mathematics Education.

Browne saw herself as a "pure" mathematician, calling herself a "pre-Sputnik" mathematician focused less on practical, real-world applications and more on the abstract philosophy of mathematics. "I always, always, *always* liked mathematics!" Marjorie Lee Browne is said to have remarked in 1979. Browne said she enjoyed her friends, but most of all she loved spending time alone with mathematical challenges. What better way to spend one's life than in the pursuit of an activity one loves best? It is a tribute to Browne's teaching and leadership that at least four of her students earned doctorates in mathematics.

On October 19, 1979, Marjorie Lee Browne died in Durham, North Carolina, apparently of a heart attack. She was 65. That same year, some of her students set up a scholarship fund in her memory, commemorating her humanitarian spirit, her own generosity, and her commitment to education. Browne often helped students financially with her own money, firmly believing that no student who really wanted an education should be denied it for financial reasons. The Marjorie Lee Browne Trust Fund provides for an annual scholarship awarded to a student in mathematics and computer science at North Carolina Central University, as well as a lecture series. In 2001, the university where she earned her doctorate—the University of Michigan at Ann Arbor—also established a lecture series in her honor.

Further Reading

Hine, Darlene Clark. *The Facts On File Encyclopedia of Black Women in America: Science, Health, and Medicine.* New York: Facts On File, 1997, 45–47.

Morrow, Charlene, and Teri Perl, editors. *Notable Women in Mathematics: A Biographical Dictionary.* Westport, Conn.: Greenwood Press, 1998, 21–25.

Warren, Wini. *Black Women Scientists in the United States.* Bloomington: Indiana University Press, 1999, 23–25.

Buggs, Charles Wesley
(1906–1991) *bacteriologist*

Years ago Charles Wesley Buggs was already concerned in his research with a topic that is still much in the news: resistance built up by bacteria to antibiotics that are intended to kill or hamper them.

Born on August 6, 1906, in Brunswick, Georgia, Charles Wesley Buggs was the son of John Wesley Buggs and Leonora Vane Clark Buggs. He did his undergraduate work at Morehouse College in Atlanta, where he majored in zoology and completed his bachelor's degree in 1928. Buggs then taught for a year as an instructor at Dover State College in Delaware before beginning graduate work at the University of Chicago, which was interrupted for financial reasons by another teaching stint at a high school in Key West, Florida. He was then able to continue his studies at the University of Minnesota, where he completed his M.S. in 1931, followed by his Ph.D. in 1934, with the help of financial aid from a Shevlin fellowship and the Julius Rosenwald Fund.

Before establishing himself at Dillard University in New Orleans in 1935, Buggs spent a year teaching chemistry at Bishop College in Mobile, Alabama. Then he joined the Dillard faculty as a biology professor and chair of the natural sciences division from 1935 to 1943. In 1943, he was able to spend a year at the Marine Biological Laboratory at Woods Hole, Massachusetts, with the help of a Rosenwald fellowship. After that he went to Wayne State

University in Detroit, Michigan, to accept a position in the College of Medicine. He stayed for six years, returning to Dillard in 1949, the same year his book, *Premedical Education for Negroes,* came out from the U.S. government, exploring interpretations and recommendations for better preparation than was currently available. Buggs remained at Dillard for seven years before moving on to Howard University in Washington, D.C., where he became professor of microbiology from 1956 to 1971 and department head from 1958 to 1970.

Meanwhile, the Charles R. Drew Postgraduate Medical School at the University of California, Los Angeles, had appointed him as project director in 1969, a position in which he served at the same time as he maintained his responsibilities at Howard. That same year, and for the next seven years, Buggs was also visiting professor at the University of Southern California. In 1971, he left Howard University for California,

serving as dean of Drew Postgraduate Medical School in 1972 and becoming professor of microbiology at California State University at Long Beach in 1973, where he remained until he retired 10 years later, in 1983.

Charles Wesley Buggs died at the age of 85, on September 13, 1991.

Further Reading

Buggs, Charles Wesley. "Antibiotic Agents and Some General Principles of Antibiotic Therapy," *Journal of the National Medical Association* (1947): 45–47.

———. *Premedical Education for Negroes: Interpretations and Recommendations Based Upon a Survey in Fifteen Selected Negro Colleges.* Washington, D.C.: Government Printing Office, 1949.

Sammons, Vivian Ovelton. *Blacks in Science and Education.* Washington, D.C.: Hemisphere Publishers, 1989.

PRESTON RIDGE LIBRARY
COLLIN COLLEGE
FRISCO, TX 75035

C

Calloway, Nathaniel Oglesby
(N. O. Calloway)
(1907–1979) *organic chemist, physician*

Nathaniel Calloway, whose father had been a slave, became respected as a physician and as a community activist in the Chicago area. He reorganized the Chicago chapter of the Urban League in the late 1950s, and late in life he taught at the University of Wisconsin, Madison, where he showed that racist white supremacy claims have no basis in scientific fact. Yet his career was highly controversial. He strove to prevent the advent of early 1960s activism in the Chicago Urban League, which led to upheaval and dissension in the group and brought on considerable criticism of Calloway. Later, the Wisconsin State Medical Examining Board brought charges against him related to a prescription drug scandal involving his medical practice in Madison.

Nathaniel Oglesby Calloway was born on October 10, 1907, in Tuskegee, Alabama. He obtained his university education at Iowa State University, completing his B.S. there in 1930, and his Ph.D. in chemistry three years later, in 1933. He began his scientific career immediately, accepting an appointment that same year as head of the chemistry department at Tuskegee Institute (now Tuskegee University). He moved on to a position of assistant professor at prestigious Fisk University in Memphis, Tennessee, in 1936. Embarking on another phase of his career, Calloway entered medical school at the University of Illinois, while simultaneously holding a position as instructor of pharmacology at the University of Chicago in 1940. He received his M.D. from the University of Illinois in 1943 and then served during World War II as a lieutenant in the U.S. Army Medical Corps.

As a chemist, Calloway studied aspects of ketone production, a type of molecule that is widely used in industrial applications of organic chemistry. (For example, acetone is a ketone.) Calloway investigated ways to improve ketone production by using metal halide catalysts or finding alternative methods for reducing unwanted reactions.

After he received his M.D., Calloway's medical career thrived. He taught at the University of Illinois Medical School, rising to assistant professor and senior physician by 1947. He also became assistant chief of medicine at Percy Jones Army Hospital and was promoted to major by 1950. He began a group medical practice in Chicago in 1958, became chief of the medical staff at the Tomah, Wisconsin, Veterans Administration Hospital in 1963, and started a private medical practice in Madison, Wisconsin, in 1966, continuing the practice until his death in 1979.

As a research scientist, once he had both the organic chemistry and medical backgrounds, Calloway was able to apply both areas of expertise. He became interested in senescence, or aging, as manifested at the cellular and tissue levels and wrote several papers on the subject.

Calloway's work as an activist and as an agent for parity for African Americans in all aspects of life is one of the most interesting facets of his career. In 1955, he was appointed president of the Chicago Urban League. Founded in 1910, with headquarters in New York City, the stated mission of the Urban League movement is to "enable African Americans to secure economic self-reliance, parity and power and civil rights." However, the Chicago chapter had become disorganized and torn apart by disagreeing factions. Calloway was able to bring peace and order to the chapter—temporarily. However, with the advent of the 1960s, a more radical type of civil rights activism was catching hold, and many Chicago Urban League members thought the Urban League should be spearheading the movement. Calloway disagreed. He believed in "working from within the system," a highly unpopular point of view, and he soon found himself lambasted from both within and outside the league. He was removed from office in a 1960 vote, and he resigned from board membership in protest in 1961. Finally, with Urban League leaders, including Calloway, publishing embarrassing criticisms of one another in the press, Calloway resigned from the National Board in 1962.

From Chicago, Calloway moved to Madison, Wisconsin, where he opened his private medical practice in 1966 and accepted a position as lecturer at the University of Wisconsin, Madison, in 1970. For eight years, until just before his death, he taught a class on genetics that debunked the racial stereotypes promoted by white supremacists. Using his knowledge of genetics, he showed that so-called racial differences are much more likely to be caused by social and economic factors than genetics. He argued that slavery and economic repression had left scars, but that these effects were not intrinsically part of being African American. As the 21st century moves farther away from the days of slavery, and as slavery's social and economic effects begin to fade, Calloway's arguments ring truer than ever.

In 1975, Calloway found himself at the center of another controversy. The State of Wisconsin Medical Examining Board handed down a decision preventing him, temporarily, from prescribing methaqualone (known commonly by the brand name Quaalude). An investigation was made into the large number of prescriptions for this drug he had written for this depressant. In 1978, an article in the *Madison Press Connection* alleged that 75 percent—60,000—of Madison's total number of prescriptions for methaqualone in 1976 were written by N. O. Calloway. In his defense, Calloway did not debate the number of prescriptions he had written. However, he said they were medically required. He asked whether any of his patients had been found to be abusing the drug. And he said that he thought racial bias was involved with the charges.

The medical board charged Calloway again in 1978, this time with endangering his patients with excessive prescriptions. However, the question was never resolved. Calloway, who had been struggling against cancer for a long time, closed his medical practice in 1979 and died.

Further Reading

Chiacchia, Kenneth B. "Nathaniel Oglesby Calloway," *Notable Black American Scientists*, Kristine Krapp, ed. Detroit: Gale Research, 1999, 54–55.

"Noted physician, activist Dr. N. O. Calloway, 72, dies," *Jet*, December 27, 1979.

Strickland, Arvarh E. *History of the Chicago Urban League;* with an introduction by Christopher R. Reed. Columbia: University of Missouri Press, 2001.

Cannon, Thomas Calvin, Jr.
(1943–) *communications engineer, inventor*

A pioneer leader in fiber optics research, Thomas C. Cannon, Jr., was instrumental in developing the first commercial fiber optic telecommunications system in the United States (using very fine glass fibers to transmit audio, video, and data information encoded as pulses of light). Today millions of people enjoy Olympics sports events in the comfort of their living rooms via cable television over fiber optic cables. In 1984, however, when Thomas C. Cannon, Jr., was one of the honorary runners carrying the Olympic torch, fiber optics was still in its pioneer stage. It was thanks to Cannon and his research team that hundreds of thousands of miles of fiber optics cables exist today.

Born in Houston, Texas, on January 28, 1943, to Thomas C. Cannon, Sr., and Lillian Bland Cannon, Cannon received his bachelor's degree in aeronautical engineering in 1964 from Purdue University in Indiana. He obtained his master's degree from Purdue in 1966 and his Ph.D. in 1970. In 1967, he married Joyce Elaine Stott. They have four sons.

Cannon's preparation for work with fiber optics began while working for the Bell Laboratories Federal Systems Division on a cable system that would help detect submarine activity. It was Cannon's job to determine if the cables of the system, made of the tough synthetic material Kevlar, could withstand the same kinds of stress and pressure as cables made of steel.

When another division of Bell Labs began experimenting with fiber optics in 1974, they needed to know how well these tiny glass fibers would withstand stress during the manufacturing and installation of the cable. Without this knowledge no one was certain whether fiber optic cables would be practical. The equations that Cannon and his team worked out, predicting the adverse forces the fibers would be subjected to, allowed manufacturers to handle the material within the safety margins of the stress.

He and his team of researchers also came up with an invention, now called the ST Connector, solving the problems related to connecting the hair-thin fibers, which previously had lost light energy at their junctions.

In addition to his expertise as an inventor, Cannon was personally dedicated to testing the solutions he found. In 1976, when an experimental fiber optic system was installed under the streets of Chicago, Cannon personally climbed down manholes and aided in splicing connections.

In addition to his commercial work with fiber optics, Cannon was also instrumental in developing the Tactical Optical Fiber Connector (TOFC), which was used by the military to transmit firing signals to the Patriot missiles used in Operation Desert Storm, during the Gulf War. Fiber optics work particularly well in battle conditions because they are lightweight, high capacity, and impervious to electrical interference. They also do not emit any radiation detectable by enemy reconnaissance. He also worked for Sandia National Laboratories for three years (1989 to 1992) on the reliability and safety of nuclear devices.

Cannon, who was an Alfred P. Sloan Fellow at Stanford University, received a master's in management science from the Stanford University Graduate School of Business in 1987. His book, *Survival Routines for Professionals: Moving Toward Corporate Success,* published that year, reflects his continuing interest in offering guidance and encouragement to minority professionals.

Further Reading
Brown, Martha. "Modern African-American Inventors," *Upscale,* February 1996, reproduced on Emeagwali.com. Available online. URL: http://emeagwali.com/inventors/index.html. Downloaded on April 13, 2002.

Cannon, Thomas C. *Survival Routines for Professionals: Moving Toward Corporate Success.* Englewood Cliffs, N.J.: Prentice Hall, 1988.

Milite, George A. "Thomas C. Cannon, Jr.," *Notable Black American Scientists,* Kristine Krapp, ed. Detroit: Gale Research, 1999, 58–59.

Carruthers, George Robert

(1939–   ) *astrophysicist, inventor*

George Robert Carruthers is best known for his major contributions to the design of ultraviolet cameras used during the *Apollo 16* mission on the surface of the Moon.

The first of four children, George Robert Carruthers was born on October 1, 1939, in Cincinnati, Ohio, to George and Sophia Carruthers. Young George was an avid science fiction reader and Buck Rogers fan and developed an early interest in science and astronomy. His father, a civil engineer in the Army Air Corps (now the U.S. Air Force) during and after World War II, encouraged his eldest son's interests. The boy delved in wholeheartedly, reading his father's books on astronomy and entering science fairs at school. At the age of 10, he built his own telescope, a simple handheld model.

Unfortunately, when George was only 12, his father died, leaving the boy without his mentor. Sophia Carruthers moved the family to Southside Chicago, where she went to work for the U.S. Post Office. There, George attended Englewood High School, where he received encouragement from his teachers, who recognized his keen interest in and talent for science. As a teenager, he received further encouragement when he won first prize at a science fair for an improved model of his telescope.

In 1957, Carruthers entered the University of Illinois at Champaign-Urbana, where he attended courses in the College of Engineering.

He completed his B.S. in aeronautical engineering there in 1961 and his M.S. in nuclear engineering the following year. In 1964, he obtained a Ph.D. in aeronautical and astronautical engineering (with minors in physics and astronomy), also from the University of Illinois, having completed research and a dissertation on the subject entitled *Experimental Investigations of Atomic Nitrogen Recombination.*

Carruthers received a postdoctoral appointment that same year in the Space Science Division of the Naval Research Laboratory, and in 1966 he went to work for the Naval Research Laboratory under a full-time civil service appointment. There, he has focused his research on ultraviolet (UV) space astronomy; ultraviolet measurements of Earth and planetary atmospheres; and design and development of electronic imaging sensors and UV instrumentation for use in space flight. UV astronomy makes use of observations made of ultraviolet, or UV, emissions from stars, planets, atmospheres, and other objects. Ultraviolet radiation is that portion of the electromagnetic spectrum that extends just beyond visible light (the near ultraviolet region) and includes wavelengths as far as the edge of the X-ray region of the spectrum (the far ultraviolet region). The work done by Carruthers has pioneered in these areas, and as of late 2002, he is head of the Ultraviolet Measurements Branch at the Naval Research Laboratory.

Carruthers was principal investigator for the Far Ultraviolet Camera/Spectrograph experiment on the *Apollo 16* mission, which took place in 1972. He developed instrumentation for this experiment, which provided the first global images of Earth's hydrogen exosphere (the outermost layer of atmosphere) and the UV airglow on the night side of the planet. Since then he has served as principal investigator or co-principal investigator on numerous experiments aboard sounding rockets, including far-UV studies of stars, nebulas, and comets, and Earth's upper atmosphere. He has also spearheaded several UV investigations carried out aboard space shuttle missions, including studies of Earth's upper atmosphere, stars, diffuse nebulas, and celestial diffuse background radiation. He has published extensive articles describing his work in professional scientific and popular astronomy journals. In 1983, Carruthers began working with the National Technical Association (NTA) as editor of the *Journal of the National Technical Association* and the *NTA Newsletter,* serving as chair of the journal's Editing and Review Committee as well.

Carruthers has also been active in education and public outreach. He served as technical editor and contributing author of a National Aeronautics and Space Administration (NASA) book, *Careers in Science and Technology,* has taught several courses for college students and teachers, and is co-producer of a series of videos on Earth and space science for high school students. He has also served on the Council of the Smithsonian Institution.

He is the recipient of numerous awards for his work, including the Arthur S. Flemming Award in 1970, awarded by the Washington, D.C. Jaycees; the Exceptional Achievement Scientific Award Medal from NASA in 1972; the Warner Prize of the American Astronomical Society; and an honorary doctorate of engineering from Michigan Technological University.

Further Reading

"Earth's Eye on the Moon," *Ebony,* October 1972, 61–63.

Kessler, James H., J. S. Kidd, Renee A. Kidd, and Katherine A. Morin. *Distinguished African American Scientists of the 20th Century.* Phoenix, Ariz.: Oryx Press, 1996, 36–39.

Sammons, Vivian Ovelton. *Blacks in Science and Medicine.* New York: Hemisphere Publishing, 1990, 49.

"Star Radiation Investigator," *Ebony,* October 1970, 6.

Carver, George Washington

(ca. 1861–1943) *biochemist, inventor, researcher*

George Washington Carver is perhaps the best-known African-American scientist, and his unflagging determination to find practical methods to improve the production of southern black farmers as well as increase the demand for their crops has commanded both widespread respect and praise. His influence in the development of Tuskegee University and its curriculum has stood as a role model for three-quarters of a century. Carver and his educational philosophy are

Astrophysicist George Robert Carruthers designed a camera used on the Moon by *Apollo 16* astronauts. *(Courtesy of George R. Carruthers)*

also at the center of an important controversy in African-American education.

Carver was born a slave in about July 1861 on German immigrant Moses Carver's 32-acre plantation near Diamond Grove, Missouri. (The date is approximate, since no real records were kept at the time. Carver himself thought he was born about January 1864, but other evidence indicates the earlier date is more likely.) Orphaned as a boy—his father was killed in a farming accident and his mother was captured by raiders—he was raised and given his earliest schooling by Moses and Susan Carver. The boy adopted the Carvers' last name and "George Washington" as his first and middle name. As a youngster of 11—by this time no longer a slave—he and the Carvers arranged for him to live and attend school in nearby Neosho, Missouri, and from that time on he resourcefully continued to extend his education despite his difficult childhood beginnings. Over the next 20 years, he found odd jobs to make a living and continue his education. He entered Simpson College in Indianola, Indiana, in 1890, transferring the following year to Iowa State Agricultural College (now Iowa State University) in Ames. He was the first African American to attend Iowa State, as well as the first black student to graduate, receiving his bachelor's degree in 1894. He went on to earn his master's degree in 1896, specializing in bacteriological laboratory work in botany.

From early childhood, Carver developed two traits that served him for the rest of his life: love of nature and frugality. Nature fascinated him and he could "see" where others only "looked." From this he developed the ability to see possibilities other people missed, and he developed a methodology that relied on observation first, then experimentation. Also, his ingrained dislike of waste led him to find uses for what seemed useless to most people.

In 1896, Carver joined the faculty of the Tuskegee Institute. This school was founded in Tuskegee, Alabama, by Booker T. Washington in 1881 for the training of black teachers, as well as industrial and agricultural instruction.

There, Carver's natural talent as a teacher quickly became apparent, and he soon became known as the "Wizard of Tuskegee," not only because of his efforts to help his students, but also because of his successes in extending the school's influence to farmers in the surrounding area.

Farmers in the South—including a large proportion of the black population—had long been dependent upon a one-crop, "Cotton is King" economy. Unfortunately, more than 100 years of growing cotton year after year on the same land had leached the nutrients from the soil. Large landowners had begun felling forestlands to grow cotton because the crop would no longer grow on existing farmlands. Small farmers, many of them African American, were out of luck. So, Carver began talking about alternative crops that didn't need the same nutrients or that gave nutrients back to the soil. But no one was listening. Then in 1914, the boll weevil destroyed field after field of cotton—completely wiping out most of what was left of cotton farming. Now, finally, farmers began to see that an alternative crop was the only way to save their farms.

Carver helped found and became head of the department of agriculture at Tuskegee, and for the next 47 years he focused his research and his teaching efforts on persuading cotton farmers to rotate their crops and use natural fertilizers to restore the worn-out soil. He visited farmers in Alabama with a traveling exhibit—which he called his "school on wheels"—to demonstrate the principles of soil enrichment. He established a State Agricultural Station. Slowly, these ideas began to make a difference.

In 1910, Carver became head of a newly created department of research at Tuskegee, and he introduced the relatively new science of chemurgy, the development of industrial uses for agricultural products. Now famous for this

Known for his enormous influence as a science educator, George Washington Carver became famous as an inventor of dozens of ways to use crops that southern farmers could grow, including peanuts. *(Tuskegee University Archives and Museums)*

approach, Carver focused his attention on peanuts after about 1914 and became known as the man who developed dozens of ways to use peanuts. Peanuts were an especially attractive crop for the depleted soils because they replenish leached nutrients, such as nitrogen. In 1921, he presented his many uses of the peanut before a congressional committee and gained national attention.

George Washington Carver was a man with practical instincts and clear priorities. He is often quoted as saying, "It is not the style of clothes one wears, neither the kind of automobile one drives, nor the amount of money one has in the bank that counts. These mean nothing. It is simply service that measures success." He died on June 5, 1943, at Tuskegee. Never married, Carver donated his life savings of $30,000 to the Tuskegee

Institute to continue his work after his death. The Institute used the money to fund the George Washington Carver Research Foundation, which continues to finance scholarship awards and a lecture series at what is now Tuskegee University.

Today, Carver's life and work are celebrated by two national monuments: the George Washington Carver National Historic Monument, a 210-acre park at the site of Carver's boyhood home, including Moses Carver's house and the Carver cemetery; and the Carver Memorial, a museum celebrating his lifework, located on the Tuskegee University campus.

Further Reading

Carver, George Washington. *George Washington Carver: In His Own Words.* Gary Kremer, ed. Columbia: University of Missouri Press, 1990.

"George Washington Carver All-University Celebration," University of Iowa. Available online. URL: http://www.lib.iastate.edu/spcl/gwc/resources/furtherresearch.html. Downloaded on August 4, 2002.

"George Washington Carver National Monument, Diamond, Missouri," National Park Service. Available online. URL: www.coax.net/people/LWF/carver.htm. Downloaded on April 19, 2002.

Spangenburg, Ray, and Diane K. Moser. *American Historic Places: Science and Invention.* New York: Facts On File, 1997, 53–66.

"Tuskegee National Historic Sites at Tuskegee, Alabama: George Washington Carver Museum," National Park Service. Available online. URL: http://www.coax.net/people/LWF/tuskegee.htm. Downloaded on April 19, 2002.

Yount, Lisa. *Black Scientists.* New York: Facts On File, 1991, 14–27.

Chambers, Vivian Murray
(1903–1984) *entomologist*

One of the first scientists to caution against the excessive use of DDT and other toxins for eradicating insect pests, Vivian Murray Chambers produced research results showing how residue runoff could end up in nearby lakes and rivers. Later, other researchers found that this residue runoff could do potentially lasting damage to the ecology.

Vivian Murray Chambers was born to Will and Elsie Chambers in Salisbury, North Carolina, on June 4, 1903. Vivian was still a baby when his father died, leaving his mother as the sole support for her three children. By the time Vivian was eight, he was lighting coal furnace fires for neighboring families to add his own earnings to his mother's income as a seamstress. Later she remarried, to the Rev. W. H. Howard, and the family moved to a house near the Livingstone College campus. Already a good student and interested in science, Vivian discovered that living near the college gave him a chance to get to know professors and students, so he never lacked for academic role models.

As an undergraduate, Chambers attended Shaw University in Raleigh, North Carolina, where he played on the football team and earned his B.S. in 1928. With his primary interest in medicine at the time, he earned a second degree, a B.A., from Columbia University in New York in 1931. By then, the United States had entered a period of extreme economic depression, and jobs were hard to find. In an effort to stimulate the economy, the federal government created several programs that provided jobs, among them the Works Progress Administration (WPA). Chambers pursued and obtained a WPA position as a researcher at the American Museum of Natural History. There, as he prepared insect specimens and studied them for his research, he developed a new interest in entomology.

Eager to pursue advanced study in the field, Chambers was accepted at Cornell University, but he ran into prejudice against blacks when he tried to enroll for work in entomology. However, Chambers had tremendous perseverance, and he obtained his master's degree in entomology in 1935.

After teaching science for a couple of years at Lincoln Normal School (now Alabama State University), he joined the biology faculty of Alabama A & M University in Huntsville in 1937—the beginning of a long and productive relationship. He completed his Ph.D. at Cornell in 1942 (becoming the only faculty member at Alabama A & M who had a doctorate, besides the president). His field was economic entomology, which includes the costs involved with controlling insect pests. He became full professor of biology at Alabama A & M in 1945, and in 1970 he became first dean of the newly established School of Arts and Sciences.

Up until the mid-20th century, little thought was given to the effects of pesticides on the ecology. Farmers needed to control insect pests, and DDT and other sprays could do the job. However, as Chambers showed in his dissertation, the residue from pesticides could run off into neighboring bodies of water. The residue, interspersed in the ground water and nearby waters, had potential for damaging other important parts of the region's ecology. The work done by Chambers served to lay the groundwork for a greater consciousness of the negative potential of human actions that otherwise might seem to have only positive effects, from the human viewpoint. His work stood at the foundation for a new way of looking at human stewardship of planet Earth, as it has begun to emerge in the 21st century.

Chambers retired in 1973 but continued his involvement with the university. On February 23, 1984, Vivian Chambers died in Huntsville. Alabama A & M has commemorated his work and life by naming the Chambers Science Building in his honor.

Further Reading

Milite, George A. "Vivian Murray Chambers: Entomologist," *Notable Black American Scientists*. Kristine Krapp, ed. Detroit: Gale Research, 1999, 62–63.

Sammons, Vivian O. *Blacks in Science and Education.* Washington, D.C.: Hemisphere Publishers, 1989, 52.

"Vivian Murray Chambers: Entomologist," Faces of Science: African Americans in the Sciences. Available online. URL: http://www.princeton. edu/~mcbrown/display/vivian_chambers.html. Updated on June 6, 2000.

Chappelle, Emmett
(1925–   ) *physical scientist, biochemist*

Holder of 14 U.S. patents, Emmett Chappelle is known as a "Renaissance Man" for his wide-ranging contributions in biochemistry, photobiology, astro chemistry, and invention.

Emmett Chappelle was born on October 24, 1925, in Phoenix, Arizona. Emmett's family raised cotton and milk cows on a small farm just outside of town. At the time, Phoenix was still a small town with very few African-American residents. Still, the schools were segregated. Emmett graduated from high school in 1942 at the top of his class of 25 students. As war was approaching, he was immediately inducted into the U.S. Army, where his good grades earned him assignment to the Army Specialized Training Program and college-level technical training. It was the beginning of a long technical and scientific career, most of it working for the U.S. government.

However, before he could finish his training he received reassignment to a black infantry corps and was shipped to Italy in 1944, where he was wounded twice in combat. After the war, his division remained during the occupation, and Chappelle did not return to the United States until January 1946.

Once home, he began a two-year program in electrical engineering at Phoenix College, going on to the University of California at Berkeley (UCB) with funding from the GI Bill of Rights. He received a B.S. from UCB in biochemistry in 1950 and an M.S. in biochemistry from the University of Washington in 1954.

Chappelle received an appointment as instructor in biochemistry from Meharry Medical College in Nashville, Tennessee, where he served from 1950 to 1952. In 1954, he became a research associate in the department of chemistry at Stanford University in California. He then served from 1958 to 1963 as staff scientist in the Research Institute for Advanced Studies at Martin Marietta Company, an aerospace and aviation firm in Baltimore, Maryland. Then from 1963 to 1965 he was Senior Biochemist at Hazelton Laboratories, Inc., in Falls Church, Virginia.

In 1966, Chappelle began a highly productive association with Goddard Space Flight Center (GSFC) at the National Aeronautics and Space Administration (NASA). There he served as exobiologist (specializing in research areas related to the possible presence of life forms on other planets) from 1965 to 1970, as astrochemist from 1970 to 1972, and as technology utilization specialist from 1972 to 1977. He also was a NASA research fellow at Johns Hopkins University from 1975 to 1977.

In 1977, he began researching the remote sensing of vegetation health through the use of laser-induced fluorescence. He worked with agricultural scientists to advance the use of this method to identify plant stress from airborne or spaceborne instruments before it destroys the plants.

Chappelle has served as a mentor for more than 100 students in high school and college, especially concentrating on encouragement of African-American students in the sciences. He retired from NASA in 2001, and he was chosen as one of the most distinguished African-American scientists and engineers of the 20th century.

Further Reading
Kessler, James H., J. S. Kidd, Renee A. Kidd, and Katherine A. Morin. *Distinguished African Ameri-*

can Scientists of the 20th Century. Phoenix, Ariz.: Oryx Press, 1996, 46–49.

"NASA Twentieth Century Renaissance Man Retires," *Goddard News*. Available online. URL: http://www.gsfc.nasa.gov/gsfc/gnews/011201/011 201.htm. Posted on January 12, 2001.

Cobb, Jewel Plummer
(Jewel Isadora Plummer)
(1924–   ) *cell biologist, cell physiologist, educator*

As president of California State University at Fullerton, Jewel Plummer Cobb became the first African-American woman to head a large university on the West Coast. Early in her career, she also participated in pioneer chemotherapy research at the Cancer Research Foundation at Harlem Hospital. She is nationally recognized as an activist for greater participation in the sciences by minorities.

Born Jewel Isadora Plummer in Chicago, Illinois, on January 17, 1924, she has said that scientific topics were part of typical dinner table conversation in her family. Her father, Frank Plummer, was a physician, and her mother, Carriebel (Cole) Plummer, taught dancing and physical education. Jewel's interest in biology dates back to the day she first looked through a microscope during her high school biology class—and caught sight of another world, a fascinating world of tiny dimensions.

After earning her B.A. at Talladega College in Alabama in 1944, Plummer continued her studies at New York University, where she obtained her master's degree in 1947 and her Ph.D. in 1950, both in cell physiology. Her studies completed, Plummer joined the research team at the Cancer Research Foundation of Harlem Hospital, in New York. There, Plummer worked with JANE COOKE WRIGHT on pioneering research in chemotherapy. The two scientists

hoped to take the guesswork out of determining the best dosage of anticancer drugs to give individual patients. To do this, they sought to develop a laboratory test method using dosages of the drugs and cells from the patient's tumor. In their collaboration, Plummer worked with the laboratory microscope, using time-lapse photography to record the effects of various dosages. Even though the researchers did not succeed in finding the answers they wanted, they did succeed in providing a record of the effects of specific drugs on tumor cells. During these years, Plummer also became associated with the Marine Biological Laboratory at Woods Hole, Massachusetts, where she researched as an independent investigator in 1949. Since that time, she has returned often. In addition to her studies of both normal and cancerous mammalian cell division and its disruption through chemotherapy and other agents, Cobb's research has involved the study of both normal and cancerous pigment cells.

In 1952, Plummer added teaching to her research activities, joining the faculty of the University of Illinois. While at Illinois, she married Roy Cobb, an insurance sales representative, in 1954, and they had a son. In 1960, she took a position at Sarah Lawrence College.

Following divorce from her husband in 1967, Cobb moved on in 1969 to Connecticut College in New London. There she accepted the positions of professor of zoology and dean, remaining for seven years. Ultimately her career moved away from the research that had formed such an important part of her life and became more involved in higher education administration. In 1976, she became dean of Douglass College (the women's college of Rutgers, the State University of New Jersey). In 1981, she accepted the presidency of California State University at Fullerton (CSUF), becoming the first African-American woman to head a university in the California state system or any institution of that size on the West Coast. There, she transformed what had been a "commuter school" into a full-fledged residency university with the construction of the school's first residence hall. She also established three new schools on campus—serving students in communications, engineering, and computer science.

After retiring as president at CSUF in 1990, Cobb became president and professor of biological science, emerita, at California State University at Fullerton, and trustee professor at California State University, Los Angeles. She is a member of the Academy of Sciences, and she has served as a member of the corporation of the Marine Biological Laboratory at Woods Hole since 1972. She has received nearly two dozen honorary doctorates, as well as numerous awards, including the Lifetime Achievement Award for Contributions to the Advancement of Women and Underrepresented Minorities in 1993 from the National Science Foundation and the Kilby Award for lifetime achievement in 1995.

Further Reading

Hawkins, Walter L. *African American Biographies.* Jefferson, N.C.: McFarland & Co., 1992.

"Jewel Plummer Cobb," Women of Science at the MBL. Available online. URL: http://www.mbl.edu/women_of_science/cobb.html. Downloaded on August 1, 2002.

Kessler, James H., J. S. Kidd, Renee A. Kidd, and Katherine A. Morin. *Distinguished African American Scientists of the 20th Century.* Phoenix, Ariz.: Oryx Press, 1996, 49–53.

Notable Black American Women. vol. 1, Jessie Carney Smith, ed. Detroit: Gale Research, 1996, 195–198.

Yount, Lisa. *A to Z of Women in Science and Math.* New York: Facts On File, 1999, 38–39.

———. *Contemporary Women Scientists.* New York: Facts On File, 1994, 72–82.

As president of California State University at Fullerton, pioneer cancer researcher Jewel Plummer Cobb became the first African-American woman to head a large West Coast institution of higher learning. *(Stan Carstensen, California State University, Los Angeles)*

Cobb, William Montague
(1904–1990) *physical anthropologist, anatomist*

For more than 40 years, William Montague Cobb taught anatomy to students of medicine and dentistry at Howard University in Washington, D.C. His scholarship also extended to the history of African Americans in medicine, a topic on which he both researched and wrote. Throughout his lifetime, he fought for integration in hospitals and equal opportunities for his students, while using his scientific knowledge base to argue against racial prejudice. Both as scholar and activist, he was recognized for his unflagging spirit.

William Montague Cobb was born in Washington, D.C., on October 12, 1904, to William Elmer and Alexzine Montague Cobb. His father was both a printer and an entrepreneur. Having moved to Washington, D.C., from Selma, Alabama, to work for the Government Printing Office, he soon opened his own print shop.

After graduating from Dunbar High School in Washington, D.C., young Cobb attended Amherst College in Massachusetts, where his abilities shone both as a scholar and as an athlete. He won championships in both intramural cross-country competition (three times) and in boxing (twice). His academic achievement was even more impressive—winning the Blodgett scholarship as best biology student. The scholarship made possible a coveted summer of research at the Marine Biological Laboratory at Woods Hole, Massachusetts.

After completing his undergraduate work at Amherst, Cobb attended medical school at Howard University, where he had the opportunity to teach a course in embryology during his senior year. The experience convinced him that he preferred teaching to clinical medicine. Cobb took his internship in 1929 at Freedman's Hospital (now Howard University Hospital).

From there Cobb went to Western Reserve (now Case Western) University in Cleveland, Ohio, where he studied physical anthropology and anatomy. He earned his Ph.D. in 1932, becoming the first African American to receive a doctorate in physical anthropology. He returned to Howard as assistant professor of anatomy in the medical school, garnering a promotion to associate professor two years later and full professor in 1942. From 1947 to 1969, he headed the anatomy department.

While at Western Reserve, Cobb got the idea from one of his professors to begin a collection of human skeletons, which he did after his return to Howard University. Over time, he col-

lected representatives from different races and compared them carefully. His study of the skeletons prompted a series of scientific papers in which he debunked the claims of anatomically based black inferiority made by white supremacists. Cobb found clear evidence in his studies that disproved the claims.

Active academically, Cobb served as president of the Anthropological Society of Washington and the American Association of Physical Anthropologists. He was also active in the American Association for the Advancement of Science (AAAS), which he served as a council member, as vice president, and as chair of anthropology. When the AAAS chose Atlanta for its convention site in 1955, Cobb objected and boycotted the meeting in protest against the segregated facilities. His point was taken, and the following year a decision was made that future meetings would not take place where facilities were segregated. Under Cobb's influence, the American Association of Anatomists adopted a similar policy in 1958.

Cobb was as dedicated to his activist commitments as he was to his teaching and research. He became president of the National Association for the Advancement of Colored People (NAACP) in 1976, a position he held until 1982, and he served on the organization's board of directors for 30 years. From within his profession, Cobb also worked to gain equal access for black doctors to hospitals and medical facilities as well as improved health care and equal access for African-American patients. In 1948, he gained entrance for black physicians into what is now D.C. General Hospital and to the Medical Society of the District of Columbia in 1952. In 1964, Cobb served as president of the National Medical Association, a medical association formed to meet the needs of African-American physicians. He used that forum to promote civil rights, as well as its journal, of which he was editor from 1949 to 1977. Cobb fought for integration in every facet of life—including art, literature, social interaction, and science. Always pressing for improvement, he was quoted by *New Direction* as remarking toward the end of his life, "When I go down, I hope I'll go down still pushing for something in the forward direction." William Montague Cobb died in Washington, D.C., on November 20, 1990. He was 86.

Further Reading

Feldman, Martin R. "William Montague Cobb," *Notable Black American Scientists*, Kristine Krapp, ed. Detroit: Gale Research, 1999, 70–72.

Hayden, Robert. *Eleven African-American Doctors*, rev. ed. New York: Twenty-First Century Books, 1992, 72–87.

"Obituary: William Montague Cobb, 1904–1990 (anatomist and civil rights leader)," *Jet*, December 10, 1990, 5.

Coleman, John William

(1929–) *molecular physicist*

John Coleman is recognized for his contributions to the development of the electron microscope at the Radio Corporation of America (RCA). He is a patent holder on electron optics research, and for his work RCA presented him with the David Sarnoff Award.

John William Coleman was born in New York City on December 30, 1929, to John William and Melissa Teresa Preston Coleman. He earned his B.S. in 1950 from Howard University in Washington, D.C. Following graduation, he received several awards in recognition of his scholastic record and abilities, including the Lucy E. Moten Award, the Göttingen Award, and a Fulbright fellowship—which combined to enable him to continue his studies abroad.

Coleman's areas of research interest centered on electron optical design, differential microspectrophotometry, electron diffraction, and light optical systems. From 1951 to 1953, he worked as a physicist for the National Bureau of Standards, after which he entered graduate school at the University of Illinois, Urbana. He received a National Science Foundation (NSF) award for the academic year 1955–56 and completed his M.S. in 1957. The following academic year, 1957–58, he taught physics at Howard University.

In 1958, he began his association with RCA as an engineer, and while working there he earned his Ph.D. in biophysics from the University of Pennsylvania in 1963. The title of his dissertation was *The Diffraction of Electrons in Ultramicroscopic Biological Particles of Ordered Structure*, a topic that was directly related to his work at RCA on development of an improved electron microscope that would be useful in examining biological specimens.

First invented in 1934 by Max Knoll and Ernst Ruska, the electron microscope is an optical instrument that uses a specialized lens to focus a beam of electrons (a type of subatomic particle). (Ruska received the 1986 Nobel Prize in physics for his work.) Because electrons have shorter wavelengths than light, they are able to magnify objects up to 1 million times their normal size. By this means, researchers can obtain greatly enlarged images of tiny objects, usually displayed through use of a fluorescent screen or photographic plate—allowing them to view very fine detail that otherwise cannot be seen. Along with several firms in Japan, RCA was at the cutting edge of commercial development of this technology in the 1940s and the following decades.

In 1969, Coleman left RCA for Forglo Corporation in Sunbury, Pennsylvania, where he became director of engineering. He remained there until 1972 when the Massachusetts Institute of Technology (MIT) hired him as a physicist to work in the Developmental Electron Optics Laboratory.

Coleman has published several articles in journals and is a member of several professional organizations, including the Electron Microscopy Society. RCA recognized the significance of his work with the David Sarnoff Award in 1963.

Further Reading

Hawkes, Peter. "One Hundred Years of the Electron," *Microscopy Microanalysis Microstructures.* 8 no. 2 (April 1997), 7. Available online. URL: http://www.ed-phys.fr/articles/mmm/abs/1997/02/editori/editori.html. Downloaded on April 17, 2002.

"John William Coleman: Physicist," Faces of Science: African Americans in the Sciences. Available online. URL: http://www.princeton.edu/~mcbrown/display/john_coleman.html. Updated on April 4, 2000.

Petrusso, A. "John William Coleman," *Notable Black American Scientists,* Kristine Krapp, ed. Detroit: Gale Research, 1999, 75–76.

Sammons, Vivian Ovelton. *Blacks in Science and Medicine.* New York: Hemisphere Publishing Corp., 1990, 158.

Cooke, Lloyd Miller

(1916–   ) *industrial chemist*

Lloyd M. Cooke achieved considerable respect among the scientific community, even though he spent his entire career as a scientist working for various firms on industrial applications of science—not on "pure" science. His book on environmental chemistry became widely adopted as a college textbook, and he was active in numerous professional scientific organizations.

Born in La Salle, Illinois, on June 7, 1916, Lloyd Miller Cooke was the son of William Wilson and Anna Miller Cooke. With a family background in technology (his father worked for the U.S. government as an engineer and architect), Cooke planned a career in science. He chose to major in chemistry, receiving his B.S. from the University of Wisconsin in 1937. However, he ran into obstacles in his employment search upon graduation, so he pursued a doctorate in organic chemistry, which he received in 1941 from McGill University in Montreal, Quebec.

With a specialization in cellulose chemistry, Cooke began his career researching starch chemistry for the Corn Products Refining Company in Illinois, later joining the Visking Corporation in Chicago in 1946 to conduct research in carbohydrate chemistry. By 1954, he had become assistant manager of a technical division of the firm. His research covered a wide range of study, including derivatives of starch and cellulose, as well as the chemistry of carbohydrates and polymers (especially those related in structure to cellulose).

Lloyd Miller Cooke's influential book *Cleaning Our Environment—The Chemical Basis for Action* (1969) sold some 50,000 copies. *(Bettmann/Corbis)*

In 1957, when Union Carbide took over Visking, Cooke became assistant director of research at Union Carbide in Chicago. In 1965, he was promoted to manager of market research and to manager of planning in 1967. In this capacity, he wrote *Cleaning Our Environment—The Chemical Basis for Action,* published in 1969 by the American Chemical Society. Intended for legislators and environmentalists, it was used by as many as 20 colleges and universities as a textbook and had an impressive sales figure, exceeding 50,000 copies.

In 1970, he became director of urban affairs for Union Carbide, a position he held until 1978. He succeeded in forging a cooperative arrangement between the company and the New York public schools and built educational programs for encouraging students in mathematics and science at the high school level. He has also served on the board of Tuskegee Institute's Carver Research Foundation (1971–78) and as a member of the National Science Board (1970–82). He also continued his work with the New York schools as an adviser to the chancellor from 1984 to 1987.

In 1970, Cooke received the William Procter Prize for Scientific Achievement for his outstanding contribution to scientific research and his ability to communicate his research results to scientists in other disciplines. Cooke is a member of the National Academy of Sciences—a body of distinguished scientists to which election is considered the capstone of a scientific career.

Further Reading

American Chemical Society, Committee on Environmental Improvement. *Cleaning Our Environment—The Chemical Basis for Action.* Washington, D.C.: American Chemical Society, 1969.

Bender, Marilyn, "A Solver of Problems: Cooke Studies Urban Crises for Carbide," *New York Times* April 25, 1971, 7.

Nagel, M.C. "Lloyd M. Cooke," *Notable Black American Scientists,* Kristine Krapp, ed. Detroit: Gale Research, 1999, 78–79.

Cowings, Patricia Suzanne
(1948–) *psychophysiologist*

Patricia S. Cowings invented a biofeedback system called the Autogenic-Feedback Training Exercise Systems and Methods (U.S. Patent 5,694,939), originally developed to facilitate human adaptation to space.

Born in New York City on December 15, 1948, Patricia Suzanne Cowings grew up in southeast Bronx, also known as Fort Apache. She had three brothers, and she has a level of energy and dedication that may have come in part from her mother, who earned a college degree at the age of 65. Her mother then became an assistant teacher of preschoolers. Her father owned a grocery store.

By the time Pat was 11 years old, she had become fascinated by science, especially astronomy. However, in college, she pursued a degree in psychology, earning her Ph.D. in that field from the University of California at Davis in 1973.

Cowings longed to become an astronaut and was one of the first women to take astronaut training at NASA. She has never gone to space, but she has made working and living in space a lot easier for those who have. By studying the ways different people adapt to space and the microgravity environment of an orbiting spacecraft, she was able to home in on some factors that were important to avoiding one of the biggest deterrents to a successful mission: space sickness. Based on her observations and her knowledge of psychology, Cowings devised a system, or systems, for teaching how to control their autonomic and instinctual physiological responses so they can adapt to space travel more quickly.

In a general sense her work involves assessing and correcting the impact of stressful environments on health, safety, and performance.

Her method has many Earth-based applications as well. Studies have shown that pilots under stress in emergency situations often are inhibited by autonomic physiological reactions that interfere with making clear decisions and acting quickly and decisively. Earth-based motion sickness can also be overcome using Cowings's Autogenic-Feedback Training Exercise (ATFE). It can also be used to reduce symptoms of nausea and fainting sometimes experienced by cancer patients during chemotherapy and other procedures.

Cowings is also an avid science fiction reader and writer. Unfortunately, she says, while she has written many published papers on space medicine, military pilots, environment, and stress, none of her science fiction writing has yet been published. Cowings married her "lab partner," William B. Toscano, more than 20 years ago, and they have a teenage son, Christopher Michael Cowings Toscano.

Further Reading

"Cowings, Patricia," *Facts On File Encyclopedia of Black Women in America: Science, Health, and Medicine,* Darlene Clark Hine, ed. New York: Facts On File, 1997.

Cowings, Patricia. "Patricia S. Cowings, Ph.D." NASA Quest: Women of NASA, NASA Ames Research Center. Available online. URL: http://quest.arc.nasa.gov/people/bios/women/pc.html. Last accessed on May 30, 2002.

McMurray, Emily, editor. *Notable Twentieth Century Scientists.* Detroit: Gale Research, 1995, 417–418.

"Patricia Cowings, Psychologist, NASA Ames Research Center," Who's Who at NASA. (February 2001.) Available online. URL: http://www.nasatech.com/NEWS/Feb01/ntb.feb01_cowings.html. Last accessed on May 30, 2002.

Warren, Wini. *Black Women Scientists in the United States.* Bloomington: Indiana University Press, 1999, 67–71.

Psychophysiologist Patricia S. Cowings invented the Autogenic-Feedback Training Exercise (AFTE) systems and methods used by astronauts to adapt more easily to living and working in space. Her work also has many uses on Earth—helping people overcome physical reactions to stress and motion. *(Photo by NASA)*

Cox, Elbert Frank
(1895–1969) *mathematician*

Elbert Frank Cox was the first African American—in fact the first black anywhere in the world—to earn a Ph.D. in pure (unapplied) mathematics. Beginning his teaching career as a high school mathematics teacher, Cox became head of the mathematics department at Howard University, where he mentored many math students who went on to graduate school and successfully attained master's degrees.

Born in Evansville, Indiana, on December 5, 1895, Elbert Frank Cox was the first of three boys born to Johnson D. Cox and Eugenia D. Cox. His father was an elementary school teacher, said to be stern, but supportive of educational goals. In high school, Elbert showed considerable talent as a violinist and was offered a scholarship at the Prague Conservatory of Music. He also had a flair for mathematics and physics, though, and he decided to pursue that course, enrolling as an undergraduate at the University of Indiana. He received his bachelor's degree in 1917, after which he served in the U.S. Army during World War I and was quickly promoted from private to staff sergeant. After the war, he became a high school math teacher in Henderson, Kentucky.

Shortly thereafter, he was appointed to the faculty of Shaw University in Raleigh, North Carolina. He enrolled in graduate school at Cornell University in Ithaca, New York, on full scholarship in September 1922. He received his doctorate in 1925, the first black student in the world to earn a Ph.D. in theoretical mathematics (rather than practical or applied mathematics). In that year, a total of only 28 Ph.D.s were awarded in the entire country.

Cox served as the head of the department of mathematics and physics at West Virginia State College, from 1925 to 1929, when he joined the faculty of Howard University in Washington, D.C. There, Cox helped develop Howard University's grading system in 1947, and he held the position of department head in mathematics until 1961. He continued to teach for another five years, remaining as full professor thereafter until he retired in 1966.

Cox's fields of specialization included difference equations, interpolation theory, and differential equations. He was a member of several educational and professional societies and associations, including the American Mathematical Society, the American Physical Society, and the American Physics Institute. Following a short illness, Cox died on November 28, 1969. In 1975,

the Howard University Department of Mathematics established the Elbert F. Cox Fellowship in his honor, and in 1980, the National Association of Mathematicians (NAM) also honored him by establishing the Cox-Talbot Address given at NAM's annual national meeting.

Further Reading

Donaldson, James A., and Richard J. Fleming. "Elbert F. Cox: An Early Pioneer," *The American Mathematical Monthly*, 107, no. 2 (February 2000): 105–128.

"Elbert F. Cox, First Black Mathematics Ph.D.," Mathematicians of the African Diaspora. Available online. URL: http://www.math.buffalo.edu/mad/PEEPS/cox_elbertf.html. Updated April 2002.

"Elbert Frank Cox," Reprinted from NAM's Newsletter, spring issue, 1995, p. 4. MAA Online: The Mathematical Association of America. Available online. URL: http://www.maa.org/summa/archive/Cox_EF.htm. Downloaded on August 1, 2002.

Harris, Lissa, "Math department honors CU pioneer Elbert Cox, first black math Ph.D.," Cornell Chronicle 33, no. 24 (February 28, 2002). Available online. URL: http://www.news.cornell.edu/Chronicles/2.28.02/ElbertCox.html. Posted on February 28, 2002.

Craft, Thomas, Sr.
(1924–) *biologist*

Thomas Craft made significant studies in skin graft rejection and, later in his career, became a consultant on science education, both in the United States and internationally.

Born on December 27, 1924, in Monticello, Kentucky, Thomas Craft was the son of Thomas M. Craft, a farmer, and Wonnie Alta Travis Craft, a teacher. Both sides of the family encouraged education. Young Tom had an older sister and a foster sister and brother. When he became fascinated as a very young child with his older sister's books, she taught him to read. So, when the precocious boy entered school, he was only five and already reading. He soon also became interested in science and wanted to pursue his education. After graduating from high school in 1941, he enrolled at Wilberforce College, founded in 1856 by the African Methodist Episcopal Church in Wilberforce, Ohio.

In 1943, however, with the United States deeply involved in World War II, Craft's studies were interrupted by the draft, as happened to many students at the time. Craft enlisted in the U.S. Marine Corps, was promoted to corporal, and trained as a drill instructor. In March 1945, he was shipped out for combat in the Pacific theater, headed for Japan. However, after the U.S. bombing of Hiroshima and Nagasaki, the war ended in September 1945, and Craft's unit did not enter combat but was assigned instead to occupation duties in Japan. Discharged in 1946 from the Marine Reserve, Craft returned to the Wilberforce campus with improved funding thanks to the GI Bill of Rights, which provided educational funds to veterans of the war.

On return to college, Craft became more interested in biology and put in extra hours in the laboratory, resulting in his appointment as a research lab assistant—his first paid work as a scientist. He completed his bachelor's degree in 1948, from Central State University, where he had transferred in his senior year. (Wilberforce had split into two schools, Central State and the original campus.) After graduating, he married Joan Hunter, whom he had met in college, and moved to Milwaukee, briefly working in a factory and later for the U.S. Post Office.

In 1949, he began graduate work in developmental biology at Kent State University in Ohio, where he also secured work as a laboratory instructor. He completed his master's degree the following year, in 1950. That same year, the Crafts had a son, Thomas Craft, Jr.

During his studies at Kent State, Craft became interested in skin grafts and the problem of graft rejection. Frequently, skin taken from one part of the body can be used to patch areas where the skin has suffered damage, as happens, for instance, in a severe burn. When successful, the new skin attaches itself to the underlying cells and grows over the damaged area. However, sometimes the body will not accept the new skin. Craft wanted to know why. He conducted research with amphibians that showed a correlation between the release of stress hormones and rejection of the skin grafts. In his experiments, he found that when stress was increased, the graft was less likely to be successful.

Craft began his teaching career in 1950 as an instructor in biology at Central State University, becoming assistant professor the following year. While teaching, he started work part-time in 1955 on a Ph.D. in zoology from Ohio State University in Columbus, which he completed in 1963. Having achieved promotion to associate professor in 1959, with his doctorate completed, he received an appointment of full professor in 1963. Three years later, in 1966, he enrolled at American University in Washington, D.C., in a National Science Foundation program on the history and philosophy of science.

Craft's continued interest in grafts and transplants led to his appointment to advisory boards for the National Institutes of Health and the Ohio state government, as well as consultant for numerous other organizations, including the National Science Foundation. He also studied melanin (the substance causing skin pigmentation) and its protective qualities. At the same time, he began developing high school and undergraduate college programs designed to interest minority students in the sciences. He worked as a volunteer district director for the Ohio Junior Academy of Science and visited India several times in 1967 and 1968 as a consultant on the training of college science instructors.

During the 1970s, Craft served as an adjunct professor at Wright State University School of Medicine in Dayton, Ohio, and in 1980, while continuing to serve as full professor at Central State, Craft also became director of the Department of Energy (DOE) program at Florida Memorial College in St. Augustine. By 1981, he had moved to Florida Memorial as chair of the Division of Natural Sciences and Mathematics and became academic dean in 1984. He retired three years later, in 1987, and returned to Ohio, where he continued his interest in furthering science education, actively serving on the boards of directors of several organizations.

In 1993, Craft was inducted into the Central State University Hall of Fame. He is also professor emeritus of biology at Central State.

Further Reading

Henderson, Ashyia N., ed. *Who's Who Among African Americans,* 14th ed. Detroit: Gale Group, 2001, 285.

Kessler, James H., J. S. Kidd, Renee A. Kidd, and Katherine A. Morin. *Distinguished African American Scientists of the 20th Century.* Phoenix, Ariz.: Oryx Press, 1996.

Croslin, Michael

(1933–   ) *inventor*

Michael Croslin holds more than 40 patents for medical inventions and has established his own company, Medtek Corporation. His inventions include a computerized, digital blood pressure measurement device; a refractometer (used to measure the index of refraction of a substance) that measures levels of urinary sugar and protein; and a pump that measures and dispenses intravenous medications.

Born in 1933 in the U.S. Virgin Islands (in Frederiksted, St. Croix), Michael Croslin was abandoned as a baby. A family named Britto gave

him a home as a child and named him Miguel (later Anglicized as "Michael"). By the time he was 12, he fled the islands for the mainland United States. He worked odd jobs, living in Georgia for a time, and he obtained a brief education at a Jesuit school. He eventually wound up in Wisconsin, where he was adopted by the Croslin family. He, in turn, adopted their name.

Despite his uneven educational opportunities during childhood, Michael Croslin was a brilliant student. By the time he was 14, he had graduated from high school. Within another three years, he had completed his B.S. degree at the University of Wisconsin.

Croslin joined the U.S. Air Force in 1950, serving in both Korea and Vietnam. Upon his return to the States and after discharge, he went back to school, earning a second B.S. degree, this one in mechanical engineering from New York University (NYU) in New York City. He has earned two additional degrees from NYU: a master's degree in electrical engineering in 1963 and a Ph.D. in biomedical engineering in 1968. Simultaneously, he earned a master's in business administration from Columbia University.

Croslin's breakthrough invention was the Medtek 410 computerized blood pressure and pulse measuring device, invented in 1978. It successfully transformed blood pressure measurement from guesswork to accuracy. The old method of measuring blood pressure levels had several drawbacks, the greatest being the possibility—even probability—for human error. A technician pumped up a pressure cuff on the patient's arm, placed a stethoscope over a blood vessel below the cuff, and then released the pressure manually, meanwhile watching a dial and listening for the heartbeat to be heard in the blood vessel. The pressure measurements were recorded from the dial at the moment when the first beat was heard and again at the last beat. However, distractions, hearing ability, extraneous sounds, visual accuracy in reading the dial, speed of release, and other factors all made inaccuracies common. Croslin's device measured the motion of the blood itself, produced results on a crystal readout, and could be calibrated digitally. In 1978, Croslin founded Medtek Corporation in Princeton, New Jersey, to produce and distribute his inventions, enabling him to profit from his own work.

Croslin and his digital blood pressure measurement invention have been showcased by the Franklin Institute Museum of Science and Invention in Philadelphia, Pennsylvania. According to an evaluation made in 1982, the Medtek blood pressure and pulse monitor model BPI 420, a later model of Croslin's original invention, was approved for use on United States Air Force aircraft in case of emergency medical evacuation by air. This was a telling tribute to the reliability of the instrument, since it needed to be capable of operating accurately at a wide range of altitudes and under many demanding circumstances. It is a small portable unit capable of measuring both systolic and diastolic arterial pressures as well as pulse rate, using an oscillometric technique in conjunction with a microprocessor. The Medtek BPI 420 controls cuff deflation automatically at a set rate. The unit automatically adjusts to the surrounding barometric pressure calibrating for a range from 1200 feet below sea level to an altitude of 30,000 feet. Surrounding noise also does not affect measurements. If an error occurs in the readout, either because of operator error or a malfunction of the unit, a message displays on the screen indicating the probable cause.

Further Reading

Moore, Patrick. "Michael Croslin," *Notable Black American Scientists*, Kristine Krapp, ed. Detroit: Gale Research, 1999, 84–85.

"Tour du Jour at the Franklin Institute: Black History Month," Franklin Institute Online. Available online. URL: http://sln.fi.edu/tfi/info/dujour/dujour3. html. Downloaded on April 22, 2002.

Crosthwait, David Nelson, Jr.

(ca. 1892–1976) *engineer*

Recipient of 34 or more U.S. patents and 80 patents internationally, David Nelson Crosthwait is best known as the designer of the heating system in Radio City Music Hall, Rockefeller Center, New York City. Crosthwait was a sought-after authority on heating, ventilation, and air conditioning (HVAC).

David Nelson Crosthwait, Jr., was born on or near May 27, 1892, in Nashville, Tennessee. (Sources list various birth years—including 1890, 1891, 1892, and 1898.) His parents were David Nelson Crosthwait, a physician, and Minnie Harris Crosthwait. Young Crosthwait grew up and attended school in Kansas City, Missouri. He studied mechanical engineering at Purdue University in Indiana, where he received his B.S. in 1913, after which he set to work as an engineer for the C.A. Dunham Company in Marshalltown, Iowa, gaining promotions in 1915 and 1919, the latter to research engineer for the firm. Meanwhile, he continued his studies at Purdue, receiving a master of science in engineering in 1920. In 1925, he became director of research at Dunham, with responsibilities for research extending to the areas of heat transfer, steam transport, and thermostat design. In 1930, he became technical adviser for the Dunham firm, which later changed its name to Dunham-Bush, Inc. He held that position until 1969, when he retired. Once retired, he returned to Purdue to teach a course in steam heating theory and control systems.

Throughout his career, Crosthwait contributed to technical magazines, such as *Power and Industrial Management* and *Heating and Ventilation* magazine. He also revised the *American Society of Heating and Ventilation Engineers Guide* for three different editions, in 1939, 1959, and 1967. He was a fellow of the American Association for the Advancement of Science (AAAS), also holding membership in several professional technical societies, including the American Society of Heating, Refrigerating and Air Conditioning Engineers (ASHRAE), the American Chemical Society, and the National Society of Professional Engineers.

Crosthwait's expertise in his field was recognized by numerous awards including the National Technological Association Medal, presented in 1936, and election as fellow in 1971 by the American Society of Heating, Refrigeration, and Air Conditioning Engineers. Crosthwait was the first African American to be so honored. In 1975,

Purdue University awarded him an honorary doctorate in technology. David Nelson Crosthwait, Jr., died on February 25, 1976.

Further Reading

McMurray, Emily, editor. *Notable Twentieth Century Scientists*. Detroit: Gale Research, 1995, 433.

Sammons, Vivian Ovelton. *Blacks in Science and Medicine*. New York: Hemisphere Publishing, 1990, 64–65.

U.S. Department of Energy. *Black Contributors to Science and Energy Technology*. Washington, D.C.: Office of Public Affairs, 1979, 9.

D

Daly, Marie Maynard
(1921–) *biochemist*

A respected researcher in biochemistry, Marie Maynard Daly was the first to identify hypertension as a precursor to arteriosclerosis. She was also the first African-American woman to receive a Ph.D. in chemistry.

Marie Maynard Daly was born to Helen Page Daly and Ivan C. Daly on April 16, 1921 in the borough of Queens in New York City. Her father had taken courses in chemistry at Cornell University, but finances became a problem and he had not been able to pursue a degree. Instead he had to settle for steady but less challenging work as a postal clerk. One of three children, Marie developed a passion for reading from her mother and became attracted to science—not only influenced by her father's interest, but also intrigued by books she read, such as Paul de Kruif's *Microbe Hunters*.

In 1942, she completed her B.S. in chemistry magna cum laude at Queens College in Flushing, New York, where she stayed on as a tutor from 1942 to 1944. Meanwhile, she worked on her master's degree from New York University in New York City, earning an M.S. in chemistry in 1943. In 1948, she completed her Ph.D. in chemistry at Columbia University in New York City.

After receiving her doctorate, Daly joined the faculty of Howard University as an instructor, where she taught for two years, from 1947 to 1949. At Howard, she taught an introductory physical science course and worked with HERMAN BRANSON. A fellowship from the American Cancer Society from 1948 to 1951 enabled her to do postgraduate work as a visiting investigator at the Rockefeller Institute (now Rockefeller University) from 1948 to 1951, becoming an assistant from 1951 to 1955. During this seven-year period she was working with A. E. Mirsky, exploring the structure of proteins within cells. Their focus centered on the cell nucleus in particular. During this period the biochemistry of cell nuclei was of particularly great interest due to the discoveries James D. Watson and Francis Crick made in 1953 about the molecular structure of DNA (deoxyribonucleic acid), the hereditary material contained in the nuclei of most cells. Suddenly, Daly and Mirsky found they were studying a very hot topic.

From her work at Rockefeller, Daly returned to Columbia University, where she served on the faculty as associate professor from 1955 to 1959. There she worked with Quentin B. Deming, who was widely respected for his work on chemical influences on the heart and its mechanics. Together, Daly and Deming examined how chemicals relate to the onset of heart attacks.

They examined the development of blockage in the arteries that supply the heart with oxygen and nutrients, and they discovered that cholesterol played a key role in this process.

In 1960, Daly and Deming moved to Yeshiva University at the Albert Einstein College of Medicine, where Daly joined the faculty as assistant professor, gaining a promotion to associate professor in 1971, and serving in that capacity until 1986. Daly also served as an investigator for the American Heart Association from 1958 to 1963 and was named career scientist at the Health Research Council of New York in 1962, a position she held for 10 years, until 1972. She retired from teaching in 1986.

Most of Daly's research involved the biochemical aspects of human metabolism and the role of the kidneys. She also examined the relationship between hypertension (high blood pressure) and atherosclerosis (arterial blockage). Later in her career, she studied the nature and function of smooth aortic (heart) muscle cells by examining them in culture.

Daly is a fellow of the American Association for the Advancement of Science (AAAS) and the Council on Arteriosclerosis of the American Heart Association. She is also a member of the Harvey Society (a society dedicated to fostering a closer relationship between the practical side of medicine and the results of laboratory investigation), the American Chemical Society, and the American Society of Biological Chemists. She also served as a member of the board of governors of the New York Academy of Sciences from 1974 to 1976.

In 1999, for her work as a researcher and professor of chemistry, Marie Daly was selected by the National Technical Association as one of the Top 50 Women in Science, Engineering and Technology.

Further Reading

Grinstein, Louise S., Rose K. Rose, and Miriam H. Rafailovich, editors. *Women in Chemistry and Physics: A Biobibliographic Sourcebook.* Westport, Conn.: Greenwood Press, 1993, 145–149.

Kessler, James H., J. S. Kidd, Renee A. Kidd, and Katherine A. Morin. *Distinguished African American Scientists of the 20th Century.* Phoenix, Ariz.: Oryx Press, 1996, 57–60.

McMurray, Emily, editor. *Notable Twentieth Century Scientists.* Detroit: Gale Research, 1995, 448–449.

Warren, Wini. *Black Women Scientists in the United States.* Bloomington: Indiana University Press, 1999, 71–73.

Who's Who Among African Americans, 14th ed. Gale Group, 2001.

Darden, Christine Mann
(1942–   ) *mathematician, aerospace engineer*

Christine Mann Darden's contributions to supersonic research—especially in the areas of sonic-boom prediction and sonic-boom minimization—have significantly increased the effectiveness of methods used to control this negative result of supersonic flight. Her work has added substantially to the advances that have been made in these areas.

Christine Mann was born on September 10, 1942, in Monroe, North Carolina. Her parents, Noah Horace Mann, Sr., and Desma Cheney Mann, were both teachers, graduates of Knoxville College in Knoxville, Tennessee. Christine began early to show the interests and talents that would later help her succeed in her chosen career. She enjoyed learning what made things work, and even as a child, she liked helping her dad change tires and work on the family car. She took her own bicycle apart and put it back together, and she learned how to change and fix the tires.

She graduated from Allen High School, where she fell in love with mathematics. As she later recalled, "From then on, I was fascinated by the power of mathematics to describe physical things in our world—and to give us answers to problems."

Darden earned her bachelor of science degree in mathematics in 1962 from Hampton Institute (now University) in Hampton, Virginia, and her master of science degree in applied mathematics in 1967 from Virginia State College (now University) in Petersburg, Virginia. In 1983, she completed her doctorate degree in mechanical engineering from George Washington University in Washington, D.C. Additionally, she obtained a Certificate of Advanced Study in Management from Simmons College Graduate School of Management in Boston, Massachusetts.

After receiving her B.S., Darden began work at one of the National Aeronautics and Space Administration (NASA) centers—the Langley Research Center, also located in Hampton, Virginia. Since its establishment in 1917 (prior to the establishment of NASA), Langley has pioneered in the development of airframe systems—constantly working at the cutting edge of aviation and space research. When Darden joined NASA, she began to see that engineering involved exactly the kind of thinking and work she enjoyed most—"a marriage," as she put it, "between mathematics and the physical things of the world." Because she already had a strong background in mathematics, she was able to switch her career path to mechanical and aerospace engineering with relative ease.

Advancement within NASA did not happen automatically, though, even once Darden had completed her Ph.D. Good assignments generally went to her male counterparts, and she found herself relegated to the role of assistant. Darden, however, did not let the discrepancies pass by without comment. Eventually, she received the chance to take on a challenging project, and she succeeded. Many women following behind Darden at NASA have her to thank for blazing the trail with her battles for equal opportunity and treatment.

As a member of the Senior Executive Service at Langley Research Center, Darden became director of the Aero Performing Center Program Management Office in 1998. In this position she oversees work at Langley in rotorcraft, aviation systems capacity, information technology, high-performance computing, and ultra-efficient engine technology. Prior to taking this position, Darden served as a senior program manager in NASA's High Speed Research Program Office—a program that was to develop the technology for building a supersonic airplane by the year 2015.

Recognized as a national expert on predicting and minimizing sonic booms and the design of supersonic aircraft wings, Darden is the author of more than 54 technical papers and articles, primarily on these topics. She has received

Christine Mann Darden, an aeronautical engineer and mathematician, thinks of her work at the National Aeronautical and Space Administration (NASA) as "a marriage between mathematics and the physical things of the world." *(Photo by NASA, by permission of Christine Darden)*

dozens of awards and honors for her work—including two NASA Medals, several NASA Outstanding Performance and Achievement Awards, the North Carolina State Brotherhood Award, the Black Engineer of the Year Outstanding Achievement in Government Award, and the Women in Engineering Lifetime Achievement Award.

Darden and her husband, Walter L. Darden, Jr., whom she married in 1963, have two daughters, Jeanne Darden Riley and Janet Christine.

In addition to her work as a NASA engineer, Darden actively encourages other young women to aim to reach their real potential. She says, "I would also like to think that my life and my work have provided an example to other young women—and especially black women that they should not let themselves be limited by what others expect of us. We should look at our own interests and aptitudes and then go for that for which we have a passion—be it engineering, medicine, or business." She counsels young people to read extensively to make themselves aware of the career choices that exist, adding, "Mold your likes, interests, and aptitudes into a career gold." She also recommends that perceiving oneself in the chosen career helps, along with following up with practical planning and preparation. Finally, she counsels persistence—because, she says, "Things don't always work the first time."

Further Reading

Austin, Hilary Mac. "Darden, Christine," *Facts On File Encyclopedia of Black Women in America: Science, Health, and Medicine,* edited by Darlene Clark Hine. New York: Facts On File, 1997, 59.

Kessler, James H., J. S. Kidd, Renee A. Kidd, and Katherine A. Morin. *Distinguished African American Scientists of the 20th Century.* Phoenix, Ariz.: Oryx Press, 1996, 60–62.

McMurray, Emily, editor. *Notable Twentieth Century Scientists.* Detroit: Gale Research, 1995, 455–456.

Warren, Wini. *Black Women Scientists in the United States.* Bloomington: Indiana University Press, 1999, 74–80.

Who's Who Among African Americans, 13th ed. Detroit: Gale Group, 2000.

Davis, Stephen Smith
(1910–1977) *mechanical engineer, educator*

Stephen Smith Davis is known for his patented design for supersonic wind tunnel nozzles. His leadership also led to establishment in 1968 of the first graduate programs in engineering at Howard University.

Born on October 24, 1910, in Philadelphia, Pennsylvania, Stephen Smith Davis was the son of Stephen Davis and Rosa Elizabeth Norris Davis. His father was a gas utility employee, which may have influenced young Stephen's early interest in engineering. The elder Davis died when his son was still a boy, though, and Rosa Davis moved to Boston—a move that gave young Davis the opportunity to attend high school at Lowell Institute, a secondary school affiliated with the Massachusetts Institute of Technology. Obtaining his high school diploma from Lowell in 1933, Davis attended Howard University in Washington, D.C., as an undergraduate, where he earned his B.S. in mechanical engineering in 1936.

Davis did not immediately find a teaching position, so he made ends meet by working as a boiler operator—keeping the heat running to the classrooms at Howard University. The only real fringe benefit was that one day when he put his head up through a manhole, he encountered a young woman sitting on a bench. She later became his wife.

Within two years, though, in 1938, he secured a position as instructor of engineering at Howard. He also became a registered professional engineer. His area of specialization was heating, ventilation, and air conditioning.

By late 1941, however, the United States had entered World War II. So, from 1943 to 1945, Davis did defense work as a mechanical engineer for the National Bureau of Standards. During this period he worked on guided missiles—missiles that are operated by remote control to attack areas that are too dangerous or inaccessible for piloted aircraft. Davis worked on a missile called the Bat. It was designed to be used by the navy, carried aboard an aircraft carrier and released from an airplane. In this way, an aircraft carrier could strike remote targets without endangering the ship itself. The Bat was used late in the war and was considered reasonably successful.

After the war was over, Davis went back to school, this time at prestigious Harvard University, where he completed an M.S. degree in mechanical engineering in just one year, receiving it in 1947. At Howard, the M.S. prompted a promotion to associate professor, a tenured (or permanent) faculty position. However, he was able to continue some of his military work at the same time. For 10 years, from 1953 to 1963, Davis did consulting as an aeronautical engineer for the Naval Ordnance Laboratory. It was during this period that he developed his wind tunnel nozzle, for which he received a patent.

Wind tunnels provide aircraft and spacecraft development engineers with a method for testing stress ratings of new designs and parts. Winds up to ultrasonic forces can be blown through the tunnel, buffeting parts or models of a design. In this way engineers can test where the weak points of the design may be before investing the time and expense of constructing a full-sized, working model. When the wind is less than the speed of sound, changing the speed of the wind is simple. However, when the test wind is faster than sound, the process is a little more difficult. To achieve a supersonic wind—that is, one faster than sound—a nozzle resembling a rocket engine is used. When an engineer needed to change the speed, the nozzle had to be changed. Davis devised a flexible nozzle. Because of its flexibility, its shape could be changed. So, just by changing the nozzle's shape, an engineer could change the speed of the supersonic air flow.

Davis also worked on development of materials that could withstand the extremely high temperatures that could be induced in a high-speed wind tunnel. He also worked on air compressors and was a coauthor of a publication on the subject put out by the Office of Naval Research.

At Howard, Davis became head of his department in 1962, and two years later he was appointed dean of the School of Engineering and Architecture, a position in which he served for six years. During his years at Howard, Davis led the university in an expansion of the engineering program, establishing graduate programs, including Ph.D. programs in engineering. This was an important step for the prestige of Howard University in this field. In 1970, he resigned as dean, but he continued to teach. Stephen Smith Davis died of heart failure on January 15, 1977.

Further Reading

Henderson, Ashyia N., ed. *Who's Who Among African Americans*, 14th ed. Detroit: Gale Group, 2001, 326.

Heppenheimer, T. A. "Stephen Smith Davis," *Notable Black American Scientists*, Kristine Krapp, ed. Detroit: Gale Research, 1999, 92–93.

Dean, Mark
(1957–) *inventor, computer scientist*

Mark Dean, an innovative inventor and researcher in electrical engineering, holds three patents on the original International Business Machines (IBM) PC chip. In 1997, Dean was inducted into the National Inventors Hall of Fame, an honor that has been awarded to only 150 inventors.

Mark Dean was born on March 2, 1957, the son of Barbara and James Dean. He attended the

University of Tennessee as an undergraduate, earning his B.S. in 1979. Subsequently, he obtained an M.S. degree from Florida Atlantic University in 1982 and then completed his Ph.D. at Stanford University in California in 1992.

The field of computer science has been criticized for including few blacks in degree programs or faculty positions. PHILIP EMEAGWALI has noted, "According to the Computing Research Association, only one out of 14 blacks that received the Ph.D. degree in 1994 was hired by academia. The same organization reported that only 3 out of 1215 (0.25 percent) full professors of computer science in the entire North America were black. Most likely, these 3 black professors are hired in predominately black universities."

Yet Mark Dean is optimistic about the future for African Americans in his discipline. Like Emeagwali, Dean has succeeded primarily in industry, not academia, but overall, he contends, "There may be obstacles, but there are no limits."

Dean began his very productive relationship with IBM in 1993, when he became director of architecture in the Power Personal Systems Division. Since then he has served as vice president of several divisions and since 2000 Dean has served as IBM fellow and vice president of systems, IBM Research.

Mark Dean has received many awards in recognition of his achievements, including the Ronald H. Brown American Innovators Award in 1977; the Distinguished Engineer Award from the National Society of Black Engineers in 1999; the University of Tennessee Founders Day Medal in 1999; the Black Engineer of the Year Award from the Career Communications Group in 2000; and from the California African American Museum's 50 Most Important African Americans in Technology Award in 2000.

As of late 2002, Mark Dean continues to serve on the Houston-Tillotson College board of trustees, of which he has been a member since 1977; the board of directors of Inroads Inc.; and the University of Tennessee School of Engineering board of advisers.

Mark Dean's three patents on the original International Business Machines (IBM) Personal Computer chip establish him as a prominent innovator in electrical engineering. His continued leadership within the hierarchy of this industry giant affirms his assertion that for African Americans in his field, "There may be obstacles, but there are no limits." *(IBM, courtesy of Mark Dean)*

Further Reading

Henderson, Ashyia N., ed. *Who's Who Among African Americans*, 14th ed. Detroit: Gale Group, 2001, 332.

Williams, Scott. "Mark Dean," Computer Scientists of the African Diaspora. Available online. URL: http://www.math.buffalo.edu/mad/computer-science/%20dean_mark.html. Updated on April 23, 2000.

Deconge-Watson, Mary Lovinia
(Sister Mary Sylvester Deconge, S.S.F.)
(1933–) *mathematician*

Sister Mary Sylvester Deconge was the 15th African-American woman to receive a Ph.D. in mathematics.

Mary Deconge was born in Wickliff, Louisiana, in 1933. When she was 16, she entered the congregation of the Sisters of the Holy Family. She later became a nun in the Holy Order of the Sisters of Saint Francis and taught elementary school in the parochial schools of the dioceses of Baton Rouge and Lafayette from 1952 to 1955 before attending Seton Hill College, a Catholic women's college in Greensburg, Pennsylvania. There she received her B.A. in mathematics and science. Subsequently she returned to Louisiana, where she attended graduate school at Louisiana State University, receiving a master's degree in mathematics in 1962.

Sister Mary Sylvester also returned to teaching with a position at Holy Ghost High School in Opelousas, Louisiana, from 1959 to 1961. After receiving her master's degree, she taught at Holy Ghost High School and Delisle Junior College in New Orleans from 1962 to 1964. She received her doctorate in mathematics, with a minor in French, from St. Louis University in 1968. Her dissertation was entitled *2-Normed Lattices and 2-Metric Spaces.*

She served as an assistant professor on the mathematics faculty of Loyola University in New Orleans from 1968 to 1971, and in 1971 she received an appointment as associate professor of mathematics at Southern University in Baton Rouge. As of 1999, she was still teaching at Southern University and also served as an executive director of the Center for Mathematics in Science, Engineering, and Technology.

Sister Mary Sylvester's several short publications have appeared in *Proceedings of the National Academy of Science* (USA), *The Notices of the American Mathematics Society,* and the *Journal of Mathematical Analytical Applications.* Sister Mary Sylvester Deconge is recognized for her achievements as a black woman in mathematics, including her teaching and her several publications relating to Cauchy's Problem for Higher-Order Abstract Parabolic Equations.

Further Reading

Brown, Mitchell C. "Sister Mary Sylvester Deconge: Mathematician." Faces of Science: African Americans in the Sciences. Available online. June 24, 2000. URL: www.princeton.edu/~mcbrown/ display/deconge.html. Downloaded on June 6, 2001.

Newell, Virgina K. ed. *Black Mathematicians and Their Works.* Ardmore, Pa.: Dorrance, 1980, 283.

Sammons, Vivian O. *Blacks in Science and Education.* Washington, D.C.: Hemisphere Publishers, 1989, 167.

Warren, Wini. *Black Women Scientists in the United States.* Bloomington: Indiana University Press, 1999, 82–83.

Williams, Scott W. History of Black Women in Mathematics. Available online. URL: http://www. math.buffalo.edu/mad/wohist.html. Downloaded on March 3, 2002.

———. "Mary Sylvester Deconge," Black Women in Mathematics, Mathematicians in the African Diaspora. Available online. URL: http://www.math. buffalo.edu/mad/PEEPS/deconge_sistermarys.ht ml. Downloaded on March 3, 2002.

Dorman, Linneaus Cuthbert
(1935–) *organic chemist*

Linneaus Dorman has had a long and productive career with Dow Chemical Company, where his research has yielded key discoveries in medicine and environmental protection. His contributions have ranged from work with peptides to methods for reducing ecological damage from use of agricultural chemicals to invention of a bone replacement substance. He was named Inventor of the Year by Dow Chemical Company in 1983 and his contributions have received recognition from the American Chemical Society.

Linneaus Cuthbert Dorman was born on June 28, 1935, in Orangeburg, South Carolina, the son of Georgia Dorman and John A. Dorman, Sr. As a youngster, he attended the laboratory school at South Carolina State College. A "laboratory school" is a school that is maintained by a university department of education to provide an ideal initial teaching situation for young teachers about to receive their credentials. Typically, a lab school has small classes, uses progressive teaching techniques, and is closely supervised by master teachers. The resulting environment tends to be highly productive educationally.

After graduating from high school, Dorman enrolled at Bradley University in Peoria, Illinois, as an undergraduate in 1952, earning his B.S. in 1956. During the summers over the next three years, he worked as a chemist at the Northern Regional Research Laboratory of the U.S. Department of Agriculture. This work not only gave him funds for continuing his education but also provided valuable experience in his field. Meanwhile, during the academic year he continued his studies at Indiana University, where he received a teaching assistantship and completed his Ph.D. in 1961. His potential had not gone unrecognized. For the academic year 1959–60 he was named Dow Research Fellow by Indiana University. In 1960, he was also corecipient of the Bond Award, given by the American Oil Chemistry Society for the best paper presented at the organization's national meeting.

Dorman began working for Dow Chemical Company directly after receiving his Ph.D., serving as research chemist from 1960 to 1968. He became a research specialist from 1968 to 1976, with continuing promotions over the ensuing years. In 1994, he was named senior associate scientist.

A frequent contributor to scientific journals and books in his field, Dorman received a patent for his invention of a bone-replacement substance having strength and flexibility very similar to natural bone. The ivory-type compound is useful in replacing bone badly damaged in accidents.

In addition to his work on the bone replacement compound, Dorman has worked in four other major areas in his research with Dow Chemical. His first studies focused on development of compounds that had potential usefulness as treatment for mental illness. From there, he moved on to the study of peptides, the building blocks of proteins, which in turn are the building blocks of living things. Peptides also have many uses as products, for example, in the production of artificial sweetener.

Dorman's third area of study focused on the need to adapt agricultural chemicals so they would not damage the environment or become ingested by people and animals in their food. Dorman found that when the chemicals were bound into pellets for distribution, using a kind of plastic binder as "glue," instead of being sprayed, that the chemicals were less concentrated, less likely to run off into water supplies, and were absorbed by the plants more slowly.

In the 1980s and 1990s, Dorman explored ways of recycling rubber and other substances that do not recycle easily. He has continued to work on this fourth area of investigation.

Dorman has served on several boards of directors and financial advisers in both industry and education, including the Comerica Bank-Midland, from 1982 to 1995; Saginaw Valley State College, from 1976 to 1987; and the Indiana University Chemistry Department financial advisers, 1994. He is a member of the National Organization of Black Chemists and Chemical Engineers, was chairman of the Midland Black Coalition in 1973 and 1977, and is a life member of the National Association for the Advancement of Colored People (NAACP).

For his work in organic chemistry, Dorman was named inventor of the year by Dow Chemical Central Research in 1983. He also received an honorary doctorate of science from Saginaw Valley State University in 1988 and the PERCY LAVON JULIAN Award from the National Organization of Black Chemists and Chemical Engineers in 1999.

Further Reading

Hawkins, Walter L. *African American Biographies, 2.* Jefferson, N.C.: McFarland & Co., 1994.

Henderson, Ashyia N., ed. *Who's Who Among African Americans,* 14th ed. Detroit: Gale Group, 2001, 325–53.

Kessler, James H., J. S. Kidd, Renee A. Kidd, and Katherine A. Morin. *Distinguished African American Scientists of the 20th Century.* Phoenix, Ariz.: Oryx Press, 1996.

Drew, Charles Richard

(1904–1950) *surgeon, blood researcher*

Charles Drew is widely recognized for his successful research on extending the shelf life of blood for transfusions. Drew conceived of the system of storage and distribution known as a "blood bank," and during World War II, he also established a blood bank in London, making blood efficiently available at a time when a supply for transfusions was urgently needed.

Charles Richard Drew, the oldest of five children of Charles and Nora Drew, was born on June 3, 1904, in Washington, D.C. His father was a carpet layer, and his mother was a teacher, a graduate of Miner Teachers College. Drew graduated with honors in 1922 from Dunbar High School. During his school years, he had gained recognition as an athlete in several sports, including swimming and running, as well as football and basketball.

The following fall, he entered Amherst University in Massachusetts, where he completed his B.A. in 1926. Drew taught biology and chemistry and served as director of athletics for two years at Morgan State College in Baltimore before continuing his education. Then, at age 24, he went on to medical school at McGill University in Montreal, Quebec, where he received his M.D. and Master of Surgery (C.M.) in 1933. During this time he began to become interested in blood research. Following his coursework at McGill, he served his two-year internship at Montreal General Hospital.

Returning to the United States, in 1936 Drew joined the faculty of the Howard University Medical School in Washington, D.C., where he taught pathology for three years and also served as an assistant in surgery. However, Drew was still thinking about doing research. In 1938, he obtained a Rockefeller Foundation research fellowship to spend two years at Columbia Presbyterian Hospital (part of Columbia University) in New York. There, he began investigating ways to preserve blood. Too often, patients died because they needed transfusions and not enough blood was on hand to save them. Drew found a method for preserving blood plasma (the pale yellow, liquid portion of the blood) for long periods of time—much longer than "whole blood" could be preserved.

Drew also served as supervisor of the blood plasma division of the Blood Transfusion Association of New York City. In 1940, he received the Doctor of Science in medicine degree from Columbia University. The first African American ever to receive the degree, he wrote a dissertation entitled *Banked Blood: A Study in Preservation.*

Meanwhile, as early as 1939, the British government had contacted Drew about setting up a military blood bank program and collecting blood to serve the British Army. World War II was close at hand, and the situation was urgent. Preserved blood plasma saw use on the battlefield for the first time. As a result of his work, the British asked Drew to set up a mass blood bank project—the first of its kind in the world.

Surgeon and blood researcher Charles Richard Drew developed techniques for preserving and storing blood plasma in large blood banks, saving thousands of lives during World War II and since. *(AP/Wide World Photos)*

By 1941, Charles Drew had become the first director of the American Red Cross Blood Bank, which supplied blood to U.S. forces. His methodology for managing a blood bank unquestionably saved thousands of lives.

However, when a controversy arose over mixing blood from African Americans with blood from white patients, Drew resigned and returned to Howard University, where he became professor and head of surgery in 1942. (The hospital used by Howard University Medical School was Freedman's Hospital, a hospital originally founded for emancipated slaves.) He served as medical director there from 1946 to 1947.

Charles Drew's life was tragically cut short. On April 1, 1950, Drew and several of his colleagues set off to attend a medical conference at the Tuskegee Institute in Alabama. A fatal automobile accident brought the trip to an abrupt end, and the famous black surgeon and blood plasma pioneer died of his injuries. Accusations ensued that Drew, because of his color, had been refused treatment at a nearby all-white hospital. In fact, he was treated in the hospital's segregated emergency room and did receive treatment promptly—his colleagues, who were doctors, attended to him. He was admitted to the hospital, but he died soon afterward of massive injuries. Since that fatal day, Drew's death has become the center of a heated controversy, and a myth has grown up around his name.

Charles Richard Drew has been widely honored by awards for his work, including the Spingarn Medal, awarded to him by the NAACP in 1944, a posthumous award of the Distinguished Service Medal of the National Medical Association in 1950, and a United States postage stamp issued in his honor in 1981.

Further Reading

Love, Spencie. *One Blood: The Death and Resurrection of Charles R. Drew.* Introduction by John Hope Franklin. Chapel Hill: University of North Carolina Press, 1996.

Wynes, Charles E. *Charles Richard Drew: The Man and the Myth.* Urbana: University of Illinois Press, 1988.

Yount, Lisa. *Black Scientists.* New York: Facts On File, 1991, 54–66.

Dunbar, Joseph Chatman, Jr.
(1944–   ) *physiologist*

As a respected authority on diabetes, Joseph Dunbar has written more than 100 published scientific articles on aspects of the disease, including the roles of insulin and the pancreas and the effect of insulin levels on the nervous and cardiovascular systems, including increased likelihood of strokes and heart attacks.

Joseph Chatman Dunbar, Jr., was born on August 27, 1944, in Vicksburg, Mississippi. Young Dunbar grew up in Port Gibson, Mississippi, where his father, J. C. Dunbar, Sr., was a department of agriculture agent and his mother, Henrienne M. Watkins Dunbar, taught school.

Dunbar attended Alcorn College in Lorman, Mississippi, a family tradition, where he earned his B.S. in 1963. He taught high school biology and band for a year to finance graduate school and then entered a master's program at Texas Southern University in Houston, where he received his M.S. degree in 1966. While at Texas Southern, Dunbar began his study of glands, an area of research that would ultimately lead to his expertise on diabetes. He joined the faculty as instructor the following academic year and then continued his graduate studies at Wayne State University in Detroit, Michigan, where he began to focus his research on diabetes. Diabetes, or more specifically, a type of diabetes known as diabetes mellitus, occurs when a gland in the pancreas fails to produce insulin, which is required by the body to maintain normal concentrations of glucose in the blood. Insulin injections are a common medical treatment for diabetes. However, Dunbar's research centered on finding appropriate chemical alternatives to the use of insulin. After earning his Ph.D. in 1970, he continued his research as a research associate at Sinai Hospital in Detroit, where he worked for eight years, from 1970 to 1978. He also joined the faculty of Wayne State University as professor of physiology in 1972 and became chair of the department of physiology in 1998.

His continued research has explored the reactions caused in the pancreas by insulin injections, how body weight relates to the functions of the pancreas, as well as the effects of certain medications on other glandular functions. Dunbar is the author of over 100 publications in his field.

In 1989, Dunbar received a Minority Achievement Award, and he received the Charles Gershenson Distinguished Faculty Fellowship in 1992.

Further Reading

Henderson, Ashyia N., ed. *Who's Who Among African Americans,* 14th ed. Detroit: Gale Group, 2001, 366–67.

Kessler, James H., J. S. Kidd, Renee A. Kidd, and Katherine A. Morin. *Distinguished African American Scientists of the 20th Century.* Phoenix, Ariz.: Oryx Press, 1996, 77–80.

E

Earls, Julian Manly
(1942–) *radiation physicist, administrator*

The first black radiation physicist to work for the National Aeronautics and Space Administration (NASA), Julian Manly Earls has blazed trails for other African Americans at NASA in many ways. Among numerous other firsts (such as first black section head, first black office chief, first black division chief), he is the first black deputy director for Operations, a position he holds at NASA's Lewis Research Center in Cleveland, Ohio. He has also made many opportunities possible for others who are underrepresented, both at NASA and among students entering majors in the sciences at U.S. colleges and universities.

Julian Manly Earls was born on November 22, 1942, in Portsmouth, Virginia, the son of Ida Earls and James Earls. During the years when young Julian was growing up in Portsmouth, he was surrounded by segregation in schools, public rest rooms, and public transportation. Although his parents had no formal education, Earls once remarked, "They were not uneducated. They were self-educated. They had something you cannot get from colleges . . . common sense." His parents encouraged their children to get a formal education, though. During his childhood, he encountered a few instances when he felt the narrow-mindedness of racial discrimination. From his parents and his own experience he concluded that education and maturity would bring about greater understanding and a more accepting society. Earls has set about, through his career, to help make that society come about sooner.

Earls was the first member of his family to attend college, and he commuted from home as an undergraduate. He received his B.S. degree in physics from Norfolk State College (now Norfolk State University) in 1964. He also received a U.S. Atomic Energy Fellowship in 1964. He studied radiation physics at the University of Rochester School of Medicine in Rochester, New York, where he completed his M.S. in 1965.

Following completion of his master's program, Earls became a physicist for NASA from 1965 to 1967. He worked for a year for the U.S. Nuclear Regulatory Agency as a radiation specialist.

In 1968, Earls returned to NASA at the Lewis Research Center. He took time out from NASA to attend the University of Michigan, where he earned his doctorate in radiation physics in 1973. Later, he was elected by his fellow employees for participation in a NASA fellowship program that enabled him to attend the business administration program at the Harvard University Graduate School of Business, where he earned a degree in Management Development in 1979.

Earls has taught in several adjunct professor positions, while climbing the ladder at NASA. In 1983, he became Health, Safety, and Security division chief at Lewis in 1983. Five years later he was promoted to director of the Office of Health Services, and as of late 2002, Earls continues to serve in the capacity of deputy director for Operations at NASA's Lewis Research Center in Cleveland, Ohio.

Earls has received numerous awards, including the Distinguished Service Award of the National Technical Association in 1981; induction into the National Black College Alumni Hall of Fame in 1986; Technical Achievement Award of the National Technical Association in 1987; Distinguished Blacks in Science Award of the Africa-Scientific Institute, 1990; and Academic Excellence Commendation, from the University of Mississippi in 1989. In 1995, he received the NASA Medal for Exceptional Achievement. For his service to his community, Earls has received many citations, most notably a resolution by the state of Ohio House of Representatives in 1974, the Humanitarian Award from Wittenberg University in 1983, the National Urban League Black College Graduate of Distinction award in 1987; the Sons of Mandela Award, Cleveland NAACP in 1990; the Strong Men and Women Excellence in Leadership award in 1996; and the Cleveland All Star Salute in 1997.

Further Reading

Henderson, Ashyia N., ed. *Who's Who Among African Americans*, 14th ed. Detroit: Gale Group, 2001, 374–75.

Easley, Annie
(1933–) *computer scientist*

Annie Easley started on the ground floor of the U.S. space program, working for the National Advisory Committee on Aeronautics (NACA) in 1955 before it became the National Aeronautics and Space Administration (NASA). She was a key member of the group of software developers who wrote the software used for the *Centaur,* a high-energy rocket used to launch space vehicles and communication satellites—most recently used to launch the spacecraft *Cassini* in 1997 on its long trip to Saturn.

Annie Easley was born on April 23, 1933, in Birmingham, Alabama. She attended Xavier University in New Orleans, after which she taught as a substitute teacher in Jefferson County, Alabama. Then she moved north to Ohio, where she started work in 1955 at what is now the Lewis Research Center, a part of NASA located in Cleveland, Ohio. At that time, however, NASA did not exist. Rocket engineers and physicists in the United States were thinking about putting an artificial satellite in orbit, but no one had succeeded yet in building a rocket powerful enough to reach escape velocity, the minimum speed required for an object to escape Earth's gravitational field and go into orbit. And the place where Annie Easley went to work was called NACA, the National Advisory Committee on Aeronautics.

Then, in 1957, *Sputnik* began orbiting Earth and everything changed. The Russians had beat the United States at the very first step in the space race. By 1958, a new organization emerged out of NACA, the organization we know today as NASA. Suddenly Easley and a lot of other talented individuals were working on a new kind of project—sending objects into space and everything required to get them there.

Many new challenges had to be met. In 1958, NASA authorized the development of a new type of booster rocket, called *Centaur.* Proposed by the air force, this rocket would be a high-energy space booster, using a powerful propulsion system that would use a mixture of liquid hydrogen and oxygen.

At that time Easley was working in the Flight Software Section of Lewis Research Center. Computer hardware was huge—a computer with a fraction of the power of an ordinary modern PC filled a room the size of a gymnasium. For space travel, everything had to be smaller—miniaturized. Easley worked on software programs that dealt with a variety of research problems, from measuring the solar wind to making various kinds of mathematical conversions. She also worked on energy problems, such as the battery life for batteries used in an electric vehicle.

While working for NASA, Easley went on with her education, earning her B.S. in mathematics from Cleveland State University in 1977. Her work on the *Centaur* software has had long-lived results. The *Centaur* technology laid the groundwork for the technology used today in launching the space shuttle. It is also used in rockets that launch satellites used for communications, weather forecasting, and defense surveillance. Most recently it was used to launch the *Cassini* spacecraft from the shuttle in 1997 and send it on its long voyage to Saturn. Easley retired from NASA in 1991, but her legacy lives on.

Further Reading

Brown, Mitchell C. "Annie Easley: Computer Scientist," Faces of Science: African Americans in the Sciences. Available online. URL: http://www. princeton.edu/~mcbrown/display/easley.html. Updated on December 15, 2000.

NASA. *"Centaur: America's Workhorse in Space."* Available online. URL: http://www.lerc.nasa.gov/ WWW/PAO/html/centaur.htm.

Notable Women Scientists. Detroit: Gale Group, 2000.

Warren, Wini. *Black Women Scientists in the United States.* Bloomington: Indiana University Press, 1999, 87–88.

Edwards, Cecile Hoover

(1926–   ) *nutritional researcher, educator*

The research contributions of Cecile Hoover Edwards in the field of nutrition have served to improve the nutritional well-being of thousands of people. She has contributed more than 150 articles to scientific journals and has received a commendation from the Illinois House of Representatives for her efforts to reduce poverty's impact on people's lives.

Cecile Hoover was born on October 20, 1926, in East St. Louis, Illinois, to Annie Jordan Hoover and Ernest Hoover. Her mother was a teacher, and her father was a manager of an insurance agency.

Edwards entered Tuskegee Institute in Tuskegee, Alabama, when she was only 15 and received her B.S. degree with honors in 1946. Her major was home economics with minors in nutrition and chemistry. She earned her M.S. in chemistry from Tuskegee the following year, in 1947. Interested primarily in improving nutrition through research, she completed her Ph.D. in nutrition at Iowa State University in 1950. She wrote her dissertation on methionine, an essential amino acid.

Edwards began her teaching and research career back at Tuskegee, where she joined the faculty in 1950 as assistant professor and a research associate of the Carver Foundation, a fund established by GEORGE WASHINGTON CARVER. Additionally, she took on the responsibilities as head of the department of foods and nutrition from 1952 to 1956, when she left for North Carolina Agricultural and Technical State University in Greensboro. She joined the faculty there as professor of nutrition and research, a position she held until 1971, while also serving as head of the department of home economics from 1968 to 1971. Finally, Edwards joined the faculty at Howard University in Washington, D.C., where she became professor of nutrition and continuing economics in 1971. She also chaired the department of home economics from 1971 to 1974, when she became dean of the School of Human Ecology. She served in that capacity for 13 years, until 1987, when she became dean of continuing education.

Edwards also served as chair of the White House Conference Panel on Community Nutrition in 1969 and president of the Southeastern Conference of Teachers of Foods and Nutrition in 1971. She chaired the National Conference on Black Youth Unemployment in 1983 and was a consultant to the University of Khartoum.

Edwards has published more than 150 articles in scholarly journals, including *American Journal of Clinical Nutrition* and *Journal of Negro Education.* She served as editor of the *Journal of Nutrition* in 1994. Her publications cover topics as widely ranging as black youth unemployment and the relationship between the use of alcohol, tobacco, drugs, and nutrients with pregnancy outcomes. She is a coauthor of a book, *Human Ecology: Interactions of Man with His Environments; An Introduction to the Academic Discipline of Human Ecology,* published in 1991. She is also the author of a monograph entitled *Quality of Life: Black Families,* published by Howard University in 1991.

Edwards has been widely recognized for her contributions to both nutritional research and community involvement. The governor of Illinois proclaimed April 5, 1984, as Dr. Cecile Hoover Edwards Day "in witness of her contribution, her professional recognition nationally and internationally and the sharing of her expertise with communities around the world including East St. Louis, Illinois." Edwards was one of 25 recent Tuskegee graduates who were honored at the Biennial Convention of the Tuskegee Alumni Association in 1984. As of late 2002, Edwards is full professor in the department of nutritional sciences at Howard University.

Further Reading

Current Knowledge of the Relationships of Selected Nutrients, Alcohol, Tobacco, and Drug Use, and Other Factors to Pregnancy Outcomes, School of Human Ecology, Howard University, 1988.

Edwards, Cecile Hoover. *Quality of Life: Black Families* (monograph), Howard University, 1991.

Edwards, Cecile Hoover, and Kendall Hunt. *Human Ecology: Interactions of Man with His Environments; An Introduction to the Academic Discipline of Human Ecology.* Dubuque, Iowa: Kendall-Hunt, 1991.

Edwards, Cecile Hoover, ed. with Linus A. Hoskins and William A. Burrell *Proceedings of the National Conference on Black Youth Unemployment: Strategies for Solutions,* Howard University, Washington, D.C., 1984.

Henderson, Ashyia N., ed. *Who's Who Among African Americans,* 14th ed. Detroit: Gale Group, 2001, 381.

Newman, Laura. "Cecile Hoover Edwards," *Notable Black American Scientists,* Kristine Krapp, ed. Detroit: Gale Research, 1999, 103–104.

Elders, Joycelyn
(Minnie Lee Jones, Minnie Joycelyn Lee)
(1933–   ) *physician, public health administrator*

Joycelyn Elders served as U.S. surgeon general from 1993 to 1994. Although that portion of her career was controversial, she took a strong position then and since in the case for universal health coverage and a practical, no-nonsense approach to public health education, including sex education.

She was born Minnie Lee Jones on August 13, 1933, in Schaal, Arkansas, the first of eight children of Haller and Curtis Jones, sharecroppers who toiled beneath the hot Arkansas sun to feed their family. They provided a loving home for their children, but Minnie and her siblings also had to work in the cotton fields to put food on the table. They lived in poverty—enjoying none of the comforts of electricity or running water—and hunted raccoons to supplement their meager income.

Both intelligent and studious, though, Minnie Lee Jones found a way out. At age 15, she won a scholarship from the United Methodist

Church, providing the means to attend college. Majoring in biology at Philander Smith College in Little Rock, Arkansas, she received her B.A. in 1952. During her college years she changed her name to Minnie Joycelyn Lee and later simplified to just Joycelyn. Following graduation, she spent several months working as a nursing assistant in the Veterans Administration hospital in Milwaukee, and then enrolled in the U.S. Army in 1953. During her three-year army career, she received training as a physical therapist. By the time of her discharge, she had decided on

A tireless campaigner in the case for universal health care, pediatric endocrinologist Joycelyn Elders was the first African-American woman to become surgeon general of the United States. *(U.S. Department of Health and Human Services)*

a career in medicine, and by 1960, she had earned her M.D. from the University of Arkansas Medical School, followed by an internship at the University of Minnesota Hospital and a residency in pediatrics at the University of Arkansas Medical Center. She also completed a master's degree in biochemistry at the University of Arkansas in 1967.

That same year, she began a teaching career as assistant professor in pediatrics at the University of Arkansas Medical Center. She received a promotion in 1971 to associate professor and to full professor in 1976. "Her research interests focused on endocrinology (the study of hormones), receiving certification as a pediatric endocrinologist in 1978. She also became an expert on childhood sexual development.

In 1987, Joycelyn Elders took the helm of the Arkansas Department of Health, appointed by Bill Clinton, who was then governor of Arkansas. During her tenure in this position she achieved significant growth in the number of children who were screened for early childhood illnesses, with a 10-fold increase. She also succeeded in nearly doubling the number of two-year-olds in Arkansas who received immunizations.

On September 8, 1993, she became the first black woman to serve as surgeon general of the United States, appointed by Bill Clinton, who by this time had been elected president. She was a strong advocate of universal health care and heartily supported Clinton's health care reform plans, which did not, however, come to fruition. She also lent her expertise and outspoken opinions to the cause of a strong sex education program. Unfortunately, controversy ensued over her stated opinion that masturbation should probably be taught in schools, and Elders was forced to resign as a result of political pressures. Her term of service came to an end on December 31, 1994.

Following her resignation, Elders returned to her position of pediatrics professor at the University of Arkansas Medical Center. She received nomination to the national board of the Civil Liberties Union in 1995, and in 1996 she published her autobiography. As of 2002, she has retired from her position at the University of Arkansas but continues her public service as a frequent speaker about health education and her favorite cause, combating ignorance with knowledge and education.

Further Reading

Elders, Joycelyn, and David Chanoff. *Joycelyn Elders, M.D.: From Sharecropper's Daughter to Surgeon General of the United States of America.* Thorndike, Me.: Thorndike Press, 1997.

Hawkins, Walter L. *African American Biographies, 2.* Jefferson, N.C.: McFarland & Co., 1994, 82–83.

"M. Joycelyn Elders (1993–1994)," Office of Public Health Services Historian, March 1999.

Smith, Jessie Carney, ed. *Notable Black American Women, Vol. 2,* Detroit: Gale Research, 1996, 200–203.

Thompson, Kathleen. "Elders, Joycelyn Jones," *Facts On File Encyclopedia of Black Women in America: Science, Health, and Medicine,* Darlene Clark Hine, ed. New York: Facts On File, 1997, 63–66.

Emeagwali, Philip

(1954–   ) *computer scientist, mathematician, inventor*

A pioneer in massive parallel computing, Philip Emeagwali developed a formula in 1989 that allowed him to link up 65,000 processors in parallel to perform 3.1 billion calculations per second. For this breakthrough achievement he was awarded the Gordon Bell Prize, the computer world's equivalent of the Nobel Prize, that same year.

Philip Emeagwali was born on August 23, 1954, in Akure, Nigeria. His father, James, was a 33-year-old nursing assistant and his mother,

Agatha, a 16-year-old homemaker. The first of nine children, Philip was already demonstrating his mathematical ability in childhood. His schoolmates nicknamed him "Calculus," and his father relieved him of some of his childhood responsibilities and began giving him extensive drills in mathematics. The object was to solve 100 math problems in an hour. Since there was not enough time to do them all on paper, Emeagwali did them in his head. "People later called me a genius," Emeagwali remarks. "But you would be a genius, too, if you had to solve 100 math problems in an hour."

Life was not easy in Nigeria, though, and life became even more difficult in 1967. By this time, Emeagwali's family was living in Biafra and became caught up in the Nigerian-Biafra war. Forced to flee for their lives, the family moved through a succession of refugee camps or sought shelter in abandoned shell-riddled buildings. "We ate only once a day. Some days we had nothing to eat," Emeagwali recalls. School was quickly forgotten. Conscripted into the Biafran army at age 14, he spent six months with the Biafran forces before the conflict finally ended and he was allowed to return to his family. By then, however, after a very brief return to classes, the state of the war-shattered economy forced Emeagwali to drop out of school altogether when his family could no longer pay his school fees. He had managed to finish only the eighth grade.

Embarking on a rigid schedule of self-discipline, he decided to continue his education on his own, studying college level physics, math, English, and chemistry through books at local libraries. He received a high school equivalency certificate from the University of London at the age of 17. That same year he received a full scholarship at Oregon State University. Despite the worries of his family, he immigrated to the United States with only $140 in his pockets. After graduation from Oregon State with a major in math, he attended Howard University, where he took civil engineering courses, and then George Washington University in Washington, D.C., where he earned a master's degree in environmental engineering in 1981. He received a second master's degree, in mathematics, in 1986 from the University of Maryland while doing additional graduate work in ocean, coastal, and marine engineering at George Washington University. In 1993, he received his doctorate in civil engineering from the University of Michigan.

Emeagwali's interest in parallel processing began in 1974 when he read a 1922 science fic-

tion article describing a scheme to use 64,000 mathematicians to forecast weather for the whole Earth. He began working out a theoretical scheme of his own, replacing the 64,000 mathematicians with 64,000 computers scattered evenly around the Earth. The idea didn't fly very well with his peers, who thought the whole idea of such a linkage "impossible," but Emeagwali's fascination with these possibilities continued to grip him. Continuing his thinking and research over the next dozen years, he laboriously worked out his theories, resulting in a thousand-page monograph describing the hypo-

Computer scientist Philip Emeagwali developed a formula for connecting 65,000 separate computer processors, enabling speeds of 3.1 billion calculations per minute. His work demonstrated the practical applications of systems allowing multiple computers to communicate, and today Emeagwali is recognized as one of the pioneers of the Internet. *(emeagwali.com)*

thetical use of a vast array of linked processors to perform super-fast calculations.

The chance to prove his theories finally came in 1987, when scientists at the Los Alamos National Laboratory became frustrated with their lack of success in programming an experimental computer containing 65,536 processors. So they decided to allow outsiders to submit their proposals for programming the machine. Worrying that the lab might not accept him because he was black, Emeagwali submitted his proposal remotely. Impressed with Emeagwali's ideas, the laboratory approved the proposal. Over the next two years Emeagwali programmed the 65,536 processors in the Los Alamos machine remotely from Michigan via the National Science Foundation Network (NSFNET), the precursor to today's Internet. His success in 1989, performing a complicated calculation three times faster than the speed of a giant supercomputer, won him immediate fame and proved the value of using many thousands of small processors linked together to solve complex problems.

Today Emeagwali is a private consultant and the recipient of more than 100 prizes and honors including the Computer Scientist of the Year Award and the Distinguished Scientist Award of the World Bank. As of 2002, Emeagwali lives near Washington, D.C., with his wife, Dale, and their 12-year-old son. Both Emeagwali and his wife, who is a distinguished microbiologist and winner of the Scientist of the Year Award of the National Technical Association for her cancer research, spend much of their time speaking to schoolchildren about the importance of continuing their education. Emeagwali served for six years as a distinguished lecturer of both the Institute of Electrical and Electronics Engineers and the Association for Computing Machinery. Recently, in addition to his other accomplishments, Emeagwali has taken up traditional African dance.

In a speech given August 26, 2000, then-president Bill Clinton called Emeagwali "one of the great minds of the information age. . . ." As for being called "a genius," Emeagwali comments, "I don't like that term. People think it only means genius in the mathematical sense or that it refers to a select group of people. . . . I think everyone of us has the power to be a genius. I was not born a genius; it was nurtured in me by my father."

Further Reading

Gillmor, Dan. "Brain to Brain: Network Links 3 Million Computers Worldwide," *Detroit Free Press.* Available online. URL: http://www.emeagwali. com/usa/michigan/brain-to-brain-detroit-free-press.html. Posted on July 8, 1991.

Kelleher, Laura. "Award Winner Cites NSFNET Reliability." Link Letter of the Merit Network, Inc. Available online. URL: http://www.emeagwali. com/usa/michigan/NSFnet-merit-network-supercomputer-centers-national-science-foundation.html. Posted in May/June 1990.

"Philip Emeagwali," URL: http://emeagwali.com/ index.html. Accessed from The Faces of Science: African Americans in the Sciences. Available online. URL: http://www.princeton.edu/~mcbrown/ display/faces.html. Updated on February 3, 2001.

"Philip Emeagwali," Computer Scientists of the African Diaspora. Available online. URL: http://www.math. buffalo.edu/mad/computer-science/emeagwali_ philip.html. Downloaded on August 1, 2002.

Rose, Sharon Walker. "Practical Math: Emeagwali Puts Math to Work in Real World," *Detroit Free Press.* Available online. URL: http://www.emeag-wali.com/usa/michigan/practical-mathematics-supercomputers-detroit-free-press.html. Posted on May 29, 1990.

The White House. "Remarks by the President in Address to Joint Assembly, House of Representatives, Chamber National Assembly Building, Abuja, Nigeria." Available online. URL: http:// clinton6.nara.gov/2000/08/2000-08-26-remarks-by-the-president-in-address-to-joint-assembly. html. Posted on August 26, 2000.

Eure, Herman
(1947–) *parasitologist*

As a parasitologist, Herman Eure has focused his research on parasites and their aquatic vertebrate hosts, using the waters and swamps of the countryside near Wake Forest University as his laboratory. He has also taken a leadership role in recruiting minority students into careers in the sciences, mathematics, and engineering.

Born in Corapeake, North Carolina, on January 7, 1947, Herman Eure was the seventh of 10 children of Grover T. Eure and his wife Sarah Goodman Eure. His father was a pipefitter at the nearby Norfolk Naval Shipyard in Portsmouth, Virginia, and his mother, in addition to raising five boys and five girls, was a domestic worker.

Of the four youngest children, all boys, Herman was the oldest, and the four brothers explored the forest, part of the Dismal Swamp area, that extended behind their home. There they were fascinated by the variety of animals and wildlife in the forest, and they studied them with great interest.

In both high school and college, Herman excelled at sports and was active in student government. He received two scholarships when he graduated from high school, enabling him to attend Maryland State College now the University of Maryland Eastern Shore (UMES), located in Princess Anne, Maryland. There he obtained his B.S. in 1969, returning to North Carolina that summer to work at the U.S. Department of Agriculture research station at Hamden, Connecticut. There he studied a weevil that attacks New England's white pine forests. The station's researchers were hoping to find ways to control the destruction caused by the weevil.

Eure entered graduate school the following fall as a Ford Foundation Fellow at Wake Forest University in Winston-Salem, North Carolina. There he centered his research on parasites that infest freshwater fish—in particular, an intestinal worm that lives in largemouth bass. He investigated the question whether heat pollution, in particular warming of the waters by industry, might make the bass more vulnerable to the parasite. He found that, in fact, the fish thrived in the warmed waters he investigated. Eure obtained his Ph.D. from Wake Forest in 1974 and then joined the faculty there. He has continued to spend his entire career at Wake Forest.

In addition to continuing his biological research, Eure has been active in recruiting minority students to careers in science on a national as well as a local level, working with the National Science Foundation, the Ford Foundation, the Graylyn Group (which encourages women to enter mathematical, science, and engineering careers), and similar organizations.

Herman Eure is a member of the American Society of Parasitology, the Southeast Society of Parasitology, and Beta Beta Beta, the National Biological Honor Society. He has also been elected to the Hall of Fame at Maryland State College (UMES). In 1991, Eure was promoted to full professor by Wake Forest University, where he continues his research, teaching, and mentoring.

Further Reading
Henderson, Ashyia N., ed. *Who's Who Among African Americans*, 14th ed. Detroit: Gale Group, 2001, 397.

Kessler, James H., J. S. Kidd, Renee A. Kidd, and Katherine A. Morin. *Distinguished African American Scientists of the 20th Century.* Phoenix, Ariz.: Oryx Press, 1996, 85–87.

Evans, Slayton Alvin, Jr.
(1943–) *organic chemist*

Slayton Alvin Evans, Jr., is a noted expert in the field of organophosphorus and organo sulfur chemistry, and he is the author of over 85 scientific publications in these subjects.

Born on May 17, 1943, in Chicago, Illinois, Slayton Alvin Evans, Jr., is the son of Corine M.

Thompson Evans and Slayton A. Evans, Sr. His family moved to Mississippi, where young Evans attended parochial school. He became fascinated with chemistry at an early age, and—inspired in the late 1950s by *Sputnik,* the first artificial satellite—he began building his own rockets and formulating some of the chemicals for their fuel. He also collected and studied plants and insects.

Evans earned both a scholastic and athletic scholarship to attend Tougaloo College, in Tougaloo, Mississippi, obtaining his B.S. in chemistry in 1965. During this time he began working summers and part-time at Abbott Laboratories in Chicago. He began a graduate course of study in 1966 at the Illinois Institute of Technology and then transferred to Case Western Reserve University in Cleveland, Ohio. During this period, he researched ways to control the disease schistosomiasis, which is caused by a parasite and is prevalent in Southeast Asia. He received his Ph.D. in chemistry from Case Western in 1970.

He had a fellowship for postdoctoral study at the University of Texas at Arlington, for the 1970–71 academic year, and he did further postdoctoral studies at the University of Notre Dame on fellowship in 1971–72, where he worked with stereoisomers, sets of compounds that are made up of the same molecule composition except that they are arranged differently atomically. The different arrangements can have very different properties. During the following academic year, 1972–73, he served as a research instructor at Dartmouth College. In 1974, Evans joined the faculty of the University of North Carolina, Chapel Hill, as Kenan Professor of Chemistry, a position he continues to hold as of late 2002.

Evans received several research grants, including Kenan Research Leave from the University of North Carolina, 1984–85; a Fulbright Fellowship, 1984–85; and a NATO Grant for Collaborative Research, 1987–89. He also held the Ralph Metcalfe, Jr., Lectureship Chair in chemistry at Marquette University, 1993–94.

Several of these fellowships have enabled him to build relationships between his research team of undergraduate and graduate students at the University of North Carolina and research teams in other countries, including France, Germany, and India.

In addition to his responsibilities as a professor and researcher, Evans has served on many committees at the state, national, and international levels. He was committee chair of the Louisiana State Board of Regents in 1990 and also served on the Regional Review Committee for Academic Programs in Chemistry of the Louisiana State Board of Regents that year. He served on the advisory committee of the National Science Foundation's Chemistry Division from 1990 to 1995 and served as its chair from 1993 to 1994. He also served on the international organizing committee for the International Conference on Phosphorous Chemistry in 1995 and 1998. In addition he has served on the National Committee for the International Union of Pure and Applied Chemistry; the advisory board of the journal *Phosphorus, Sulfur, and Silicon;* the advisory board of the International Council on Main Group Chemistry; and the National Advisory Council of the National Institutes of Health (NIH), as well as serving as chair of the NIH BI-4 Study Section.

Evans was also awarded the Science Skills Center "Minds in Motion Award: A Tribute to Outstanding African-American Scientists" in 1992; the National Science Foundation Creativity Award in 1994; and the Howard University Outstanding Achievement Award.

Further Reading

Henderson, Ashyia N., ed. *Who's Who Among African Americans,* 14th ed. Detroit: Gale Group, 2001, 401.

Kessler, James H., J. S. Kidd, Renee A. Kidd, and Katherine A. Morin. *Distinguished African American Scientists of the 20th Century.* Phoenix, Ariz.: Oryx Press, 1996, 87–91.

PRESTON RIDGE LIBRARY
COLLIN COLLEGE
FRISCO, TX 75035

F

Falconer, Etta Zuber
(1933–2002) *mathematician, educator*

Etta Zuber Falconer was considered, above all, a great educator and teacher of mathematics. She contributed considerably to the development of the highly productive science program at Spelman College. Through her influence and as a role model, she substantially increased the number of minorities and women entering majors—and ultimately, careers—in mathematics and the sciences.

Etta Zuber was born in Tupelo, Mississippi, in 1933, the second of two daughters. Her father, Walter A. Zuber, was a physician. Her mother, Zadie L. Montgomery Zuber, was a musician who had attended Spelman College in Atlanta. Coincidentally, Spelman would become her daughter's teaching home for most of her lifetime.

Etta Zuber graduated Phi Beta Kappa and summa cum laude with an A.B. in mathematics from Fisk University in Nashville, Tennessee, in 1953. During that time she met two important mentors, EVELYN BOYD COLLINS GRANVILLE and Lee Lorch. Granville taught at Fisk only one year, but that one year was important—providing a career role model at a time when most mathematics instructors were men. Lorch encouraged Zuber to go on to graduate school.

The following year, Zuber entered graduate school at the University of Wisconsin, where she earned her M.S. in mathematics in 1954. In that year, she joined the faculty of Okolona Junior College in Okolona, Mississippi, where she taught from 1954 to 1963. During this time, she met and married her lifetime partner, Dolan Falconer. The couple had two sons, who became an engineer and a physician, and a daughter, who also became a physician.

Etta Falconer taught briefly in the Chattanooga, Tennessee, public school system during 1963 and 1964 and then joined the faculty at Spelman College in Atlanta, Georgia, as assistant professor in 1965. During this period she also attended the University of Illinois, Champaign-Urbana during the summers of 1962 through 1965 and attended a National Science Foundation (NSF) Teaching Teacher Training Institute during the academic year 1964–65, continually building her knowledge of mathematics and teaching techniques. Falconer also received an NSF fellowship from 1967 to 1969, enabling her to complete her Ph.D. in algebra in 1969 at Emory University, also in Atlanta. Her thesis adviser, Trevor Evans, was said to have remarked that she was the best of the numerous Ph.D. students he had in his 30 years at Emory. In 1980, she attended a workshop at the University of California at Santa Barbara on the use of microcomputers in the undergraduate mathematics curriculum.

During the 1971–72 academic year, Falconer taught at Norfolk State College as assistant professor of mathematics, returning to Spelman as chair of the department of mathematics in 1972. As of late 2002, she continues to teach at Spelman as the Fuller E. Callaway Professor of Mathematics, a position she assumed in 1990, as well as serving as associate provost for science programs and policy since 1991.

During her years of teaching, Falconer consistently found ways to raise the number of students from underrepresented groups, such as minorities and women, in the study of both mathematics and the sciences. At Spelman College, she fostered remarkably successful programs for encouraging students to enter the sciences. Under her leadership, some 38 percent of the students at Spelman pursued mathematics, computer science, chemistry, biology, physics, or dual engineering degrees—an extraordinarily high percentage for a liberal arts college.

Included among her successful efforts are a Summer Science Program for students entering college, an annual Science Day, and Spelman College's National Aeronautics and Space Administration (NASA) Women in Science and Engineering Program (WISE), which promotes science and engineering to women. More than 150 women students have participated in WISE since its establishment on campus in 1987. Both WISE and the NASA Undergraduate Scholar Awards program coordinated by Falconer allow students to use NASA facilities for research.

Among Falconer's many awards, two stand out. In 1995, the Association of Women in Mathematics (AWM) awarded her the Louise Hay Award for Contributions to Mathematics Education. In part, the citation stated: "Her many years of service in promoting mathematics at Spelman College and her efforts to enhance the movement of minorities and women into scientific careers through many forums in the math-

Dedicated to the principle of lifelong learning and nationally recognized as a master teacher in mathematics, Etta Zuber Falconer remarked in 1995, "My entire career has been devoted to increasing the number of African American women in mathematics and mathematics-related careers." *(Courtesy of Etta Zuber Falconer)*

ematics and science communities are extraordinary." In 1999 she was elected a fellow of the American Association for the Advancement of Science (AAAS), and in 2002 she received the AAAS Mentor Award for Lifetime Achievement.

When she received the AWM Louise Hay Award, Falconer remarked, "I have devoted my entire life to increasing the number of highly qualified African Americans in mathematics and mathematics-related careers. High expectations, the building of self-confidence, and the creation of a nurturing environment have been essential components for the success of these students. They have fully justified my beliefs."

Etta Zuber Falconer died on September 18, 2002, from complications from pancreatic cancer. She was 68.

Further Reading

Narayanan, Nisha. "Award Recipients Honored at AAAS Meeting," American Association for the Advancement of Science. Available online. URL: http://www.aaas.org/news/releases/aaasawards. shtml. Downloaded March 4, 2002.

Newell, V. K., J. H. Gipson, L. W. Rich, and B. Stubblefield, *Black Mathematicians and their Works*, Ardmore, Pa.: Dorrance & Company, 1980, 286.

Warren, Wini. *Black Women Scientists in the United States*. Bloomington: Indiana University Press, 1999, 96–98.

Ferguson, Angella Dorothea

(1925–) *medical researcher, pediatrician*

A distinguished pediatrician and researcher in sickle-cell anemia, Angella Ferguson also managed the development and construction of medical facilities that became the Howard University Hospital, built on the site in Washington, D.C., where Freedmen's Hospital once stood.

The daughter of Mary Burton Ferguson and George Alonzo Ferguson, Angella Dorothea Ferguson was born in Washington, D.C., on February 15, 1925, one of eight children. When Angella was a sophomore in high school, she developed an interest in chemistry and mathematics. Even though her family lived in poverty, she determined she would go to college and pursue a career in science. In 1951, after graduating from high school, she entered Howard University.

Once at Howard, Ferguson's interests shifted to biology and she decided to become a physician. After receiving her bachelor's degree from Howard in 1945, she immediately entered the Howard University Medical School, where she took a course in pediatrics (treatment and prevention of disease in children) from Roland Scott. Scott later became her mentor. Ferguson completed her M.D. in 1949 and entered her internship at Freedmen's Hospital (which was part of the Howard medical school). During an internship, interns spend time in each of several medical disciplines, a process referred to as a rotation. When Ferguson's rotation took her to pediatrics, she settled on the direction of her career. She went on to her residency at Freedmen's Hospital.

After receiving her license, Ferguson opened a private pediatrics practice. However, she felt hampered by the lack of information about the normal developmental progress of African-American babies. At the time, the only results available were based on studies of European children. At Howard, Roland Scott obtained funding for pursuing the needed studies and brought Ferguson on staff as a research associate. The project began by gathering data from well-baby clinics.

However, in the process, Ferguson noticed how prevalent sickle-cell anemia was among African-American babies. Sickle-cell anemia is a painful and potentially serious disease that is genetically transmitted. In 1949, Linus Pauling discovered that an abnormal (S) hemoglobin (the oxygen-carrying red blood cells) was the molecular cause of the disease. Children of parents who both carry the gene may inherit the most common form of the disease (SS). When the abnormal hemoglobin releases oxygen, it forms a type of sticky polymer that makes the red blood cells stiff and they take on a sickle-like shape (hence the name) instead of their normal donut-like shape. The sickle-cells are brittle and tend to break up, causing anemia (an insufficient supply of red blood cells). Blood vessels become clogged, blood flow slows, and tissues and organs can become damaged. The main symptoms are attacks of pain, and resulting infections and damage to the lungs can cause death. African Americans are the primary victims of sickle-cell anemia, although it sometimes also appears among people of Mediterranean, Middle Eastern, and Asian Indian descent. Some 60,000 Americans have sickle-cell disease and another 2.5 million are healthy carriers of the gene.

Ferguson studied sickle-cell anemia during the 1950s and early 1960s and became a respected authority on the subject. In 1953, she accepted a position as instructor in the pediatrics department at the Howard University school of medicine, and she received a promotion in 1959 to assistant professor. She also served at Freedmen's Hospital as an assistant pediatrician.

Beyond her training at Howard, Ferguson completed postgraduate training at Bethesda Naval Hospital in Maryland, where she studied the effects and uses of radioisotopes. (An isotope is a form of an element that varies from the most common atomic structure in that it has the same number of protons, but a different number of neutrons—so they have the same atomic number but a different atomic mass. A radioisotope is an isotope of a radioactive element.) Tiny amounts of radioisotopes can be injected and tracked by instruments that can detect the radiation, providing information to the physician about biological processes.

Ferguson also obtained a fellowship that allowed her to do postgraduate work in hematology (the study of blood and blood-forming tissues) at Cornell University Hospital.

Ferguson set up guidelines for diagnosing sickle-cell anemia in young children under age 12. She advised administration of blood tests to infants to identify the presence of the disease early. She recommended a daily glass of soda water for children under five who suffered from the disease—so that blood volume would increase and the damaged blood cells could flow through blood vessels more easily. She also recommended increased oxygen during surgery for patients having sickle-cell anemia, since the trauma of surgery increased the disease symptoms.

Ferguson received certificates of merit twice for this work from the American Medical Association. She also received a promotion to associate professor from Howard University and she became associate pediatrician at Freedmen's Hospital in 1963, and in the same year joined the staff of D.C. General Hospital as attending physician.

In 1965, what might be called the "hard-hat" portion of Ferguson's career began. A new medical center for Howard University school of medicine was to be built to replace Freedmen's Hospital, by then nearly a century old. Angella Ferguson was given the job of overseeing the construction of the new facility. Initially she was just in charge of the pediatric wing development, but eventually she oversaw the entire project. In May 1975, the hospital was completed and patients were moved in from the old Freedmen's Hospital. The first baby was born 15 minutes after his mother moved in.

Ferguson continued to serve the university and its medical school. As of 1996, Dr. Angella Ferguson had returned from retirement to act as associate vice president for health affairs. Her record of service to the field of pediatrics has spanned more than 45 years.

Further Reading

Hayden, Robert. *Eleven African-American Doctors,* rev. ed. New York: Twenty-First Century Books, 1992, 154–169.

Kessler, James H., J. S. Kidd, Renee A. Kidd, and Katherine A. Morin. *Distinguished African American Scientists of the 20th Century.* Phoenix, Ariz.: Oryx Press, 1996.

Sammons, Vivian Ovelton. *Blacks in Science and Medicine.* New York: Hemisphere Publishing, 1990.

Ferguson, Lloyd Noel
(1918–   ) *chemist*

In 1983, a Smithsonian Living History presentation about Lloyd Noel Ferguson noted that "his research on the sense of taste, on structure-bioactivity relationships and on cancer chemotherapy . . . give evidence of the tremendous contributions Lloyd Noel Ferguson has made to his profession." Ferguson's stature as both a researcher and a mentor has received widespread recognition.

Born on February 9, 1918, in Oakland, California, Lloyd Noel Ferguson was the second generation of his family to be born in California. Following the Civil War, his grandparents had moved to California, so both his mother and father were native Californians. Ferguson suffered a severe childhood illness at the age of seven, when he came down with both diphtheria and pneumonia and nearly died. The experience left

The author of more than 50 publications in scientific journals and seven books, chemist Lloyd Ferguson was the subject of an oral history interview conducted in 1992, *Increasing Opportunities in Chemistry, 1936–1986. (Stan Carstensen, California State University, Los Angeles)*

a lasting impression on the young boy's memory and probably increased his sense of the value of life. He made up for lost time, despite missing a year of school with his illness, graduating from high school at age 16. He also had a keen curiosity. He bought himself a chemistry set at age 12 and did chemistry experiments in a backyard shed. It was the beginning of his lifelong career as a chemist. He put together a moth repellent, invented a spot remover and a silver polish, and a developed a lemonade mix. A budding entrepreneur, as well, he sold his inventions to his neighbors.

Ferguson couldn't go straight on to college—the financially difficult years of the depression kept his family in financial straits, as happened to many people during the 1930s. For a while he worked for the Works Progress Administration on a dock construction project in Berkeley, California. Later, he took a job as porter on the Southern Pacific Railway. The job paid well, and within two years, Ferguson was able to begin his undergraduate studies at the University of California at Berkeley (UCB). In 1940, he received his B.S. degree. Three years later, in 1943, he had completed his Ph.D. in biochemistry, also from UCB. He was the first African American to receive a Ph.D. in chemistry from UCB. During and after his studies at Berkeley, he worked as a research assistant for the National Defense Project at UCB from 1941 to 1944.

He joined the faculty at North Carolina Agricultural and Technical College (now University) in Greensboro, North Carolina, in 1944, moving on to Howard University the following year, where he remained on the chemistry faculty for 20 years. He served as department head as well from 1958 to 1965. In this capacity, he built the first doctoral program in chemistry at any black college in the nation.

During his years at Howard, Ferguson had two opportunities to conduct research in Europe. In 1953, he received a Guggenheim Fellowship through which he traveled to Copenhagen, Denmark, to the Carlsberg Laboratory, which had a reputation for studies in fermentation. In 1960, he was awarded a National Science Foundation Fellowship, which made possible a year of teaching at the Swiss Federal Institute of Technology in Zurich, Switzerland.

Upon leaving Howard University, Ferguson joined the faculty at California State University at Los Angeles as full professor, serving as chemistry department chair from 1968 to 1971.

Ferguson is the author of more than 50 journal articles and seven textbooks, including: *Electron Structures of Organic Molecules* (Prentice-Hall, 1952), *Textbook of Organic Chemistry* (D. Van Nostrand, 1958; 2nd edition, 1965); *The Modern Structural Theory of Organic Chemistry* (Prentice-Hall, 1963), *Organic Chemistry: A Science and an Art* (Willard Grant Press, 1972), *Highlights of Alicyclic Chemistry*, two volumes (Franklin Publishing, 1973), and *Organic Molecular Structure: A Gateway to Advanced Organic Chemistry* (Willard Grant Press, 1975).

Ferguson's research included investigation of the structure of carbon-based molecules, the relationship between structure and biological activity, and cancer chemotherapy. Over a span of 20 years, he also explored the functioning of the human sense of taste. In particular, he investigated the molecular differences between substances that taste sour and those that taste sweet—and tried to find out why some molecules of very similar structure do not produce any taste.

In addition to his teaching and research, Ferguson was chairman of the American Chemical Society's Division of Chemical Education, served as director of Cal State L.A.'s Minority Biomedical Research Support program for more than 10 years (1973–84) and was program director for many National Science Foundation teaching and research participation programs.

California State University recognized Ferguson's contributions to chemistry and his excellence as a teacher in 1981 by naming him the 1980–81 California State Universities and Colleges Trustees' Outstanding Professor, both at the Cal State L.A. and statewide levels. The Lloyd N. Ferguson Scholarship in chemistry and biochemistry has been established in his name. The Lloyd N. Ferguson Young Scientist Award has also been created in his honor, a CibaGeigy Corporation "Exceptional Black Scientists" Poster was published to celebrate his career and his work, and his birthdate appears in the "Milestones in Chemistry" calendar. In 1995, California State University at Los Angeles established the Lloyd Ferguson Distinguished Lecture in his honor.

Ferguson has also received recognition for his mentoring of minority students. In 1998, he received the Quality Education for Minorities in Mathematics, Science and Engineering (QEM/MSE) Network's Giants in Science Award. This award is given to outstanding mentors, teachers, and researchers who are strong advocates of quality math, science, and engineering education for all students, along with a particular commitment to students who are underrepresented in the educational system. Ferguson is recognized as having served as a role model for many hundreds of minority students, encouraging them to enter and excel in careers in science and technology.

Lloyd Noel Ferguson retired in 1986 and became professor emeritus in chemistry at Cal State L.A., a position he continued to enjoy as of late 2002.

Further Reading

Ferguson, Lloyd Noel. *Increasing Opportunities in Chemistry, 1936–1986,* oral history conducted in 1992 by Gabrielle Morris, Regional Oral History Office, Bancroft Library, University of California, Berkeley, 1992. Available online. URL: http://sunsite.berkeley.edu:2020/dynaweb/teiproj/oh/blackalum/ferguson/@Generic__BookView. Downloaded on November 3, 2002.

"Giant in Science," *University Reports*, California State University, Los Angeles, 27 No. 2 (winter 2000), 1. Available online. URL: http://www.calstatela.edu/univ/ppa/ur/ur2w00.pdf. Posted in February 2000.

Hawkins, Walter L. *African American Biographies*. Jefferson, N.C.: McFarland & Co., 1992.

Forde, Evan B.

(1952–   ) *oceanographer*

In his capacity as oceanographic researcher for the National Oceanic and Atmospheric Administration (NOAA), Evan Forde discovered a massive submarine sediment slide along the Atlantic Coast during a research cruise. The discovery led to curtailment of oil company off-shore drilling rights near Cape May, New Jersey, by the Department of the Interior. Forde was also the first black oceanographer to participate in submersible dives aboard research submersibles *Alvin* (1980), *Johnson Sea Link* (1981), and *Nekton Gamma* (1979).

Born on May 11, 1952, in Miami, Florida, Evan B. Forde was the son of two teachers—his father was a high school science teacher and his mother an elementary schoolteacher. Forde grew

During research dives inside the *Johnson Sea Link* submersible, oceanographer Evan Forde investigated Norfolk Submarine Canyon off the shore of Delaware and New Jersey. *(NOAA, courtesy of Evan Forde)*

up watching *The Undersea World of Jacques Cousteau* and became fascinated by the science of the underwater world. Forde attended Columbia University in New York, specializing in oceanography within his geology major. He received his B.S. in 1974. While completing his undergraduate curriculum at Columbia, Forde first began working for NOAA (a branch of the U.S. Department of Commerce) during the summer of 1973, under a student appointment as a scientific technician.

After winning a NOAA Fellowship to attend graduate school, he became a full-time, permanent NOAA employee in 1974. He returned to Columbia University for his master's degree, studying at the Lamont-Doherty Earth Observatory there. He completed his M.S. in marine geology in 1976, after which he returned to Miami to work at NOAA's Atlantic Oceanographic and Meteorological Laboratory (AMOL). This laboratory is charged with conducting both basic and applied research programs in oceanography, tropical meteorology, atmospheric and oceanic chemistry, and acoustics. Its purpose is to gain understanding of the physical characteristics and processes of the ocean and the atmosphere, both separately and as a coupled system. During the late 1970s, Forde's research focused on such topics as the geology of the ocean floor along the Atlantic coastline, including submarine canyons, slides, sedimentary textures, and processes.

In 1982, he began working for the Ocean Chemistry Division, when he began investigating aspects of hydrothermal plumes. As of July 2001, he became research oceanographer in the laboratory's Remote Sensing Division. In that capacity, he has worked on methods for using a new satellite, QuikSCAT, to locate hurricanes in their early formation stages. Forde has authored or coauthored numerous published articles on these and other topics. Forde was selected NOAA Research Employee of the Year in 2001.

Forde has taken a leadership role in outreach, educational outreach, and Equal Opportunity Employment (EEO) for the laboratory. He is coordinator of outreach and is chair of the educational outreach committee, and he is the webmaster for the AMOL website, as well as the EEO page for the AMOL. He is also a member of the EEO Committee and is manager of the Community Outreach Program. Involved in numerous community programs, Forde has given many talks to Miami-Dade county schoolchildren on science careers and other topics.

In keeping with his continuing interest in science education, from 1982 to 1983, Forde wrote a column for *Ebony, Jr.* on topics ranging from magnets, static electricity, and chemistry to light, air, compasses, and magnifying lenses.

Further Reading

"Evan B. Forde, Oceanographer," Evan B. Forde's Homepage. Available online. URL: http://www.aoml.noaa.gov/od/people/forde/. Updated 2001.

Milite, George A. "Evan B. Forde," *Notable Black American Scientists*. Kristine Krapp, ed. Detroit: Gale Research, 1999, 119.

Francisco, Joseph Salvadore, Jr.

(1955–   ) *atmospheric scientist, physical scientist*

Joseph Salvadore Francisco, Jr., is known for his work relevant to ozone depletion in the atmosphere and is a respected scientist in atmospheric and Earth studies.

He was born on March 26, 1955, in New Orleans, Louisiana, the son of Lucinda Baker Francisco and Joseph Salvadore Francisco, Sr. However, his home soon became Beaumont, Texas, where he was raised by his grandparents, Merlin and Sarah Walker. They gave him a part-time job as a teenager doing bookkeeping for their real estate business. He also had a part-time job in a pharmacy, which enabled him to get a feel for the way chemicals combined.

Backed by encouragement from his high school science teachers and his own enthusiasm for chemistry, Francisco entered the University of Texas at Austin, from which he earned his B.S. with honors in 1977. Although he was accepted to graduate school at the Massachusetts Institute of Technology (MIT), he was not able to continue straight on to graduate studies because of financial strains caused by the death of his grandfather. Francisco took a job in the private sector as a chemist for Monsanto Chemical Company. When he had gathered sufficient funds, Francisco entered the doctoral program in chemistry at MIT in Cambridge, Massachusetts, in 1978.

At MIT, he worked with a research team that was investigating how laser beams affected chemical reactions. Prior to completion of his Ph.D., Francisco spent a year as visiting lecturer at the University of Sydney in Sydney, Australia, in 1981. At Sydney, Francisco gained insights about the effects of laser beams on chemical bonds, an experience that contributed to the research on laser energy he was doing at MIT. He received his Ph.D. from MIT in 1983.

Following completion of his doctorate, he attended Cambridge University at Cambridge, England, as a research fellow from 1983 to 1985. He returned to MIT as a provost postdoctoral fellow during the 1985–86 academic year. Francisco taught as assistant professor of chemistry at Wayne State University in Detroit, Michigan, from 1986 to 1990, receiving a promotion to associate professor in 1990. He simultaneously held a position as research associate on a fellowship at the California Institute of Technology's Jet Propulsion Laboratory (JPL) in 1991. A John Simon Guggenheim Fellowship enabled him pursue research as a visiting scientist at JPL from 1993 to 1994.

During this period he conducted key research about the causes of ozone depletion in Earth's upper atmosphere. He showed that chemicals emitted by aerosol sprays and types of refrigeration and air conditioning used at the time had caused chemical reactions that removed ozone molecules from the upper atmosphere. The ozone layer in the upper atmosphere

provides a shield that protects Earth and its biosphere from the Sun's harmful ultraviolet (UV) radiation. Francisco received an Alfred P. Sloan Research Fellowship in 1990 for his research in this area, as well as several other awards.

In 1995, he became professor of chemistry and professor of earth and atmosphere sciences at Purdue University in West Lafayette, Indiana, and in 1998, he served as the Sterling Brown Visiting Professor at Williams College in Williamstown, Massachusetts.

Francisco has coauthored a book in his field, *Chemical Kinetics and Dynamics*, published in 1989.

Francisco has earned numerous fellowships and awards, including Research Fellow, St. Edmund's College, Cambridge University, 1983–85; Presidential Young Investigator Award by the National Science Foundation, 1988; Alfred P. Sloan Research Fellow, Alfred P. Sloan Foundation, 1990–92; the Camille and Henry Dreyfus Teacher-Scholar Award, Dreyfus Foundation, 1990–95; the Percy Julian Research Award, 1995; Sigma XI National Lecturer, 1995–97; Purdue University Faculty Scholar, 1998; and Fellow of the American Physical Society, 1998.

Additionally, for excellence in teaching, Francisco received the Wayne State Faculty Award at Wayne State University in 1986, the National Organization of Black Chemists and Chemical Engineers Outstanding Teacher Award in 1992, and the American Association for the Advancement of Science (AAAS) Mentor Award in 1994.

He continues to teach, research, and mentor at Purdue University.

Further Reading

Henderson, Ashyia N., ed. *Who's Who Among African Americans,* 14th ed. Detroit: Gale Group, 2001, 437.

Kessler, James H., J. S. Kidd, Renee A. Kidd, and Katherine A. Morin. *Distinguished African American Scientists of the 20th Century.* Phoenix, Ariz.: Oryx Press, 1996, 103–106.

Franklin, Renty Benjamin
(1945–) *physiologist*

Renty Benjamin Franklin is an internationally recognized expert on glandular functions and processes, in particular of the prostate gland. He is the author of more than 80 scientific articles and abstracts.

Renty Franklin was born on September 2, 1945, to Pinkie Smith Franklin and George Franklin in Birmingham, Alabama. His family owned a small grocery store, and every member of the family took turns taking care of the store, including Renty and his brother, when they were old enough. Renty's father took his turn in the evening after a full day's work at another job. The family was closely knit and attended up to three church services a week together.

Renty's mother had formerly been a teacher, and she taught the boys the basics of reading, writing, and arithmetic in the evenings. The extra lessons put the Franklin boys ahead in their classes, and Renty started high school two years early, graduating in January 1962, when he enrolled at Morehouse College at the age of 16. His plan was to become a physician. Meanwhile, though, the important and compelling events of the 1960s Civil Rights movement were taking place throughout the South, and young Franklin became involved in the demonstrations. As a result, his activism took up time that he might otherwise have spent studying, and his grades suffered somewhat. His adviser, Roy Hunter, pointed out that his middle-of-the-road grades could keep him out of medical school, and Franklin turned his focus back to his studies.

Hunter also turned Franklin's attention to the unsolved problems of the biological sciences, with the result that Franklin began to think in terms of a research career instead of his original plan for a medical career.

Franklin received his B.S. degree from Morehouse College in Atlanta, Georgia, in 1966, and his M.S. degree from Atlanta University the fol-

lowing year. He was able to support his master's studies with a graduate research assistantship. While at Atlanta University, Franklin was asked to fill in for one of his professors when the professor became seriously ill. Franklin not only taught the undergraduate courses, but a graduate seminar as well, which whetted his appetite for the challenges of teaching at the graduate level.

After receiving his master's degree, Franklin needed to take time off from his studies to build up his financial resources. He joined the faculty of St. Augustine's College in Raleigh, North Carolina, where he served as an instructor for two years. In 1969, he was able to return to graduate studies and chose Howard University in Washington, D.C. There he again received a graduate assistantship that covered most of his expenses, and he also received a National Science Foundation grant for his doctoral research, which explored various questions about glands and how they marshal the body's energy resources through the secretion of hormones and enzymes. He also examined how specific chemicals, such as vitamins, might influence this process, and he studied the vulnerability of glands to specific diseases. He completed his Ph.D. in physiology in 1972.

Franklin became assistant professor of physiology at Howard University College of Medicine in 1972, teaching a basic course in physiology for medical, dental, and allied health students (physical therapists for example).

He received another research grant in 1974, from the Porter Foundation, in support of advanced medical research at Harvard University Medical School, where he was able to investigate how minerals affect the way the body functions. His research centered on the relationship between high levels of calcium in the bloodstream and the inception of cancer and other diseases. He returned to Howard, receiving a promotion to associate professor in 1977.

In 1980, Franklin joined the faculty of the University of Maryland Dental School in Baltimore. The school had offered him a tenured (permanent) position as associate professor of physiology, and he received a promotion to full professor in 1986. There he was able to expand his studies of glands, centering on investigation of the prostate gland, which commonly causes health problems for older men. During this period, Franklin was extremely productive, producing two or more research reports each year, resulting in a growing international recognition of Franklin as an expert in the study of the prostate gland. The NIH awarded Franklin and his research team a series of grants for continued work.

Awards garnered by Franklin include the Outstanding Faculty Research Award from Howard University College of Medicine in 1976 and the Howard Hughes-Morehouse Distinguished Scientists Award in 1994. Franklin also received further recognition of his scientific reputation when he was named chair of the NIH Scientific Review Group.

Further Reading

Henderson, Ashyia N., ed. *Who's Who Among African Americans,* 14th ed. Detroit: Gale Group, 2001, 440.

Kessler, James H., J. S. Kidd, Renee A. Kidd, and Katherine A. Morin. *Distinguished African American Scientists of the 20th Century.* Phoenix, Ariz.: Oryx Press, 1996, 106–109.

Fuller, Almyra Oveta
(A. Oveta Fuller)
(1955–) *microbiologist*

A. Oveta Fuller's research as a microbiologist has centered on the study of viruses and the methods they use to attach to the cells they infect. Her research revolves around two major questions: First, how do viruses and cells interact and how can knowledge of this relationship enable scientists to control viral diseases? Second, how might viruses be used in genetic engineering?

Almyra Oveta Fuller was born on August 31, 1955, in Mebane, North Carolina, to Deborah Woods Fuller, a junior high school teacher, and Herbert R. Fuller, a farmer. Known as Oveta, she grew up on the farm where her family lived near Yanceyville. The household included a large extended family including Oveta, her two brothers and parents, her grandmother, and four of her uncles.

Growing up on a farm, Oveta saw nature close up, and time spent with her grandmother gave her early firsthand knowledge of suffering caused by her grandmother's diabetes and arthritis. When Oveta was in high school, she was chosen to attend the North Carolina Governor's School, a summer program for promising students selected from all over the state.

Upon graduation from high school, Fuller received a four-year scholarship to the University of North Carolina at Chapel Hill (UNC), where she majored in biology. During the summer of 1976, she worked in a local health clinic, half-time as a physician's assistant and half-time as a laboratory assistant. She found she was more drawn to the research side of the experience. An outbreak of a deadly disease at a Philadelphia convention of the American Legion in 1976 further confirmed Fuller's interest in the detective work of research. Now known as Legionnaires' disease, the disease and its cause were unknown prior to the outbreak. A total of 221 people became seriously ill and 34 died. Finally, the cause was discovered to be the *Legionella pneumophila* bacterium. The importance of the research detective work that led to the discovery of the cause was not lost on Fuller, who was in her senior year at UNC. Fuller received her B.A. in 1977.

Fuller settled on UNC for her graduate work, recognizing UNC's strong microbiology program as well as the numerous other research centers in the "Research Triangle" area, which included North Carolina State, North Carolina Central University, Duke University, and numerous government research agencies and private research firms. Fuller received a graduate fellowship from the university and worked as a research assistant at UNC from 1980 to 1982 while she pursued her doctorate in microbiology, which she received in 1983. Her doctoral thesis studied the interaction of two plant toxins: Abrin, an eye irritant, and Ricin, a blood coagulant.

After receiving her degree, Fuller received a one-year postdoctoral grant from the Anna Fuller Cancer Fund, enabling her to join Patricia G. Spear's research team at the University of Chicago, where Fuller conducted research during the 1984–85 academic year. Her continued research there for the next four years was funded by a National Institutes of Health (NIH) Postdoctoral Research Award, 1984–86, and a Ford Foundation Postdoctoral Research Award, 1986–87. During this period her studies focused on the herpes virus, a group of viruses that cause many illnesses, including cold sores, genital herpes, mononucleosis, shingles, and chicken pox, to name just a few. Fuller investigated the method used by the virus to penetrate the cell wall. Because herpes attacks soft tissues exclusively, she postulated that the molecular structure of soft tissue cells might be different from other cells in some way that facilitated the virus's attachment to the cell walls. Once attached, the virus passes through the cell wall to the cell's interior. Fuller also studied the question of whether, once inside, the virus could introduce new genetic material into the cell. Spear and Fuller also examined the molecular differences between cells that appeared to be immune to herpes viruses and those that were not immune. They did not arrive at a cure or prevention for herpes; however, their work provided a foundation for further studies.

In other studies, Fuller showed that each virus requires the presence of specific amino acids—the building blocks of proteins. So for each pair of virus and host cell, the host cell must have the specific amino acids required by the virus or the virus cannot attach itself to the cell wall. Information about how viruses function in conjunction with their hosts can open up new understanding of how specific viruses, such as the AIDS virus, might be defeated. Fuller also taught genetics courses during this period at the University of Chicago.

In 1988, Fuller joined the faculty as assistant professor at the medical school at the University of Michigan at Ann Arbor. While teaching at the graduate school, as well as the medical and dental schools, she continues her work in research, now the head of her own research team, funded in part by the NIH and the National Science Foundation. She has begun to build an international reputation, and in 1992 she co-chaired a technical session at an International Herpes Conference in Edinburgh, Scotland.

Further Reading

Henderson, Ashyia N., ed. *Who's Who Among African Americans,* 14th ed. Detroit: Gale Group, 2001, 449.

Kessler, James H., J. S. Kidd, Renee A. Kidd, and Katherine A. Morin. *Distinguished African American Scientists of the 20th Century.* Phoenix, Ariz.: Oryx Press, 1996, 112–116.

Fuller, Solomon Carter

(1872–1953) *neurologist*

Solomon Carter Fuller, the grandson of slaves, became the first eminent black psychiatrist. He studied the degenerative brain disease known as Alzheimer's disease and made significant contributions to the understanding of its processes. He also saw the connection between body and mind, recognizing that many mental illnesses have physical causes.

Solomon Carter Fuller was born in Monrovia, Liberia, on August 11, 1872. His father was Solomon Fuller, a coffee plantation farmer and government administrator. Young Solomon Carter Fuller's grandfather, John Lewis Fuller, had been a slave in the United States, had bought himself out of slavery, and had traveled with his family across the ocean to the newly formed African republic, founded in 1847 to provide a homeland to freed American slaves.

Fuller's mother was Anna Ursula James, the daughter of missionaries. She established a small school to teach her son and neighboring children. Fuller attended school there until he was 10, then attended the College Preparatory School of Monrovia for six years, graduating in 1888. He sailed for the United States in 1889. Once arrived, he continued his education by enrolling in Livingstone College in Salisbury, North Carolina, graduating in 1893. He then went on to medical school at Long Island College Hospital in Brooklyn, New York, transferring to Boston University School of Medicine (BUSM), where he earned his M.D. in 1897.

Fuller completed his internship at the pathology laboratory at Westborough State Hospital in Massachusetts. He received an appointment as pathologist there in 1899 and simultaneously joined the faculty at BUSM as a pathology instructor. He continued to teach pathology for the next 10 years.

Few scientific studies of mental illness and its pathology and psychology had been done at the time, and Fuller became determined to change that situation following a lecture by neurologist S. Weir Mitchell at a meeting of the American Medico-Psychological Association. Mitchell called for increased scientific attention in this area, and Fuller began to initiate a study of mental patients. He also enrolled at Carnegie Laboratory in New York in 1900, where he studied psychiatry. In 1904, he traveled to the University of Munich in Germany, where he studied in the psychiatric clinic under Emil Kraepelin

and Alois Alzheimer, who two years later would become the first to identify the disease now known as Alzheimer's disease. In 1905, he also had a conversation with Paul Ehrlich, whose work on immunity would win him the 1908 Nobel Prize in physiology or medicine.

In 1909, Fuller began teaching neurology instead of pathology at BUSM. He continued his study of mental patients, focusing on Alzheimer's disease and other aspects of neurology. In this year, he also met Sigmund Freud when the well-known neurologist from Austria was visiting in the United States. In that year, he also married Meta Vaux Warrick, a sculptor who had studied in France under Auguste Rodin, celebrated for his statues, including his famed piece "The Thinker."

Fuller became editor in 1913 of the *Westborough State Hospital Papers*, which focused on mental illness, and he published numerous articles on aspects of psychiatry, pathology, and neurology, both there and in other journals.

Fuller was one of the first researchers to investigate the chemical causes of several mental disorders, including schizophrenia and manic-depressive psychosis, or bipolar disorder. He continued to follow his premise of a physical-mental link in mental disorders, at a time when most psychiatrists were not thinking in those terms. Since then, Fuller's position has become much more accepted in the psychiatric community.

He continued his investigation of Alzheimer's—first identified by his former teacher in 1906 and now considered the most prevalent cause of dementia in adults. Its cause remains undetermined early in the 21st century. At the time of Fuller's work the favored theory was that Alzheimer's was caused by arteriosclerosis (an inflexibility of the arterial walls, often called hardening of the arteries). Fuller did not agree but could not prove his position. Not until 1953 did confirmation come that no link existed between arteriosclerosis and Alzheimer's.

Fuller continued teaching until 1937, ultimately achieving the status of professor and then professor emeritus upon retirement. He continued to serve as neuropathologist on several hospital staffs and practiced psychiatry for the rest of his life. He died on January 16, 1953. He was 80 years old.

Since his death, Fuller has been recognized by several honors. The Black Psychiatrists of America honored him in May 1971 by presenting his portrait to the American Psychiatric Association in Washington, D.C. The two organizations established the Solomon Carter Fuller Institute in 1972. The following year, BUSM, Fuller's alma mater, held a conference in his honor, and the university renamed its mental health center the Dr. Solomon Carter Fuller Mental Health Center.

Further Reading

Hayden, Robert. *Eleven African-American Doctors,* rev. ed. New York: Twenty-First Century Books, 1992, 18–35.

Kaufman, Martin, et al., eds. *Dictionary of American Medical Biography, Volume I,* Westport, Conn.: Greenwood Press, 1984, 268.

Sammons, Vivian Ovelton. *Blacks in Science and Medicine.* New York: Hemisphere Publishing Corp., 1990.

G

Gillam, Isaac Thomas, IV
(1932–) *aerospace engineer, administrator*

As manager for the Delta rocket program, Isaac Thomas Gillam IV, helped develop one of the most reliable launch vehicles in NASA history. Delta rockets have launched countless weather and communication satellites, as well as military satellites, over the years since inception of the program. Gillam also directed shuttle operations during the critical flight tests of the shuttle orbiter *Enterprise* during the development phase of that program. He became director in 1978 of the National Aeronautics and Space Administration (NASA) flight test center at Dryden Flight Research Center, located at Edwards Air Force Base in California. He also worked on the early development of what is now the *International Space Station*.

Born in Little Rock, Arkansas, on February 23, 1932, Isaac Gillam was the son of Isaac Thomas Gillam III and Ethel McNeal Reynolds Gillam. As a boy, young Gillam lived with his grandparents in Little Rock, where his grandfather was a high school principal. He spent summers with his parents, who worked for the government in Washington, D.C., and he attended Dunbar High School in Washington, enrolling after graduation in undergraduate classes at Howard University. (Both his grandfather and father had also attended Howard University.) Inspired by the Tuskegee airmen, Gillam joined the Air Force ROTC at Howard and aspired to become a pilot. In 1952, he received his bachelor's degree in mathematics.

After graduation, Gillam joined the Air Force, becoming an Air Force pilot in 1953. He taught as an ROTC instructor at Tennessee State University, where he studied mathematics and physics. He served as commander of a Strategic Air Command missile crew from 1961 to 1963. However, grueling long hours caused him to leave the Air Force at the end of that period, having achieved the rank of captain.

Gillam's career with NASA began in 1963. He began as a resources management specialist, and by 1968 he was manager of the Delta program. He was program manager for small launch vehicles and international projects from 1971 to 1976, coordinating the many launches NASA did for governments of other countries that had no launch capability. Gillam also oversaw launching of many communication satellites for private companies, such as the Radio Corporation of America (RCA), Comsat, and Western Union, when these satellites were still a new but growing concept. For his work with the Delta launch vehicle, Gillam received the NASA Distinguished Service Medal in 1976.

Gillam moved on to director of shuttle operations at Dryden Flight Research Center from 1976 to 1979. There, he directed the first flight tests of the shuttle. These tests were carried out by using a big Boeing 747 jet to transport the shuttle into flight. The shuttle was then released from the 747 and glided to a landing. Since the shuttle would ultimately be launched using vertical rockets (as it is launched today) and was never designed to take off from an airstrip like an airplane, this was the best way to test landing capability. Assuring the ability of the shuttle to land safely, in a glide, was a key step in its development, since the shuttle has no engine power for landing. Gillam served as director of Dryden from 1979 to 1981, when he went back to Washington, D.C., to work in NASA Headquarters, accepting a post as special assistant. There he helped shape national space policy in the Office of Science and Technology Policy. He became assistant associate administrator for NASA in 1982 and assistant administrator in charge of commercial programs from 1984 to 1987.

Although Gillam left NASA in 1987, his expertise continues to be available through his work for consulting firms that support the space agency's complex operations. In 1987, Gillam joined the Orbiting Astronomical Observatory Corporation (OAO), a space technology consulting firm. There, he became vice president of the Aerospace Systems Group, Missions and Computing Support Division, directing 450 personnel responsible for providing engineering, operational, and maintenance support to NASA's Jet Propulsion Laboratory (JPL) in Pasadena, California. By 1989, he was senior vice president of the Aerospace Systems Group, directing five operating divisions of OAO. Remaining in that position for the next eight years, he also served from 1994 to 1997 as chairman and chief executive officer of SECON, Inc., a wholly owned subsidiary specializing in systems engineering support to the aerospace and intelligence communities.

In early 1998, Gillam joined Allied Signal Technical Services (ASTS), where he became director of Pasadena operations, serving as program manager for the Deep Space Network communications facilities used by NASA for tracking and communicating with spacecraft in distant regions of the solar system. In late 1998, after ASTS became part of Honeywell Technology Solutions, Inc. (HTSI), Gillam became the multicompany Consolidated Space Operations Contract (CSOC) team's link with JPL, serving as CSOC associate program manager.

Throughout his career, Gillam has garnered many awards and citations for his contributions to the space program and the space industry. In addition to NASA's award for his work with the Delta program, Gillam received two Exceptional Service Awards from NASA, in 1981 and 1982. He has also received the Outstanding Contributions Award from the National Technical Association, the American Institute of Aeronautics and Astronautics (AIAA) Space Commerce Award, the National Society of Black Engineers Achievement Award, the National Association for the Advancement of Colored People (NAACP) Outstanding Technological Achievement Award, and the Tuskegee Airmen's Achievement Award, among others. In 1981, Howard University honored him as a distinguished alumnus, and he received the Presidential Meritorious Excellence Award in 1986.

As of late 2002, through his position at HTSI as the CSOC team's main interface with JPL, Gillam continues to contribute from his wealth of some 40 years of aerospace management experience.

Further Reading

Hallion, Richard P. *On the Frontier: Flight Research at Dryden, 1946–1981.* Washington, D.C.: National Aeronautics and Space Administration, 1984.

Moite, Sally M. "Isaac Thomas Gillam, IV," *Notable Black American Scientists.* Kristine Krapp, ed. Detroit: Gale Research, 1999, 128–129.

Sammons, Vivian Ovelton. *Blacks in Science and Medicine.* New York: Hemisphere Publishing, 1990.

Gillyard, Cornelia Denson
(1941–) *organic chemist*

Cornelia Gillyard has built her reputation as an organic chemist around her research identifying and eliminating compounds, such as toxins and pollutants, that are harmful to the environment.

Born in Talladega, Alabama, on February 1, 1941, Cornelia Denson was the firstborn of three children in the Denson family. Her father was a steel worker and her mother was a nurse. Cornelia became fascinated by chemistry while in high school, put in extra hours studying with her chemistry teacher, and graduated as valedictorian of her class.

She continued her studies at Talladega College, where she earned her bachelor's degree in chemistry, although she began thinking she would pursue a degree in biology. Ultimately, her career has combined both interests.

After graduation, she needed to take time off from her studies to work and save money for further education. She took a position at the nuclear medicine laboratory at Ohio State University Hospital, where she learned techniques of working with radioactive tracers for observing internal biological processes. In 1964, she went to work for the Children's Hospital in Columbus, Ohio, where she gained experience in setting up and running a new nuclear medicine laboratory.

Returning to school for graduate studies, she completed her master's degree in organic chemistry at Clark Atlanta University in 1973. Her research there explored the chemistry of vitamin B_{12}. After completing her studies, she returned to Columbus, where she worked for

Battelle Memorial Institute. However, she went back to Atlanta after marrying in 1974.

There, in about 1977, Gillyard went back to graduate school at Clark Atlanta University to work on her doctorate. She also began teaching organic chemistry and a chemistry course for nonscience majors at Spelman College, a private college for women located in Atlanta. Gillyard completed her doctoral degree in organic chemistry in 1980 and joined the Spelman faculty full-time, where she became associate professor of chemistry and chair of the chemistry department.

As of 2002, Gillyard's research has focused on the study of both the synthesis and characterization of organoarsenicals. Organoarsenicals are arsenic compounds that organisms ingest and break down into metabolites (products of metabolism). They are used as growth stimulants in feed for poultry and livestock, and they are also used as antibacterial agents to help fight disease. She also has used spectroscopic analytical methods to monitor pollutants and toxins in the environment, and she looks for ways not only to identify them but also to destroy toxic contaminants in the environment.

Research and training grants have been awarded to Gillyard by several agencies, including the U.S. Department of Energy, the National Institutes of Health, the National Science Foundation, and the Kellogg Foundation.

Gillyard serves on several national committees, including the Women Chemists Committee, American Chemical Society Scholars Selection Committee, and the Blue Ribbon Panel for Minority Affairs of the American Chemical Society. She is also a member of the National Organization for the Professional Advancement of Black Chemists and Chemical Engineers. She has served as director of the National Aeronautics and Space Administration (NASA) Women in Science and Engineering Scholars Program and codirector of the National Science Foundation's Research in Chemistry for

Minority Scholars Program. She has served as director of the Spelman College Summer Science and Engineering Program since 1995.

Further Reading

Kessler, James H., J. S. Kidd, Renee A. Kidd, and Katherine A. Morin. *Distinguished African American Scientists of the 20th Century.* Phoenix, Ariz.: Oryx Press, 1996, 116–120.

Sandoval, Steve. "Chemistry professor Gillyard to deliver Martin Luther King Jr. Day talk Jan. 14 at Laboratory," Daily News Bulletin, Los Alamos National Laboratory. Available online. URL: http://www.lanl.gov/orgs/pa/News/010802.html. Posted on January 8, 2002.

Gipson, Mack, Jr.
(1931–1995) *geologist*

Mack Gipson worked in industry as a petroleum explorer for major oil companies and located vitally needed sources of oil. As a professor at the University of South Carolina, he relayed to his students his knowledge of the working world of a geologist and the knowledge they would need as professional geologists. He also provided an important role model for African-American students.

Born in Trenton, South Carolina, on September 15, 1931, Mack Gipson, Jr., grew up on his grandmother's farm. His parents, Artie Mathis Gipson and Mack Gipson, Sr., were sharecroppers, and young Mack's grandmother cared for him and his sister while their parents farmed. His country environment provided opportunities for his early interest in rocks, land formations, and the world of geology. However, he did not think of himself as interested in science until he studied geology in junior high school. He read a book called *The Earth and Life upon It,* which showed him that science provided methods for finding answers to questions he had about how rocks formed and the detective work involved with finding out about their history.

The rural school in his area did not continue beyond 11th grade, but he was able to persuade his grandmother to move to Augusta, Georgia, so he could complete high school. They moved in December 1947 and Mack enrolled in high school a few weeks later, in January 1948, graduating in the spring of 1949.

Though supportive of Gipson's ambition to continue to college, his family had little money and could not provide much financial help. His mother borrowed money, though, to get him started at nearby Paine College, and Gipson also worked part-time while pursuing a major in science and mathematics. He received his bachelor's degree from Paine College in 1953. He was drafted into the army in June 1954, becoming a radio technician during his service from 1954 to 1956. During this time he realized that his original plan to become a high school science teacher or even a laboratory technician would keep him cooped up indoors. During his rural childhood, he had come to love the outdoors and so he decided to pursue graduate studies in geology.

Gipson attended the University of Chicago under a stipend provided by University of Georgia, where African-American students were not accepted to study but promising students could receive financial aid to attend another college or university. His wife, the former Alma D. Gadison, was a psychiatric nurse and she helped support his graduate studies as well. Gipson also worked part-time as a substitute teacher, as a geologist for the Walter H. Flood Company in Chicago, and as a research assistant in geophysical sciences at the university. He completed his master's degree in 1961 and began research for his Ph.D., which studied deep rock layers near coal fields in central Illinois. Overseen by University of Chicago professors in chemistry, physics, and geology, Gipson's doctoral dissertation was entitled *A Study of the Relations of Depth, Porosity, and Clay Mineral Orientation in Pennsylvanian Shales.* He completed his doctorate in 1963.

Gipson continued his work for the Walter H. Flood Company, which involved core sampling to determine runway locations for O'Hare International Airport in Chicago. A core sample removes a narrow vertical section of rock and earth so that the layering of soils and rocks can be studied. Through this type of examination, the stability of an area of land can be determined.

Gipson also worked with a research team at the University of Chicago during this period, helping with a study of samples taken from the sea floor. By examining these samples, the team was able to determine facts about the formation and evolution of the oceans during a span of time extending millions of years into the past.

In 1964, Gipson joined the faculty at Virginia State University. Over the next 11 years, he taught at Virginia State and was promoted to full professor and chair of the department of geological sciences. An understanding of geological formations on Earth can also help with understanding formations on other rocky planets, such as Mars. During his time at Virginia State, the National Aeronautics and Space Administration (NASA) asked Gipson and a group of other geologists to help explain some pyramid-like formations on the surface of Mars. They determined that extensive sandstorms sweeping across the surface of Mars had worn extinct volcanoes into conelike shapes that resembled pyramids.

In 1973 and 1974, while on sabbatical from Virginia State University, Gipson worked for Exxon Company conducting oil exploration. In 1975, he resigned from teaching and went to work for Exxon as a research associate, using seismic stratigraphy to locate oil fields. Traveling to wide-ranging locations, Gipson ran tests by simulating earthquake waves and conducting measurements to determine the formations at deep levels of rock. He explored for oil in such far-flung areas as Alaska, Florida, Mexico, Czechoslovakia, and Pakistan. In the 1980s, he worked for several other oil companies, including ERCO Petroleum, Aminoil, Inc., and Phillips Petroleum Company.

Gipson returned to teaching in 1986, when he joined the faculty of the University of South Carolina in Columbia as professor of geology. For his students, Mack Gipson provided a living demonstration of the opportunities for success for minorities in the geological sciences. Among the awards he received during the course of his career were the Elmer Thomas Fellowship in Geology, which he received for his studies in the years 1961 to 1963, and the Outstanding Scientist Award from the National Consortium for Black Professional Development in 1976.

Mack Gipson died of cancer in Columbia, South Carolina, on March 10, 1995. He was 63. After Gipson's death, colleagues, students, and friends founded the Dr. Mack Gipson, Jr., Memorial Fund at the University of South Carolina. Its purpose is to provide stipends for graduate work in the geological sciences, with first preference to outstanding minority candidates.

Further Reading

Kessler, James H., J. S. Kidd, Renee A. Kidd, and Katherine A. Morin. *Distinguished African American Scientists of the 20th Century.* Phoenix, Ariz.: Oryx Press, 1996, 120–123.

Sammons, Vivian Ovelton. *Blacks in Science and Medicine.* New York: Hemisphere Publishing, 1990.

Teitler, Robert J. "Mack Gipson, Jr.," *Notable Black American Scientists.* Kristine Krapp, ed. Detroit: Gale Research, 1999, 130–131.

Gourdine, Meredith Charles
(1929–1998) *inventor, engineer*

Meredith C. Gourdine pioneered research in the area of electro-gas dynamics (involving the generation of electricity through the kinetic energy produced by an ionized combustion gas that is both in motion and under pressure). An expert on gas dispersion, he also developed a technique for removing smoke from buildings and advanced methods for clearing fog from airport runways. As an engineer and physicist, he held more than 70 patents related to thermal management and the conversion of gas to electricity.

Meredith Charles Gourdine was born in Newark, New Jersey, on September 26, 1929. He grew up in Brooklyn, New York, and attended Brooklyn Technical High School. After classes, he worked an eight-hour day with his father as a painter. Gourdine once recalled, "My father said, 'If you don't want to be a laborer all your life, stay in school.' It took." After high school, Gourdine entered college at Cornell University in Ithaca, New York. (Even though he had won a swimming scholarship to the University of Michigan, he elected to attend Cornell, where he had to work part-time to earn his way for at least the first two years.) He earned his B.S. in engineering physics from Cornell in 1953.

An outstanding runner and long jumper, Gourdine won four titles in competition in the Intercollegiate Association of Amateur Athletes of America championships, and he won five titles in the Heptagonal Games. He was also the silver medalist in the long jump competition at the 1952 Olympics, missing the gold medal by an inch and a half. "I would rather have lost by a foot," he later remarked. "I still have nightmares about it."

After graduating, Gourdine served in the U.S. Navy for several years. From 1957 to 1958, Gourdine worked on the technical staff of the Ramo Woolridge Corporation, leaving there to work on his doctorate at California Institute of Technology (Caltech), where he had a Guggenheim Fellowship and served as Senior Research Scientist at Caltech's Jet Propulsion Laboratory (run by Caltech for NASA) from 1958 to 1960. Gourdine completed his doctorate in engineering physics at the California Institute of Technology in 1960.

Holder of more than 70 patents, inventor and engineer Meredith Gourdine was honored in 1991 by the National Academy of Engineering for his "outstanding contributions in the field of electro-gas dynamics and the development of practical devices derived therefrom." *(AP/Wide World Photos)*

Gourdine spent the next four years in private industry. He then borrowed funds, mostly from friends and, operating out of Livingston, New Jersey, established his own research and development firm, Gourdine Systems. In 1973, he formed another company, Energy Innovations, which produced direct-energy conversion devices. He served as its president and chief executive officer until his death.

Gourdine's first patents were awarded from 1971 to 1973 for various systems that cleared the air, including "Incineraid," a device that helps remove smoke from burning buildings. His method for removing fog from airport runways received a patent in 1987. These systems apply a negative charge to airborne particles.

The particles then are attracted to the ground through electromagnetic attraction. They drop out of the air, and fresh air replaces them.

Gourdine applied electro-gas dynamics to other systems having very practical applications, such as circuit breakers and systems for applying coatings. He also invented a device called the "Focus Flow Heat Sink," used to cool down computer chips.

For his "outstanding contributions in the field of electro-gas dynamics and the development of practical devices derived therefrom," Gourdine was elected to the National Academy of Engineering in 1991, a high distinction in the engineering profession.

Gourdine died on November 20, 1998, at St. Joseph's Hospital in Houston. He was 69.

Further Reading

Litsky, Frank. "Meredith Gourdine, 69, Athlete and Physicist," *New York Times* (November 24, 1998) Late Edition Final, Section B, 10.

"Meredith Gourdine," The Lemelson-MIT Program's Invention Dimension. Available online. URL: http://web.mit.edu/invent/www/inventorsA-H/gourdine.html. Posted in March 1998.

U.S. Department of Energy. *Black Contributors to Science and Energy Technology.* DOE/OPA-0035. Washington, D.C.: Office of Public Affairs, 1979, 16–17.

Granville, Evelyn Boyd Collins
(1924–) *mathematician*

When Evelyn Boyd Granville completed her doctorate at Yale University in 1949, she also earned the distinction of becoming one of the first African-American women ever to receive a Ph.D. in mathematics. Since that time she has not only contributed to her field, but has served as a strong role model for many others, both men and women, who have followed in her footsteps.

In Washington, D.C., on May 1, 1924, Evelyn Boyd was the second daughter born to William and Julia Walker Boyd. Her mother and father separated when Evelyn was in high school, resulting in financial insecurity, as well as emotional upheaval. Her mother obtained work in the U.S. Bureau of Engraving and Printing, which allayed some of the financial problems. Encouraged by teachers and her mother to pursue a professional career, Boyd initially thought of teaching high school mathematics. However, her talent for mathematics was so apparent that her teachers encouraged her to seek greater challenges.

When she graduated from high school, Boyd won a partial scholarship to Smith College. She economized by living in a cooperative and worked for the National Bureau of Standards during the summers. Her mother and Louise Walker, an aunt, also helped with expenses. The effort paid off in 1945, when she received her bachelor's degree, graduating summa cum laude and Phi Beta Kappa.

Boyd contin1ued her studies at Yale University in New Haven, Connecticut, for which she received fellowships from both the Julius Rosenwald Foundation and the Atomic Energy Commission. She completed her M.A. in mathematics at Yale in 1946, and in 1949, she completed her Ph.D. with a specialty in functional analysis and was elected to the scientific honorary society Sigma Xi. MARJORIE LEE BROWNE, another black female mathematician, received her Ph.D. that same year, just a few months later, from the University of Michigan at Ann Arbor.

Following her graduate studies at Yale, Boyd spent a year as a research assistant doing postdoctoral research at the New York University Institute of Mathematics. She was also a part-time instructor in the mathematics department of New York University. In 1950, she received an appointment as associate professor of mathematics at Fisk University in Nashville, Tennessee, where she remained for only two years, but while she was there she taught two students—ETTA ZUBER FALCONER and VIVIENNE LUCILLE MALONE MAYES—who continued on, in turn, to earn Ph.D.s in mathematics.

In 1952, Boyd left Fisk University to work in industry, which she did for the next 15 years. She worked as an applied mathematician for Diamond Ordnance Fuze Laboratories for four years, and then moved on to International Business Machines (IBM), where she worked from 1956 to 1960 on the National Aeronautics and Space Administration's (NASA's) Project Vanguard (which put some of the first U.S. satellites into orbit) and Project Mercury (the first U.S. astronaut flights). For these projects, Boyd calculated orbits and set up computer procedures, including real-time calculations as satellites were being launched.

In 1960, Boyd met the Reverend Gamaliel Mansfield Collins, whom she married, and the couple settled in Los Angeles. In 1967, the couple divorced.

While living in Los Angeles, she worked at the Computation and Data Reduction Center of the U.S. Space Technology Laboratories. There she worked on rocket trajectories and orbit calculations. Still working on space-related projects in applied mathematics, she moved in 1962 to the Space and Information Systems Division of North American Aviation. There she worked on similar projects for the Apollo Program (which took astronauts to the Moon)—including celestial mechanics, computations of trajectories and orbits, numerical analysis, and digital computer techniques. After a year at North American, she spent four additional years as a senior mathematician for IBM.

However, IBM moved its operation in 1967, and Boyd wanted to stay, so she took a teaching position at California State University at Los Angeles. At this point, she became deeply and enthusiastically involved in mathematics education at all levels. She observed that her college mathematics students were poorly prepared. So she began working on programs for teaching elementary schoolchildren, and she personally taught some of the children in after-school classes for students kindergarten through fifth grade. She also taught in a National Science Foundation Institute for Secondary Teachers of Mathematics summer program that took place in 1972 at the University of Southern California. In addition she coauthored a textbook used at more than 50 colleges, *Theory and Application of Mathematics for Teachers,* which saw two editions, the first in 1975 and the second in 1978.

Among numerous other awards, Evelyn Granville received an honorary doctorate in science from Yale University in May 2001. *(Yale University)*

In 1970, Evelyn Boyd married Edward V. Granville, a real estate broker. After Evelyn Boyd Granville retired from teaching at California State University at Los Angeles in 1984, the couple moved to Texas, where they raise chickens on a 16-acre farm.

There Granville taught mathematics and computer science from 1985 to 1988 at Texas College in Tyler. She received an appointment to the Sam A. Lindsey Chair at the University of Texas at Tyler (1990–91) and an honorary doctorate from Smith College in 1989.

In 1994, when asked by interviewer Loretta Hall what she considered her most significant accomplishments, Evelyn Boyd Granville replied: "First of all, showing that women can do mathematics." To that she added, "Being an African American woman, letting people know that we have brains too."

Further Reading

Granville, Evelyn Boyd. "My Life as a Mathematician," *SAGE A Scholarly Journal on Black Women* 6, no. 2 (fall 1989): 44–46.

Hine, Darlene, ed. *Facts on File Encyclopedia of Black Women in America: Science, Health, and Medicine.* New York: Facts On File, 1997, 79–80.

Kessler, James H., J. S. Kidd, Renee A. Kidd, and Katherine A. Morin. *Distinguished African American Scientists of the 20th Century.* Phoenix, Ariz.: Oryx Press, 1996, 127–131.

Williams, Scott W. "Black Women in Mathematics: Evelyn Boyd Granville," *Mathematicians of the African Diaspora.* Available online. URL: http://www.math.buffalo.edu/mad/PEEPS/granville_evelynb.html. Updated in June 2001.

Green, Harry James, Jr.

(1911–) *chemical engineer*

Despite obstacles caused by racial barriers and the Great Depression, Harry James Green, Jr., persevered in a successful career as a chemical engineer in industry.

Harry James Green, Jr., showed promise as a young engineer as early as high school, when he built a steam engine, using it to power a boat. He was born in St. Louis, Missouri, on December 7, 1911. His father was Harry James Green, Sr., a U.S. postal clerk, and his mother, Olivia Jones Green, worked at home as a housewife. Young Green was not attracted to the vocational training other boys were encouraged to pursue, and he made use of the school library and opportunities to develop more academic skills, even taking college algebra as a high school student.

Upon graduation from high school in 1928, Green entered college at Ohio State University, majoring in chemical engineering. He recognized that prejudice against a black scientist might hamper him less in this field, thanks to rapid growth caused by the rising importance of the oil industry and increasing use of chemicals in industry. Unfortunately, he graduated with his B.S. in chemical engineering in 1932. The nation—and many parts of the world—was in the throes of the Great Depression, and thousands of people were out of work. Green could not obtain a position in industry, but almost every student who graduated from college in that year had the same problem. Jobs were extremely scarce.

Green did, however, secure a position as instructor of chemistry at North Carolina Agricultural and Technical College, a historically black college where he knew he would be welcome.

By 1937, Green was ready to continue his studies, entering Massachusetts Institute of Technology (MIT), where he completed his M.S. degree in 1938, and he received a promotion to assistant professor at North Carolina A&T. Three years later, Green went to Ohio State University on a Julius Rosenwald fellowship to earn his doctorate in chemical engineering, which he completed in 1943. Green's dissertation dealt with aspects of dialysis, a process for separating particles in solution by passing them through a membrane. (Dialysis would become useful medically several years later in the development of the artificial kidney.) After completion of his dissertation, Green returned to honor his teaching obligation at North Carolina A&T, where he was promoted to full professor.

He left the following year, however, to pursue his career goal of becoming a chemical engineer. His timing was good—World War II had created a demand for many industrial products. Green joined the Rochester, New York, firm of Stromberg-Carlson as a senior engineer. The company built radios and later merged with General Dynamics, continuing as the electronics branch of the larger firm. Green worked on telephone transmitters there, and in 1959 he became supervisor of manufacturing research and development in the production engineering department.

Green worked with metals and the usefulness of magnetic materials in development of electronics. He studied plastics and their electrical properties, and he also worked with packaging challenges for microelectronic circuits. As a member of the American Society of Metals, he helped edit a handbook on metallurgy, and he also worked on a publication on copper alloys.

In 1970, when General Dynamics moved its location to California, Green joined Xerox Corporation and stayed in Rochester. He worked in the research department as staff scientist there, remaining until his retirement in 1976.

His advice to young scientists, he told interviewer T. A. Heppenheimer, is to remain flexible and "move into whatever the situation is, whatever the barriers."

Further Reading

Heppenheimer, T. A. "Harry James Green, Jr.," *Notable Black American Scientists*. Kristine Krapp, ed. Detroit: Gale Research, 1999, 137–138.

Sammons, Vivian Ovelton. *Blacks in Science and Medicine*. New York: Hemisphere Publishing, 1990.

Gregory, Frederick Drew

(1941–   ) *astronaut, engineer, inventor*

In 1985, Frederick Drew Gregory piloted the space shuttle *Challenger* on mission STS 51-B, becoming the first African American to pilot the space shuttle. For his second and third missions he served as commander, the highest responsibility aboard a shuttle spacecraft.

Born on January 7, 1941, in Washington, D.C., Frederick Drew Gregory was the son of Francis Gregory and Nora Drew Gregory. His mother was the sister of CHARLES RICHARD DREW, the famous blood bank organizer and plasma specialist, who was therefore Frederick Gregory's uncle.

Gregory graduated from Anacostia High School in 1958, later entering the United States Air Force Academy, from which he graduated with a B.S. in 1964. From 1965 to 1970, Gregory served in the United States Air Force, receiving pilot training, and in 1965 he received certification as a helicopter pilot. He became certified as a fighter pilot in 1968 and flew F-4 Phantoms. After graduating from the United States Naval Test Pilot School in 1971, he was assigned as a research and engineering test pilot. Three years later, he began flying test flights for the National Aeronautics and Space Administration (NASA). Meanwhile, he completed his master's degree at George Washington University in 1977. Finally, in 1978, he was accepted as an astronaut candidate, one of the first three black astronauts, who all were inducted into the corps at that time. (The others were GUION STEWART BLUFORD, JR., and RONALD ERWIN MCNAIR.)

In all, Gregory completed three missions in space. The first, STS-51B, was aboard the orbiter *Challenger*, with Robert Overmyer in charge as commander. Gregory was the second in command as pilot and became the first African American to pilot the shuttle. The shuttle

Frederick Drew Gregory was the first African-American space shuttle pilot and also served as commander of two shuttle missions. In 2002, he accepted NASA's number-two administrative position, deputy administrator. *(Photo by NASA)*

launched on April 29, 1985, from Kennedy Space Center in Florida, carrying *Spacelab-3,* a scientific laboratory developed by the European Space Agency, in its cargo bay. The astronauts carried out scientific experiments and deployed a satellite, and the shuttle landed without incident on the dry lake bed at Edwards Air Force Base in California on May 6, 1985.

On his second space flight, STS-33, Gregory served as commander, with full responsibility for the success and safety of the mission. The orbiter *Discovery* lifted off at night on November 22, 1989. This mission was classi-

fied, carrying Department of Defense payloads. *Discovery* landed five days after liftoff on November 27, 1989, also landing at Edwards Air Force Base.

Gregory's third and final mission again was a Defense mission, STS-44 aboard the orbiter *Atlantis.* With Gregory as commander, the shuttle lifted off on November 24, 1991, touching down a week later, on December 1, 1991, again landing in California. Onboard experiments during flight included tests to see how well a spaceborne observer could gather information about ground troops, equipment, and facilities. The crew also ran studies to test medical countermeasures that might be taken by astronauts during long-duration space flight.

On April 28, 1992, Gregory was appointed associate administrator of the Office of Safety and Mission Assurance at NASA Headquarters in Washington, D.C. In that capacity he led the redesign of the shuttle cockpit in addition to working on the development of an innovative landing system that utilizes microwave instrumentation. He has also consulted on NASA safety studies and on the coordination of the Shuttle–*Mir* joint missions that took place in the late 1990s. In August 2002, Gregory was sworn in as NASA's deputy administrator, the agency's second in command. Gregory has written or cowritten several papers on cockpit design and handling qualities for aircraft.

In addition to numerous military commendations, Gregory has earned many awards. He was selected as Distinguished National Scientist by the National Society of Black Engineers in 1979. He is also the recipient of the NASA Outstanding Leadership Award, as well as NASA's Distinguished Service Medal, three NASA Space Medals, and two NASA Space Flight Medals. In 1990, he was chosen one of the Top 20 Minority Engineers, and he was awarded an Honorary Doctor of Science by University of the District of Columbia as well as the Distinguished Alumni Award from George Washington University and the President's Medal from Charles R. Drew University of Medicine and Science.

Further Reading

"Biographical Data: Frederick D. Gregory," Lyndon B. Johnson Space Center. Available online. URL: http://www.jsc.nasa.gov/Bios/htmlbios/gregory-fd.html. Updated in July 1993.

Burns, Khephra, and William Miles. *Black Stars in Orbit: NASA's African American Astronauts.* San Diego, Calif.: Harcourt Brace and Company, 1995.

Hawkins, Walter L. *African American Biographies.* Jefferson, N.C.: McFarland & Co., 1992, 172–173.

H

Hall, Lloyd Augustus
(1894–1971) *food chemist, inventor*

Pioneer inventor Lloyd Augustus Hall revolutionized the meatpacking industry through his research on improved curing salts—resulting in marked improvements in meat preservation.

Lloyd Augustus Hall was born on June 20, 1894, in Elgin, Illinois, to second-generation Chicago residents. On his father's side, Hall's grandfather had lived in Chicago since at least the late 1830s and was one of the founding members as well as the pastor of the first African-American church in Chicago, the Quinn Chapel African Methodist-Episcopal (A.M.E.) Church. Also in the 1830s or early 1840s, Hall's maternal grandmother had come to Chicago via the Underground Railroad, the secret chain of houses, barns, and hideaways used to hide slaves escaping from the South.

Hall developed an interest in chemistry in high school, and after he graduated he attended Northwestern University, majoring in chemistry and receiving his B.S. degree in 1914. Two years later, he had also earned his master's degree, which secured him a position as a junior and then senior chemist in the Chicago Department of Health Laboratories, where he worked from 1915 to 1919. He was chief chemist for John Morrel Foods of Ottuma, Illinois, for two years,

then moved on to become president of the Chemical Products Corporation in Chicago, a position he held from 1921 to 1924. In 1925, he worked for Griffith Laboratories as a consultant and later joined the staff, becoming technical director and later chief chemist. During his 34 years at Griffith's, he earned more than 100 U.S. and foreign patents in food chemistry.

Before Hall did his work, food preservation using chemicals had received little scientific attention and the process as well as its results had a lot of problems. Either the preservation did not work and the food spoiled, or it was effective and the food tasted bitter. In 1932, Hall combined sodium chloride (table salt) with very small crystals of sodium nitrate and nitrite. These compounds kept the nitrogen in check that cause food spoilage. He patented his method and it is still used today in packaged cold cuts, hot dogs, and other cured meats.

Another common origin of food spoilage is the reaction of foods' fats and oils with oxygen. Hall developed antioxidants, such as lecithin, that stopped this process.

Since the early Middle Ages, people had covered up food spoilage by using spices to mask the bad taste. However, while some people thought they were preserving the food when they used spices such as ginger and cloves, Hall discovered that these and other spices often carry bacteria and mold that speed up the deterioration process. Hall invented a method using ethylenoxide gas inside a vacuum chamber to kill these bacteria, making the food safe to eat. The same process later came into use for sterilization of cosmetics and pharmaceuticals.

Hall returned to graduate school in the 1940s to obtain his doctorate, earning his Ph.D. from Virginia State College in 1944. He continued to work for Griffith's until 1959, when he retired. Lloyd Augustus Hall died on January 2, 1971, in Pasadena, California, where he and his wife had moved after his retirement.

Further Reading

"Lloyd Augustus Hall," Journal of Chemical Education: JCE Online: Biographical Snapshots. Available online. URL: http://jchemed.chem.wisc.edu/JCEWWW/Features/eChemists/Bios/Hall.html. Downloaded on April 8, 2002.

"Lloyd Augustus Hall (1894–1971)," Inventor of the Week. Available online. URL: http://web.mit.edu/invent/www/inveotrsA-H/hall2.html. Posted in February 1998.

Harris, Bernard Anthony, Jr.

(1956–   ) *astronaut, biologist, medical researcher*

The first African American to walk in space, Bernard Harris is a physician, biologist, and medical researcher.

Born on June 26, 1956, in Temple, Texas, Bernard Anthony Harris, Jr., is the son of Bernard A. Harris, Sr., and Gussie H. Harris (now Burgess), who resides in San Antonio, Texas, with Harris's stepfather, Joe Roye Burgess. Harris graduated in 1974 from Sam Houston High School in San Antonio, Texas. He entered the University of Houston, completing his B.S. degree in biology in 1978. He earned an M.D. in 1982 from Texas Technological University School of Medicine, followed by his residency in inter-

nal medicine at the Mayo Clinic, completed in 1985. He conducted research under a National Aeronautics and Space Administration (NASA) fellowship at NASA's Ames Research Center in Mountain View, California, in 1987. He also received training as a flight surgeon at the Aerospace School of Medicine, at Brooks Air Force Base in San Antonio, Texas, in 1988.

In 1990, NASA selected Bernard A. Harris as an astronaut candidate, and after testing and training, he became an astronaut in July 1991. Harris has flown aboard two shuttle missions. The first, STS-55, lifted off aboard the orbiter *Columbia* on April 26, 1993. Harris conducted experiments in both the life sciences and the

Medical researcher Bernard Anthony Harris, Jr., became the first African American to walk in space. *(Photo by NASA)*

physical sciences aboard the Spacelab D-2 module the shuttle carried in its cargo bay for the mission. *Columbia* landed on May 6, 1993.

Harris's second spaceflight was STS-63, aboard *Discovery*. After lifting off on February 2, 1995, Harris was assigned to perform a space walk, during which he and crew-mate Michael Foale practiced moving a large object in space. The exercise was part of the preparation necessary for building the *International Space Station* in the early 21st century. Handling large objects, grappling tools, guiding objects into position, and securing them all were movements that had to be tested out in space, since the process of moving objects and doing jobs in microgravity is very different from doing the same tasks on Earth. Harris and Foale also tested modifications to their extravehicular activity suits (space suits) that were added to improve protection against the extreme cold and heat experienced in space. On this mission, Harris became the first African American to "walk in space"—that is, to exit the spacecraft and engage in an "extravehicular activity," or EVA, in the harsh environment of space.

Harris was also payload commander aboard STS-63. During the mission, the *Discovery's* crew docked the orbiter with the Russian space station *Mir*, conducted several experiments, and deployed and retrieved a satellite. *Discovery* touched down on February 11, after a nine-day flight.

After his space walk, Harris told an interviewer, "I get emotional when I think about it. And I'd like to dedicate this space walk—my first space walk as an African American, to all African Americans, to African-American achievement."

Harris left NASA in April 1996 to become chief scientist and vice president of Science and Health Services. He also earned an M.S. in biomedical science in 1996 from the University of Texas Medical Branch at Galveston. Harris has served on the faculties of several universities, including the University of Texas School

of Medicine, Baylor College of Medicine, the University of Texas School of Public Health, and the University of Texas Medical Branch. He has also received honors and awards, including an honorary doctorate of science from the Morehouse School of Medicine in 1996; the Challenger Award from the Ronald McNair Foundation in 1996; and the Award of Achievement from the Association of Black Cardiologists in 1996.

Further Reading

"Biographical Data: Bernard A. Harris, Jr. (M.D.)," Lyndon B. Johnson Space Center. Available online. URL: http://www.jsc.nasa.gov/Bios/htmlbios/harris.html. Updated in January 1999.

Burns, Khephra, and William Miles. *Black Stars in Orbit: NASA's African American Astronauts*. San Diego, Calif.: Harcourt Brace and Company, 1995.

"Harris Becomes First African-American to Walk in Space," NASA News. Available online. URL: http://www.jsc.nasa.gov/pao/news1995/95-007.html. Posted on February 2, 1995.

"Houston physician is first black to walk in space," *Jet*, February 27, 1995, 47.

Harris, Don Navarro
(1929–) *biochemist*

Don Navarro Harris has produced more than 60 scientific articles on subjects relating to his research work for Bristol-Meyers Squibb Research Institute near Princeton, New Jersey. He also is co-holder of five patents for products he has developed.

Don Navarro Harris was born on June 17, 1929, in New York, New York, to Margaret Vivian Berkley Harris and John Henry Harris. Harris's parents were originally from Virginia but had moved to New York a few years before Harris was born. He attended integrated New York schools, but when the time came to go to college, he attended Lincoln University in rural Pennsylvania, the oldest historically black university in the country. There he received his A.B. in chemistry in 1951. He worked in New York for a couple of years, before being drafted in 1953. The Korean War was just over, and Harris served as a medical technician, first in Texas, at Fort Sam Houston, and then in France, returning in 1955, when he was discharged.

Upon his return to New York, Harris worked for the New York Public Health Service, moving soon afterward to do basic research at Columbia University, where he worked with a team that was looking at the relationship between cholesterol and cardiac health.

He enrolled in the graduate program in biochemistry at Rutgers University, located in New Brunswick, New Jersey, obtaining his M.S. in biochemistry in 1959 and his Ph.D., also in biochemistry, in 1963. His graduate research focused on ribonucleic acid (RNA), which is key to the synthesis of protein and the transmission of genetic information from a cell nucleus to the rest of the cell. Specifically, he examined how RNA directs the construction of amino acid units.

After completion of his degrees, Harris went to work from 1963 to 1964 as a senior researcher at the Colgate Palmolive Research Center, returned to Rutgers as an assistant research specialist the following year, and finally became a research fellow in 1965 at Bristol-Meyers Squibb Research Institute near Princeton, New Jersey. There the work was interesting and challenging, and he stayed. He has worked on many varied research projects, including methods for analysis of how hormones and complex proteins are built, the effects of sex hormones on protein synthesis, the effects of enzymes on processes such as blood clotting, and the relationship of cholesterol to heart attacks. He authored or coauthored some 60 scientific papers and is coholder of several U.S. patents.

In 1993, Harris left full-time employment at Squibb, consulting part-time in human resources areas, including recruitment. He also accepted an appointment as associate professor on the faculty of Temple University School of Medicine.

Further Reading

Sankaran, Neeraja. "Don Navarro Harris," *Notable Black American Scientists.* Kristine Krapp, ed. Detroit: Gale Research, 1999, 145–146.

Henderson, Ashyia N., ed. *Who's Who Among African Americans,* 14th ed. Detroit: Gale Group, 2001, 549.

Harris, James Andrew
(1932–) *chemist*

James Andrew Harris codiscovered two chemical elements: element 104 (unnilquadium, also known as rutherforium) and element 105 (unnilpentium, also known as dubnium). He was the first African American to take part in a major program for identifying new elements.

James A. Harris was born on March 26, 1932, in Waco, Texas. However, when his parents divorced, Harris moved to California, where he graduated from McClymond High School in Oakland, in the San Francisco Bay Area.

Harris attended Huston-Tillotson College in Austin, Texas, where he received his B.S. in chemistry in 1953. He then joined the U.S. Army, where he served as a sergeant from 1953 to 1955. After his discharge from the army, Harris worked as a radiochemist at Tracerlab, Inc., in Richmond, California, where he worked for five years. He left there to join the Nuclear Chemistry Division of the Lawrence Radiation Laboratory at the University of California, Berkeley. There, as a nuclear chemist, he became part of the team that discovered and identified elements 104 and 105 in 1969 and 1970.

For any practical purpose, only 92 elements occur in nature—number 92 is uranium, the heaviest natural element. However, others have been created through the use of nuclear reactors. In 1940, chemist Glenn Seaborg at the University

Codiscoverer of elements 104 and 105, nuclear chemist James Andrew Harris was the first African American to participate in a major program to identify new elements. *(Ernest Orlando Lawrence Berkeley National Laboratory)*

of California at Berkeley bombarded uranium and created element 94, plutonium. (This was actually the second "transuranium" element found beyond uranium. The first was neptunium. Very small traces of both natural plutonium and neptunium have been found in nature, but not of any of the others.) Since 1940, other "human-made," or synthesized, elements have been created. The process allows chemists to expand their understanding of chemical properties and physicists to understand atomic structure better.

In 1964, a Soviet team claimed to have created element 104. Considerable competition between Soviet and U.S. scientists went on in the 1960s, and discoveries of elements were no exception. At the same time, one of the basic principles of science is that in order to be valid, an experiment must be repeatable. The Berkeley

lab hoped to duplicate the Soviet discovery but could not without better equipment. Finally, when they obtained a machine called the Heavy Ion Linear Accelerator (HILAC), they thought they would be able to duplicate the work. But they never succeeded. Other scientists at the Los Alamos National Laboratory in New Mexico and at the Lawrence Radiation Laboratory in Livermore, California, were also not able to duplicate the Soviet element 104. However, they were able to duplicate the Berkeley work, which came up with a different element 104.

Harris's work was key to the process. He devised the target that was to be bombarded. The group had decided to use californium, element 98, and Harris's job was to prepare an extremely pure target from which the new element would be created through interaction with the bombarding substance. Harris described it to interviewer T. A. Heppenheimer as "a very thin, small dot." His colleagues said it was the best target ever produced by their lab.

Another part of Harris's job was to help identify the substance, and tests derived from both chemistry and physics were used. Once they had element 104, they went on to element 105, which the Soviets also claimed to have created.

Controversy stirred over the naming of the elements. The Soviets wanted to name 104 kurchatovium, named for Igor Kurchatov, director of the Soviet atomic bomb program. The Berkeley group wanted rutherfordium, after the great British physicist Ernest Rutherford. The International Union of Pure and Applied Chemistry (IUPAC) tried to settle the dispute by using a generic name, unnilquadium, another way of saying "104." However, rutherfordium stuck. For 105, the Soviets wanted nielsbohrium after the Danish physicist Niels Bohr. The Berkeley lab wanted hahnium after the German chemist Otto Hahn, who first split a uranium atom. Again IUPAC suggested a generic unnilpentium for "105." This time, scientists ended up calling it dubnium, after the Russian research site, Dubna.

Harris, who says he always wanted to retire early, left the Berkeley Laboratory in 1988. "Too busy working," as he once remarked, he never took time to obtain a Ph.D. Yet he has done some of the most exciting work any nuclear chemist could engage in. He is a member of the National Society of Black Chemists and Chemical Engineers, has been a lecturer at several universities and colleges, and has been featured in a display at the Oakland Museum. He has received a certificate of merit from the National Urban League; a Scientific Merit Award from the City of Richmond, California; an Outstanding Achievement Award from the Marcus Foster Institute; and the key to the city of Oakland, California, in 1988.

Further Reading

Heppenheimer, T. A. "James Andrew Harris," *Notable Black American Scientists.* Kristine Krapp, ed. Detroit: Gale Research, 1999, 146–148.

"James A. Harris," Journal of Chemical Education: JCE Online: Biographical Snapshots. Available online. URL: http://jchemed.chem.wisc.edu/JCEWWW/Features/eChemists/Bios/Harris.html. Downloaded on April 23, 2002.

Henderson, Ashyia N., ed. *Who's Who Among African Americans,* 14th ed. Detroit: Gale Group, 2001, 551.

Harris, Mary Styles

(1949–) *geneticist*

Mary Styles Harris, a biologist and geneticist, has researched genetic connections with disease, such as sickle-cell anemia. She has become a spokesperson for African-American health concerns, hosting a weekly radio program, "Journey to Wellness: African American Health Radio," to make health information both available and widely understandable.

Mary Styles was born on June 26, 1949, in Nashville, Tennessee. Her father, George Styles, was a physician. She grew up in Florida and had a keen interest in science, somewhat influenced by her father. He died when she was only nine, but she continued to pursue science. She received her B.A. in biology in 1971 from Lincoln University in Pennsylvania. Soon thereafter, she met and married Sidney E. Harris. Both attended Cornell University in Ithaca, New York, he in engineering while she completed her Ph.D. in genetics in 1975. Under a postgraduate research grant from the National Cancer Institute, Mary Harris spent two years studying viruses at the New Jersey University of Medicine and Dentistry.

Harris served as executive director for the Sickle Cell Foundation of Georgia from 1977 to 1979, and in 1978 she joined the faculty of Morehouse College School of Medicine as assistant professor. From 1979 to 1980, she also served as scientist in residence for WGTV Channel 8, a public television station sponsored by the University of Georgia. For the 1980–81 academic year, she received an appointment as assistant professor of biology at Atlanta University. Under a grant from the National Science Foundation, she wrote, produced, and narrated an educational science series for Georgia television. She also produced a 40-minute television special, *To My Sisters . . . A Gift for Life,* examining the problem of breast cancer particularly as it affects the African-American community.

In her media productions, both on television and on radio, Harris has focused on health issues of particular concern to African Americans, heightening a consciousness of the problems and their solutions—for example, the need for early detection of breast cancer, the genetic burdens of sickle-cell anemia, and the resources available for understanding diabetes. Other topics she has explored include AIDS, cervical cancer, colon cancer, hypertension, and prostate cancer.

Harris is a member of the Congressional Black Caucus Health Brain Trust, the Governor's Advisory Council on Alcohol and Drug Abuse, and the Georgia Human Genetics Task Force.

She has established a consulting firm, Harris & Associates Ltd., of which she is president and genetics consultant.

Further Reading

"Doctor Gets Grant to Simplify Medicine on TV," *Jet*, February 21, 1980, 27.

Kessler, James H., J. S. Kidd, Renee A. Kidd, and Katherine A. Morin. *Distinguished African American Scientists of the 20th Century.* Phoenix, Ariz.: Oryx Press, 1996.

Sammons, Vivian Ovelton. *Blacks in Science and Medicine.* New York: Hemisphere Publishing, 1990.

Henderson, Ashyia N., ed. *Who's Who Among African Americans,* 14th ed. Detroit: Gale Group, 2001, 553.

Harris, Wesley Leroy

(1941–   ) *aerospace engineer*

Wesley Leroy Harris has written more than 100 technical papers and presentations and has substantially contributed to research in the areas of unsteady aerodynamics, aeroacoustics, and rarefied gas dynamics. At three major universities, he has advanced engineering education, has worked with industry and government to build cooperative research and development programs, and has encouraged cultural diversity.

Wesley Leroy Harris was born on October 29, 1941, in Richmond, Virginia, one of three children in the family of Rosa M. Minor Harris and William M. Harris. His parents, who worked in a tobacco factory, encouraged the children to learn and obtain an education. As a boy, "Wes" loved airplanes, built models, and read about flying. He dreamed of a career as a test pilot. When young Harris was just about to turn 16, the Soviet Union's launch of *Sputnik* on October 4, 1957, spurred his interest even further.

In 1960, after graduating from high school in Richmond, Harris enrolled at the University of Virginia at Charlottesville. There he completed his B.S. with honors in aerospace engineering in 1964. He went on to earn an M.A. and Ph.D. in aerospace and mechanical sciences at Princeton University in 1966 and 1968. He returned to the University of Virginia, this time to join the faculty as the school's first African-American professor.

From 1972 to 1985, he held several positions on the faculty and administration at the Massachusetts Institute of Technology (MIT) in Cambridge, Massachusetts. He taught aeronautics, astronautics, and ocean engineering. While at MIT, he established an Office of Minority Ed-

Wesley Leroy Harris is a respected aerospace engineer who has made significant contributions to research in the areas of unsteady aerodynamics, aeroacoustics, and rarefied gas dynamics. In 1993, as associate administrator for aeronautics, he became responsible for overseeing research and technology development in aeronautics for the National Aeronautics and Space Administration (NASA). *(Photo by NASA)*

ucation to serve as a resource for students needing encouragement. In 1985, he was appointed dean of the School of Engineering and professor of mechanical engineering at the University of Connecticut in Storrs, Connecticut. Then he received an appointment as vice president and chief administrative officer at the University of Tennessee Space Institute in Tullahoma, Tennessee, where he served from 1990 to 1993.

In 1993, the National Aeronautics and Space Administration (NASA) appointed Harris the associate administrator for aeronautics. In that capacity Harris shouldered the responsibility for directing NASA research and technology development in support of the American aeronautics industry—including fundamental research in aerodynamics, materials and propulsion, flight tests with advanced aircraft, and efforts to improve safety. After leaving NASA in 1995, Harris became Charles Stark Draper Professor of Aeronautics and Astronautics at MIT, where he continues to serve as of late 2002.

Harris has served on numerous committees and boards of the National Research Council, the National Science Foundation, and the U.S. Army Science Board. He is an elected fellow of the American Institute of Aeronautics and Astronautics and the American Helicopter Society. In honor of Harris's 60th birthday, in 2001 MIT established the Wesley Leroy Harris Scholarship fund for outstanding minority students in science.

Further Reading

"Dr. Wesley L. Harris," RE&D Advisory Committee Biographies. Available online. URL: http://www.faa.gov/aar/red/bios/Harris.htm. Downloaded on April 23, 2002.

"Harris, Freeman Named Heads of NASA Offices," NASA News Release. Available online. URL: http://spacelink.nasa.gov/NASA.News/NASA.News.Releases/Previous.News.Releases/92.News.Releases/92-12.News.Releases/92-12-21. Posted on December 22, 1992.

Hawkins, Walter Lincoln
(1911–1992) *chemical engineer*

W. Lincoln Hawkins is most widely recognized as coinventor of an antioxidant additive that made inexpensive telephone wire insulation possible. By saving telephone and power companies billions of dollars, this invention revolutionizes the communications industry and made universal telephone service possible. Hawkins, the first African-American scientist at Bell Laboratories, received 147 U.S. and foreign patents for his inventions and published more than 50 scientific papers and three books. He was also the first African-American member of the prestigious National Academy of Engineering.

Walter Lincoln Hawkins was born on March 21, 1911, in Washington, D.C., where his mother, Maude Johnson Hawkins, was a science teacher, and his father, William Langston Hawkins, was a lawyer for the Census Bureau. Hawkins was a curious child—and resourceful. He wanted to know what made things work, and he usually figured it out. He constructed model boats powered by springs. A baseball fan, he wanted to listen to the games. So he built his own radio.

Hawkins went to Dunbar High School, a segregated school that by all accounts was one of the best by any standard, especially in the sciences. Ironically, discrimination was the probable cause of Dunbar's excellence. Many of the teachers at Dunbar had doctorates, but because of prejudiced hiring practices in many colleges and universities, a Dunbar High School teaching job was the best position they could find. Many of the nation's best African-American scientists came from the classes at Dunbar, where a strong high school education was the rule.

In addition to the discipline and perseverance he learned at Dunbar, Hawkins also discovered that his tinkering inclinations could be profitable. One of his teachers drove a new car every year. Hawkins found out that this unlikely wealth in a high school teacher came from profits from an automatic automobile starter he had invented. For a boy whose parents hoped he would become a doctor, not an engineer, this was heady news.

After graduating from Dunbar in 1928, Hawkins took the stiff entrance exam at Rensselaer Polytechnic Institute in Troy, New York. He passed and so did a classmate from Dunbar. They were the only two African Americans in the school, until the following year, when two more Dunbar graduates joined them. Despite Rensselaer's two-thirds dropout statistics, all four of the Dunbar alumni completed their studies in four years and received their bachelor's degrees. Unfortunately, Hawkins graduated in 1932, when the Great Depression made jobs scarce. So he continued on to graduate school, completing his master's degree in chemistry from Howard University in Washington, D.C., in 1934. After teaching briefly in a trade school, Hawkins won a scholarship from McGill University in Montreal, Quebec, completing his Ph.D. in chemistry there in 1938. He received a postgraduate fellowship in alkaloid chemistry from the National Research Council and went to Columbia University, where he stayed for four years.

Hawkins joined the research team at Bell Laboratories at Murray Hill, New Jersey, in 1942. He was the first African American ever to work there. Hawkins described the place to an interviewer as "a world of excitement," and he thrived on the high energy level of his colleagues. He liked it so much, in fact, that he remained there for the next 34 years—until company regulations compelled him to retire in 1976.

During his highly productive career, the most far-reaching of the 147 patents he held was an invention he shared with a colleague, Vincent Lanza. Lead was used as insulation for telephone wires at the time, but it was expensive. British inventors had developed a polymer that was much less expensive, but it became brittle under extreme changes in temperature. The innovation Hawkins came up with was an additive that stabilized the polymer so the insulation could withstand temperature changes without becoming brittle and could last up to 70 years without being replaced. This invention was one of the most important breakthroughs in telephone communications history. Saving telephone and power companies billions of dollars, the nonoxidizing additive made stringing telephone wires inexpensive and opened the door to universal telephone service.

Hawkins became supervisor of applied research at Bell Labs in 1963, and in 1972, he gained promotion to department head. He garnered literally hundreds of awards. Even after leaving Bell, Hawkins continued working—teaching at New York's Polytecnic Institute, consulting for chemical and pharmaceutical companies, and serving as research director for the Plastics Institute of America.

Hawkins also advocated passionately for expansion of the national pool of minority scientists and inventors. He helped black youngsters develop science skills. He worked to expand science programs in black colleges. He believed that minority students had much more to give than the sports and entertainment successes for which they usually found role models and praise. He also believed that they deserved more than that.

Just before Hawkins died in 1992, President George H. W. Bush awarded him the National Medal of Technology to add to his already large collection of awards. Hawkins died of heart failure on August 20, 1992. He was 81.

Further Reading

"African-American Inventors of Our Times: Continued successes, improving opportunities," The Lemelson-MIT Awards Program's Invention Dimension: Inventor of the Week Archives. Available online. URL: http://web.mit.edu/invent/www/inventorsA-H/AAweek4.html. Posted in February 1997.

Sammons, Vivian Ovelton. *Blacks in Science and Medicine.* New York: Hemisphere Publishing, 1990.

"Two Esteemed Rensselaer Graduates: Garnet Baltimore and W. Lincoln Hawkins," *Issues & Views.* Reprinted from *Issues & Views* (Fall 1992). Available online. URL: http://www.issues-views.com/index.hph/sect/1000/article/1005. Posted on April 23, 2002.

"W. Lincoln Hawkins, Class of 1932: Chemist, Inventor, Advocate, 1911–1992." Rensselaer Alumni Hall of Fame. Available online. URL: http://www.rpi.edu/dept/NewsComm/sub/fame/inductees/wlincolnhawkins.html. Downloaded on April 23, 2002.

Haynes, John Kermit

(1943–)   *biologist, educator*

An authority on sickle-cell membranes and mechanisms used by cells to regulate volume, John Kermit Haynes has received recognition for both his research and his commitment to science education.

Born on October 30, 1943, in Monroe, Louisiana, John Kermit Haynes is the son of Grace Quanita Ross Haynes and John Kermit Haynes, Sr. As a high school student, Haynes planned to become a doctor, and after high school graduation, he enrolled at Morehouse College in Atlanta, Georgia, to pursue a premedical program of study. However, the research possibilities in biology became apparent to him as he began to take courses in the life sciences, and he became excited about a career as a biological researcher. He received his bachelor's degree from Morehouse in 1964, pursuing graduate studies at Brown University in Providence, Rhode Island. He completed his Ph.D. in developmental biology there in 1970, following up with postdoctoral studies at Brown and the Massachusetts Institute of Technology (MIT) in Cambridge, Massachusetts.

In 1973, Haynes accepted a position teaching medical students as assistant professor in the Division of Genetics and Molecular Medicine at Meharry Medical College in Nashville, Tennessee. He remained at Meharry for five years, moving on to Morehouse College as professor and director of health professions from 1979 to 1990, also serving as chair of the department of biology. In 1985 he was appointed to the David E. Packard Professor in Science Chair at Morehouse College, and in 2000 he became dean of science and mathematics.

Haynes has been selected for numerous professional responsibilities. He has served as a peer reviewer for the National Science Foundation and served as a member of the Graduate Record Examination (GRE) Biochemistry, Cell and Molecular Biology Committee of Examiners from 1989 to 1992. In 1999, he was selected as a member of the National Research Council's Committee for Advanced Mathematics and Science Programs in American High Schools. Additionally, he has served on the board of directors of the Sickle Cell Foundation in Georgia since 1980, on the board of trustees for Morehouse College from 1984 to 1987, and chair of the board of directors for the Afro Arts Center from 1970 to 1972. He also serves as adjunct professor of physiology at both Brown University and Clark Atlanta University.

Haynes has received numerous awards, including election to the Phi Beta Kappa honor society in 1999, and selection in 1996 as one of the Distinguished African American Scientists of the 20th century.

Haynes continues his involvement in sickle-cell and other cell research and has garnered grants as principal investigator from the Howard Hughes Medical Institute, the National Science Foundation the Centers for Disease Control, and the National Institutes of Health. He is also coinvestigator on a grant from the U.S. Department of Defense.

Further Reading

Longe, Patrick J. "John Kermit Haynes," *Notable Black American Scientists.* Kristine Krapp, ed. Detroit: Gale Research, 1999, 153–154.

Henderson, Ashyia N., ed. *Who's Who Among African Americans,* 14th ed., Detroit: Gale Group, 2001.

Henderson, James Henry Meriwether

(1917–   ) *botanist, plant physiologist*

James H. M. Henderson's research in plant physiology centered on the study of auxins (a group of plant hormones that regulate growth) and other areas of plant tissue biology—an area of study that holds implications regarding the growth processes of human cancer cells. During his lifelong teaching career, Henderson has served as a mentor and role model to hundreds of students. Additionally, his community and political activism round out a picture of a man committed to intellectual and personal growth, as well as equality in the democratic process.

On August 10, 1917, James Henry Meriwether Henderson was born in Falls Church, Virginia, into a family of famous individuals. His father, Edwin Bancroft Henderson, became the first African American in Washington, D.C., to teach physical education professionally. His mother, Mary (Meriwether) Henderson, was the daughter of James Henry Meriwether, descended from Meriwether Lewis, cocommander of the Lewis and Clark Expedition, which set out in 1804 to explore the overland route to the Pacific Ocean. Additionally, Booker T. Washington, founder of what is now Tuskegee University, was James H. M. Henderson's great uncle.

Henderson studied botany as an undergraduate at Howard University, earning his B.S. in 1939. He went on to graduate studies at the University of Wisconsin-Madison, where he earned a M.Ph. degree (1940) and Ph.D. in plant physiology (1943). His doctoral research focused on the tomato's ability to regulate nutrients and water through its roots.

As part of the war effort during World War II, Henderson worked at the Badger Ordnance Works on the development of propellants for rockets during his last two years of graduate studies, from 1942 to 1943. Following completion of his studies at Wisconsin, he worked at the Toxicity Laboratory of the University of Chicago from 1943 to 1945, studying poisons produced by plants to repel predators.

After the war, Henderson joined the faculty at Tuskegee University, beginning his lifelong academic career in 1945. There Henderson's research work and teaching has focused primarily on the biological and agricultural sciences. His research in plant biology has revolved primarily around tissue culture and plant cell structure, mostly with sunflowers and sweet potatoes.

During the course of his career, Henderson published more than 50 professional publications, including journal articles, review articles, and abstracts.

Henderson became senior research professor in the department of biology at Tuskegee University and chair of the Division of Natural Sciences. He also directed the George Washington Carver Foundation at Tuskegee University from 1968 to 1975. (Founded in 1938 by GEORGE WASHINGTON CARVER, the Carver Foundation continues to fund scholarships for students pursuing science careers.)

Always concerned with mentoring, Henderson shifted his focus almost entirely to this key pursuit in about 1990. Henderson has spearheaded several programs to encourage high school students to pursue higher education. One, ENHANCES, funded by the Howard Hughes Medical Institute, has encouraged more than 40 students to pursue a college education. Since 1945, he has served as a mentor and role model to many undergraduate students at Tuskegee who have gone on to graduate studies in the biological and medical sciences. He says he especially encourages researchers, telling them, "Look what Salk did for humanity. If you are a surgeon, you might help 200 people a year, but a researcher can make a discovery that can save millions of lives."

He has served on the Commission on Undergraduate Biological Sciences for the American Association for the Advancement of Science (AAAS). He has also been active in the American Society of Plant Physiologists, the Botanical Society of America, the National Institutes of Science, the American Institute of Biological Sciences, the Society for the Study of Development and Growth, and the Tissue Culture Association. For many years, he has also served as an active member of the Board of Trustees of Stillman College in Tuscaloosa, Alabama.

Henderson has received awards almost too numerous to count. He has twice received the Tuskegee Institute Eminent Faculty Award, in 1976 and 1980. For his many years of work with the Boy Scouts, he received the Boy Scouts of America Silver Beaver Award.

In September 2001, upon his retirement as professor emeritus at Tuskegee Institute, Henderson received a commendation from the state legislature of Alabama, celebrating his "long and distinguished record of professional service with Tuskegee Institute," including his many years of service as teacher, productive biological researcher, and unexcelled leader in professional organizations and the community.

For his "impact on increasing diversity in science and engineering," the AAAS named him one of two scientists to receive the Mentor Award for Lifetime Achievement in February 2002. (The other was ETTA ZUBER FALCONER.) According to the AAAS press release at the time, "His efforts have helped rank [Tuskegee University] among the top five historically black institutions from which black scientists with doctorate degrees received their undergraduate degrees."

Further Reading

"AAAS Awards," Available online. URL: http://www. aaas.org/news/releases/aaasawards.shtml. Posted on February 16, 2002.

"AAAS names Etta Z. Falconer and James H. M. Henderson to receive the Mentor Award for Lifetime Achievement," AAAS Public Release. Available online. URL: http://www.eurekalert. org/pub_releases/2002-02/aaft-ane020602.php. Posted on February 6, 2002.

"Commending Dr. James H. M. Henderson for His Outstanding Professional Achievements," Resolutions, Congratulatory, House of Representatives of the Legislature of Alabama. Available online. URL: http://www.legislature.state.al.us/ SearchableInstruments/2001TS/Resolutions/HR 160.htm. Posted on September 18, 2001.

Petrusso, A. "James H. M. Henderson," *Notable Black American Scientists.* Kristine Krapp, ed. Detroit: Gale Research, 1999, 154–156.

Henry, Walter Lester, Jr.
(1915–   ) *endocrinologist*

During his 35-year career on the faculty of Howard University, Walter Lester Henry, Jr., distinguished himself as a researcher into diabetes and its causes, as well as the function of insulin. He is also a respected physician and educator.

Walter Lester Henry, Jr., was born to Vera Robinson Henry and Walter Lester Henry, Sr., on November 19, 1915 in Philadelphia, Pennsylvania. Lester, as he was known, received his A.B. from Temple University in 1936. Five years later, he graduated first in his class with an M.D. from Howard University Medical School. That same year, though, in 1941, the nation had entered World War II and during the war years, Henry served as a major in the U.S. Marine Corps. He received the Bronze Star and cluster for distinguished service from 1942 to 1944. When he returned to civilian life, he opened up his practice as a physician.

In 1953, Henry joined the faculty at Howard University as an assistant professor, later promoted to associate professor and, in 1963, to full professor. In 1962, he also became chair of the department of medicine, a responsibility he held for 11 years. In 1973, he became John B. Johnson professor of medicine, retaining that position until his retirement in 1988.

Henry was certified in Endocrinology and Metabolism by the American Board of Internal Medicine, and he made his greatest mark by his work in that field, in particular his studies of insulin, how it works, and the causes of diabetes. Diabetes develops when the pancreas is unable to secrete enough insulin to maintain a normal sugar glucose concentration in the blood. Even though African Americans have a higher incidence of diabetes than other groups in the nation, only about 25 black physicians in the country had specialized in diabetes at the time. Of those, Henry was the most active and respected—the "dean," according to *Ebony* magazine.

Henry wondered why blacks seemed to have a disproportionately high risk for diabetes, and he studied the question to see if he could isolate any factor that would contribute to high risk. He concluded that the cause was diet choices and lifestyle, rather than genetics or any physical factor unique to blacks. A diet of rich foods, especially sweet foods, and the weight gains that go with that diet, as well as a tendency to become less active, all contribute to obesity. If one were writing a set of instructions for becoming diabetic, that scenario would sum them up—and being black really has nothing to do with it, Henry concluded. Obesity leads to resistance to insulin and, often, diabetes. In talking with *Ebony* in 1979, he said that, in a way, obese people were "digging their graves with their teeth."

One of Henry's most telling arguments in support of his premise was the low incidence of diabetes among Africans compared to the high incidence among African Americans. The African diet is simple and low in foods that pro-

mote the onset of diabetes. The African-American diet is high in those foods.

Henry extended his research to a study of methods for making use of insulin the body secretes, thereby minimizing the need for insulin injections for individuals suffering from diabetes.

Henry became a regent of the American College of Physicians in 1974, the first black regent ever to be selected. He served in that capacity until 1980 and was later selected as a regent laureate in 1993. He was also a member of the board of governors of the American Board of Internal Medicine from 1971 to 1978. In 1987, Henry also became the first black physician to be elected a Master by the American College of Physicians, and in 1997 he received the American College of Physicians Distinguished Teacher Award.

Further Reading

Henderson, Ashyia N., ed. *Who's Who Among African Americans,* 14th ed. Detroit: Gale Group, 2001, 584.

Henry, Walter Lester, with Kirk A. Johnson. *The Black Health Library Guide to Diabetes.* New York: Henry Holt, 1993.

Howell, Ron. "Diabetes: Black Women Are Its No. 1 Victim," *Ebony,* March 1979, 65–71.

Sammons, Vivian Ovelton. *Blacks in Science and Medicine.* New York: Hemisphere Publishing, 1990.

Henry, Warren Elliott
(1909–2001) *physicist, physical chemist, inventor, educator*

Warren E. Henry spent nearly seven decades researching the fields of magnetism, low temperature physics, and solid state physics, and during his long and productive career he authored 75 published scientific papers and coauthored 29. He also mentored hundreds of students, who, he once said, afforded him the greatest honor anyone could by following in his footsteps.

Warren Elliott Henry was born on February 18, 1909, in Evergreen, Alabama. His parents, Nelson E. Henry and Mattye McDaniel Henry—both graduates of Tuskegee Institute (now University) and both teachers—farmed near this rural community. His father applied farming methods he learned from GEORGE WASHINGTON CARVER from his days at Tuskegee. Young Warren grew up in his parents' classroom, playing in a corner at the age of three. And the exposure took. By the time he was four, he had learned to read. He was interested in science, and when he left home to board at the Alabama State Normal School in Montgomery, Alabama, his mother made sure he enrolled in a chemistry course.

At age 18, Henry enrolled at Tuskegee Institute, completing his B.S. degree in 1931. The following fall, Henry began his career as a teacher of mathematics, French, physics, and chemistry, as well as principal at Escambia County Training School in Alabama. He served as a teacher of mathematics from 1934 to 1936 at Spelman and Morehouse Colleges in Atlanta, then moved back to Alabama to become an instructor at Tuskegee Institute from 1936 to 1938, taking time to complete his M.S. from Atlanta University in 1937.

He took time off from teaching during the years 1938 to 1941 to earn his Ph.D. at the University of Chicago. These were exciting years at Chicago—many famous scientists were there, many having fled the atrocities of the Holocaust in Germany and Italy. Enrico Fermi (who received the Nobel Prize in physics, 1938) was his tennis partner. He took quantum mechanics from Arthur Compton (Nobel in physics, 1927) and Wolfgang Pauli (Nobel in physics, 1945) taught nuclear forces, while Robert Millikan (Nobel Prize in chemistry, 1960) taught molecular spectra. Henry soaked up all the learning he could from these and some dozen other world-class scientists who were there at that time.

In 1941, Henry completed his Ph.D., returning to Tuskegee to teach from 1941 to 1943.

Then Henry had an opportunity to serve as a staff member in the radiation laboratory at the Massachusetts Institute of Technology (MIT), which he did for three years during World War II, from 1943 to 1946. While there he worked on radar systems and invented a video amplifier that strengthened and clarified the signal on the screen.

He returned to the University of Chicago as an instructor in the 1946–47 academic year and did postdoctorate research at the Institute for the Study of Metals. There, he studied the problem of metal fatigue. He was able to show which alloy would last the longest and avoid the dangers of metal fatigue, and he was able to predict how long the alloy would hold up. After leaving Chicago, Henry became acting head of the department of physics at Morehouse College during the following academic year.

The next few years served up the most productive opportunities for Henry to research topics in physics that most interested him. He spent 12 years as a physicist at the Naval Research Laboratory in Washington, from 1948 to 1960. While there he explored aspects of superconductivity and solid-state physics. During this period he also taught evening courses at Howard University.

The following nine years he spent at Lockheed Missiles and Space Company, from 1960 to 1969. While there he worked on guidance systems for detecting submarines and helped develop a hovercraft used during the Vietnam War.

Finally Henry joined the faculty at Howard University as full professor of physics in 1969, where he remained until his retirement in 1977.

Included among the many awards presented to Henry are honorary doctorates from Lehigh University and Atlanta University; the Carver Award; the National Technical Achiever Award given by the National Technical Association in 1997; and the Excellence at Howard Award presented by the libraries of Howard University, also in 1997. However, Warren Henry once remarked warmly that of all his successes he felt most honored by the students who followed in his footsteps—becoming scientists and mentoring those who follow after them. Warren Henry died on October 31, 2001.

Further Reading

Carwell, Hattie, "Dr. Warren Henry, Pioneering Physicist." Available online. URL: http://www.bamit.org/warrenhenry.htm. Downloaded on February 15, 2001.

Henderson, Ashyia N., ed. *Who's Who Among African Americans,* 14th ed. Detroit: Gale Group, 2001.

Williams, Scott. "Warren E. Henry," Physicists of the African Diaspora. Available online. URL: http://www.math.buffalo.edu/mad/physics/henry_warren.html. Downloaded on February 2, 2002.

Hill, Henry Aaron
(1915–1979) *chemist*

Henry A. Hill pioneered in the chemistry of polymers and the flammability of fabric. He was particularly interested in resins, rubber, and plastics, and he also directed research on fluorocarbons. A recognized authority in the field of chemical regulation and safety, he served on the National Commission on Product Safety, appointed by President Lyndon Johnson. In 1977, he also became the first African American to be elected president of the American Chemical Society.

Henry Aaron Hill was born on May 30, 1915, in St. Joseph, Missouri, located on the Missouri River north of Kansas City. He attended Johnson C. Smith University in Charlotte, North Carolina, earning his B.A. in 1936. Hill continued with his studies at the Massachusetts Institute of Technology (MIT), completing his Ph.D. in chemistry in 1942.

Focusing much of his research on polymers and fluorocarbons, Henry Hill spent his career working in industry. However, landing his first job was not easy, probably because of prejudice.

Henry Aaron Hill was a pioneer in the chemistry of polymers and fabric flammability and a recognized authority on chemical regulation and safety. *(AP/Wide World Photos)*

After sending out 54 résumés, he was finally hired as a research chemist by North Atlantic Research Corporation of Newtonville, Massachusetts, in 1942. There he researched the development of water-based paints, fire-fighting foam, and synthetic rubber. He became director of research in 1943 and vice president in charge of research from 1944 to 1946. Hill then joined the Dewey & Almy Chemical Company, where from 1946 to 1952 he served as supervisor of research. He founded his own entrepreneurial firm in 1952, National Polychemicals, Inc., and 10 years later he became founder and president of the Riverside Research Laboratory. In 1976, he served as director for the Rohm & Haas Company. The firm provided research, development, and consulting on polymer production.

In addition to becoming the first African-American president of the American Chemical

Society in 1977, Hill chaired the chemistry section of the American Association for the Advancement of Science (AAAS).

On March 17, 1979, Aaron Hill died of a heart attack in Haverhill, Massachusetts. He was 63.

Further Reading

Brown, Mitchell C. "Henry Aaron Hill: Chemist," *Faces of Science*. Available online. URL: http://www.princeton.edu/~mcbrown/display/hill.html. Updated on June 4, 2000.

Massie, Samuel P. "Henry A. Hill: The Second Mile," *Chemistry* (January 1971): 11.

Young, Herman, and Barbara Young. "Henry Hill Dead of Heart Attack at 63," *Chemical and Engineering News* (March 26, 1979): 6–7.

Hill, Mary Elliott

(1907–1969)   *chemist*

One of the few notable women in chemistry in her time, and practically the only notable black woman chemist, Mary Elliott Hill is not well known and her career is sparsely documented. Her interests centered on two challenging areas of research, ultraviolet spectrometry and ketene synthesis.

Mary Elliott was born in South Mills, North Carolina, on January 5, 1907. She was 22 when she earned her bachelor of science degree from Virginia State College in Petersburg, Virginia, in 1929. Following completion of her degree, she taught in the Virginia State College Laboratory School for two years, from 1930 to 1932. Joining the faculty at Hampton Institute in Hampton, Virginia, she taught there for four years, until 1936. She apparently took a break from teaching for two years, joining the faculty at Virginia State College in 1938.

She married Carl McClellan Hill, although exactly when is not clear. She also continued her studies in science, earning her M.S. degree from the University of Pennsylvania in 1941. Mary Hill subsequently joined the faculty of Bennett College in Greensboro, North Carolina, for the academic year 1942–43. In 1944, she joined the faculty at Tennessee A&I State University in Nashville. There, she served as assistant professor in chemistry and as acting head of the chemistry department for 11 years, from 1951 to 1962. Finally, she moved to Kentucky State College in Frankfort in 1962.

Hill's research revolved in part around the properties of ultraviolet light. She explored the use of ultraviolet spectrometry, the measurement of electromagnetic waves that are shorter than visible light waves and longer than X rays. She also worked with ketenes and ketene synthesis, a complex area of organic chemistry involving a pungent, colorless, toxic gas that is used as an agent in acetylation (the process of introducing an acetyl group, that is, the acetic acid radical CH_3CO).

Mary Elliott Hill died in 1969.

Further Reading

Sammons, Vivian Ovelton. *Blacks in Science and Medicine*. New York: Hemisphere Publishing Corp., 1990.

Who's Who of American Women, 4th ed., 1966–67. Chicago: Marquis Who's Who, 1965.

Hill, Walter Andrew

(1946–)   *agronomist*

With his colleagues including his wife Jill Harris, Walter Hill has pioneered in development of food processing techniques and crop varieties useful for long-term human spaceflight. As dean of the College of Agricultural, Environmental, and Natural Sciences and director of the George Washington Carver Agricultural Experiment Station at Tuskegee University, he has also developed effective and far-reaching agricultural education programs. A strong mentor, he has also encouraged many minority students to pursue careers in the sciences.

Born on August 9, 1946, in New Brunswick, New Jersey, Walter Andrew Hill moved as a small child with his parents to North Little Rock, Arkansas. His parents, a schoolteacher and a minister, both set a high value on education. Because no high schools for blacks were available in the surrounding rural areas, they organized a network of neighborhood families in North Little Rock who would provide a place for the rural children to stay while they attended school there. Young Walter was impressed by this dedication to the cause of education for all, and he also had begun to read about GEORGE WASHINGTON CARVER and his work in science and science education. The two influences helped set him on his future path as agronomist and educator.

Hill's high marks in high school earned him a scholarship to Lake Forest College in Lake Forest, Illinois, where he majored in chemistry. He completed his bachelor's degree there in 1968, continuing his studies on a Ford Foundation Fellowship at the University of Chicago, where he completed a master of arts in teaching degree in 1970. He spent a few years teaching chemistry and general science in the Chicago public school system, but he soon yearned to expand his scientific training. He earned a master's degree in soil chemistry at the University of Arizona in 1973 and a Ph.D. in agronomy at the University of Illinois College of Agriculture in 1978.

That fall, Hill moved to Alabama to teach soil science at Tuskegee Institute (now University). There, he encouraged his students to join his research projects and in 1980, his teaching was honored when he was named a Danforth Associate. In 1990, he also received the Outstanding Education Award from the American Society of Agronomy for his excellence in teaching.

Hill has especially explored uses and attributes of the sweet potato. His work garnered an award in 1983 from the International Society of Tropical Root Crops. His work has also gained attention from the U.S. National Aeronautics and Space Administration (NASA), which provided a grant to explore the usability of the sweet potato in a self-sustaining environment, for example, on a long-term space mission to Mars. Hill devised a method for overcoming the problems of growing a root crop in a water tank, which had never been done successfully before. He earned a patent for this method.

Hill is a member of several professional societies, including the American Society of Gravitational and Space Biology. At Tuskegee, he serves as full professor, dean, and research director of the School of Agriculture and Home Economics. The U.S. secretary of agriculture has recognized his work with the Group Honors Award for Professional Excellence. In 2001, he received an honorary doctorate of science from Forest Lake College, in addition to election to Phi Beta Kappa and a Distinguished Service Citation, previously bestowed by his alma mater.

Further Reading

Kessler, James H., J. S. Kidd, Renee A. Kidd, and Katherine A. Morin. *Distinguished African American Scientists of the 20th Century.* Phoenix, Ariz.: Oryx Press, 1996.

Sammons, Vivian Ovelton. *Blacks in Science and Medicine.* New York: Hemisphere Publishing, 1990.

"Walter Andrew Hill," Lake Forest College Honorary Degree Candidates. Available online. URL: http://www.lfc.edu/news/events/commencement01/program/honorary/hill.html. Downloaded on April 23, 2002.

Hinton, William Augustus
(1883–1959) *medical researcher*

William Augustus Hinton became the first black professor to join the faculty at Harvard University in 1949. He was the author of *Syphilis and Its Treatment,* published in 1936.

William Augustus Hinton was born on December 15, 1883, in Chicago, Illinois. He began his college education at the University of Kansas, where he enrolled from 1900 to 1902, transferring to Harvard University, where he completed his bachelor of science degree in 1905. He intended to enter medical school, but did not have the funds, so he taught, first at Walden University in Nashville, Tennessee, and then at State School (now Langston University) Langston, Oklahoma, for a total of four years. He spent summers at the University of Chicago, where he studied bacteriology and physiology.

In 1909, Hinton entered Harvard Medical School, where he earned his M.D. with honors three years later. In 1912, he joined the staff at the Wassermann Laboratory—at the time a part of Harvard Medical School. He began to teach serology at the laboratory, and when Wassermann Laboratory became part of the Massachusetts Department of Public Health in 1915, he was appointed assistant director of the Division of Biologic Laboratories as well as chief of the Wassermann Lab. In 1918, he received a simultaneous appointment as instructor in preventive medicine and hygiene at the Harvard Medical School. From 1921 to 1949, Hinton moved through the ranks until in 1949, he became the first black professor at Harvard Medical School in its 313-year existence. In this capacity, Hinton would teach for the next 36 years, retiring in 1950.

The Hinton test for syphilis, which William A. Hinton developed, proved to be as effective as the Wassermann test—sometimes more so. The army used this test widely during World War II. With J. A. N. Davies, Hinton also formulated the Davies-Hinton test of blood and spinal fluid, also a widely used test for syphilis.

William Hinton died on August 8, 1959 in Canton, Massachusetts. He was 75.

As chief of the Wassermann laboratory at Harvard, in 1935 William A. Hinton published the first major text on syphilis, *Syphilis and Its Treatment.* Hinton was codeveloper of the Davies-Hinton test to detect syphilis in spinal fluids. *(Courtesy of the Harvard University Archives)*

Further Reading

Hinton, William Augustus. *Syphilis and Its Treatment,* Macmillan Medical Monographs. New York: Macmillan, 1936.

Kessler, James H., J. S. Kidd, Renee A. Kidd, and Katherine A. Morin. *Distinguished African American Scientists of the 20th Century.* Phoenix, Ariz.: Oryx Press, 1996.

"William Hinton—His Life and Times," The Public Health Museum in Massachusetts. Available online. URL: http://www.publichealthmuseum.org/more-exhibits-williamHinton.html. From *American Men of Science.* 1944, 816.

Hubbard, Philip Gamaliel
(1921–2002) *electrical engineer, educator*

When Philip G. Hubbard first enrolled at the University of Iowa as a student in 1940, black men were not permitted to live in university housing. By 1947, Hubbard became the University of Iowa's first black professor, and in 1971 he became vice president of the university. Always a civil rights advocate, Hubbard spoke out in support of fair housing and other issues of the emerging Civil Rights movement of the 1960s. Hubbard was recognized internationally for his work as scholar, inventor, and consultant in his fields of electronics and hydraulics.

On March 4, 1921, Philip Gamaliel Hubbard was born in Macon, Missouri, a small town in the central region of the state. His mother, who was a teacher, did not want her children to attend segregated schools, so she moved her family to Iowa, where schools were integrated, and she worked in Des Moines as an elevator operator. When Phil Hubbard graduated from North High School in 1939 in Des Moines, he was a member of the National Honor Society and he had $252.50 saved for college from shining shoes.

Hubbard entered the University of Iowa, where tuition was $50 a semester. He still had to shine shoes as a student to stay in school. Because black men could not reside on campus, he and the other African-American students lived in the homes of families and they formed a network among them. However, in 1943 he joined the army reserves after three years of classes at the University of Iowa. This gave him a real income and he obtained army certification in electrical engineering from Pennsylvania State University. He then returned to the University of Iowa to conduct war research in 1945.

Hubbard graduated from Iowa with honors in 1947, receiving a B.S. in electrical engineering. He also accepted a position as research engineer at the university that year, becoming the first African American on the University of Iowa faculty. Meanwhile, Hubbard also continued with his education at Iowa, completing an M.A. in mechanics and hydraulics in 1949.

In 1951, Hubbard expanded his prospects by founding his own consulting company, Hubbard Instrument Company, and during this period he invented two devices to measure fluid turbulence. His company consulted for many clients, including three branches of the military (army, navy, and air force), as well as several in the private sector, including General Electric and General Motors.

He completed his doctorate in engineering at the University of Iowa in 1954, and from 1954 to 1966, he taught mechanics and hydraulics in the University of Iowa College of Engineering.

In 1963, Hubbard received an appointment from the university president to serve on a committee to develop the first human rights code for the university. Hubbard became dean for Academic Affairs in 1965, and in 1967 he accepted additional responsibilities as vice president for Student Services. He additionally took a leadership role in development of the Iowa Center for the Arts. He also created the Opportunity at Iowa program, designed to make the university experience available to as many people who could benefit from it as possible. In 2002, former university president Willard Boyd remarked, "Mr. Hubbard played an incomparable role in building the university by working constantly to open it to all people and to treat each person individually and humanely."

At age 69, Hubbard retired on December 31, 1990. Philip G. Hubbard died on January 10, 2002, at the University Hospitals in Iowa City. He was 80 years old.

Further Reading
"Census," *Jet*, March 4, 2002, 18.
"Hubbard dies on January 10, 2002, in Iowa City, Iowa, at the age of 80." *Chicago Tribune* (January 14, 2002), sec. 2, 6.

Hubbard, Philip G. *My Iowa Journey: The Life Story of the University of Iowa's First African American Professor.* Iowa City: University of Iowa Press, 1999.

———. *New Dawns: A 150-Year Look at Human Rights at the University of Iowa.* Iowa City: University of Iowa Press, 1996.

"Philip G. Hubbard Papers," University of Iowa Archives, Iowa City, Iowa. Available online. URL: http://www.lib.uiowa.edu/spec-coll/Archives/guides/hubbard.htm. Updated on December 21, 2001.

Hudson, Roy Davage
(1930–) *neuropharmacologist*

Roy Davage Hudson is a pharmacologist who is noted for his research on the interaction of various chemical agents with neurons, resulting in some 25 publications and numerous citations in sources such as the Merck Index. Hudson also served as the 10th president of Hampton Institute.

Born on June 30, 1930, in Chattanooga, Tennessee, Roy Davage Hudson is the son of Everence Wilkerson Hudson and James Roy Hudson. His mother, a teacher, passed on to him her love of learning and the pursuit of excellence. Hudson told an interviewer in 1998 that his mother liked to remind him: "Not to equal, but to excel." As a boy, Hudson was fascinated with living things he observed on his grandfather's farm, and much of his advanced studies were in the disciplines of biology and zoology. He always had curiosity about how toys, gadgets, and organisms worked.

In the years 1948 to 1952, Hudson served in the U.S. Air Force. Stationed in Alaska, he worked on engine maintenance and repaired aircraft that had sustained damage during combat in the Korean War. This experience made him unflappable later in life when laboratory equipment broke down.

Following discharge from the military, Hudson enrolled at Livingstone College in Salisbury, North Carolina, where he played football for the college and earned his B.S. in biology in 1955. Named all-conference guard, he was later honored as one of Livingstone's all-time top 22 football players. Hudson received a Danforth Fellowship to continue his study of zoology at the University of Michigan, where he completed his M.S. in zoology in 1957 and entered the doctoral program in zoology.

During this period, Hudson took a summer job as a technician in the pharmacology department. He handled the work so well that he gained the attention of faculty members, and so began his career as a pharmacologist. He changed his emphasis and was teaching pharmacology at the University of Michigan in 1961, completing his Ph.D. in pharmacology in 1962.

In 1966, Hudson became associate professor of neuroscience at Brown University in Providence, Rhode Island, where he also served as dean of the graduate school until 1969. In 1970, he became president of Hampton University in Hampton, Virginia, meanwhile continuing to teach pharmacology at the University of Virginia.

In 1976, Hudson shifted from university research and teaching to industry, where he worked for the pharmaceutical research division of several major firms. He served as vice president for pharmaceutical research at Warner-Lambert/Parke-Davis (1977–79) and director of central nervous system research at Upjohn Company (1981–87). He served as vice president of Upjohn's pharmaceutical research and development in Europe (1987–90) and served as corporate vice president for public relations for Upjohn (1990–92). He retired in 1992, but accepted an interim appointment as president at Livingstone College from 1995 to 1996.

Hudson has received honorary degrees from several universities, including Brown University, Lehigh University, and Princeton University.

Further Reading

O'Mathúna, Dónal P. "Roy Davage Hudson," *Notable Black American Scientists*. Kristine Krapp, ed. Detroit: Gale Research, 1999, 165–166.

Henderson, Ashyia N., ed. *Who's Who Among African Americans*, 14th ed. Detroit: Gale Group, 2001.

Hunt, Fern
(1948–) *mathematician*

As a recipient of the Arthur S. Flemming Award in 2000, Fern Hunt has been honored for her consistent and sustained contribution to her field. A former professor at Howard University, she had authored 19 peer-reviewed technical publications in mathematics by 2001, and she is a respected senior researcher at the National Institute of Standards and Technology (NIST).

Born in New York City in 1948, Fern Hunt is the daughter of Daphne Lindsay and Thomas Edward Hunt. When Fern was seven, a younger sister, Erica, was born, who would later become a published poet and writer. The girls' grandparents had emigrated from Jamaica prior to World War I to escape the limitations placed on blacks in that country. They hoped to find greater opportunities in New York.

The Hunt family lived in a mid-Manhattan housing project, a primarily black community. Her father worked for the postal service, and her mother was a typist for the Welfare Department. No one in her family was a college graduate—her father had not finished high school. However, for two years her mother had attended Hunter College. After that she had not been able to continue because of the financial cost.

As a youngster growing up, Fern had little reason to look ahead to a career as a mathematician—she was born just before the first African-American woman in history had received a Ph.D. in mathematics, a field dominated in the United States by white males. As Hunt likes to say, "I was no one's fair-haired boy."

Yet, as a girl she was fascinated by science and liked to experiment with a chemistry set given to her by her mother. Soon she became engrossed with mail-order electrical kits. In ninth grade, she had a science teacher, Charles Wilson, who saw her potential and talked her into entering science fairs and attending the Saturday Science Program at Columbia University. There, she learned to look at mathematics with a new, high level of interest. This exposure was a pivotal point in her life—and she calls Wilson's influence the "single most important event in my individual career."

After graduating from the Bronx High School of Science, thanks in part to encouragement by her mother, Hunt attended Bryn Mawr College, a private four-year liberal arts college for women in Pennsylvania. She earned her A.B. degree from Bryn Mawr in 1969, continuing on to graduate programs in mathematics at the Courant Institute of Mathematics at New York University. There she received her master's degree, followed by her Ph.D. in mathematics in 1978.

Hunt taught briefly at the University of Utah and then joined the faculty at Howard University as assistant professor of mathematics. While teaching there, she also worked for the National Institutes of Health in the Laboratory of Mathematical Biology from 1981 to 1982 and for the National Bureau of Standards from 1986 to 1991. She enjoyed the mix of teaching with research in mathematical biology and applied mathematics.

Along the way, Hunt encountered discrimination and setbacks. However, she says, she usually tried to put these incidents in perspective, recognizing that specific incidents would have less importance in the long run. She thought in terms of a "final review" of her life "when the curtain comes down," and that, she says gave her courage to continue. She has said, "So several things helped me: I took a longer view. I had inspirational resources, and I also have a very stubborn personality that says, Well, I'll show them!"

She thinks the constant challenges caused her to search within herself for understanding about who she really was at a fundamental level. So, in a sense, she thinks that the suffering contributed to her personal growth.

In her teaching, Hunt celebrates the life of the mind. She tells students that mathematics is about ideas and how to work with them, how to create structure and develop an appreciation for ideas. She evokes the existence of an intellectual life that is bigger than material possessions and financial success—and she tries to instill an appreciation for intellectual challenges and structure. She says she likes to impart three lessons: Have confidence. Enjoy intellectual activity. Blacks can and should do mathematics.

In 1993, Hunt accepted a position at NIST, where she is a mathematician in the ITL Mathematics and Computational Sciences Division. There she works on mathematical problems that arise in research on the physics and chemistry of materials that are important to U.S. industry. She also considers pure research important. Her job constantly demands creativity and wide-ranging capabilities with various techniques in analysis and applied mathematics. So she tries to continue to do mathematical research that does not have immediate application to a NIST project, focusing on the area of ergodic theory of dynamical systems.

She continues to encourage undergraduate students in mathematics by lecturing at colleges and universities and by working with summer students. Hunt is strongly interested in mentoring minority students interested in careers in mathematics. In 1998, she was one of four instructors in EDGE (Enhancing Diversity in Graduate Education), a summer seminar program for graduating high school seniors who are entering graduate programs. The program is hosted by the mathematics department at her alma mater, Bryn Mawr, and sponsored by the Andrew W. Mellon Foundation and the National Science Foundation.

Hunt has said she thinks educators should be thinking in terms of encouraging the talents people have, instead of focusing on those they lack. Regarding mathematics in particular, she adds, "No matter how good you actually are, there is definitely somebody who can run rings around you. It can be intimidating." Mathematics as a field should minimize this aura of intimidation and the effects caused by the "math anxiety" problem by being, as Hunt puts it, "a little more inclusive."

In 2000, Hunt was one of 12 federal employees to receive the prestigious Arthur S. Flemming Award sponsored by George Washington University and Government Executive magazine. Those receiving the award come from three categories: scientific, administrative, and applied science. Hunt's award recognized her sustained contributions to probability and stochastic modeling, mathematical biology, computational geometry, nonlinear dynamics, computer graphics, and parallel computing.

Hunt's expertise has been sought in other ways as well. She served as a member of the Graduate Record Examination (GRE) Mathematics Advisory Board for the Educational Testing Service from 1988 to 1991. She has also been a member of the board of trustees of Bryn Mawr College since 1992 and a member of the Biological and Environmental Research Advisory Committee for the Department of Energy since 1994.

Further Reading

"Chaos expert Fern Hunt '69," Alumnae Bulletin. Available online. URL: http://www.brynmawr.edu/Alumnae/bulletin/hunt.htm. Last accessed on May 31, 2002.

Henrion, Claudia. Women in Mathematics: The Addition of Difference. Bloomington: Indiana University Press, 1997, 212–233.

PRESTON RIDGE LIBRARY
COLLIN COLLEGE
FRISCO, TX 75035

Hunter, John McNeile
(1901–1979) *physicist, chemist, educator*

John McNeile Hunter's singular contributions as an educator in physics and chemistry resulted in the instruction of more than 4,000 students in these fields, more than 50 of whom became physicists and engineers.

John McNeile Hunter was born on January 23, 1901, in Woodville, Texas. He enrolled for undergraduate studies at the Massachusetts Institute of Technology (MIT), receiving his B.S. degree in 1924. Following his graduation, he began his lifelong career teaching at Virginia State College (now Virginia State University in Petersburg, Virginia).

Hunter started out as an instructor of electrical wiring and operated the power plant for the college. However, that was just a beginning. He pursued graduate studies at Cornell University in Ithaca, New York, completing his M.S. degree there in 1927. During the course of his teaching career, Hunter became full professor of physics, as well as director of the Division of Graduate Studies and Research and dean of the College. His administrative efforts resulted in the reshaping of the college.

In the meantime, he had returned to Cornell to complete his Ph.D., receiving the doctorate in physics from that institution in 1937. His research focused on thermoionics, the study of electrically charged particles (usually electrons) emitted at high temperatures by a conducting substance. Hunter's dissertation examined the anomalous Schottky effect for oxygenated tungsten. In solid-state physics, the Schottky effect is an effect observed in thermoionic emitters in which the work function is reduced in the presence of an electric field. The Schottky anomaly, however, produces the opposite effect, an excess contribution to the heat capacity of a solid.

Hunter retired in 1968 at age 67. In 1973, he received a Distinguished Service Citation from the American Association of Physics Teachers for his exceptional contributions to the teaching of physics. The citation noted that John Hunter had touched the lives of more than 4,000 students with his teaching, and that of the more than 50 who became physicists and engineers, 10 became teachers and one became a university president. John McNeile Hunter died in Petersburg, Virginia, in July 1979.

Further Reading
"AAPT Distinguished Service Citations for 1973," *The Physics Teacher* (May 1974): 292.

Sammons, Vivian Ovelton. *Blacks in Science and Medicine.* New York: Hemisphere Publishing, 1990.

Who's Who in America. 38th ed., vol. I. Marquette, Ill.: Marquis Who's Who, 1974.

I

Imes, Elmer Samuel
(1883–1941) *physicist*

In 1918, when Elmer Samuel Imes received his doctorate from the University of Michigan, he became the second African American to receive a Ph.D. in physics. (The first, EDWARD ALEXANDER BOUCHET, received his Ph.D. from Yale University in 1876.) Imes gained international recognition for his research on infrared spectra.

The city of Memphis, Tennessee, was hometown to Imes, who was born there on October 12, 1883. His father was a graduate of Oberlin College and Theological Seminary—one of the earliest colleges in the nation to admit black students. He and Imes's mother were missionaries who pioneered in the work of the American Missionary Association in the South. Both young Imes and his father taught in schools established by the American Missionary Association.

Elmer Samuel Imes earned his B.A. in 1903 from Fisk University in Nashville, Tennessee, and his M.A. in 1907. He entered doctoral studies at the University of Michigan on a fellowship from 1916 to 1918, receiving his Ph.D. in physics in 1918. He was the second African American to receive a Ph.D. in physics. His dissertation topic was *Measurements of the Near Infra-red Absorption of Some Diatomic Cases,* and it was published the following year in the *Journal of Astrophysics.*

Imes used infrared light (invisible light just beyond the red end of the visible light spectrum) to probe the size and structure of molecules, making the first accurate measurement of distances between atoms in a molecule. Using near infrared radiation (the shortest infrared wavelengths), he produced spectra of HCl (hydrogen chloride), HBr (hydrogen bromide), and HF (hydrogen fluoride) that supported quantum theory and showed that chlorine occurs in two forms (isotopes) with different atomic masses.

Spectra (plural of spectrum) are displays of light or radiation that are separated into their component parts. Scientists have found that different wavelengths (such as infrared, X ray, gamma ray, and so on) are useful for probing the properties of matter in different ways and observing how the spectra are absorbed. Gamma rays, for example, are absorbed by atomic nuclei, so gamma ray spectra are useful in studying atomic nuclei. Imes was using near infrared wavelengths to probe the diatomic (two-atom) molecules of HCl, HBr, and HF.

During the time when Imes was working on his doctorate and the years just after receiving his Ph.D., he served as a consulting chemist and engineer in New York. From 1922 until 1930, he worked in industry for several firms, accepting positions with the Federal Engineer's Development

Corporation, the Burrows Magnetic Equipment Corporation, and E.A. Everett Railway Signal Supplies.

In 1930, he returned to Fisk University to accept a position as professor and head of the department of physics, retaining that position for the rest of his life. Imes died at Memorial Hospital in New York on September 11, 1941. Fisk University has established the Elmer S. Imes Memorial Scholarship in his honor to en-courage students showing outstanding promise in either physics or mathematics.

Further Reading

Obituary. *New York Times*, September 12, 1941, 22.

Sammons, Vivian Ovelton. *Blacks in Science and Medicine*. New York: Hemisphere Publishing, 1990, 127.

Swann, W. F. G. "Elmer Samuel Imes," *Science* (December 26, 1941): 600–601.

J

Jackson, Shirley Ann
(1946–) *physicist*

Shirley Jackson is one of the most distinguished scientists in the United States. A theoretical physicist, she is the author of some 100 published scientific papers, and she has completed a fruitful career of nearly 20 years as a research physicist in solid-state physics and other branches of physics at Bell Laboratories. Since then she has begun a second career as an accomplished administrator. In 1995, she became chairman of the United States Nuclear Regulatory Commission (NRC). Since 1999, she has headed the prestigious Rensselaer Technological Institute in Troy, New York.

The second daughter of George and Beatrice Jackson, Shirley Ann Jackson was born on August 5, 1946, in Washington, D.C. She attended Roosevelt High School, where she participated in accelerated programs in math and science, graduating in 1964 as valedictorian.

She went on to attend undergraduate classes at the Massachusetts Institute of Technology (MIT), where she was the only African-American woman majoring in theoretical physics. She completed her bachelor's degree in 1968. She chose to stay at MIT to complete her doctorate, although several other excellent opportunities were open to her. She completed her Ph.D. in theoretical physics at MIT in 1973, with a thesis on elementary particle theory, entitled *The Study of a Multiperipheral Model with Continued Cross-Channel Unitarity.* The thesis was published in 1975 by *Annals of Physics.* She was one of the first black women to earn a Ph.D. in physics, and she was also the first black woman to earn a Ph.D. in any subject at MIT.

Jackson's area of interest in physics centered on subatomic particles, which are found within atoms and most of which are very unstable, making them difficult to study. One method of study involves the use of a particle accelerator. In this device, atomic nuclei are accelerated to very high speeds. Then they are collided with a target material. The collision separates the nucleus into its tiny constituent parts—subatomic particles. A second method of study uses certain types of nonconducting solids. When such solids are exposed to high-energy particles, the structure of their atoms becomes distorted. The distortion serves as a track left behind by the subatomic particle. By examining highly enhanced photographs of these tracks, Jackson and other theoretical physicists can decipher information about the tiny, unstable particles that made them.

These studies require complex, sophisticated equipment, and Jackson spent several years of

Shirley Ann Jackson is author of some 100 published scientific papers on solid-state physics, semiconductor systems, and related topics that she pursued during her 20 years as a research physicist at Bell Laboratories. In 1999, she became president of Rensselaer Polytechnic Institute, one of the most respected technological institutions in the nation. *(© Gary D. Gold, 2002)*

postgraduate research conducting studies at some of the most prestigious physics laboratories in the world. In 1973 and 1974, she studied hadrons at the Fermi National Accelerator Laboratory (Fermilab) in Batavia, Illinois, outside Chicago. Hadrons are medium to large in size (for subatomic particles) and the group includes particles known as baryons and mesons. She was a visiting scientist in 1974 at the accelerator laboratory at the European Center for Nuclear Research (CERN) in Geneva, Switzerland. Using the CERN equipment, she was able to investigate theories of strongly interacting elementary particles. In 1976, she lectured at the Stanford Linear Accelerator Center in Stanford, California, and in 1976 and 1977 she was visiting scientist at the Aspen Center for Physics in Aspen, Colorado.

The year 1976 also marked the beginning of a productive period as research scientist for Bell Laboratories in Murray Hill, New Jersey. There, her research focused on four main areas of physics: optical, solid state, quantum, and theoretical. She remained with AT&T for nearly 20 years. From 1991 to 1995, she also served as professor of physics at Rutgers University in New Jersey. During this period, she met and married Morris A. Washington, who is also a physicist, and they have one son, Alan.

In 1995, she received a nomination from President Bill Clinton to chair the Nuclear Regulatory Commission (NRC)—an agency run by a board of commissioners charged with ensuring that the health and safety of the public is not endangered by the peaceful use of nuclear energy. Although many of Clinton's nominations were deeply contested, Jackson's appointment was quickly confirmed by Congress and she was sworn in on May 2, 1995. She assumed the position two months later, becoming the first African American to head the NRC.

As chair of the NRC, she said, "We must demonstrate vigilance, objectivity and consistency." She meant it. During her tenure, she had several Northeast Utilities plants shut down for safety violations and placed several others under close surveillance. In fact, she was known as "the toughest [NRC] chairman we've seen," according to Bill Megavern, director of the Critical Mass Energy Project at Ralph Nader's Public Citizen group.

In July 1999, Shirley Ann Jackson became president of Rensselaer Polytechnic Institute in Troy, New York, after a unanimous vote by the university's board of trustees. She is the first black woman to become president of a major research institution. In this position, she hopes to increase the representation of African Americans and women among science students at Rensselaer and she also hopes to attract a larger number of African-American faculty members.

Jackson has received many awards and honors, and her stature has been confirmed by her selection to serve on many national boards and commissions. In 1998, she was inducted into the National Women's Hall of Fame for her contributions not only as a distinguished scientist, but also as an advocate for science, education, and public policy. In late 2002, she was elected president of the American Association for the Advancement of Science.

Further Reading

Hawkins, Walter L. *African American Biographies.* Jefferson, N.C.: McFarland & Co., 1992.

Hayden, Robert C. *Seven African-American Scientists.* Brookfield, Conn.: Twenty-First Century Books, 1992, 148–167.

Pooley, Eric. "Nuclear Safety Fallout." *Time,* March 17, 1997, 34–36.

Yount, Lisa. *A to Z of Women in Science and Math.* New York: Facts On File, 1999.

Jay, James Monroe

(1927–   ) *microbiologist*

Author of several publications in his field, including *Modern Food Microbiology* (Van Nostrand, 1970), Jay has also contributed to *Journal of Bacteriology, Applied Microbiology, Journal of Food Science,* and *Canadian Journal of Microbiology.*

James Monroe Jay was born on September 12, 1927, in Fitzgerald, Georgia, the son of Lizzie W. Jay and John B. Jay. James Jay has said that he always was interested in nature and wanted to be a scientist. Even though each of his parents harbored other hopes for him (his father envisioned a minister; his mother, a dentist), they encouraged him. Jay graduated from high school in 1945 and enlisted in the army, earning the rank of sergeant and serving from 1946 to 1947. After his discharge, he attended Paine College in Augusta, Georgia. He received an A.B. degree in natural sciences and mathematics

cum laude from Paine College in 1950, continuing to Western Reserve University in Cleveland, Ohio, where he had planned to study chemistry. However, a course in bacteriology changed all his plans—he was hooked. He transferred to Ohio State University in Columbus, where he earned a master's in science degree in 1953 and his Ph.D. in bacteriology and biochemistry in 1956. Jay continued his studies at Ohio State University under a postdoctorate fellowship in the Department of Agricultural Biochemistry during the 1956–57 academic year.

In the fall of 1957, Jay joined the faculty of Southern University in Baton Rouge, Louisiana, first as assistant professor, soon followed by promotions to professor. He stayed at Southern for four years, from 1957 to 1961, moving on to the Department of Biology at Wayne State University in Detroit, Michigan, in 1961, where he became assistant professor, later promoted to full professor. He continued to teach there until his retirement in 1994, taking on the mantle of professor emeritus at that time. He also taught as adjunct professor at the University of Nevada, Las Vegas, since 1994. He keeps a laboratory in his home in Henderson, Nevada, where he continues his research, which currently centers on the *Escherichia coli* bacterium.

During Jay's career, he has developed a respected reputation as a watchdog on the consumer's behalf. As such, he served as a member of the National Advisory Committee for Microbiological Criteria for Foods for the U.S. Department of Agriculture (USDA) from 1987 to 1994. He also served as a committee member for the National Academy of Sciences from 1984 to 1987. He was a member of the editorial board of the *Journal of Food Protection* from 1981 to 1997, and he served as a panel member for the Institute of Food Technology from 1991 to 1995.

Among the many awards with which Jay and his work have been honored the following stand out: the Probus Award, Wayne State University (1969); Distinguished Alumni Award,

Paine College (1969); Michigan Science Trailblazer Award, Detroit Science Center (1987); Faculty Research Award, Sigma Xi Chapter, Wayne State University (1988); Fellow, Institute of Food Technologists (1996–); Outstanding Teacher Award, Society for Industrial Microbiology (1996); Fellow, American Society for Microbiology (1997); and Fellow, International Association for Food Protection (1999).

Further Reading

Jay, James Monroe. *Modern Food Microbiology.* New York: Van Nostrand, 1970.

———. *Negroes in Science: Natural Science Doctorates, 1876–1969.* Detroit: Balamp Publishing, 1971.

Who's Who Among African Americans, 14th ed. Detroit: Gale Group, 2001.

Jearld, Ambrose, Jr.

(1944–) *marine biologist*

Ambrose Jearld, Jr., is a fisheries biologist and chief of Research Planning and Coordination at the Northeast Fisheries Science Center's Woods Hole Laboratory, a research laboratory for the National Oceanic and Atmospheric Administration (NOAA).

Jearld was born to Ambrose Jearld, Sr., and Katherine Marie Smith Jearld on March 6, 1944, in Annapolis, Maryland. Jearld's mother was alone at the time, raising young Ambrose and his sisters while their father was away at war. Ambrose went to North Carolina to live with his grandmother and uncles on the family farm, and he imagined himself growing up to be a farmer like them. He stayed with them until he was 10, when he returned to Annapolis.

He graduated from high school in 1961 and enrolled in Maryland State College (later the University of Maryland, Eastern Shore—UMES) in Princess Anne. To pay expenses, he found a job in the biology laboratory, which worked well with his biology major. He completed his bachelor's degree in 1964, receiving a senior biology achievement award.

After working for a chemical company in Philadelphia, Jearld enrolled at the University of Oklahoma in Stillwater to begin graduate studies and research in the school's fisheries research program. For his dissertation, he monitored and recorded fish behavior as part of an ongoing census project. The draft and the Vietnam War interrupted his work when he was inducted into the army. Because of his scientific training, the army stationed him where he could do the most good—at a research laboratory in Maryland. During his off-duty time, he was able to work on his master's degree, which he completed, long-distance, in 1971, while also taking course work in psychobiology at Johns Hopkins University, which was nearby.

After his military discharge, Jearld returned to Oklahoma, completing his Ph.D. in 1975. He accepted a teaching position in biology at Lincoln University in Oxford, Pennsylvania, followed by a position teaching zoology at Howard University in Washington, D.C. He spent summers on field research in various locations, such as New Jersey and San Francisco. In 1978, he accepted a position as a fisheries biologist at the Northeast Fisheries Science Center's Woods Hole Laboratory and has been there ever since. He also is an adjunct professor at UMES since 1983.

The Northeast Fisheries Science Center where Jearld works is the research arm of NOAA Fisheries in the region. Jearld has said that the laboratory has moved away from just assessing stocks of types of fish and now takes a more holistic, ecological view of the fish, their environment, and impacts by humans and other forces on both. The Center plans, develops, and manages a multidisciplinary program of basic and applied research. In the process, the effort is hoped to increase understanding of living marine resources of the region and the habitat they need to live and produce. The laboratory's research also has an outreach aim—communicating with management, industry, and the public what the options are for both conservation and utilization of the area's fish and restoration of the environment.

Jearld has also been active in outreach, education, and human rights issues. He is a strong advocate for the development of diversity and equity in employment at NOAA. Also, since 1994, he has provided links between NOAA and the national and international affairs in South Africa, particularly relating to human resources corrective actions. For over 10 years, he has also provided leadership in NOAA science and technical support for six West African countries around the Gulf of Guinea. Within the United States, Jearld has worked at establishing a link between graduate programs in oceanic and atmospheric sciences and historically minority-serving colleges. He also has worked on building outreach programs to the general public, industry, and management that bridge the different outlooks between operational and educational fields in oceanic and atmospheric research.

In 2001, Jearld received a NOAA Administrator's Award "For contributions to the conservation of the world's fisheries and protected marine resources, improvement of global fisheries science and management, and international acclamation for NOAA administrative leadership."

Further Reading

"Ambrose Jearld, Jr." Woods Hole Black History Month Committee, USGS Woods Hole Field Center. Available online. URL: http://woodshole.er.usgs.gov/outreach/WHBHMC/HTMLdocs/ambrose.htm. Updated on January 17, 2002.

Kessler, James H., J. S. Kidd, Renee A. Kidd, and Katherine A. Morin. *Distinguished African American Scientists of the 20th Century.* Phoenix, Ariz.: Oryx Press, 1996.

Jemison, Mae Carol
(1956–) *physician, astronaut*

On September 12, 1992, Mae Jemison lifted off into space aboard the Space Shuttle *Endeavor* and became the first African-American woman in space. Before and since, she has made contributions as an engineer, physician, social scientist, educator, and advocate for women and African Americans in science.

The youngest of three children, Mae Carol Jemison was born on October 17, 1956, to Charlie and Dorothy Jemison in Decatur, Alabama. She grew up in Chicago, Illinois, where her mother taught English and math and her father worked as a maintenance supervisor. Jemison developed an early interest in science and was a strong student. After graduating in 1973 from Morgan Park High School in Chicago, she earned both a B.S. in chemical engineering and a B.A. in African-American studies in 1977 from northern California's Stanford University, one of the foremost U.S. educational institutions. She went on to receive her M.D. from Cornell University in 1981, also traveling during these years to Cuba, Kenya, and Thailand, where she provided primary medical care. She completed her internship the following year at the Los Angeles County/University of Southern California Medical Center.

Jemison worked briefly as a general practitioner with the INA/Ross Loos Medical Group in Los Angeles, prior to two years of Peace Corps service (1983–85) in Sierra Leone and Liberia in West Africa, where she served as the area Peace Corps medical officer. There she managed medical service for both the Peace Corps and the U.S. embassy, supervising the medical staff as well as laboratory and pharmacy personnel. During this time she also worked with the Centers for Disease Control (CDC) and the National Institute of Health on vaccine research for hepatitis B, schistosomiasis ("snail fever," considered the most widespread parasitic disease after malaria) and rabies.

Following her return from the Peace Corps in 1985, Jemison worked as a general practitioner for CIGNA Health Plans of California, while pursuing graduate engineering studies in Los Angeles. In 1987, the National Aeronautics and Space Administration (NASA) selected her as one of 15 successful astronaut candidates from a field of 2,000 applicants. When she completed her training in 1988, she became qualified as a "mission specialist," or scientist-astronaut, the first black female astronaut in NASA history and NASA's fifth black astronaut.

The thundering external rockets of the space shuttle *Endeavor* roared as the huge spacecraft lifted off from Kennedy Space Center in Florida on September 12, 1992. It was the 50th U.S. space shuttle mission, the first major joint mission between the United States and Japan, and the first time a black woman had ever flown in space. The mission focused on experiments in materials processing and life sciences, which took place in the Spacelab J module, a scientific laboratory designed to ride in the shuttle bay, the large cavity in the main body of the spacecraft. Jemison conducted an experiment on frogs' eggs, observing that eggs fertilized in micro-gravity developed normally into tadpoles, just as they do on Earth. In an experiment she designed, she also studied the loss of calcium in her crewmates' bones during the flight, one of the major concerns for human health during prolonged spaceflights. Also, instead of using preventative medication against motion sickness during her spaceflight, Jemison successfully used biofeedback methods and meditation strategies for controlling motion sickness, an affliction that hampers the work of about 50 percent of all astronauts.

After leaving NASA in 1993, Jemison established The Jemison Group, Inc., a private organization founded to integrate socially responsible principles with technology. Jemison's commitments to social equality and the importance of science are both evident in the organization's work. Recent projects include a satellite-based telecommunications system that enables health care to be brought more efficiently to developing countries; development of a science and literature curriculum in South Africa; and The Earth We Share, an international science camp to promote basic science literacy.

Also in 1993, Jemison joined the faculty of Dartmouth College as professor of environmental studies. She is also director of The Jemison Institute for Advancing Technology in Developing Countries at Dartmouth, where she uses her richly varied background as an engineer, physician, astronaut, social scientist, and educator to

Astronaut and physician Mae Carol Jemison became the first African-American woman in space. *(Photo by NASA)*

promote the design and use of technology in real-life situations.

Jemison once remarked, "I believe at the heart of science are the words, 'I think, I wonder, and I understand.'" During her career, she has contributed powerfully by her expertise, enthusiasm, and energy to the spread and use of the positive possibilities that science and those concepts can produce.

Further Reading

Hawkins, Walter L. *African American Biographies.* Jefferson, N.C.: McFarland & Co., 1992.

Jemison, Mae. *Find Where the Wind Goes: Moments from My Life.* New York: Scholastic, 2001.

Yannuzzi, Della A. *Mae Jemison: A Space Biography* (Countdown to Space). Springfield, N.J.: Enslow Publishing, 1998.

Yount, Lisa. "Jemison, Mae Carol." *A to Z of Women in Science and Math.* New York: Facts On File, 1999, 103–104.

Johnson, Katherine G.
(1918–) *mathematician, physicist*

Katherine G. Johnson was in on the ground floor of the space program. In 1953, she began work at Langley Research Center, now part of the National Aeronautics and Space Administration (NASA)—but at that time NASA did not even exist. No one had even launched a satellite. Russia's *Sputnik* had not been developed.

Katherine Johnson was born in White Sulphur Springs, West Virginia, on August 26, 1918. She was the youngest of four children. Schools were segregated at the time, and classes for African Americans did not go beyond eighth grade in Katherine's hometown, so she traveled to Institute, West Virginia, to complete her high school education. She also attended West Virginia State College in Institute, where she graduated summa cum laude and received her bachelor's degree in mathematics and French in 1937.

She worked in a high school teaching position in Virginia for several years, but in 1953 she found a better job working at Langley Research Center as a "pool" mathematician. That is, whenever the researchers needed some calculations carried out, they drew on the resources of the pool, and the available mathematician got the job. Most of the mathematicians in the pool were women and the pools were segregated. Johnson was "loaned"—transferred, really, to work on a flight research program. In this position, she had the opportunity to make significant contributions to space program development.

She worked on problems that challenged her skills—interplanetary trajectories, space navigation, orbital mechanics. She mapped out orbits for numerous spacecraft, including the Earth Resources Satellite that has helped locate underground minerals. During the Apollo missions to the Moon, Johnson analyzed data from satellite tracking stations that are located strategically in Australia, Spain, and California. She investigated improved navigation procedures to apply them to tracking manned and unmanned space missions.

In 1970, 1980, and 1985, with her colleagues in the Lunar Spacecraft and Operations Division, Johnson received the Group Achievement Award for her contributions to the lunar space program and her pioneering work on navigation problems. In 1998, the State University of New York at Farmingdale awarded her an honorary doctor of laws degree, and in 1999, West Virginia State College named her Outstanding Alumnus of the Year. Katherine G. Johnson retired in 1986.

Further Reading

Brown, Mitchell C. "Katherine G. Johnson," Faces of Science: African Americans in the Sciences. Available online. URL: http://www.princeton.edu/~mcbrown/display/katherine_johnson.html. Updated on July 18, 2000.

Hine, Darlene, ed. *Facts On File Encyclopedia of Black Women in America: Science, Health, and Medicine.* New York: Facts On File, 1997, 89–90.

Jones, Eleanor Green Dawley
(1929–   ) *mathematician, educator*

When Eleanor Green Dawley Jones received her doctorate in 1966, she became one of the first dozen African-American women to earn a Ph.D. in mathematics. Respected as a resource for mathematics curriculum development, she has served on national committees charged with setting curriculum goals. She has also taken an active role as an advocate for women and minorities in mathematics and science.

The second of six children, Eleanor Green was born in Norfolk, Virginia, on August 12, 1929. Her father, George Herbert Green, worked for the postal service, and her mother, Lillian Vaughn Green, had been employed domestically prior to their marriage. They valued education and expected their children to attend college, and they all did. Eleanor graduated as valedictorian from a segregated high school in Norfolk. She enrolled on scholarship at Howard University in Washington, D.C., with a major in mathematics. There, the first math course she took was taught by ELBERT FRANK COX, the first African American to earn a Ph.D. in pure mathematics. She also took a course from DAVID HAROLD BLACKWELL, another highly respected mathematician. She graduated cum laude with minors in education and physical education in 1949 and continued on, again on scholarship, to complete her master's degree in 1950.

Following her studies at Howard University, Green taught high school in Norfolk, Virginia, and then took time out from her teaching career when she married Edward Dawley, Jr., and they began to raise a family. Eleanor Dawley returned to teaching in 1955, after her two children were born, accepting a position at Hampton Institute (now University).

Civil rights issues loomed large in the late 1950s, and in 1957 black students in Norfolk had no schools to attend due to forced integration that resulted, ironically, in closed schools.

So Dawley helped tutor the students in a local church. An outspoken civil rights activist, she also became vice chair of CORE (Congress for Racial Equality) for Virginia from 1958 to 1960.

Since she was then teaching at the college level, pursuing a doctorate was more attractive than ever, since it would mean promotion—and the security of tenure—as well as opportunities to expand her work in mathematics. The natural choice would be the University of Virginia. However, the state university did not accept black graduate students at the time. Instead the university paid tuition and travel expenses for out-of-state studies. So, Dawley, now divorced, moved with her two sons to Syracuse, New York, where she enrolled at Syracuse University. With a stipend from Hampton Institute and money she made grading papers, she managed to support the family and attend classes. The first year was the hardest. After that, from 1963 to 1966, she had a National Science Foundation faculty grant and a teaching assistantship to help with the finances. She completed her dissertation and received her Ph.D. in 1966. Her dissertation, on an aspect of algebra, warranted publication of an abstract in the May 1967 issue of *American Mathematical Monthly*.

On her return to Virginia, Dawley became an associate professor at Hampton and taught for the 1966–67 academic year. That summer, she and Everette Benjamin Jones were married, and she became Eleanor Jones. The couple would have one son. The marriage ended in divorce in 1982.

In the fall of 1967, Jones became associate professor of mathematics at Norfolk State University, where she spent the next 33 years of her career—teaching calculus, abstract algebra, linear algebra, and mathematics for nonscience majors. She retired in 2000.

Jones has been active on national committees or boards of several professional organizations, including the National Association of Mathematicians, the Mathematical Association of America, and the Association for Women in Mathematics. In 1990, she began work with the American Mathematical Society on creating opportunities in math for underrepresented minorities. She was elected to the science honor society Sigma Xi in 1965, while at Syracuse, becoming a full member in 1985. The National Association of Mathematicians (NAM) honored Eleanor Green Dawley Jones in 1994 with the NAM's Distinguished Service Award.

Further Reading

American Men and Women of Science, 1995–96, 19th ed. New Providence, N.J.: Bowker, 1994.

Kenschaft, Patricia C. "Black Women in Mathematics in the United States." *American Mathematical Monthly* (October 1981): 592–604.

Sammons, Vivian Ovelton. *Blacks in Science and Medicine.* New York: Hemisphere Publishing, 1990.

Jones, Frederick McKinney (Fred Jones)
(1892–1961)   *inventor*

Frederick McKinney Jones invented a refrigerator that could be used by military field units and mechanical techniques for refrigerated railroad

Fred Jones was the king of mobile refrigeration inventions, and his systems and devices transformed food transportation. Two-thirds of Jones's 60 patents were for inventions in the field of refrigeration. *(Thermo King Corporation)*

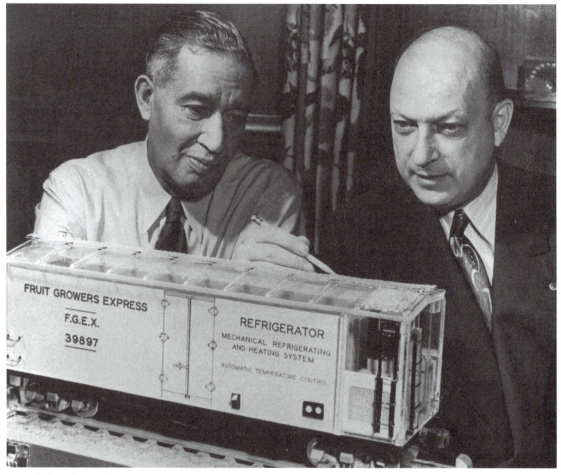

Jones (left) cofounded Thermo King Corporation with Joe Numero (right) to market Jones's refrigeration inventions, including the refrigerated railroad car. *(Thermo King Corporation)*

cars and trucks. He received more than 60 patents during his lifetime, more than 40 patents in the field of refrigeration alone. He was the first black inventor to receive the National Medal of Technology.

Fred Jones was born on May 17, 1892, in Cincinnati, Ohio. His mother was African American and his father was an Irish-American railroad worker. Jones's mother apparently died while he was still a young child, and his father raised him until he was eight. At that age, his fa-

ther asked Father Edward A. Ryan at St. Mary's Catholic Church in Cincinnati, Ohio, to take his son in and give him a good education. Fred did chores around the church in return for room and board, but he was always curious about how toys and gadgets worked. By the age of 12, he had run away to become a garage mechanic at the R. C. Crothers Garage.

During World War I, Jones served in the U.S. military operations in France. After the war, he found a job as a garage mechanic. He had little or no training—he had always either figured out how things worked on his own or learned from on-the-job experiences. Early automobiles were awkward to start—a crank at the front of the car had to be wound to start the engine. Then the driver or an assistant had to run around and climb into the driver or passenger seat. Jones had the idea of inventing an automatic starter for a gas engine. His experience working as a mechanic helped him in the invention process.

Another early invention addressed the growing pains of another industry: the movies. In the late 1920s, most movie theaters were switching from silent films to "talkies." However, for the small theater owners, investing in new projection equipment to run the films that now had sound was a big financial problem. Jones invented a series of devices to adapt existing silent film projectors to sound projectors. The movie theater box office also benefited from Jones's innovation—an invention that spit out the tickets and also gave the customers back their change.

However, Jones's most famous and lucrative inventions supplied automatic refrigeration for mobile application. He invented a refrigerator that could be used for storing blood banks in military field hospitals. He also invented the first automatic refrigeration system for long-haul trucks and later ships and rail cars. Before he started experimenting with refrigeration devices in the late 1930s, truck refrigeration units were too big and wasted space inside the truck. Jones succeeded in reducing the size of the unit.

Along with Joseph Numero, Jones also founded the U.S. Thermo Control Company (later Thermo King) to manufacture his automatic air coolers for trains, ship, and airplanes, as well as other devices. Jones also developed ways to keep the air surrounding food at a constant temperature, devices that produced special atmospheric conditions to prevent fruit from drying out or becoming overripe before reaching supermarkets, and parts for existing refrigeration equipment.

Jones also invented an air-conditioning method (1954); starter generator for cooling gas engines (1949); two-cycle gasoline engine (1950); and thermostat design (1960).

Jones continued inventing and improving his designs in a productive, innovative lifetime of invention. He died on February 21, 1961. In a posthumous ceremony, he was awarded the National Medal of Technology, one of the highest and most coveted honors an inventor can receive.

Further Reading

Aaseng, Nathan. *Black Inventors*. New York: Facts On File, 1997.

"A cool man. A cool inventor. A cool project." Thermo-King website. Available online. URL: http://www.thermoking.com/features/mod/sum99/coolman.asp. Posted in summer 1999.

"Frederick M. Jones (1893–1961)," The Lemelson-MIT Prize Program: Inventor of the Week Archives. Available online. URL: http://web.mit.edu/invent/wwwjones.html. Posted in November 1996.

"Fred Jones," Black Inventor. Available online. URL: http://www.blackinventor.com/pages/fredjones.html. Downloaded on August 1, 2002.

Julian, Percy Lavon
(1899–1975)   *organic chemist*

As a research chemist, Percy Lavon Julian conducted trailblazing research on the synthesis of complex organic chemicals that have proved useful in both medicine and industry. His synthesis of the drug physostigmine has helped treat glaucoma, an eye ailment that often causes blindness. He synthesized a low-cost cortisone that helps relieve arthritis pain. His research facilitated the manufacture of the hormones testosterone and progesterone in large quantities. His research on the uses of soybeans led to the availability of many low-cost drugs and other new products, such as the use of soya protein to create a foam useful for fighting fires.

Born in Montgomery, Alabama, on April 11, 1899, Percy Lavon Julian was the first of six children in the Julian family. His father, James Julian, was a railroad mail clerk who expected nothing less than excellence from his children. Percy developed an early interest in chemistry, but his high school did not cover chemistry in its curriculum. In fact, young Julian had to take make-up high school classes when he entered DePauw University in Greencastle, Indiana, as a freshman in 1916. Despite this disadvantage and loss of time spent working part-time, when Julian graduated in 1920, he was elected to Phi Beta Kappa and was class valedictorian. However, finding a graduate school that would accept a black student turned out to be a discouraging task. So, instead of pursuing graduate studies, he took a position on the faculty of Fisk University, a highly respected black university in Nashville, Tennessee. To his surprise, he found teaching both challenging and rewarding.

In 1922, Julian won a one-year graduate fellowship to attend Harvard University, earning his master's degree in chemistry in one year. Denied a teaching assistantship because he was black, Julian put together enough small fellowships and scholarships to continue his studies at Harvard until 1926. He traveled to Austria and received his doctorate from the University of Vienna in 1931, returning to DePauw to continue his research in organic chemistry.

In 1935, with Josef Pikl, Julian first synthesized a chemical called physostigmine, or esserine, which could reduce pressure inside the eyeball, slowing or stopping the blinding effects of glaucoma, a disease that causes pressure to build up in the eye. The breakthrough brought him international recognition as a scientist. However, no university asked him to join its faculty as a professor.

A highly productive organic research chemist, Percy Lavon Julian (right) is best known for his synthesis of the drug physostigmine, which helps treat glaucoma, a serious eye ailment that can cause blindness. *(AP/Wide World Photos)*

Finally, he gave up trying to gain a faculty position and went to work for the Glidden Company as laboratory director. While there, he found a way to synthesize male and female hormones, testosterone and progesterone, from soy sterol. Julian also invented a foam made from soy protein that the military adopted for use against oil and gas fires.

When the Mayo Clinic announced in 1948 the discovery that the steroid cortisone was useful for treatment of rheumatoid arthritis, it was a big breakthrough but prohibitively expensive at hundreds of dollars for just a drop. Within months, Julian had found a way to synthesize a substitute for cortisone that was inexpensive to manufacture—yet fully as effective. The cost was just a few pennies an ounce.

By the end of his career, Julian owned more than 100 chemical patents and he had published dozens of technical and scientific papers describing his research. Among his many awards, the National Association for the Advancement of Colored People (NAACP) awarded him the Spingarn Medal in 1947. He was elected to the Distinguished Members Gallery Academy membership in 1973, and in 1974 he was winner of the Lemelson-NUT Prize Program. He founded Julian Laboratories, Inc., which maintained laboratories in both the United States and Mexico and a chemical plant in Guatemala.

Julian and his family moved to Oak Park, Illinois, in 1951. They were the first black family in town, and their house was firebombed twice. Today, however, Percy Julian Junior High School in Oak Park is named in his honor. Percy Lavon Julian died on April 19, 1975.

Further Reading

Hayden, Robert C. *Seven African-American Scientists.* Brookfield, Conn.: Twenty-First Century Books, 1992, 148–167.

Yount, Lisa. *Black Scientists.* New York: Facts On File, 1991, 41–53.

Just, Ernest Everett

(1883–1941) *zoologist, marine biologist, physiologist*

Often referred to by other scientists, as "a scientist's scientist," Ernest Everett Just was a pioneer researcher in the field of marine invertebrate embryology.

Just was born to Charles Frazier Just and Mary Matthews Just in Charleston, South Carolina, on August 14, 1883. Charles Just was a dockworker who died while Ernest was still a young boy. Mary, a teacher, took charge of Ernest's education at home during his childhood, raising him by herself after his father's untimely death.

Just began his formal schooling at age 13 and left South Carolina at 16 to attend Kimball Union Academy, a college-preparatory high school in Meriden, New Hampshire. One of the few African-Americans in the school, Just graduated from the four-year course in three years and enrolled in Dartmouth College in 1903.

Although his primary interest in prep school had been Greek and Latin, he began to find his life's work when he took his first science course, "The Principles of Biology," in his sophomore year. Once he had discovered science, Just never looked back. Gifted with natural curiosity, a strong sense of self-discipline, and a love of research, he had taken all the courses in biology the school had to offer by the time he received his bachelor's degree in zoology in 1907. Having graduated magna cum laude, Just accepted a teaching appointment at Howard University in Washington, D.C. It was the beginning of a long, if not always happy, association with the predominantly black university.

Although Just was a fine teacher, his first love was research, especially research into the development and growth of animal egg cells. This fascination, along with his desire to pursue work toward a Ph.D., led Just to Frank R. Lillie, head of the department of zoology at the University of

Working at the Marine Biological Laboratory in Woods Hole, Massachusetts, Ernest Everett Just completed thousands of experiments in his study of fertilization of the marine mammal cell. He challenged some of the leading theories of the time, and his work attracted international recognition. *(Marine Biological Laboratory Archives)*

Chicago. Lillie, who was also the head of the Marine Biological Laboratory at Woods Hole, Massachusetts, was immediately impressed with Just and invited him to spend the summer of 1909 at the Woods Hole Lab. Then, as today, Woods Hole was a world-renowned seaside lab that hosted many highly skilled scientists during the summer months, allowing them ample time for research away from their teaching or other chores. It was a perfect opportunity for Just to pursue his research interests in animal eggs. Over the next 20 years, he spent every summer except one at Woods Hole. With its idyllic setting, leisurely pace, and fine collection of stimulating minds, it became not only a perfect research laboratory for the scientist but a refuge as well.

When Just received a promotion to head the Department of Zoology at Howard in 1912, his

teaching load grew even heavier, and although he took a keen interest in his students, he was not really a teacher at heart. More fitted to hours of intense concentration in the laboratory with his beloved marine animal eggs, his most productive work was done at Woods Hole. In 1911, he had begun working at the lab as assistant to Lillie, researching the breeding habits and fertilization of sandworms and sea urchins. It was arranged that Just would receive credit toward his Ph.D. at the University of Chicago for his work at Woods Hole, and Lillie, by then a friend as well as coworker and supervisor, also encouraged Just to follow up on his own research interests.

On June 26, 1912, Just married Ethel Highwarden, who also taught at Howard, in the German department. Together they had three children, with whom Ethel Just usually remained in Washington, D.C., rather than travel with her husband during his research trips.

In 1912, Just published his first research paper in the *Biological Bulletin*, the laboratory's official journal. Over the years he would publish many more papers, becoming recognized by the scientific community as a leader in understanding the complexities of egg fertilization and development in marine animals.

In 1915, Just was honored by the National Association for the Advancement of Colored People (NAACP) as recipient of the first Spingarn Medal, an award given to recognize the achievements of men and women of African descent. The award would later be given to such prominent African Americans as Bill Cosby, Jesse Jackson, and Lena Horne. The Spingarn Medal brought Just national attention, but the quiet and studious biologist was uncomfortable with the publicity. In fact, in a letter to the NAACP prior to the award he wrote, "My contributions have been meager. It rather upsets me to learn that I am expected to be present at the award ceremony, doubtless in the presence of a large audience. I feel deeply that I ought not to court publicity, since courtship ought to be incompatible with scientific endeavor."

Always more interested in pure science than the honors and publicity that he often saw others assiduously cultivating, he knew that if he wanted to continue to expand his scientific work he would have to complete his Ph.D. He began taking classes at the University of Chicago in the academic year 1915–16 and, thanks to the credits that he had already earned while working at Woods Hole, received his Ph.D. in June of that year.

Just continued his research work at Woods Hole and his teaching duties at Howard over the next few years. His work at the marine laboratory continued to set standards and break new ground for other scientists to follow, but his teaching duties at Howard also absorbed much of his time and energy. Consequently, he began to seek grants from philanthropic foundations that would allow him to spend more time with his research. It was a bold step at the time, since no black scientist before him had ever received a grant for pure research in science. It was a tribute to the high esteem the scientific community had for Just that he was able to secure a series of grants during the 1920s. Most provided short-term funding, but they did allow him to cut his teaching duties at Howard in half and spend the rest of his time in pure research.

By 1929, however, Just began to feel he needed to expand beyond both Woods Hole and Howard. Few pure scientific research positions were open to African Americans, either in commercial or academic laboratories in the United States, and so he began to look toward Europe as a place where he might continue his career. Offered a position at the Zoological Station in Naples, Italy, he began work there that same year. The decision would mark a major change in his life.

The Zoological Station was in many ways like Woods Hole, but Just felt that working there included fewer of the discomforts and difficulties that he had often encountered as a black scientist in the United States. Although he had achieved eminence through his Woods Hole work and had even become a member of the corporation of the Marine Biological Laboratory and an editor of the *Biological Bulletin,* he had grown tired of fighting the prejudice against blacks, both obvious and subtle, that he found everywhere in American society and science. His work was well known and highly respected in Europe and a six-month stay the following year at the Kaiser Wilhelm Institute in Berlin as visiting professor became a personal high point in his life. The institute had a great history of Nobel Prize winners and many of them were still on its staff. Proud and demanding, the institute had never before invited an American to serve as a visiting professor.

In 1930 Just resigned his positions at both Woods Hole and Howard, feeling more comfortable and free with European society than with American. Although he would return very briefly to Woods Hole that same year for a party celebrating the 60th birthday of his friend and teacher, Frank Lillie, Just spent the rest of his professional scientific life at European institutes and universities.

Ironically, although he felt more at ease in Europe and enjoyed greater professional opportunities, most of his appointments were short ones. Grants were hard to come by in the depression-ridden 1930s, and the rise of the Nazi Party in Germany ended his work in that country after 1933. In permanent self-imposed semi-exile from the United States, he continued his research in Italy and France. Deciding to move to France for good in 1938, he took up an appointment at a marine research station operated by the Sorbonne, France's oldest academic institution. When Nazi Germany invaded France in 1940, the French government ordered all non-French scientists to leave the country. Just tried to comply but was cut short by the fall of Paris. Held briefly in a prisoner-of-war camp, he eventually was allowed to leave the country and return to the United States. Short on money and with nowhere else to go, he returned to Howard, where he was again immediately assigned to a strict teaching schedule. Ill and disillusioned, he died of stomach cancer on October 27, 1941.

Ernest Everett Just was a scientist who loved science more than anything else, a pure researcher who during his lifetime published more than 50 papers and two major books, *The Biology of the Cell Surface* and *Basic Methods for Experiments in Eggs of Marine Animals*. Yet, sadly, Just often tried to discourage his black students from following careers in pure science, advising them instead to go into other fields such as medicine, where he felt they would have a greater chance to succeed than in the rarified atmosphere of the white-dominated scientific world.

"Just's scientific career was a constant struggle for opportunity for research, the breath of his life," Frank Lillie wrote in the journal *Science* shortly after Just's death. Lillie went on to add, "An element of tragedy ran through all Just's scientific career due to the limitations imposed by being a Negro in America, to which he could make no lasting psychological adjustment despite earnest efforts on his part." In his own country, Just never received a position in a research institute or large university with the facilities he needed for his work. "He felt this a social stigma," Lillie wrote, "and hence unjust to a scientist of his recognized standing."

The fact that Just was ever expected to make a "psychological adjustment" to this injustice serves to emphasize the true tragedy of his life and career.

Further Reading

"Ernest Everett Just," Charleston Science Walk. Available online. URL: http://web2.ccpl.org/scienceproject/ScienceWalk/Ernest%20Everett%20Just.html. Downloaded on August 1, 2002.

"Ernest Just: Exploring the Human Cell," Inventor's Museum, © 1999. Available online. URL: http://www.inventorsmuseum.com/ErnestJust.htm. Downloaded on August 1, 2002.

"Ernest Everett Just," Faces of Science: African Americans in the Sciences. Available online. URL: http://www.princeton.edu/~mcbrown/display/just.html. Updated June 4, 2000.

Hayden, Robert C. *Seven African-American Scientists*. Brookfield, Conn.: Twenty-First Century Books, 1992.

Lillie, Frank R. "Ernest Everett Just," *Science* 95 (February 2, 1942): 10–11.

Manning, Kenneth R. *Black Apollo of Science: The Life of Ernest Everett Just*. New York: Oxford University Press, 1983.

Yount, Lisa. *Black Scientists*. New York: Facts On File, 1991, 28–40.

K

King, James, Jr.

(1933–) *physical chemist*

James King, Jr., has gained a reputation for expertise in the interactions of gases, both natural and synthetic. He has become an authority on atmospheric science and pollution. His management skills were key to his past successes in managing complex research programs at the Jet Propulsion Laboratory (JPL), as well as a research study for the Office of Manned Space Flight at the National Aeronautics and Space Administration (NASA).

James King, Jr., was born on April 23, 1933, in Columbus, Georgia, and that is where he grew up, went to elementary school and high school, and where his family lived. When he graduated from high school and enrolled in college at age 16, he chose nearby Morehouse College, a historically black college for men in nearby Atlanta. Although he initially set out to become a physician, he found he enjoyed chemistry and changed his major.

At age 20, King graduated with highest honors, receiving his B.S. in chemistry and mathematics from Morehouse. He decided it was time for a change. He had never been far from home and he had never attended an integrated school. So he chose a small university on the opposite coast with a nationally respected program in physical chemistry—California Institute of Technology (Caltech) in Pasadena, California. Because of his excellent record at Morehouse, he had the support of a General Education Board Scholarship from the Rockefeller Foundation and a Danforth Foundation Fellowship.

The experience produced a sizable culture shock. Far from home and just off a four-hour flight, he arrived in Pasadena only to be told there was no room available for him in the dormitory, an unpleasant surprise, since an arrangement had been made in advance, and the people behind him in line received rooms. He finally found a place to sleep on the gymnasium floor at the Young Men's Christian Association (YMCA).

During his studies at Caltech, he became interested in iron and how it combines with oxygen to form different types of rust under different conditions. For his dissertation, King investigated how iron and similar metals react with the complex organic molecules found in living cells. He received his master's degree in chemical physics in 1955 and his doctorate in chemistry and physics in 1958, both from Caltech.

After completing his doctorate, King joined Atomics International (a division of North American Aviation, Inc.), as a research engineer in electrochemistry. There, he devised a method for measuring temperature inside an atomic reactor—since an ordinary thermometer would not survive in that environment. As the Middle East oil crisis drove gasoline prices up in the 1960s, King joined a company that was engineering solar-powered cars. The potential market was short-lived, however, once the oil prices dropped. So King took a position at the JPL, managed by Caltech for NASA.

JPL provides NASA with consultant services, specializing primarily in solar system exploration. At JPL robot spacecraft are designed, built, and readied for spaceflight, although some aspects of the process are outsourced. JPL also tracks space probes as they travel to remote locations at other planets and return reports via radio signals and imaging. Engineers, scientists, and technicians there also build robots for exploring the ocean depths and satellite telescopes that look out into the universe from Earth orbit. The lab is also working on future space habitats and new propulsion systems.

King's project involved investigating the physical chemistry of hydrogen, a common ingredient in fuels. The study expanded to explore how gases, including hydrogen, react in the human body—an investigation that led King to devise a new theory for gas anesthesia and how it works.

The remaining body of King's scientific work involves gases and how they interact with other substances, including the influences that unreactive gases such as xenon can have on chemical reactions.

In 1969, James King became manager of the physics section of JPL. In 1974, in a sense "on loan" to NASA, King moved to Washington, D.C., where he directed the space shuttle environmental effects program for NASA's Office of Manned Space Flight. His experience with investigating gases and their reactions contributed insights to directors who wanted to make sure that the shuttle would not disturb important atmospheric conditions during launch, orbiting, or descent.

After two years in Washington, King returned to JPL, where he obtained experience managing several different research programs, including atmospheric science, astronomy and astrophysics, and general space science and its applications to practical problems. He gained a reputation as an outstanding manager, and the experience both broadened his knowledge of these subjects and sharpened his management skills.

In 1984, King left on a two-year project at his alma mater, Morehouse College. There he helped set up a new curriculum for teaching and research in atmospheric science.

In 1988, after his return to JPL, King was named as senior technical manager for the Space Science and Applications Program. In 1993, he became director of engineering and science at JPL, where he oversaw more than 4,000 personnel—including scientists and engineers. In this capacity, one of his policy concerns revolved around pollution control, again drawing on his knowledge of natural and synthetic gases and their interactions. He has also worked on pollution reduction in the Los Angeles area.

In 1993, King was named Technologist of the Year by the National Technical Association.

Further Reading

Hawkins, Walter L. *African American Biographies, 2.* Jefferson, N.C.: McFarland & Co., 1994.

Kessler, James H., J. S. Kidd, Renee A. Kidd, and Katherine A. Morin. *Distinguished African American Scientists of the 20th Century.* Phoenix, Ariz.: Oryx Press, 1996.

Sammons, Vivian Ovelton. *Blacks in Science and Medicine.* New York: Hemisphere Publishing, 1990.

King, Reatha Belle Clark
(1938–) *chemist, educator, administrator*

Trained in thermochemistry (a branch of physical science that studies the energy changes that occur when a chemical reaction takes place), Reatha

Clark King has published numerous papers on fluorine flame calorimetry and other aspects of her field. As an educator, she has shown her dedication to the educational process in her vocal advocacy and her years as a college chemistry teacher and academic dean. As an administrator of an international grant-making organization, she has guided commitments to education, continuing education, family life, health and nutrition, arts, and cultural affairs.

Reatha Belle Clark was born on April 11, 1938 in Pabo, a town in rural Georgia. She was the middle child of three sisters born to Willie and Ola Watts Campbell Clark. The girls and their mother moved to Moultree, Georgia, after the parents divorced. During her childhood, Reatha and her sisters worked long and tiring summer hours in the cotton and tobacco fields to earn money. She has said that perhaps this arduous work helped build her stamina and give her the perseverance to keep going.

Clark originally thought she might teach home economics in her local high school. However, when she attended Clark College in Atlanta, she fell in love with chemistry and decided to change goals. She received her B.S. in chemistry and mathematics in 1958 from Clark College. She received a Woodrow Wilson Fellowship to continue with graduate studies in chemistry at the University of Chicago, where she obtained her M.S. in 1960 and her Ph.D. in thermochemistry in 1963. In 1961 she married N. Judge King, Jr., and they later had two sons.

Reatha King began her first professional work as a research chemist with the National Bureau of Standards in Washington, D.C., from 1963 to 1968. Her early research centered on fluoride chemistry that became useful in the space program. Her work involved the development of a substance that could be used to protect containers of the highly corrosive substance oxygen difluoride. She also researched other fluoride compounds and similar compounds that had applications for use in rocketry in the space

program. Willing to work long hours, even overnight if rush results were needed, King was known for both her perseverance and professionalism. For a paper she wrote on fluoride flame calorimetry she won the Meritorious Publication Award.

In 1968, she joined the chemistry faculty of York College of the City University of New York. She also served as associate dean for the division of Natural Sciences and Mathematics from 1970 to 1974 and as associate dean for academic affairs from 1974 to 1977.

For 11 years, from 1977 to 1988, she was president of Metropolitan State University at St. Paul and Minneapolis, Minnesota. During this time she obtained an M.B.A. in 1977 from the

As a young research chemist, Reatha Clark King's work with fluoride contributed to the space program. *(Courtesy of Reatha Clark King)*

King holds both a Ph.D. in thermochemistry from the University of Chicago (1963) and an M.B.A. from the Columbia University Graduate School of Business (1977). After several years as a science educator and university administrator, in 1988 King took the helm of the philanthropic General Mills Foundation. There she has shown her gifts as a persuasive spokesperson for the sciences and education, especially in the lives of minorities. *(Courtesy of Reatha Clark King)*

Columbia University Graduate School of Business in New York, with concentrations in finance and management of organizations.

In November 1988, King was named president and executive director of the General Mills Foundation, and she is also vice president of General Mills, Inc. The foundation was established in 1954 to make grants to tax-exempt organizations in support of positive civic efforts, such as education, planned low-cost housing, health, and nutrition. King is CEO of the organization and she is responsible for directing the company's $45 million citizenship and charitable giving program.

King is a member of the American Association for the Advancement of Science, the American Chemistry Society, the National Organization of Professional Advancement of Black Chemists and Chemical Engineers, the science honorary society Sigma Xi, and the Exxon/Mobil Corporation board of directors.

She has served on many committees, councils, and boards. King has also received many awards and honors, including 14 honorary doctorate degrees. She received the Exceptional Black Scientist Award from the CIBA-GEIGY Corporation in 1984, and the University of Chicago Alumni Association presented her with the Professional Achievement Award in 1988. In 1999, the Minneapolis *Star Tribune* named her as one of the 100 Most Influential Minnesotans of the Century, and in 2001 she was inducted into the National Black College Alumni Hall of Fame.

Reatha Clark King has really had three careers, but she believes that her training as a scientist formed a vital part of her education. She has said, "Young people especially often fail to realize that scientific education is flexible and that it can prepare one to function in various careers."

A strong advocate for universal education, King is often quoted as saying, "I realized early in life that education is our best enabling resource, that technical skills are important, and that my stamina for championing educational opportunity for all people is inexhaustible."

Further Reading

Hawkins, Walter L. *African American Biographies.* Jefferson, N.C.: McFarland & Co., 1992.

Henderson, A. N., ed. *Who's Who Among African Americans,* 14th ed. Detroit: Gale Group, 2001.

Narins, Brigham, ed. *Notable Scientists: From 1900 to the Present,* 2nd ed. Farmington Hills, Mich.: Gale Group, 2001, 1225–26.

Warren, Wini. *Black Women Scientists in the United States.* Bloomington: Indiana University Press, 1999, 150–153.

Kittrell, Flemmie Pansy

(1904–1980) *nutritionist, educator*

An internationally influential nutritionist and home economist, Flemmie Pansy Kittrell helped transform home economics from farmhouse adjunct of the farm to a respected, scientific discipline that applied results from scientifically controlled studies to real-world problems. A woman of great energy and vision, she applied her insights to nutrition deficiencies in Africa and the phenomenon of "hidden hunger." She encouraged cooperation among people to solve problems, whether at the national level or at the cross-disciplinary academic level. And she recognized the importance of the early childhood environment, helping to start the beginnings of the Head Start program.

Flemmie Kittrell was born to Alice Mills Kittrell and James L. Kittrell on December 25, 1904, in Henderson, North Carolina. She was the seventh of nine children. After graduating from high school with honors, Kittrell entered Hampton Institute (now University) in Hampton, Virginia. She majored in home economics and her professors were impressed with her abilities, encouraging her to enter the graduate program at Cornell University in Ithaca, New York, after completing her B.S. from Hampton in 1928.

However, Kittrell was not so sure about graduate school—she knew it would be lonely in Ithaca and Cornell had no graduate program in home economics per se, just nutrition. Nutrition had always been her least favorite area of home economics. Also, not only were there few African-American graduate students at Cornell, but there were even fewer female African-American students. She decided to face the challenge, however, and she earned her M.A. in 1930 and her Ph.D. in nutrition with honors in 1938.

Before leaving for Ithaca, Kittrell had been offered a teaching position by Bennett College in Greensboro, North Carolina, and she went back there in 1938, moving to Hampton Institute in 1940 to fill the position of dean of women and head of the home economics department.

In 1944, she received an offer from the president of Howard University in Washington, D.C., for a position as head of the home economics department. Especially with this appointment Kittrell saw ways she could begin to change the way people viewed home economics as a university discipline. She did not accept any of the usual classifications. It was not just a smattering of biology, simplified chemistry, and developmental psychology. Nor did it have to be the distaff side of agriculture, although the discipline had been viewed this way at many land grant colleges because extension services from the U.S. Department of Agriculture extended to home economics. To Kittrell, home economics was, or should be, more like engineering and medicine—a field of research producing results that are applicable to real-life problems. Kittrell also saw a special need for trained home economists in rural areas, where low-income and minority families could become very isolated and would have need of the services of research outreach programs. At Howard, she began to redesign the curriculum along these lines and made use of her position to gain leadership in the field.

At Howard, Kittrell established one of the earliest cross-disciplinary efforts at the university level. She encouraged communication among the departments and schools at the university and shared resources and encouraged course offerings that supported other disciplines.

She also established a nursery school program at Howard. It was the basis for child development studies and similar research, and it also provided a training ground for students. Kittrell did carefully controlled scientific studies that eventually led the way to programs such as Head Start.

In 1946, the extension of Kittrell's range of influence to a worldwide audience began. The U.S. Department of State invited her to head a six-month survey of nutrition in Liberia, in West Africa. She found undernourishment and

PRESTON RIDGE LIBRARY
COLLIN COLLEGE
FRISCO, TX 75035

extensive deficiencies in protein and vitamins. Out of this study emerged international recognition of a condition known as "hidden hunger," malnourishment on a full stomach. The sufferer may feel full but is not ingesting the nutrients his or her body needs.

The worldwide significance of the studies and the concept of "hidden hunger" rapidly spread internationally. Kittrell set to work trying to facilitate ways to provide informational support and training for organizations and governments that wanted to help improve conditions in areas where hidden hunger was rampant.

Again at the request of the State Department, in 1950 Kittrell helped establish a college-level training program for home economists in India. In 1962, at the establishment of independence in the Congo, a Methodist group invited Kittrell to help start new institutions for higher learning—in particular with a curriculum for home economics, ensuring that women would be allowed to enroll in the schools.

At Howard, Kittrell also encouraged the university to recruit international students, especially in home economics, and as the international community at Howard began to grow, the university began to build an international reputation in the field.

Kittrell retired from Howard in 1972, becoming professor emeritus of nutrition. She continued to work, however, serving as a Visiting Senior Fellow at Cornell from 1974 to 1976 and as Moton Center Senior Research Fellow in 1977. In 1978, she traveled to India as a Fulbright lecturer.

Among the many honors awarded her, the American Home Economics Association founded a scholarship fund in her honor. Flemmie Pansy Kittrell died of a heart attack on October 3, 1980, in Washington, D.C.

Further Reading

Kessler, James H., J. S. Kidd, Renee A. Kidd, and Katherine A. Morin. *Distinguished African American Scientists of the 20th Century.* Phoenix, Ariz.: Oryx Press, 1996.

Sammons, Vivian Ovelton. *Blacks in Science and Medicine.* New York: Hemisphere Publishing Corp., 1990.

Warren, Wini. *Black Women Scientists in the United States.* Bloomington: Indiana University Press, 1999, 153–174.

Knox, William Jacob, Jr.
(1904–1995) *chemist*

William Knox's contributions to chemistry span two different areas. Early in his career, Knox worked on the Manhattan Project during World War II. He was charged with preparing the uranium for use in the nuclear weapon that was under development. After the war, working for Eastman Kodak, Knox became an expert on surfactants, a type of chemical that plays a key role in manufacturing photographic film. During his years at Kodak, Knox received patents at a rate of nearly one per year—21 patents in about 25 years.

Born in New Bedford, Massachusetts, on January 5, 1904, William Jacob Knox, Jr., was the oldest of three boys. All three attended Harvard, and William's two brothers earned Ph.D.s from Harvard. Everett, who took his degree in history, enjoyed a diplomatic career. Lawrence completed a degree in chemistry. William attended Harvard as an undergraduate and received his B.S. in chemistry in 1925. Then, he taught chemistry for three years at Johnson C. Smith University, from 1925 to 1928, returning to school for graduate studies at the Massachusetts Institute of Technology (MIT). In just one year he had completed his M.S. degree in 1929. After teaching at Atlanta University for a couple of years, he returned to MIT and completed his Ph.D. in physical chemistry in 1935. During the following eight years he served as head of the department of chemistry at the Agricultural and Industrial College of North Carolina and later at Talladega College in Alabama.

As the United States became deeply involved in World War II, William Knox received a call in 1943 to join a team at Columbia University in New York that was working on an atomic bomb. The team needed Knox to help solve a fundamental problem with the uranium ore they planned to use. Uranium ore contains uranium, but like any ore it is not pure. Also, uranium occurs in nature in one of two natural isotopes: U235 or U238. The second, U238, weighs a little more but is chemically the same as U235, but with one big difference: U238 can sustain the chain reaction that is needed. U235 cannot. The question was: how could they separate the two isotopes so they could have pure U238?

Since the two types of uranium were chemically the same, no chemical method for separating them would work. The weight difference, though tiny, was the only avenue open. The Manhattan Project team ended up using gaseous diffusion, a complex process that made use of uranium hexafluoride, an extremely corrosive material, to achieve the separation of the two types of uranium. As a result, corrosive substances became Knox's area of expertise.

After the war, in 1945, Knox accepted a position on the research staff of Eastman Kodak in Rochester, New York. There, he began a lengthy study of surfactants, or wetting agents. Photographic film requires the use of various emulsions to do its job. Wetting agents help emulsions to wet or spread out and cling to the surface beneath them. This promotes a good bond. If the surfactants work well, the various layers of emulsion spread evenly and a clear image is produced. Because so many factors are involved in the complicated process of manufacturing film, the studies required for answering all the "what-if" questions took many years. Knox, who became known as Kodak's surfactant expert, continued

to work on questions related to surfactants until he retired in 1970.

William Jacob Knox, Jr., died of prostate cancer in July 1995 at the age of 91.

Further Reading

Henderson, Ashyia N., ed. *Who's Who Among African Americans,* 14th ed. Detroit: Gale Group, 2001.

Heppenheimer, T. A. "William Jacob Knox, Jr.," *Notable Black American Scientists.* Kristine Krapp, ed. Detroit: Gale Research, 1999, 191–192.

Sammons, Vivian Ovelton. *Blacks in Science and Medicine.* New York: Hemisphere Publishing, 1990.

Kornegay, Wade M.
(1934–) *engineering physicist*

Wade Kornegay, a recognized expert on ballistic missile defense, served as head of the Radar Measurements Division of the Lincoln Laboratory at the Massachusetts Institute of Technology (MIT) from 1993 to 2000. For more than 30 years he has researched technical issues affecting bodies as they re-enter Earth's atmosphere during ballistic flight. He has served on several advisory committees for the U.S. Department of Defense and in 1991 he was appointed to the Army Science Board.

Wade Kornegay was born on January 9, 1934 in Mt. Olive, North Carolina, the sixth of nine children. At an early age, he and his brothers and sisters suffered the death of both their parents, Estelle Williams Kornegay and Gilbert Kornegay. After the death of their mother in 1940, the children lived with their maternal grandmother in rural North Carolina. As a young man, Wade Kornegay knew that success required a good education and, encouraged by his teachers, he entered North Carolina Central University, graduating summa cum laude. After a year of study as a Fulbright Fellow at Bonn

University in Germany, he returned to the United States to work on his doctorate at the University of California at Berkeley (UCB), receiving his Ph.D. in 1961. He received a Danforth Fellowship that covered all his graduate years, and then a National Science Foundation postdoctoral fellowship supported an additional year of study at UCB, and a research associateship in 1962 provided another half year of postgraduate work.

At Berkeley, Kornegay investigated the processes by which inert gases, such as xenon and krypton, can form new compounds, even though ordinarily they are nonreactive and do not combine. However, heating these elements to very high temperatures can cause reactions.

In 1962, Kornegay embarked upon a lifelong career researching aspects of ballistic missile defense, serving as a technical staff member at MIT from 1962 to 1971, and becoming technical group leader of Radar Signature Studies from 1971 to 1986. Kornegay's earlier work with chemical compounds had led into examination of radar signature recognition—recognizing objects on a radar screen by identifying properties called a signature. An object's chemical makeup and the trail it produces when traveling in the atmosphere at several times the speed of sound are part of its radar signature, so military researchers made use of these concepts in missile detection and retaliation, a process of particular concern during the cold war period when the U.S. military maintained continual preparedness for possible missile attacks from the Soviet Union. Much of Kornegay's work in this area and other investigations he has made into ballistic missile detection and reentry physics are classified and not available in the open literature.

Kornegay completed a program of study at the MIT Sloan School of Management in 1979, and in 1986, he became associate division head and then head of Radar Measurements at MIT's Lincoln Laboratory from 1993 to 2000, where he is now division fellow.

Kornegay received an honorary doctorate from Lowell University in 1969, as well as the Black Achiever Award from the Boston Young Men's Christian Association (YMCA) in 1979, the M. L. King, Jr., Achievement Award from the Massachusetts Institute of Technology in 1980, and the Scientist of the Year award from the National Society of Black Engineers in 1990.

Further Reading

"Ballistics expert speaks on 21st century challenges for minority engineers," *University of California at Berkeley Engineering News* (summer 1998). Available online. URL: http://coe.berkeley.edu/EPA/EngNews/98S/EN10S/kornegay.html. Updated on March 30, 1998.

Edwards, K. R., and W. M. Kornegay, "Measurements, Phenomenology and Discrimination," *Lincoln Laboratory Journal* 12, no. 1 (2002): 75–108.

Henderson, Ashyia N., ed. *Who's Who Among African Americans*, 14th ed. Detroit: Gale Group, 2001, 762.

Kessler, James H., J. S. Kidd, Renee A. Kidd, and Katherine A. Morin. *Distinguished African American Scientists of the 20th Century.* Phoenix, Ariz.: Oryx Press, 1996.

Norwood, R. L., and V. P. Manuel, "Standing on the Frontline," *Journal of the National Technical Association*, spring 1989, pp. 15–16.

Kountz, Samuel Lee, Jr.
(1930–1981) *medical researcher, surgeon*

Renowned as a kidney transplant specialist, Samuel Kountz transplanted more than a thousand kidneys. He developed a method for monitoring the blood supply to the transplanted kidney following surgery so that drugs can be administered to control rejection at the moment when needed and in the necessary amount. His journey from a small rural town in Arkansas that had no doctor to become an internationally recognized expert and consummate surgeon is remarkable.

Samuel Lee Kountz, Jr., was born on October 20, 1930, in Lexa, Arkansas, a tiny, poor, entirely African-American town having a population of fewer than 100 people. Because the town had no doctor, Kountz's father, Samuel Lee Kountz, Sr., used to function as a nurse when neighbors became ill. Educational resources in the town were also poor, and even though young Kountz hoped to become a doctor, he failed to pass the entrance exam for Arkansas A&M College. However, he appealed to the college president, who made an exception and admitted him. It was soon obvious it was a good decision since Kountz graduated third in his class, even though he had needed to work waiting tables to support himself.

Kountz attended Arkansas Medical School in Little Rock on scholarship—the first African American ever to enroll there. He completed an M.S. in biochemistry in 1956 and his M.D. in 1958, traveling across the country to the West Coast to intern at San Francisco General Hospital for two years. He completed his residency at Stanford Medical Center near Palo Alto, California in 1965.

During his internship, he had assisted in 1959 at the first West Coast kidney transplant. At that time, renal (kidney) transplant surgery was still new and seldom successful. Transplants in animals had been done since 1902 (Austria), and the first human transplant was performed in the Soviet Union (now Russia) in 1936. However, only since 1954 had kidney transplants succeeded in humans, and then only between either identical (preferably) or fraternal twins. The overwhelming problem was that the human body tends to reject transplanted organs. Not until immunosuppressant drugs became available did successes begin to occur between donor-recipient pairs who were not siblings. While in residency at Stanford, Kountz began investigating the rejection process. He found that by administering large amounts of methylprednisolone, a steroid, following surgery, the rejection process could be reversed.

Kountz also discovered, through close observation, that rejection took place on the cell level—and that uncommitted cells in the host body actually attacked and destroyed the fine network of blood vessels connecting the kidney to the rest of the body. As a result, the kidney died from lack of blood. By monitoring blood levels in the transplanted kidney, the surgical team can tell when to administer reversing drugs and what dosage to use. Before Kountz and his colleagues developed this system for arresting rejection, 95 percent of renal transplant patients did not survive for more than two years.

In 1967, Kountz also worked with a colleague, Folker Belzer, to design a method that could maintain a donated human kidney in functioning condition for more than 48 hours, allowing time for transportation to an appropriate recipient. It was another important step to help more patients in need of a renal transplant.

After his residency, Kountz remained at Stanford as associate professor of surgery until 1967, when he became associate professor at the University of California at San Francisco. There he built one of the largest centers in the country for training and research in kidney transplant surgery. In 1972, Kountz accepted a position of full professor of surgery and department chair at the State University of New York Downstate Medical Center in Brooklyn. He also served as chief of surgery at Kings County Hospital Center. During the course of his career, he wrote some 179 scientific published papers documenting his research.

Tragically, Kountz sustained brain damage from a disease he contracted while teaching in South Africa in 1977 and never completely recovered. On December 23, 1981, he died at home in Great Neck, New York. He was 51, a great pioneer whose surgical skill saved hundreds of lives and whose innovations for overcoming rejection and extending transport time for replacement kidneys create a legacy that secures his place in medical history.

Further Reading

Brown, Mitchell C. "Dr. Samuel Lee Kountz, Jr.: Kidney Specialist," Faces of Science: African Americans in the Sciences. (Contains bibliography of 172 scientific publications by Kountz.) Available online. URL: http://www.princeton.edu/~mcbrown/display/kountz.html. Updated on June 4, 2000.

"Dr. Samuel Kountz," *San Francisco Chronicle*, December 25, 1981, 42.

Kessler, James H., J. S. Kidd, Renee A. Kidd, and Katherine A. Morin. *Distinguished African American Scientists of the 20th Century*. Phoenix, Ariz.: Oryx Press, 1996.

LIBRARY
COLLIN COLLEGE
FRISCO, TX 75035

L

Langford, George Malcolm
(1944–) *cell biologist*

Through research completed primarily at Dartmouth College, cell biologist George Langford and his research team have made breakthrough discoveries on intracellular motility—movement processes with cells.

Born to Maynard and Lillie Langford on August 26, 1944, in Halifax, North Carolina, George Malcolm Langford grew up in a nurturing, rural environment. He attended Fayetteville State University as an undergraduate, receiving his B.S. degree in biology in 1966. He then traveled to Illinois Institute of Technology for graduate studies, completing his M.S. degree there in 1969 and his Ph.D. degree in cellular biology in 1971. He continued with postgraduate studies for two years at the University of Pennsylvania.

Langford accepted his first academic appointment at the University of Massachusetts at Boston in 1973, joining the faculty as an assistant professor. From 1977 to 1979 he taught at Howard University, and then joined the faculty at the University of North Carolina at Chapel Hill in 1979 as associate professor, with a promotion to full professor in 1988. In 1991, he became E.E. Just Professor (named for ERNEST EVERETT JUST) of Natural Sciences in biology

and physiology on the faculty at Dartmouth (where his wife Sylvia is a dean).

In his research on intracellular motility, Langford has had a particular interest in nerve cells, first introduced to him by the famous embryologist Jean Dan, whom Langford met when they were both in Chicago. He has continued exploring this field ever since. In 1992, he had what he has described as a "Eureka!" moment. Late one night, he was looking through his microscope when he noticed a system of movement within the cells that no one else had ever documented. "I could see bundles of proteins moving along like trucks on invisible highways," he later remarked. He found that the mechanism was a protein that resembles myosin, the motor protein in muscles. The implications of Langford's discovery are of great interest for scientists studying the movements within cells and trying to understand how the traffic is controlled or what the mechanism is that causes and directs the movements.

Langford's work has earned him several honors. He was appointed program director for Cell Biology for the National Science Foundation in 1988 and 1989. Since early in his career he has had a summer laboratory at the prestigious Marine Biological Laboratory at Woods Hole, Massachusetts. He also served as chair of the Woods Hole council for a time.

Langford is also a strong advocate for building the minority presence in the sciences. He founded an internship program for minorities at Dartmouth, the E. E. Just Program, named after zoologist and marine biologist Ernest Everett Just, a Dartmouth graduate. He also chairs the Minorities Affairs committee of the American Society for Cell Biology, which is concerned with attracting minorities to the sciences. However, Langford is critical of the reception minorities receive. Obstacles still exist, he says, and, like E. E. Just, minority scientists still struggle for recognition and funding for their research. Langford has found that exchanges and research trips to other countries, where these prejudices are less pronounced to nonexistent, can be helpful.

Further Reading

"George M. Langford, Ph.D." Dartmouth College Faculty. Available online. URL: http://www.dartmouth.edu/dms/physiol/faculty/langford.html. Downloaded on April 23, 2002.

Gibbons, Ann. "Building a global lab," *Science* 262 (November 12, 1993): 1,111.

Kessler, James H., J. S. Kidd, Renee A. Kidd, and Katherine A. Morin. *Distinguished African American Scientists of the 20th Century.* Phoenix, Ariz.: Oryx Press, 1996.

Latimer, Lewis Howard

(1848–1928) *inventor*

Lewis H. Latimer began in the world of invention by using his skills in drafting to draw up the patent design for Alexander Graham Bell's telephone. Before long, he had begun to develop inventions of his own, including a long-lasting filament for the electric lightbulb—an important improvement over the filament used by Thomas Edison.

Lewis Howard Latimer was born on September 4, 1848, in Chelsea, Massachusetts. His parents, George and Rebecca Latimer, were escaped slaves from Virginia who settled in Boston in 1842. The couple's fourth child, Lewis attended school until the age of 10 when the family's lack of money forced him to quit and aid his father, who worked days in a barbershop and evenings as a paperhanger. When his father abandoned the family shortly afterward, Rebecca had to take a job as a steward on an oceangoing ship and Lewis was sent to a farm school in the western part of Massachusetts. He hated the school and ran away after a few years, finding his way back to Boston. Although the Civil War was nearing its conclusion, Latimer succeeded in joining the Union navy by lying about his age. When the war ended in 1865, he returned to Boston and began to seek work, along with many other black and white former enlisted men.

After fruitless months of searching, he finally found a job as an office helper in the patent firm of Crosby and Gould, which specialized in preparing the legal documents and detailed drawings for patent applications. The job changed the direction of his life.

Latimer soon became fascinated with the work of the draftspeople in the office as they prepared the complex and intricate drawings necessary to explain various inventions. He watched their work as he went about his own daily job and spent his evenings teaching himself until he was able to duplicate their careful, accurate drawings. Finding a chance one day to show what he could do, Latimer demonstrated his newly acquired skill and was promoted to draftsperson, soon becoming one of the most skilled in the office.

One of Crosby and Gould's clients was Alexander Graham Bell, then seeking a patent on his telephone. It was Latimer who was assigned to work with the inventor and execute the finely detailed drawings necessary for Bell's patent application. The two men spent long hours together, days and nights, carefully going over all the invention's details.

By this time Latimer had also begun to work on inventions of his own. At the age of 26 he was awarded his first patent for an improvement on water closets in railway cars. It was electricity, however, that most captured his interest—in particular, Thomas Edison's 1879 invention of the electric lamp.

That same year, Latimer left Crosby and Gould to go to work for another firm that appeared to offer better opportunities. Unfortunately, the firm went bankrupt shortly after Latimer joined it. His luck tuned better when, after months of seeking employment, he found a position as draftsperson in a small machine shop. There, a visitor to the shop took notice of his work. The visitor was Hiram Maxim, the inventor of the machine gun, and also the founder and chief electrician for the U.S. Electric Lighting Company. Immediately impressed with Latimer's skill, Maxim was doubly impressed to find that Latimer had previously worked for Crosby and Gould, a firm whose work he knew and respected. Maxim was looking for highly skilled draftspeople at the time and offered Latimer a job.

Maxim's company was one of the earliest to get involved in the electrical industry, quickly building up in the wake of Edison's inventions, and Maxim was hoping to take over Edison's lead in the field to reap the obvious rewards. One of the biggest problems in the fledgling industry centered on the electric lightbulb. The problem was the short life span of the carbon filament that heated up inside the vacuum bulb to produce light. The filament tended to burn out so quickly that the electrical lightbulb was little more than an interesting gadget. It was this problem that occupied much of the attention of Maxim's company at the time.

Although officially a draftsperson, Latimer's interest in the problem, along with his extensive knowledge based on his reading, soon secured him a place on Maxim's development team. Hundreds of experiments and failures later, La-

timer found the answer. His improved carbon filament was given a patent in September 1881. Not included in the patent, but of great importance to the U.S. Electric Light Company, were the methods Latimer devised for producing the filaments both faster and cheaper.

Promoted to the position of chief engineer in the company, Latimer soon was placed in charge of supervising the installation of electrical lights in businesses, railroad stations, city facilities, and city streets all over the country.

The son of escaped slaves, Lewis Latimer received his first patent at age 26. He is best known for inventing an improved, longer lasting filament for Edison's newly invented electric lightbulb. *(The Queens Borough Public Library, Long Island Division, and Latimer Family Collection)*

The honeymoon with U.S. Electric soon came to an end, however, when Maxim began taking credit for innovations and inventions proposed by Latimer. It was not, and still is not, an uncommon practice for an employer or company to claim credit for an employee's work, but to Latimer it seemed an extremely unjust policy. He left U.S. Electric in 1882.

Two years later, in an ironic twist of fate Latimer found himself working for Thomas Edison. Working with Edison's legal department, Latimer had the job of inspecting and investigating patent claims made by Edison's rivals in upcoming court cases against Edison. As part of the job, Latimer also prepared the technical drawings that were to be used as supporting evidence for Edison during court trials and often was called upon as an expert witness. One of his biggest victories was against Maxim, by then one of Edison's major rivals.

Latimer left Edison's employment in 1912, after serving 30 years in the company. In his final years with Edison, he found time to write the first major handbook on electric lighting, *Incandescent Electric Lighting: A Practical Description of the Edison System,* published in 1890.

Lewis Latimer died on December 11, 1928. On May 10, 1968, the Lewis H. Latimer Public School in Brooklyn, New York, was named in his honor.

Further Reading

Aaseng, Nathan. *Black Inventors.* New York: Facts On File, 1997.

"African-American Inventors Database," Great Lakes Patent and Trademark Center. Available online. URL: http://www.detroit.lib.mi.us/glptc/aaid/index.asp?Inventor=Latimer&Invention=. Downloaded on February 5, 2002.

Hayden, Robert. *Nine African-American Inventors.* New York: Twenty-First Century Books, 1992.

"Lewis Howard Latimer," Faces of Science: African Americans in the Sciences. Available online. URL: http://www.princeton.edu/~mcbrown/display/latimer.html. Updated on June 4, 2000.

"Lewis Howard Latimer," The Lemelson-MIT Prize Program: Inventor of the Week Archives. Available online. URL: http://w3.mit.edu/invent/www/inventorsI-Q/latimer.html. Posted on November 1996.

"Lewis Latimer: Bringing Light to the World," The Inventor's Museum. Available online. URL: http://www.inventorsmuseum.com/LewisLatimer.htm. Updated in 1999.

"Lewis H. Latimer—Super Scientist Biography," California State Energy Department Energy Quest. Available online. URL: http://www.energy.ca.gov/education/scientists/latimer.html. Downloaded on February 15, 2001.

Sullivan, Otha Richard. *African American Inventors.* Black Stars series, Jim Haskins, ed. New York: John Wiley & Sons, 1998.

Lawson, James Raymond
(1915–1996) *physicist, educator*

As a physicist, James Raymond Lawson made his mark in the field of experimental infrared spectroscopy, building an impressive infrared spectroscopy program at Fisk University. He also took the helm at Fisk as president during turbulent times and later served as director of the University Affairs Office for the National Aeronautics and Space Administration (NASA).

Born in Louisville, Kentucky, on January 15, 1915, James Raymond Lawson was the son of Daniel Lamont Lawson and Daisy Harris Lawson. Daniel Lawson was a teacher, a Fisk University graduate, and a former member of the Jubilee Singers, a group of gospel singers at Fisk, which is located in Nashville, Tennessee.

James Lawson chose Fisk University as well for his undergraduate studies, completing his bachelor's degree in physics in 1935. At Fisk, he studied under ELMER SAMUEL IMES, the department chair, who had done his graduate work at the University of Michigan, where Lawson also chose to pursue his graduate studies. After completing his master's degree in 1936, Lawson received a Julius Rosenwald fellowship, which helped him continue with his doctoral work.

For his dissertation, Lawson chose far infrared spectroscopy. (Imes had done his work in *near* infrared spectroscopy—using the shortest infrared wavelengths. Lawson examined objects using the far infrared portion of the spectrum, the longest infrared wavelengths.)

Historically, the first spectroscopy was done with visible light waves, and this choice worked very well for identifying atoms of specific elements. However, Lawson and his dissertation adviser, Harrison M. Randall, were interested in examining complex molecules, such as methyl alcohol. These molecules could not be detected using visible light spectroscopy, or even the near infrared, which worked so well on simple molecules. However, at the time, new instruments had to be developed for examination in the far infrared, and new techniques and innovations were required. Lawson succeeded in solving these problems and received the Ph.D. degree in 1939 for his pioneering work in this field.

Lawson began his career in college teaching and research at Southern University at Baton Rouge, Louisiana, where he was assistant professor for one year, 1939–40. The following year he became associate professor at Langston University in Langston, Oklahoma, where he taught from 1940 to 1942. In the fall of 1941, Imes had died and Fisk invited Lawson to head the physics department as of the following academic year. Lawson accepted.

As department head, Lawson had a vision. Fisk had always held a flagship position among the historically black colleges and its reputation was well deserved. But Lawson realized that a program in infrared spectroscopy could put Fisk at the cutting edge of this exciting field. He found out that the University of Michigan was having two new infrared spectrometers built by a team of researchers. These instruments would be research-grade equipment, capable not only of observing infrared radiation emissions but also would be equipped to measure their intensity. Lawson checked to see if the team could build a third spectroscope of the same caliber. Then he obtained approval to purchase it for the Fisk physics department. The maneuver had real possibilities for attracting excellent students who would be interested in pioneering in this field. Few instruments of this type or of this quality existed anywhere. Lawson applied for research grants and convinced five seniors to accept a grant to stay and work with the new spectroscope while earning a master's degree. He founded the Fisk Infrared Research Laboratory, which by 1950 had become the Fisk Infrared Research Institute, adding a summer program that offered training to other scientists on the new equipment.

Oddly, though, at about this time Lawson accepted an offer to chair the department of a rival school, Tennessee Agricultural and Industrial State University. It was a strange move to make in the midst of his plans for building the Fisk Infrared Research Institute, and he had not discussed it with Fisk. Angered, the Fisk president fired him.

At Tennessee Agricultural and Industrial State University, Lawson started building another infrared laboratory. By 1957, Lawson was back at Fisk as department chair.

Ten years later, Lawson received a promotion to vice president in 1967, and by the end of 1968 he was asked to take charge of the university as president. However, times were changing. Riots took place on college campuses all over the nation. Tens of thousands of students were involved and hundreds of campuses suffered serious disturbances. Anger surged over civil rights, over the Vietnam War, and confrontation became a daily part of campus life. Students gathered in demonstrations, yelled epithets, threw rocks, and sprayed graffiti. Police forces retaliated with tear gas and batons. Sometimes guns were fired and people were killed.

At Fisk, a group of students felt that black colleges should not accept funds and grants from white donors. They wrote insulting letters to philanthropic organizations and benefactors. They yelled obscenities in demonstrations. Finally, in May 1970 a group of demonstrators burned down Livingstone Hall on the campus. Funds dried up and Fisk was soon in serious financial trouble.

Lawson tried to stem the tide, but he did not succeed. Drastic measurements had to be taken, including 20 percent salary reductions and big budget cuts. Still, half the endowment fund had drained away. Finally, Lawson, who had been ill, resigned in 1975, and he never went back. He worked for 20 years for NASA as director of university affairs, which was part of the equal opportunity office. In this capacity he was able to encourage contracts for minority institutions and function as an advocate for hiring of minorities and women. However, he never recovered his health. James Raymond Lawson died on December 21, 1996, of colon cancer. He was 81.

Further Reading

Heppenheimer, T. A. "James Raymond Lawson." *Notable Black American Scientists.* Kristine Krapp, ed. Detroit: Gale Research, 1999, 201–203.

Mickens, Ronald E. "James Raymond Lawson," *Physics Today* 50 (Oct 1997): 128.

Leevy, Carroll Moton

(1920–) *physician, medical researcher*

Through his internationally recognized research on liver disease and his communication with the public about the damage done to the liver by alcohol, Carroll Moton Leevy has changed public understanding of this illness and its relationship to alcoholism. He has published more than 500 articles and several books, established the first clinic in the world for alcoholics with liver disease, and has made detection of liver disease simpler through development of better technology for testing.

Born on October 13, 1920, in Columbia, South Carolina, Carroll Moton Leevy developed a sense of mission early in life. As a small child, Leevy became very ill with pneumonia and felt sure he owed his life to his doctors. He also saw unnecessary deaths in his family and in his neighborhood. He developed an appreciation for what a knowledgeable and caring doctor can accomplish and also a recognition of the need for better medical care in many cases. He resolved then to become a doctor.

Leevy's grandparents were freed slaves, and members of his family had embraced the freedom of knowledge and education quickly. Both his parents had a college education and they both had been teachers. Leevy knew he would need a good academic record from high school in order to fulfill his dream of becoming a doctor. He worked hard and graduated at the top of his class. He was accepted by Fisk University in Nashville, Tennessee, one of the best historically black universities in the country. At Fisk he was active in the Young Men's Christian Association (YMCA) and attended a racially integrated YMCA conference in 1940. For the grandson of former slaves, a young man who had always lived with segregation, this was an invigorating experience, as he saw that people of diverse cultures and backgrounds could work together for common goals. Leevy received his bachelor's degree summa cum laude in 1941.

By December of that year, the United States had entered World War II. However, because physicians were badly needed, Leevy continued with his medical education. He entered the University of Michigan's medical school at Ann Arbor and he also entered the Army Specialized Training Program, which helped with the financial burden of his medical training. He completed his M.D. degree in 1944 and moved east to New Jersey, where he completed his internship and his residency at Jersey City Medical Center.

During his years in Jersey City, he saw many patients with liver disease, often also suffering from alcoholism. Neither methods of diagnosis nor treatments were available, however. Struck by their plight and disturbed by the large numbers of victims, with the encouragement of the Medical Center physicians with whom he was training, Leevy set about chipping away at the problem. He invented and patented a method for diagnosis of liver ailments that was simple to use. He also devised a nearly painless method for taking minute liver biopsies that could be examined microscopically.

Once his residency was concluded in 1948, Leevy technically was required to fulfill his military obligation. However, by that time the war had ended, so that requirement was postponed while he continued his work with liver disease in Jersey City. Six years later, in 1954, Leevy received orders to report to the U.S. Naval Hospital in St. Albans, New York. He just brought his liver research with him, and within 24 months he had set up a liver disease research center, where he could continue his work, also writing a textbook on liver disease, *Practical Diagnosis and Treatment of Liver Disease* (1957).

Also during this period, in 1956, Leevy married his lifetime partner, Ruth Secora Barboza. A chemist, Ruth Leevy took an interest in his research and helped with it in later years. The couple had a daughter, Maria, and a son, Carroll Barboza Leevy, M.D., who also became involved in liver research and went to work at the Sammy Davis, Jr., National Liver Center.

Leevy garnered two postdoctoral grants—one in 1952 for work at the University of Toronto, where he was able to compare notes with other liver experts, and the second in 1958–59 from the National Institutes of Health for studies at Harvard Medical School. During this time he researched relationships between diet and liver disease, as well as environmental contaminants and liver disease.

Meanwhile, Jersey City Medical Center went through several transformations while Leevy was at the U.S. Naval Hospital and continued to undergo mergers and growth, moving to Newark in 1970, when it became the College of Medicine and Dentistry of New Jersey. Leevy continued with his work and published his findings. From the rank of full professor he became chair of the department of medicine and physician-in-chief from 1975 to 1991. In 1990, he was offered the position of director of the New Jersey Medical School Liver Center, and since 1984 he has simultaneously held the position of scientific director of the Sammy Davis, Jr., National Liver Center.

Further Reading

American Men & Women of Science 1998–99. New Providence, N.J.: R. R. Bowker, 20th vol. 4, 832.

Kessler, James H., J. S. Kidd, Renee A. Kidd, and Katherine A. Morin. *Distinguished African American Scientists of the 20th Century.* Phoenix, Ariz.: Oryx Press, 1996.

Leffall, LaSalle D., Jr.
(1930–) *medical researcher, surgical oncologist*

An internationally acclaimed oncologist and gifted surgeon, LaSalle D. Leffall, Jr., has devoted his life to the study of cancer. As chair of the Department of Surgery at Howard University College of Medicine, he has worked effectively to build the caliber of training offered there. He has raised awareness of the disproportionate percentage of African Americans who are stricken by cancer. As the first African American to become national president of the American Cancer Society, Leffall launched a program that focused on the increasing incidence of soft-part sarcoma and cancers of the breast, colorectum, head, and neck in African Americans.

Born on May 22, 1930, in Tallahassee, Florida, LaSalle Leffall, Jr., was the son of Martha Jordan Leffall and LaSalle Leffall, Sr. Young Leffall attended public school and graduated from high school in 1945, valedictorian of his class. He completed his undergraduate studies at Florida A&M University in just three years, earning his B.S. summa cum laude in 1948. He enrolled in the College of Medicine at Howard University in Washington, D.C. and graduated first in his class in 1952. Over the next seven years he first completed his internship at Homer G. Phillips Hospital in St. Louis, then served as assistant resident in surgery in Washington, D.C., at D.C. General Hospital and Freedmen's Hospital. Finally, attracted by the dynamic nature of the field, he completed his medical training as a senior fellow in cancer surgery from 1957 to 1959. For this phase of his training, he chose Memorial Sloan-Kettering Cancer Center in New York because of the exciting state-of-the-art techniques in use there.

Leffall served one year of military service, from 1960 to 1961, first as captain of the Medical Corps, then as chief of General Surgery at the U.S. Army Hospital in Munich, Germany. After his discharge, finally he was ready to go back to Howard and begin to give back what he felt the school had given him. When he began his medical training in 1948, he has pointed out, predominantly white medical schools did not often welcome black students. Had Howard not been there to provide the training he needed, he has said, he would not have been able to pursue his goals of becoming a physician and surgeon.

Since returning to Howard in 1962, for many years he served as chair of the Department of Surgery. He has trained hundreds of medical students and has saved thousands of lives, sometimes seeing as many as 60 patients a week. He has focused in his research on cancer of the breast, colorectum, head, and neck, and he has authored or coauthored more than 130 articles and chapters published in professional journals or forums. Leffall has also lectured tirelessly on cancer at more than 200 medical institutions in the U.S. and other parts of the world.

In addition to his election to serve as president of the American Cancer Society, Leffall has also served as president of the American College of Surgeons, and in 1980 President Carter appointed him to serve a six-year term as a member of the National Cancer Advisory Board. A consultant to the National Cancer Institute, diplomate of the American Board of Surgery, and fellow of the American College of Surgeons and American College of Gastroenterology, Leffall has received many awards, including the St. George Medal and Citation from the American Cancer Society. In 1987, M.D. Anderson Hospital and Tumor Institute in Houston established the Biennial LaSalle D. Leffall, Jr., Award in his honor, and Howard University honored him in 1995 by establishing a chair in surgery in his name.

Leffall has written an autobiography, *Equanimity Under Duress: A Surgeon's Memoirs*, to be published in 2003. To Leffall, the title has an especially powerful significance. Just prior to the book's publication, he remarked, "The book represents one of the highest standards of surgical discipline: maintaining that degree of calmness or tranquillity that allows one to exercise the best judgment, even in the most trying situations."

As of late 2002, Leffall held the title of Charles R. Drew Professor of Surgery (named for CHARLES RICHARD DREW) at Howard. He also served as a professorial lecturer in surgery at Georgetown University.

Further Reading

Leffall, LaSalle D., Jr. *Equanimity Under Duress: A Surgeon's Memoirs*. Washington, D.C.: Howard University Press, 2003 (forthcoming).

"Winning the Battle Against Cancer," *Black Enterprise*, October 1988, 76.

Lewis, Harold Ralph
(1931–   ) *theoretical physicist*

A researcher in theoretical physics, H. Ralph Lewis worked for the Los Alamos National Laboratory in New Mexico for 30 years—but he often was not actually at the lab. His work took him to theoretical physics laboratories and universities located in far-flung locations, including England, Wisconsin, southern France, and South Africa. Having spent two years in Germany on a postgraduate fellowship, he was also fluent in German and helped translate several volumes of the lectures of Austrian physicist Wolfgang Pauli (1900–58), the 1945 Nobel laureate in physics.

Harold Ralph Lewis was born on June 7, 1931, in Chicago, Illinois, to Harold Lewis, an electrical engineer, and Lena Lewis, a teacher. Young Lewis grew up in a household where getting an education was just expected—but Lewis welcomed the idea, since he had a curious mind, liked reading and learning, and did well in school. By the time he was in high school, he knew he wanted to study physics.

He finished high school a semester early and began taking courses at Wilson Junior College in Chicago, then received a scholarship offer that enabled him to enroll at the University of Chicago. There he completed a bachelor of arts degree in three years but stayed to earn a second bachelor's degree, this one in science, which he completed in two additional years, receiving it in 1953.

For his graduate work, Lewis chose the University of Illinois at Champaign-Urbana, where the faculty included several outstanding researchers. Lewis completed his M.S. in 1955, followed by his Ph.D. in 1958. His dissertation dealt with the use of nuclear radiation to measure magnetic fields found in superconductors. (Superconductors are special materials that conduct electricity almost completely without resistance when cooled to very low temperatures;

however, the presence of a magnetic field tends to mitigate superconductivity. Lewis was exploring this puzzle.)

Lewis's dissertation had dealt with a topic in experimental physics, but theoretical physics fascinated him, too, and after receiving his Ph.D. he received a postdoctoral fellowship to study as a research associate in Germany at the Institute for Theoretical Physics in Heidelberg. He studied there for two years and then returned to the United States to accept a position as instructor in the department of physics at Princeton University in New Jersey, where he taught from 1960 to 1963. There he explored aspects of plasma physics. A plasma is a collection of unattached or unbound electrons and positive ions that are almost completely in balance and therefore more or less neutral. This substance is sufficiently different from solids, liquids, and gases to be considered a fourth state of matter. Yet, its study is relatively new. Lewis also examined the possibility of engaging thermonuclear energy for useful purposes—for generating electricity, for example.

In 1963 Lewis became interested in the thermonuclear fusion project at the Los Alamos National Laboratory. In that year he began a long and ongoing relationship with Los Alamos and collaboration with colleagues at the University of Wisconsin, the U.S. Department of Energy, and the Witwatersrand University in Johannesburg, South Africa. He worked with a variety of topics, including magnetic fusion theory and plasma physics, along with the controlled-thermonuclear fusion project, on which he worked from 1963 to 1990.

After teaching for one year at St. John's College in Santa Fe, New Mexico, in 1991 H. Ralph Lewis became professor of physics in the department of physics and astronomy of Dartmouth College in Hanover, New Hampshire, where he was professor emeritus as of late 2002.

Further Reading

"H. Ralph Lewis: Professor of Physics, Emeritus," Dartmouth Arts and Science Physics Faculty. Available online. URL: http://www.dartmouth.edu/artsci/physics/faculty/lewis.html. Updated on February 4, 2002.

Kessler, James H., J. S. Kidd, Renee A. Kidd, and Katherine A. Morin. *Distinguished African American Scientists of the 20th Century.* Phoenix, Ariz.: Oryx Press, 1996.

Lewis, Julian Herman

(1891–1989) *physiologist, pathologist*

Not allowing himself to be bound by academic disciplinary boundaries, Julian Herman Lewis pursued scientific research in both diverse and overlapping fields, making memorable contributions in several. His investigations delved into immunology, anthropology, pathology, physiology, and psychology. He investigated the nature of African-American physiology and anatomy and wrote a detailed account of African ancestry, published in his book *The Biology of the Negro.* He explored questions related to immunity. He also was the first recipient of a Guggenheim Award for study abroad.

Julian Lewis, the son of John Calhoun Lewis and Cordelia O. Scott Lewis, was born on May 26, 1891, in Shawneetown, Illinois. Julian's father was a freed slave, and both his parents taught in public schools, having met at Berea College in Berea, Kentucky. Berea was originally established in 1855 to educate freed slaves, but ironically a new law barred African Americans by the time Julian was ready to attend college. So he went to the University of Illinois, where few black students attended and Lewis was isolated, but at least no state law kept him out.

Lewis did extremely well and graduated Phi Beta Kappa in 1911. He completed his M.A. the following year and continued on with his Ph.D. at the University of Chicago, which he completed in 1915 (becoming the first African-American Ph.D. in physiology at the University of Chicago). His dissertation, a study of the role played by lipids in immunity, was not only published that same year in the *Journal of Infectious Diseases,* but also won the Ricketts Prize. Lewis completed an M.D. two years later at Rush Medical College and received an appointment the same year to the physiology faculty of the University of Chicago. Ultimately, he became an associate professor (but not a full professor), a position he retained until 1943.

Throughout his career, Lewis caught the attention of discerning individuals and groups. In 1926, he received the first John Simon Guggenheim Fellowship for study abroad, which he used to travel to Basel, Switzerland, where he conducted research. He consistently presented his results at professional scientific conferences. Coverage of his work appeared in *Life* and *Time.* Always ready to experiment, he even participated in a study to examine whether beef plasma could be used instead of human blood in a transfusion. He belonged to scientific societies, such as the Society for Experimental Pathology, the American Association of Immunologists, and the American Association of Pathologists and Bacteriologists. In 1971, he received the Benjamin Rush Medal in honor of his outstanding achievements.

Lewis's book, *The Biology of the Negro,* grew out of his own need to know more about his ancestry and dispel any myths not based in observable evidence. A reviewer in the *Journal of the National Medical Association* called it a "fair, impartial, scientific and masterly study and analysis." Most important, the reviewer indicated that, for him, the case was closed: "It is noteworthy that the author has failed to discover any fundamental evidence to show that the Negro is biologically inferior to other groups in the genus *Homo.*"

Lewis later became director of the pathology department at Our Lady of Mercy Hospital in

Dyer, Indiana—a position he would retain until a little before his death on March 6, 1989, just months before his 98th birthday.

Further Reading

"Review of *The Biology of the Negro*," *Journal of the National Medical Association* (July 1942).

Sammons, Vivian Ovelton. *Blacks in Science and Medicine*. New York: Hemisphere Publishing, 1990.

Lloyd, Ruth Smith
(1917–) *anatomist*

The first African-American woman to earn a Ph.D. in anatomy, Ruth Smith Lloyd focused her research on fertility, the female sex cycle, and related endocrinology.

Ruth Smith, the youngest of three daughters born to Mary Elizabeth Smith and Bradley Donald Smith, was born on January 25, 1917, in Washington, D.C. She graduated from Dunbar High School in Washington, noted for its academic program, and she traveled to Massachusetts, where she entered undergraduate studies at Mount Holyoke College, a private liberal arts college for women in South Hadley. There, she completed her A.B. in 1937. Returning to Washington, she earned her master's degree at Howard University. She had planned to look for a high school teaching position in zoology after completing her studies at Howard. However, the Howard professors convinced her to pursue advanced studies in anatomy, recommending Western Reserve University (now Case Western Reserve University), a private coeducational school in Cleveland having strong anatomy and medical programs. In the interim, she married Sterling M. Lloyd, a physician, in 1939. She and Lloyd raised a family of three children, but she nonetheless managed to "do it all," attending Western Reserve, where she completed her Ph.D. in anatomy in 1941. She

thereby earned the distinction of becoming the first African-American woman to earn a Ph.D. in anatomy.

Ruth Lloyd investigated fertility in the Western Reserve laboratories, which kept colonies of monkeys for research. Ultimately, she would center her research and teaching in endocrinology, specifically the study of sex-related hormones, and medical genetics. After receiving her Ph.D., she returned to Washington, accepting a position on the faculty at the Howard University College of Medicine as an assistant in physiology. She also taught zoology at Hampton Institute (now Hampton University) in Hampton, Virginia.

After a brief hiatus to begin raising her family, Lloyd returned to Howard University in 1942, receiving a promotion to instructor. Sixteen years later, she had advanced to assistant professor of anatomy, later moving to the graduate school at Howard as associate professor. She continued teaching in that capacity until she retired.

Further Reading

Bruno, Leonard C. "Ruth Smith Lloyd." *Notable Black American Scientists*. Kristine Krapp, ed. Detroit: Gale Research, 1999, 208.

Warren, Wini. *Black Women Scientists in the United States*. Bloomington: Indiana University Press, 1999, 179.

Logan, Joseph Granville, Jr.
(1920–) *physicist, inventor*

Joseph Logan invented a small jet engine with improved fuel economy that was useful for helicopters and guided missiles. He brought a physics background to the aeronautical and aerospace firms for which he worked during much of his career and ultimately he became director of the physics department at California Polytechnic University in Pomona, California.

Joseph Granville Logan, Jr., was born on June 8, 1920, in Washington, D.C. His parents were Lula Briggs Logan and Joseph Granville Logan, Sr., who was a junior high school principal in Washington, D.C. Logan earned his B.S. degree in 1941 from Miner Teachers College in Washington.

Logan taught math and science in Baltimore and then in Washington, D.C., until 1945. Meanwhile, he had also taken on a position working as a physicist in the aerodynamics department at the U.S. Bureau of Standards from 1943 to 1946.

The year 1946 brought a move to Buffalo, New York, where Logan joined the firm of Cornell Aeronautical Laboratories as a research physicist. During his work at Cornell, in 1950, he developed his new jet engine, a valveless pulse engine. He also helped develop a new gas turbine during this period. At the same time, he had returned to graduate school while working at the lab. While in Washington, he had already completed some of his work at Howard University and later at Cornell University. Then he completed the work at the University of Buffalo and received his Ph.D. in physics in 1955.

In 1957, Logan went to work for Space Technological Labs, Inc., where he was head of the aerophysics laboratory and then manager of the propulsion research department. In 1960, he moved to the Aerospace Corporation to become director of the Aerodynamic and Propulsion Laboratory in El Segundo, California, where he stayed until 1967. In that year, he joined the western division of McDonnell Douglas Aircraft Company, where he became a special assistant to the director of research and development. Among other positions he held at McDonnell Douglas, he was manager of vulnerability and hardening development engineering for three years and chief engineer of nuclear weapons effects for two years. From 1974 to 1978 he held management and administrative positions at Apple Energy Sciences, Inc. (president, 1974–78),

and West Coast Research Corporation (vice president, research and development, 1978). He also chaired the physics department at California Polytechnic Institute for a year (1978–79). In 1979, he became director of the Urban University Center at the University of Southern California, which he held until his retirement in 1989.

Further Reading

Petrusso, A. "Joseph Granville Logan, Jr.," *Notable Black American Scientists.* Kristine Krapp, ed. Detroit: Gale Research, 1999, 208–209.

Lu Valle, James Ellis
(1912–1993) *chemist*

A 1936 Olympic Games bronze medalist in the 400-meter race, James E. Lu Valle received a Ph.D. in chemistry and mathematics at the California Institute of Technology (Caltech) in 1940, probably becoming the first African American to do so. Lu Valle's research interests centered on photochemistry, electron defraction, and magnetic resonance. He had a varied career, including teaching, research positions in industry, work for the Office of Scientific Research and Development (OSRD) during World War II, and direction of the undergraduate chemistry laboratories at Stanford University.

James Ellis Lu Valle was born on November 10, 1912, in San Antonio, Texas. His family later moved to Los Angeles, where Lu Valle attended Los Angeles Polytechnic High School. He received his bachelor's degree from the University of California at Los Angeles (UCLA) in chemistry and mathematics in 1936, graduating Phi Beta Kappa. He was also inducted into Sigma Xi, the science honorary society, and *Atlantic Monthly* published a short story he had written. That summer, he won the bronze medal in the 400-meter run at the Olympic Games in Germany. He earned his M.S. the following year, also at UCLA, where he had become the first president of the school's newly formed Associated Graduate Students. He completed his Ph.D. in chemistry and mathematics three years later.

After teaching at Fisk University in Nashville, Tennessee, for a year, he worked for Eastman Kodak from 1941 to 1942. During World War II he worked for the Office of Scientific Research and Development first at the University of Chicago for a year and then for two years at Caltech, where he helped to develop the atomic bomb.

After the war, Lu Valle worked in the research laboratories at Eastman Kodak from 1945 to 1953; for Technical Operations, Inc., from 1953 to 1959; and became director of basic research for Fairchild Camera and Instrument in Syosset, New York, in 1959. In 1975 he became director of undergraduate chemistry laboratories at Stanford University.

James Lu Valle died on January 30, 1993, of a heart attack while on vacation in New Zealand. The student commons building at UCLA is named Lu Valle Commons in his honor.

Further Reading

Brown, Mitchell C. "James Ellis Du Valle," Faces of Science: African Americans in Science. Available online. URL: http://www.princeton.edu/~mcbrown/display/luvalle.html. Updated on November 25, 2000.

"James E. Lu Valle: Student Leader, 1936 Olympic Medalist," Los Angeles Times, February 12, 1993, Part A, 30.

M

Macklin, John W.
(1939–) *analytical chemist*

Since 1980, John Macklin has been working with the National Aeronautics and Space Administration (NASA) to examine meteorites and cosmic dust to see if he can find evidence of organic molecules—a project that connects with the question of whether carbon compounds from space may have originally supplied the ancestor molecules from which all living things on Earth developed. The need to examine specks of cosmic dust led to development of techniques for examining and analyzing microscopic samples, a procedure that also has applications in many other circumstances.

Born in Fort Worth, Texas, on December 11, 1939, John W. Macklin spent his early childhood in Texas on his grandmother's farm. His father had died when John was very young, and the Texas farm seemed the best place for the young boy. He rejoined the rest of his family in Seattle, Washington, when he was seven years old. By then he already had a reputation for curiosity and wanting to find out how things work and what they are made of.

After graduating from high school, Macklin chose Linfield College in McMinnville, Oregon, for his undergraduate studies and at first chose a major in chemical engineering, but he quickly found he preferred more theoretical research than engineering offered. He also had a minor in music, sang in the choir, and played on the varsity football team. He received his bachelor of arts degree from Linfield in 1962.

Macklin continued his graduate studies in analytical chemistry at Cornell University in Ithaca, New York, where he had a six-year research assistantship. Analytical chemistry involves identifying substances, often using very small samples—for example, trying to find out about a meteorite's makeup and its past by examining a tiny chip. It often requires highly intriguing detective work and innovative techniques for finding answers. In Macklin's research project, he focused on trying to find new techniques for analysis, for example using lasers. He completed his Ph.D. in inorganic chemistry in 1968.

After finishing his work at Cornell, Macklin accepted a position on the faculty of the University of Washington in Seattle. During his first decade there—the 1970s—he continued to explore the use of laser beams to identify atoms in a molecule and see how they fit together. He used a fascinating technique known as Raman spectroscopy, named after the scientist from India who first devised it. It involves using a laser beam to disturb all the atoms in the molecule very slightly, causing them to emit energy, which can then be analyzed for its identity through the use of a spectroscope. The use of a spectroscope in this kind of analysis relies on the fact that each element emits a different "fingerprint" of spectral lines. The pattern of light also shows the arrangement of the atoms within the molecule.

During the 1980s, Macklin worked with NASA and Stanford University scientists to determine whether meteorites and cosmic dust particles from outer space contained complex carbon-based molecules. Macklin showed that tiny crystals of clay could support the construction of complex carbon-based molecules. Investigations such as these may lead in the future to breakthroughs in solving the mystery of how life may have begun on Earth.

Recently, Macklin has also been involved in trying to improve the quality of science teaching in Washington State at both the elementary and high school levels.

Further Reading

"John W. Macklin, Associate Professor of Chemistry," University of Washington Department of Chemistry. Available online. URL: http://depts. washington.edu/chemfac/macklin.html. Downloaded on April 23, 2002.

Kessler, James H., J. S. Kidd, Renee A. Kidd, and Katherine A. Morin. *Distinguished African American Scientists of the 20th Century*. Phoenix, Ariz.: Oryx Press, 1996.

Maloney, Arnold Hamilton

(1888–1955) *pharmacologist*

Arnold Hamilton Maloney is best known for his discovery that a substance called picrotoxin can be used to reverse the effects of barbiturate poisoning. He was also the first black professor of pharmacology.

Born on July 4, 1888, in Cocoye Village, Trinidad, British West Indies, Arnold Maloney was the oldest of 10 children born to Estelle Evetta Bonas Maloney and Lewis Albert Maloney. The family owned several grocery stores, which were run by Estelle Maloney, while her husband pursued his business as a building contractor. As a youth, Arnold Maloney did well in school and showed an aptitude for learning, as well as skills in writing and public speaking.

Maloney attended Naparima College in Trinidad (affiliated with Cambridge University in England), obtaining his A.B. degree in 1909. It would be the first of many academic degrees. He initially set out to run a drugstore on the island of Trinidad. However, on the advice of an uncle in the United States, he immigrated to the U.S. in hope of finding more profitable opportunities. After a brief enrollment at Lincoln University in Pennsylvania, he attended General Theological Seminary in New York, where he earned a bachelor of science degree in theology in 1912. In the meantime, he also obtained a master's degree in philosophy from Columbia University in 1910. He became ordained as a priest in the Episcopal Church, later changing to the African Orthodox Church, in which he became a bishop. However, his life as a pastor was plagued with misgivings and by 1920 he had withdrawn completely from the ministry.

In that same year, Maloney accepted a position as professor of psychology at Wilberforce University in Ohio, a profession that he greatly enjoyed, remaining in that position for five years. In 1925, he decided to take a new career path, combining his medical interests with his enthusiasm for teaching, and he entered medical school at Indiana University School of Medicine in Indianapolis, Indiana. He completed his M.D. in 1929. Always gifted with a flair for writing, he also wrote a column called "The Indianapolis Negro" for the *Indianapolis Recorder* during this period.

Although Maloney began an internship at Provident Hospital in Baltimore, he interrupted that process to pursue an opportunity at

Howard University in Washington, D.C. Howard was expanding its medical school and offered Maloney a faculty position and a fellowship for graduate studies in pharmacology at the University of Wisconsin in Madison. Maloney's research centered on the effects some drugs (such as morphine or barbiturates) can have on particular parts of the brain, resulting in either stimulation or depression of the breathing process. He completed his Ph.D. in 1931 and began teaching at Howard University, where he also became dean of pharmacology. He remained on the Howard faculty for 22 years, from 1931 to 1953. During that time he engaged in further research on the effects of drugs on breathing. Of particular concern was the danger of barbiturate overdose, which can depress breathing to the extent of causing coma or death. Maloney made the very useful discovery that picrotoxin—a natural substance derived from seeds of the plant *Anamirta cocculus*—could reverse the effects of a barbiturate overdose, also known as barbiturate poisoning.

Maloney wrote more than 50 published scientific articles as well as several books on topics such as religion and politics. He also wrote an autobiography. He also was active in several professional scientific organizations, including the American Association for the Advancement of Science, the New York Academy of Sciences, and the National Medical Association. Arnold Hamilton Maloney died on August 8, 1955, in Washington, D.C. He was 67.

Further Reading

McMurray, Emily, ed. *Notable Twentieth Century Scientists*, vol. 3. Detroit: Gale Research, 1995, 1305–06.

Narins, Brigham, ed. *Notable Scientists: From 1900 to the Present,* 2nd ed. Farmington Hills, Mich.: Gale Group, 2001.

Sammons, Vivian Ovelton. *Blacks in Science and Medicine.* New York: Hemisphere Publishing, 1990.

Massey, Walter Eugene
(1938–) *physicist, administrator*

In 1990, Walter Eugene Massey became the first African American to head the National Science Foundation (NSF). The NSF, which is the federal government's primary presence in scientific, mathematical, and engineering research, distributes billions of dollars in grants for some of the most important scientific research in the nation. Massey has also held administrative positions at the University of California, as provost and senior vice president of academic affairs; at the University of Chicago, as vice president for research and as director of the Argonne National Laboratory; and at Brown University, as dean of the college. Massey became president of Morehouse College in 1995.

Walter Eugene Massey was born on April 5, 1938, in Hattiesburg, Mississippi, to Almar and Essie Nelson Massey. After graduating from high school, he attended Morehouse College in Atlanta, Georgia. There he encountered a prejudice among students from other states against black students like himself who came from Mississippi, which the more sophisticated students viewed as a "backwater" state. To prove his intellectual mettle, Massey took the most difficult courses he could find, such as physics and calculus—and excelled at them. He later remarked that he didn't even know what calculus was when he began the course, and that, he says, is how he ended up in physics. To his surprise, though difficult, he found the subject compelling. He received his bachelor's degree from Morehouse in 1958.

The following year, Massey received a National Defense Education Act (NDEA) fellowship to attend Howard University in Washington, D.C., where he also taught for one year. Then, under an NSF fellowship, Massey went on to earn a master of science and Ph.D. in physics from Washington University in St. Louis, Missouri, both in 1966.

For his thesis, Massey worked at the Argonne National Laboratory in Illinois, a U.S. Department of Energy laboratory run by the University of Chicago and Washington University. There, he studied quantum solids and liquids. His thesis topic was "Ground State of Liquid Helium—Boson Solutions for Mass 3 and 4."

He remained at Argonne from 1966 to 1968 as a staff physicist, then moved on to become assistant professor of physics at the University of Illinois at Urbana. During his stay in Illinois, Massey helped organize the Illinois Science and Mathematics Academy, a high school for gifted students. He also was a trustee for the Academy for Mathematics and Science Teachers, a laboratory that has trained some 17,000 Chicago public school teachers in these subjects.

In 1970, Massey became associate professor on the physics faculty at Brown University in Providence, Rhode Island, with a promotion to full professor in 1975. From the mid-1970s to the mid-1980s he was director of Argonne National Laboratory and vice president for research at the University of Chicago. In 1990, when President George H. W. Bush appointed him president of the National Science Foundation, Massey became the first African American to hold this important policy-making position. (He likes to point out that Bush appointed him, even though Bush is a Republican and Massey is a Democrat.) Following that position, he served as senior vice president and provost of the University of California system (governing all the universities in the system). In 1994, he returned to his alma mater to accept the position of president.

About his return to Morehouse, Massey has said, "At this point in my career, I wanted to get back to an environment where I have more direct contacts with students and faculty. . . . [T]he opportunity to get back in the classroom appeals to me. I've been involved in programs around the country, at the national level, to try to promote more opportunities for minorities in

Walter Eugene Massey's early work in quantum physics and extensive teaching and science administration experience at Brown University, Argonne National Laboratory, and the University of Chicago set the stage for his appointment to head the National Science Foundation, the nation's independent agency for promoting science. *(Courtesy of Walter E. Massey)*

science and to encourage minority youngsters to pursue science, and I decided that I should go back and get more involved at a grass-roots level."

Further Reading

Hawkins, Walter L. *African American Biographies, 2.* Jefferson, N.C.: McFarland & Co., 1994.

Hoke, Franklin. "Former NSF Director Massey Returns to Alma Mater, Morehouse College, As Institution's New President," *The Scientist* 9, no. 16 (August 21, 1995): 14.

Massie, Samuel Proctor

(1919–   ) *organic chemist, educator*

Samuel Massie is recognized for his leadership in the field of chemistry education. He was also the first African-American member of the faculty at the United States Naval Academy in Annapolis, Maryland.

Samuel Proctor Massie was born in North Little Rock, Arkansas, on July 3, 1919. A remarkable student, he had graduated from high school at age 13, attended Dunbar Junior College for two years, and completed his B.S. in chemistry summa cum laude from the University of Arkansas at Pine Bluff by the time he was 18. With the help of a National Youth Administration Scholarship, he continued on to Fisk University in Nashville, Tennessee, where he completed his master's degree in chemistry in 1940. He was only 21.

Next he went for his doctorate in chemistry at Iowa State University in Ames, Iowa, arriving for enrollment in 1941. As Massie was nearing the end of his doctoral program, however, he lost his draft deferment. The United States had entered World War II in 1941. By this time, Henry Gilman had already invited Massie to join his research group, which was working on research connected to the Manhattan Project, so Massie did not join the army, but his own studies were now on hold. After the war was over in 1945, he was able to finish up his work, and he received his Ph.D. in 1946.

Massie taught at Fisk University for one year and then took a position on the faculty at Langston University in Langston, Oklahoma, becoming full professor of chemistry and chair of the department. In six years, he was able to strengthen the department both in teaching and in research. In 1953, he was elected president of the Oklahoma Academy of Sciences.

Later in 1953, Massie accepted an offer from Fisk University to take the chair of the chemistry department there. He stayed for seven years, and toward the end of that period, he persuaded the American Chemical Society to hold its national meeting at Fisk—the first time a historically black institution had ever hosted a major scientific meeting.

During his years at Fisk, Massie's research focused on phenothiazine, and he wrote a major review article on the subject. Massie's remarks changed the view chemists had of the compound. It had previously been used as a precursor for dyes, insecticides, and medicines. Now researchers saw that it had more varied applications. It could also be used for preparation of drugs used for mental diseases and cancer therapy.

Massie received an appointment in 1960 to serve as associate director of special projects in science education at the National Science Foundation in Washington, D.C. After he completed that work, he accepted the chair of pharmaceutical chemistry at Howard University, also in Washington. Then in 1963 he became president of North Carolina College at Durham.

In 1966, he received an appointment from Lyndon Baines Johnson as professor of chemistry at the Naval Academy in Annapolis, Maryland. Massie was the first African-American science professor at the academy. In 1977, he also became the first African-American department chair at the academy.

Massie had a difficult time finding a place to live near the academy, but he succeeded and he plunged into teaching. He also began important research at the academy. He received awards for his work on drugs to combat malaria and meningitis, and he also received a patent for work he did on gonorrhea. He worked to formulate drugs to treat herpes, as well as a foam that could be used against nerve gasses. While he was there, teaching mostly white students, he established a black studies program on campus.

At one time, the University of Arkansas had turned down his application to attend there, but in 1970, the University of Arkansas awarded him an honorary doctorate. He received the Distinguished Achievement Citation from Iowa State University in 1981. Without doubt the greatest honor is the establishment of a Dr. Samuel P. Massie Chair of Excellence, which is a $14.7 million grant, awarded to 10 universities to enhance "groundbreaking environmental research and the production of top-level graduates."

Among chemists, Samuel P. Massie is considered one of the greats—one of the 75 greatest chemists of all time, according to a 1998 issue of the journal *Chemical and Engineering News*. The list includes GEORGE WASHINGTON CARVER, Marie Curie, Linus Pauling—and Samuel P. Massie.

Further Reading

"Contributors to the Chemical Enterprise: C&EN's Top 75," *Chemical and Engineering News*. January 12, 1998. Available online. URL: http://pubs.acs.org/hotartcl/cenear/980112/top.html. Posted on January 12, 1998.

Hawkins, Walter L. *African American Biographies, 2.* Jefferson, N.C.: McFarland & Co., 1994.

Matzeliger, Jan
(1852–1889) *inventor*

Tennis shoes, walking shoes, hiking boots, dress shoes—today we walk into department stores or shoe stores and take our pick from the shelves, try them on for size, and walk out with our purchases. But shoe shopping was not always this easy. As late as the 1870s, shoemaking in America was a slow and difficult process, accomplished primarily by hand. Good, dependable shoes were expensive and often in short supply. Jan Matzeliger changed all this with a single invention, the lasting machine—revolutionizing the shoe industry and making shoes less expensive and widely available to consumers.

Jan Matzeliger was born on September 15, 1852, in Paramaribo, Surinam, a Dutch colony on the northeast coast of South America. His father was a Dutch official and his mother a former slave. Matzeliger's mother died when he was three years old and he was raised by his aunt. Thanks to his father's position, the family was fairly well off. Opportunities for education were rare for blacks in Surinam, though, and at age 10 Matzeliger began work as an apprentice at one of the machine shops supervised by his engineer father.

At age 19 he signed onto an East Indian merchant ship as a common seaman, serving two years aboard ship before quitting his job when the ship docked at Philadelphia, Pennsylvania, in 1873. Even though he did not speak English, Matzeliger began looking for work. He had been fascinated by machinery since childhood and had worked on ship engines while at sea. However, he found work difficult to find in Philadelphia. He was grateful when he finally found a job working a small machine in a shoemaker's shop. Matzeliger quickly proved himself an expert with machines and his employer, impressed with his abilities, suggested that he might find better opportunities farther north in Lynn, Massachusetts, then a large shoemaking center in the United States.

Arriving in Lynn, Matzeliger managed to find a job at Harney Brothers, one of the town's many shoe manufacturers. A machine operator part-time, he spent the rest of his workday sweeping floors. During his free hours, spent alone in an unheated room, and often without food, he learned English and read all that he could about physics and machinery. He soon began to prove his worth at Harney Brothers, making repairs on some of the company's machines and suggesting improvements on others.

The biggest problem for shoe manufacturers in those days was the "lasting" process. To fit properly, measurements had to be made of the customer's feet and molds created over which the top portions of the shoes were shaped in leather. The leather then had to be stretched and fitted and finally fixed permanently to the shoe soles. It was this final attachment of the uppers to the lowers that was the biggest problem in the industry. The quality, thickness, and individual contours of the leather used in the shoe's upper portions meant that each upper had to be carefully and individually fixed to its sole by hand. A careless job could mean rips in the leather, improper fits, and poor quality shoes. This was the job of the "lasters." A good laster could turn out 50 shoes

Inventor Jan Matzeliger's automatic shoe lasting machine transformed the Massachusetts shoe industry by automating one of the most difficult steps in the shoe manufacturing process. Only 37 when he died, Matzeliger was posthumously awarded a gold medal at the 1901 Pan American Exposition and was honored by a United States postage stamp in 1992. *(Lynn Museum)*

a day and consequently was highly paid and in great demand. Unfortunately, they could also bottleneck the industry, or go on strike as they often did, bringing shoemaking to standstill and raising prices beyond the ability of many customers to pay.

The solution, obviously, was a machine that could do the lasting, but most shoe manufacturers believed that no one could possibly devise a machine to handle the complexities of the job. A few people had tried, but all had failed. By the time Matzeliger became interested in the problem, firms in the industry had long since given up hope for the invention of such a machine.

The first step Matzeliger decided was to understand the hand motions used by lasters as they did their work. Lasters formed a close, tightly knit group, however, and they knew their power lay in their exclusive knowledge and skills. So, quite naturally, they resisted any attempts made by outsiders to observe them at work.

Matzeliger secured a job as a millwright, an all-around specialist whose job it was to inspect and keep all the machines in the factory working properly, and in this capacity he managed to get closer to the lasters as they worked. Little by little, he succeeded in picking up their patterns of movement, method, and procedure. Once he thought he understood well enough, he began working in his off time on designing a machine that could perform the lasting process.

It was a long and arduous process, involving him in the study of the design of many other machines, especially those used in wrapping various products. Working with models roughly put together with scraps of wood, nails, and cigar boxes, at first the job appeared to be as impossible as everyone had said. But by this time he was determined to meet the challenge and solve the problem.

Matzeliger's progress was slow but steady as each new rough model showed improvement over its predecessor. Word of his project began to get around the industry. Twice in the machine's development, other inventors who had tried and failed with their own models offered to buy in, but Matzeliger refused even though he could have used the money.

Finally, in 1880 Matzeliger had a good enough working model that he was able to find financial backers—C. H. Delnow and M. S. Nichols—who each took a third ownership in the process in exchange for their backing. With his newly obtained financing, Matzeliger was finally able to complete a full-scale working model and apply for a patent in 1882. The diagrams for the machine were so complex that a patent officer was sent to Lynn to examine the model itself. On March 20, 1883, Matzeliger was awarded patent number 274,207.

Almost overnight Matzeliger's lasting machine revolutionized the shoemaking industry. Where previously a laster could turn out 50 shoes a day, with Matzeliger's new machine a company could turn out from 150 to 700. Shoe prices dropped dramatically, sales rose, workers' wages increased, and customers suddenly could choose from an array of higher quality shoes in more styles and varieties than ever before.

Jan Matzeliger died of tuberculosis on August 24, 1889. He was 37 years old. Few Americans, then or now, have realized the impact the self-educated black immigrant from Paramirabo had on their lives. In 1901, he was posthumously awarded a gold medal at the Pan American Exposition, and in 1992 a U.S. postage stamp honored him and his invention.

Further Reading

Aaseng, Nathan. *Black Inventors.* New York: Facts On File, 1997.

Hayden, Robert. *Nine African-American Inventors.* New York: Twenty-First Century Books, 1992.

"Jan Matzeliger." Inventors Museum. Available online. URL: http://www.inventorsmuseum.com/JanMatzelilger.htm. Updated in 1999.

Sullivan, Otha Richard. *African American Inventors.* Black Stars series, Jim Haskins, ed. New York: John Wiley & Sons, 1998.

Mayes, Vivienne Lucille Malone
(1932–1995) *mathematician*

Vivienne Malone Mayes, a student of EVELYN BOYD COLLINS GRANVILLE and Lee Lorch, was an influential teacher whose high expectations and infectious enthusiasm for mathematics both challenged and engaged her students. In 1985, at Baylor University, she was voted Outstanding Teacher of the Year.

Vivienne Lucille Malone was born on February 10, 1932, in Waco, Texas. Her father could add long columns of figures in his head and was gifted at mathematics, although he did not have a formal education. He helped his daughter with her homework, and Vivienne always knew she would go to college. Her parents felt college was an investment in her future. She graduated from A. J. Moore High School in Waco in 1948, when she was only 16.

She entered Fisk University in Nashville, Tennessee, where she received her B.A. in mathematics in 1952. There, she studied under Evelyn Boyd Granville (the first African-American woman to obtain a Ph.D. in mathematics), of whom she wrote, "I believe that it was her presence and influence which account for my pursuit of advanced degrees in mathematics." Mayes went on to complete her M.A. two years later, in 1954. At Fisk, she also met and married J. J. Mayes, a dental student at nearby Meharry College. The marriage ended in divorce 33 years later.

Vivienne Mayes obtained her first teaching job at Paul Quinn College in Dallas, Texas, where she accepted a position as associate professor and chair of mathematics in 1954, remaining there until 1961. She had mapped out her teaching goals early in her career: to build self-respect in her students through an attitude of respect and support; teach them how to read mathematics and also identify and solve problems, as a way to think for themselves; and help them find and use opportunity.

She applied for admission to Baylor University in Waco, where she was frankly told the university was not yet ready for racial integration. The state university, however, was required to desegregate, so she completed her doctoral studies at the University of Texas in Austin with the help of a fellowship from the American Association of University Women for the 1964–65 academic year. It was a lonely time, about which she later wrote, "It took a faith in scholarship almost beyond measure to endure the stress of earning a Ph.D. degree as a black, female graduate student"—especially, one might add, in a field that was not highly receptive to females at the time. One mathematics professor refused to have her in his class because he "did not teach blacks." She was unable to join other students at the campus café because it did not serve blacks. So, always outspoken and courageous, she joined the civil rights picket lines outside. She earned her Ph.D. in mathematics in 1966, the fifth African-American woman in the United States to do so. She was also the second African American and the first black woman to receive a Ph.D. in mathematics from the University of Texas.

Having completed her graduate work, she accepted a faculty position as associate professor of mathematics in 1966 at Baylor University—in the very school that had refused her admission just a few years earlier. She spent the rest of her teaching career there.

Mayes served on the resolution committee of the Mathematical Association of America, as well as on the program committee in 1973, and she served on the board of directors of the National Association of Mathematicians (organized to serve black mathematicians). She was the first African American to serve on the executive committee of the Association for Women in Mathematics (AWM). Her professional memberships also included the American Mathematical Society and the National Council of Teachers of Mathematics. Mayes also consulted in the development of a textbook, *Pre-Calculus: Algebraic and Trigonometric Functions*, published by Individual Learning Systems, 1971.

Vivienne Lucille Malone Mayes retired because of illness in 1994, and she died on June 9, 1995, in her hometown of Waco, Texas. Colleagues, friends, and family established a scholarship fund in her name.

Further Reading

Henrion, Claudia. *Women in Mathematics: The Addition of Difference*. Bloomington: Indiana University Press, 1997, 192–211.

Leggett, Anne. "Vivienne Malone-Mayes in Memoriam," *AWM Newsletter* 25 no.6. Reproduced by permission by the MAA Online, Mathematical Association of America. Available online. URL: http://www.maa.org/summa/archive/MLNMAYS. HTM. Downloaded on February 4, 2002.

Warren, Wini. *Black Women Scientists in the United States*. Bloomington: Indiana University Press, 1999, 193–195.

McAfee, Walter Samuel
(1914–1995) *astrophysicist*

As mathematician for the U.S. Army's Project Diana, Walter S. McAfee made the calculations that led to the first human contact with the Moon, a radar signal bounced off the surface in January 1946. The experiment was a first step toward developing a trajectory for spacecraft sent to the Moon.

Born on September 2, 1914, in Ore City, Texas, Walter Samuel McAfee was the second of nine children born to Luther F. McAfee and Susie A. Johnson McAfee. After completing his bachelor's degree at Wiley College in 1934 and his M.S. from Ohio State in 1937, McAfee could not afford to continue, so he took a break from school for a couple of years. During that time he first taught physics at a junior high school in Columbus, Ohio, from 1939 to 1942.

Then, in May 1942 McAfee received an interesting job offer. The theoretical studies unit of the Electronics Research Command—a part of the U.S. Army's Signal Corps at Fort Monmouth, New Jersey—needed a civilian physicist. McAfee took the job. It turned out to be his lifelong job, requiring all the things he was good at—studying and experimenting in theoretical nuclear physics, working with electromagnetic theory, quantum optics, and laser holography. In 1946, McAfee received a Rosenwald fellowship that enabled him to enroll in the doctoral program at Cornell University at Ithaca, New York, to finish up his education. There he studied with the great theoretical physicist Hans Bethe. He received his doctorate in physics from Cornell in 1949, continuing his work for the Electronics Research Command.

The idea behind Project Diana was to bounce a radar signal off the Moon's surface. No one knew much about the Moon. Maybe a high-frequency radio signal would not penetrate the Moon's ionosphere or stratosphere. Experiments with low- and medium-frequency radio waves had already failed. To be sure the signal would actually arrive at the Moon, and not at the place where the Moon was when the signal left Earth, some careful calculations had to be made. An accurate calculation of the Moon's speed had to be made—and just to make things difficult, it happens that the speed at which the Moon travels relative to Earth varies. McAfee was the project mathematician, so he made the calculations. On January 10, 1946, using a special 40-foot-square antenna, a laser beam was sent traveling toward the Moon. A faint radar echo came back, just 2.5 seconds later. Project Diana had succeeded.

McAfee's name was never in the report that was publicized at the time, though. Not until the 25th anniversary of Project Diana did he finally receive credit and a moment of fame. Later, though, Wiley College inducted McAfee into its Science Hall of Fame. Sometime after that, McAfee established a math and physical science fellowship at Wiley College to encourage minority students in those fields.

McAfee continued working for the Electronics Research Command until he retired in 1985. He was also a lecturer in nuclear physics at Monmouth College, where he taught both graduate and undergraduate courses for 17 years. Walter S. McAfee died at his home in South Belmar, New Jersey, on February 18, 1995.

Further Reading
Accardo, Carl A. "Walter S. McAfee" (obituary). *Physics Today* (June 1995): 72, 74.

Gates, Henry Louis. "Who calculated the speed of the moon?" Little Known Black History Facts. Available online. URL: http://www.infoage.org/mcdonalds2000.html. Updated on February 5, 2002.

McBay, Henry Ransom Cecil
(1914–1995) *chemist*

Out of Henry McBay's research with acetyl peroxide—a volatile substance that many scientists refused to work with—came a synthesized protein now used in the treatment of prostate cancer. As compelling in the classroom as he was persevering in the laboratory, McBay had an impressive record for recruiting students to his field, with 45 of his students earning Ph.D.s in chemistry.

Henry Cecil Ransom McBay was born in Mexia, Texas, on May 29, 1914. McBay's plan at the beginning of his career was to become a physician, but along the way he decided on chemistry instead, earning his bachelor of science degree in 1934 from Wiley University in Marshall, Texas. For his master's degree he enrolled at Atlanta University, completing that degree in 1936. Before going on to earn his doctorate, he returned to Wiley as an instructor of chemistry for two years, then taught at various locations at the college and high school level in Kansas and Huntsville, Alabama, picking up a laboratory research project at nearby Tuskegee Institute (now University). He had attended some summer courses at the University of Chicago, finally enrolling there full-time for his doctoral studies in chemistry in 1942 and completing his Ph.D. in chemistry in 1945. He also won the Elizabeth Norton prize for research he completed in the 1944–45 academic year.

McBay returned to Atlanta in 1945 to become an instructor of chemistry at Morehouse College, a private historically black college for men. He became chair of the department of chemistry in 1960, a position he retained until 1981.

In 1949, he received a $5,000 grant from the Research Corporation of New York for research on chemical compounds. He also served as technical expert on a United Nations Educational, Scientific, and Cultural Organization (UNESCO) mission to Liberia, West Africa, in 1951.

After leaving Morehouse, McBay became Fuller E. Callaway professor of chemistry at Atlanta University in 1982, retiring to professor emeritus in 1986.

Henry Cecil Ransom McBay died on June 23, 1995. At the time of his death, WALTER EUGENE MASSEY, president of Morehouse College and former student of McBay, remarked, "More than a half century, Henry McBay tutored and taught, educated and inspired hundreds of young Morehouse men with an interest in and aptitude for the sciences . . . for me and so many other young men, he was a role model, mentor, and hero rolled into one."

Further Reading

Chandler, David L. "Black Chemist Steers Students to Achievement." *Boston Globe*, January 25, 1991, Metro Section, 21.

Frierson, Chaundra. Obituaries: "Henry R. C. McBay, 81, Professor of Chemistry at Atlanta Colleges." *Atlanta Constitution*, June 2, 1995, Local News, C6.

Sammons, Vivian Ovelton. *Blacks in Science and Medicine*. New York: Hemisphere Publishing, 1990.

McCoy, Elijah
(ca. 1843–1929) *inventor, mechanical engineer*

Elijah McCoy invented a simple but inspired automatic lubricating device that revolutionized the railroad and machine industries.

As escaped slaves, McCoy's parents had managed to find freedom in Canada by way of the Underground Railroad, an escape route composed of secret hideaways and helpers aiding former slaves who sought safety in the North. Elijah McCoy was born in Colchester, Ontario, Canada, on May 2 in either 1843 or 1844. His parents, George McCoy and the former Mildred Goins, at first found the going tough in their newly adopted country. Things changed, however, after George served as an enlisted soldier in the Canadian Army. As reward for his exceptional services in battle, upon honorable discharge he received 160 acres of farmland. George was an excellent farmer and the family's lot quickly improved. One of 12 children, Elijah worked on the farm and attended school until his parents felt safe enough from bounty hunters to venture back to the United States, settling in Ypsilanti, Michigan, a few miles west of Detroit.

Elijah had always shown a keen understanding of machinery, so the family took advantage of connections made in Canada to arrange an apprenticeship for him in mechanical engineering in Edinburgh, Scotland.

On his return to the United States young McCoy soon found, like many other blacks, that even a good education in a trade was of little value when it came to finding work in white-dominated businesses and industries. Although he was a certified mechanical engineer, the best job he could find was work as a locomotive fireman—shoveling coal into the firebox that fed the coal-burning steam locomotive engines used by railroads at the time.

The work was both backbreaking and boring, and although it occasionally offered advantages to whites who could slowly work their way up to driving the big locomotives, few black men ever found themselves given that opportunity. McCoy found he needed something to keep his mind active, so he carefully studied engines and other machines and how they worked.

Besides shoveling coal into the mouth of the hot, hungry firebox, the fireman's job also entailed keeping the engine oiled to keep it running smoothly, limit wear and tear on its parts, and prevent overheating due to friction. During every run a locomotive had to make frequent stops for oiling, at which point, the fireman would jump off with an oilcan in hand and lubricate all of the engine's moving parts. Without constant lubrication, the heavy machinery parts would grind away against each other, requiring frequent repair and replacement. It was obvious to the railroads that a better system was needed, but so far no one had come up with one.

To exercise his mind and reduce the boredom of his job, McCoy started trying to picture ways to solve the problem. The trick, he saw, was to get a steady and regulated supply of oil

Elijah McCoy invented an automatic lubricating device for steam engines that helped streamline railroad operations. He had imitators, but McCoy's invention was the original and the best. According to legend, that is the origin of the expression "the real McCoy"—meaning "not an imitation." *(Burton Historical Collection, Detroit Public Library)*

into the moving parts of the engine without having to stop the train. McCoy began to give forms to some of his ideas in a small machine shop in his home in Ypsilanti.

By 1872, he had patented his new system under the title, "Improvement in Lubricators for Steam Engines." The idea was wonderfully simple but elegant: a lubricating cup consisting of a piston set inside an oil-filled container. Driven by steam from the engine, the piston forced oil under pressure down special channels to the engine's moving parts.

At first some railroad companies refused to have anything to do with a device invented by a black man, no matter how useful it might be. However, the "McCoy Lubricator" proved so successful that any company that decided not to use it soon found itself in danger of economic collapse.

McCoy continued to improve his lubricators and began adapting them to work with machines and engines outside the railroad industry. Before long, McCoy Lubricators were being used in applications ranging from ocean liners to factories.

Although hundreds of companies profited by his invention, McCoy never became a rich man. He received more than 70 patents in his lifetime, but he was often forced to sell them away to finance time and material for further improvements on the lubricators and other new inventions. By the end of his life, only a few patents remained in his name.

In 1920, along with a group of financial backers, Elijah McCoy, at approximately age 77, formed the Elijah McCoy Manufacturing Company in Detroit, Michigan. The name McCoy was proudly stamped on all the company's lubricators, which by then were being used not only in the United States but also around the world.

According to some lexicographers, the expression "the real McCoy" (meaning the genuine article) originated when inferior imitations of McCoy's lubricating cup caused concerned buyers to inquire, "Is this the real McCoy?" However, that's only one of several possible origins of the expression. The phrase "the real Mackay," used in the mid- to late 1800s to advertise a Scottish whiskey, may be the oldest and most likely source. Word experts William and Mary Morris contend that "Kid McCoy" Selby, a welterweight world boxing champion, coined the expression to distinguish himself from other boxers who imitated his style—at about the same time that the McCoy Lubricator became widely used. Wherever the expression originated, though, it undoubtedly was also ap-

plied by railroaders to Elijah McCoy's innovative device.

Elijah McCoy died on October 10, 1929. In recent years, his accomplishments have become celebrated, and in May 2001, he was one of 10 honorees inducted into the National Inventors Hall of Fame, located in Akron, Ohio.

Further Reading

Aaseng, Nathan. *Black Inventors*. New York: Facts On File, 1997.

"Elijah McCoy," Inventors Assistance League. Available online. URL: http://www.inventions.org/culture/african/mccoy.html. Updated in 1999.

"Elijah McCoy," Inventors Museum. Available online. URL: http://www.inventorsmuseum.com/ElijahMcCoy.htm. Updated in 1999.

Heppenheimer, T. A. "Elijah McCoy," *Notable Black American Scientists*. Kristine Krapp, ed. Detroit: Gale Research, 1999, 225–227.

Sullivan, Otha Richard. *African American Inventors*. Black Stars series, Jim Haskins, ed. New York: John Wiley & Sons, 1998.

McKinney, Roscoe Lewis
(1900–1978) *anatomist*

When Roscoe Lewis McKinney earned his Ph.D. in anatomy in 1930, he became the first African American to do so. He also established the anatomy department at the Howard University School of Medicine and served as its chair for the next 17 years. For more than 50 years, he taught at Howard and lectured throughout the world.

Roscoe Lewis McKinney was born on February 8, 1900, in Washington, D.C., where he spent much of his life. He was the son of Blanche Hunt McKinney and Lewis McKinney, who worked for the U.S. Government Office in Washington. Young McKinney attended local public schools.

After serving in the U.S. Army during World War I, McKinney earned his B.S. in 1921 from Bates College in Lewiston, Maine. Before continuing on to graduate school, he taught biology for two years at Morehouse College in Atlanta, returning to Washington in 1923 to teach zoology as an instructor at Howard University. It was the beginning of a 53-year relationship with Howard.

With the support of a Rockefeller Foundation fellowship, McKinney began working on his doctorate in the late 1920s at the University of Chicago and received his degree in 1930. His area of research centered on the development of reticulum (a network of cells within an organ) into collagenous fibers in cultures of adult rabbit lymph nodes.

With his doctoral work behind him, McKinney became a full professor of anatomy at Howard University. He also established the anatomy department within the School of Medicine and served as its first chair, from 1930 to 1947. He became vice dean of the School of Medicine in 1931, serving as both chair and dean for 15 years, until 1946.

During the 1950s and 1960s, McKinney made several international trips, some of which amounted to several years of teaching in such divergent locales as the Royal College of Medicine in Baghdad, Iraq (1955–56 on a Fulbright and again in 1956–57); Osmania Medical College of Hyderabad, in south-central India (1960–62); and University of Saigon, Vietnam (1969–71).

McKinney continued to teach at Howard, after he stepped down as department chair, until he retired in 1968. However, he began teaching again in 1971 after returning from Vietnam and continued until 1976.

McKinney's legacy in anatomy has several aspects. The work on reticulum that he did for his doctorate in 1930 was included in the 1952 edition of the *Textbook of Histology*. Two of his tissue samples were included for many years in the standard anatomy reference and text, *Gray's Anatomy*. Along with the establishment of a department of anatomy at Howard, he also founded the first tissue-culture laboratory in the entire Washington area, making Howard a focal point for advice in tissue-culture technique. McKinney's other research areas also included tissue-culture cytology (the study of cells), motion picture photography at the microscopic level, and the use of radioactive isotopes in cell and tissue studies. McKinney also studied ligaments and other connective tissue in vitro.

Roscoe Lewis McKinney died on September 30, 1978.

Further Reading

Knight, Judson. "Roscoe Lewis McKinney," *Notable Black American Scientists*. Kristine Krapp, ed. Detroit: Gale Research, 1999, 227–228.

Sammons, Vivian Ovelton. *Blacks in Science and Medicine*. New York: Hemisphere Publishing, 1990.

McNair, Ronald Erwin
(1950–1986) *physicist, astronaut*

Ronald Erwin McNair and the rest of the crew of shuttle mission STS-51L were upbeat the morning of January 26, 1986. It was to be the first spaceflight ever of a non-astronaut civilian, a schoolteacher named Christa McAuliffe. For McNair, it would be his second mission. For all of them, it was a great moment, full of promise. However, on that sad morning, something went terribly wrong. McNair became the first black astronaut ever to die during a space flight or on the job.

Born on October 21, 1950, in Lake City, South Carolina, Ron McNair was the son of Carl McNair, an auto mechanic, and Pearl McNair, a teacher. McNair attended Carver High School, where he played the saxophone, graduating in

1967. He enrolled at North Carolina Agricultural and Technical University, initially with a music major, but a counselor convinced him to change to physics. He earned his B.S. in 1971, enrolling at the Massachusetts Institute of Technology for graduate work in physics. There, he completed his Ph.D. in 1976, with a dissertation on the generation of laser beams.

McNair married Cheryl Moore shortly after that, and they moved to Malibu, California, where he went to work for Hughes Research Laboratories. At Hughes, he extended his familiarity with lasers, working on satellite communications using lasers.

One of the first three African-American astronauts, Ronald McNair lost his life in the *Challenger* accident in 1986. *(Photo by NASA)*

National Aeronautics and Space Administration (NASA) had become aware that the astronaut corps lacked diversity and had begun actively recruiting black astronauts. McNair's application to the training program was both sought out and accepted, and in 1978, the McNairs moved to Houston, Texas, where McNair began the six-year training program for shuttle astronauts.

McNair's first spaceflight took place in February 1984 aboard the orbiter *Challenger*. The mission was successful, and McNair tested a mechanical retrieval unit, monitored space gases, and tested solar cells—and he played his saxophone, undoubtedly the first saxophone player to play in space. On his second mission, scheduled for January 1986, also aboard *Challenger*, McNair's main job was to be deployment of a spacecraft with a telescopic camera that was going to study Halley's comet. But the flight ended tragically. The morning was icy cold, and a rubber O-ring that was supposed to seal an area of a rocket fuel tank became rigid and brittle and did not seal. *Challenger* exploded and all seven crew members were killed. Carver High School, where McNair had attended, was renamed in his honor. A street in Brooklyn is also named in his memory.

Further Reading

Burns, Khephra, and William Miles. *Black Stars in Orbit: NASA's African-American Astronauts.* 1st ed. San Diego: Harcourt Brace, 1995.

Hawkins, Walter L. *African American Biographies.* Jefferson, N.C.: McFarland & Co., 1992.

Mickens, Ronald Elbert
(1943–   ) *mathematical physicist*

As a mathematical physicist, in his work Ronald Mickens emphasizes the quantitative side of physics and the usefulness of mathematics to describe processes. He is best known for his work with difference equations, useful in working with chaos theory, a relatively new field that provides a framework for understanding irregular and erratic functions in nature. He has written several textbooks on mathematics, as well as editing a biography of EDWARD ALEXANDER BOUCHET.

Ronald Elbert Mickens was born on February 7, 1943, in Petersburg, Virginia, to Joseph and Daisy Brown Williamson Mickens. As a boy he showed aptitude for science and received a full scholarship to attend Fisk University in Nashville, Tennessee, for his undergraduate studies. He graduated with a B.S. in mathematics and physics in 1964. Having earned both Woodrow Wilson and Danforth scholarships, he enrolled at Vanderbilt University, also in Nashville, where he earned a Ph.D. in theoretical physics in 1968. He pursued postdoctorate studies at the Massachusetts Institute of Technology from 1968 to 1970.

In 1970, Mickens returned to Fisk University to serve on the faculty as a professor of physics. He remained there until 1982, when he accepted an appointment at Clark Atlanta University in Atlanta, Georgia, as professor of physics. Three years later, in 1985, he was named Callaway Professor of Physics at Clark Atlanta.

His work as a researcher has been honored by his election to fellowship in the American Physical Society, an honor limited to 0.5 percent of the society membership. Under several federally sponsored grants from various agencies, including the National Science Foundation, the National Aeronautics and Space Administration, the Department of Energy, and the U.S. Army, Mickens has pursued research at several prestigious institutions, including the Los Alamos National Laboratory in New Mexico; the Stanford Linear Accelerator Center in California; the Aspen Center for Physics and the Joint Institute for Laboratory Astrophysics at Boulder, both in Colorado; and the European Organization for Nuclear Research in Geneva, Switzerland. His research topics range from non-linear equations and numerical analysis to mathematical biology and the history of science.

In addition to his research and teaching, Mickens has worked to open physics to blacks, and he is historian for the National Society of Black Physicists. In *Mathematics and Science*, which he edited, he has drawn together a series of some 20 essays by scientists and philosophers that help show how mathematics contributes to the understanding of "sloppy old reality," as one reviewer put it. He has also celebrated the life of Edward Bouchet in *Edward Bouchet: The First African-American Doctorate*, published in 2002 and edited by Mickens.

Mickens has written some 170 published papers and 5 books on mathematics (including two editions of a text on difference equations). As of late 2002, he continued to teach as Callaway Professor of Physics at Clark Atlanta University.

Further Reading

Mullig, A. "Ronald Elbert Mickens," *Notable Black American Scientists*. Kristine Krapp, ed. Detroit: Gale Research, 1999, 229–230.

Williams, Scott W. "Ronald E. Mickens," Mathematicians of the African Diaspora. The Mathematics Department of the State University of New York at Buffalo. Available online. Includes bibliography of publications. URL: http://www.math.buffalo.edu/mad/PEEPS/mickens_ronalde.html. Updated in April 2002.

Milligan, Dolphus Edward
(1928–) *chemist*

Dolphus Milligan investigated the spectroscopic study of free radicals and reactive molecules, and for this work in physical chemistry, he received international acclaim.

Dolphus Edward Milligan was born in Brighton, Alabama, on June 17, 1928. He received his bachelor's degree from Morehouse College in Atlanta in 1949, continuing with graduate studies at Atlanta University, where he earned his M.S. in 1951.

Milligan then took time off from his studies to teach for a couple of years, accepting a position as chemistry instructor at Fort Valley State College (now Fort Valley State University) in Fort Valley, Georgia. In 1954, he moved to California, where he joined the faculty of the University of California at Berkeley as a chemistry instructor, while working on his doctorate. Sometimes spending long hours in the lab, he and another student helped each other with experiments, and 1996 Nobel laureate Robert F. Curl, Jr., later expressed his appreciation for Milligan's help with some of his rather volatile materials. "If I had tried to do these experiments involving liquid hydrogen without help, I believe there is a good chance an explosion would have resulted," he wrote at the time of his Nobel award. "However, a fellow student, Dolphus Milligan, helped me tremendously with these experiments and with his aid I was able to collect the necessary data. . . ." Milligan received his doctorate in chemistry in 1958. His focus of research was the spectroscopic study of reaction intermediates at extremely low temperatures.

After completing his doctoral studies, Milligan joined the Mellon Institute of Industrial Research in Pittsburgh, where he conducted basic research. In 1963, he joined the National Bureau of Standards as a physical chemist. He also became adjunct resident professor at Howard University in 1970, while retaining his position at Mellon. He became chief of the photochemistry section of the National Bureau of Standards in 1971.

For his work with free radical research Milligan received the Arturo Miolati Prize for Free Radical Research from the University of Padua in Italy in 1965. In 1968, he received the Washington Academy of Sciences Award in Physical Science. Additionally the United States Department of Commerce awarded him the Gold Medal for Distinguished Service in 1970. A member of both the American Chemical Society and the American Physical Society, Milligan is now retired.

Further Reading

"Robert F. Curl, Jr., Autobiography," Nobel e-Museum. Available online. URL: http://www.nobel.se/chemistry/laureates/1996/curl-autobio.html. Updated on November 9, 2001.

Sammons, Vivian Ovelton. *Blacks in Science and Medicine*. New York: Hemisphere Publishing, 1990.

Mishoe, Luna Isaac
(1917–1989) *mathematician*

Luna I. Mishoe has an established name in two areas of mathematics—applied and theoretical. He created mathematical methods for solving some of the problems faced initially by the United States in developing its first satellites. He also served for 27 years as the president of Delaware State College (now Delaware State University) and was an influential figure in the state's educational policies.

Luna Isaac Mishoe was born on January 5, 1917, in Bucksport (Horry County), South Carolina. His father was Henry Mishoe and his mother was Martha Oliver Mishoe. Like many black families in the South at the time Mishoe was born, his family was poor, trying to scratch a living out of soil that had been leached of all its nutrients. His father left for New York to find work, and Mishoe's mother and the rest of the children stayed behind. Martha Mishoe encouraged her children to get an education, even though there was no money for it. She knew it was the best way—perhaps the only way—out of the poverty they lived in.

Mishoe always had to work his way through school. He actually began teaching while he was still taking courses for his undergraduate degree. His first appointment was as a professor of mathematics and physics at Kittrell College in Kittrell, North Carolina, from 1934 to 1942. Meanwhile, he received his bachelor of science degree from Allen University in Columbia, South Carolina, in 1938, continuing his studies during summer courses at the University of Michigan, where he completed his M.S. in mathematics and physics in 1942.

During World War II, Luna Mishoe served as a photographic intelligence and communications officer in the "Tuskegee Airmen," the all-black 99th Squadron. After the war, Mishoe accepted a position on the faculty of Delaware State College in Dover, Delaware, where he taught mathematics and physics from 1946 to 1948. He then served as associate professor of physics at Morgan State College in Baltimore, Maryland, from 1948 to 1954.

Meanwhile, he received his doctorate in mathematics from New York University in 1953 and was promoted to full professor at Morgan State the following year. He did postdoctoral research in mathematics at Oxford University in England in the 1955–56 academic year, returning to his position at Morgan State, where he was appointed chair of the division of natural science, where he served from 1956 to 1960.

Mishoe put together a complicated schedule, with summers as research mathematician at the Ballistics Research Laboratory, Aberdeen Proving Ground, from 1952 to 1957. From April 1957 to October 1960, he served as a consultant (in math and ballistics) for the Ballistics Research Laboratories. During this time he developed equations for development of missiles and satellites.

Then he embarked on the phase of his career for which most people remember him: the presidency of Delaware State College (now Delaware

Specializing in applied mathematics and mathematical physics, Luna I. Mishoe helped solve problems related to ballistics and the early development of missiles and satellites. He also served for 27 years as president of Delaware State College, now Delaware State University. *(Courtesy of Wilma Mishoe)*

State University), which he filled for 27 years from 1960 to 1987. During that time he took what had been a poorly endowed black college and made it bloom into a major state university system.

After his retirement, Mishoe began another project, a housing construction project in Dover, Delaware, for low-income families and handicapped tenants. Funding for this project was nearly impossible to find. Mishoe was turned down by religious groups, charities, government agencies—no one wanted to take it on. With the help of his son, Luna, a city planner, he did finally get it going. Finally, because of Mishoe's long service at Delaware State, a state senator sponsored a bill to provide a bond. Then Mishoe needed to find a bank that would purchase the bond, but he did succeed. Unfortunately, before the project was finished, Luna Mishoe died in January 1989. But he knew the project was going to succeed.

Today, on the campus of Delaware State University, the Luna I. Mishoe Science Center stands in his memory, housing offices, classrooms, and facilities for natural sciences and mathematics.

Further Reading

Chiacchia, Kenneth B. "Luna Isaac Mishoe," *Notable Black American Scientists.* Kristine Krapp, ed. Detroit: Gale Research, 1999, 231–233.

Newell, Virginia K., et al., ed. *Black Mathematicians and Their Works.* Ardmore, Pa.: Dorrance & Company, 1980, 291–292.

Mitchell, James Winfield

(1943–   ) *analytical chemist*

As an analytical chemist and senior scientist at Lucent Technologies, Bell Labs Innovations at Murray Hill, New Jersey, James Mitchell has made contributions to methods for ensuring that optic fibers are not exposed to chemical contamination. He is expert in using high-technology techniques for synthesis and analysis of materials and directs Bell Labs' Materials, Reliability, and Ecology Research Laboratory, and he has lectured internationally on these topics.

James Winfield Mitchell was born on November 16, 1943, in Durham, North Carolina. He was the only boy and the oldest of the five children born to Willie Lee Mitchell and Eunice Hester Mitchell. His parents divorced when the children were still small, and Eunice Mitchell brought them up on her own. James attended segregated public schools in Durham and he took the college preparatory program at Hillside High School there. He had the opportunity to attend a summer program sponsored by the National Science Foundation that provided some excellent insights about chemistry, his favorite subject. He developed the sense that chemistry was straightforward and dependable, and those qualities appealed to him as a young man for whom perhaps life had not been so dependable thus far.

In 1961, he entered undergraduate classes at North Carolina A&T College (now the Agricultural and Technical State University of North Carolina at Greensboro), where he became fascinated with analytical chemistry. In 1964, he married Alice Jean Kea, who had been his laboratory partner and had shared in his research for the first three years of college. They both received their B.S. degrees in chemistry in 1965, and they both had summer internships at Oak Ridge National Laboratory in Tennessee. They also attended graduate school at Iowa State University in Ames. The analytical chemistry program there was highly regarded, the university had offered Mitchell a teaching assistantship, and he would have a chance to work at the Ames Laboratory in the summer, where some interesting work was taking place in the area of isolation of rare elements.

Jean Mitchell enrolled in Iowa State's program in nutrition, completing her master's degree in 1966. Later that year, the couple had a daughter, Veronica D. Mitchell. James Mitchell completed his dissertation and earned his Ph.D. in 1970. His dissertation demonstrated the usefulness of some new solvents in the process of extraction and isolation of rare elements from certain mixtures.

James Mitchell received a job offer from Bell Laboratories, which offered him an opportunity to work in an environment with a reputation for supporting both basic and applied research. The labs are also known for their interest in engineering design, development, and testing. He also knew his colleagues would be highly professional and that it was an environment in which he would both be learning constantly and have the freedom to define his own projects.

At Bell, one of Mitchell's first projects involved purifying the environment for manufacture of fiber optics so that contaminants would not degrade their signal-carrying abilities. Mitchell developed a new analytic technique by focusing radioactive rays on the substances used in the core of the fibers. Then he recorded the electronic reactions of the foreign chemicals. He also designed a new technique for purifying the raw chemicals.

Mitchell's work on this project provided some breakthroughs for fiber optics and he received a promotion to supervisor of another team, this time working on noncarbon-based molecules. By 1975 he headed the Analytical Chemistry Department, and the following year, in 1976, he received a patent for his method of purification. He and a colleague, Morris Zief, published a book on the subject.

More recently, his work has made use of microwave discharges and plasmas for synthesis and analysis of materials using spectroscopy and nuclear radiation to develop high-accuracy methods for ultratrace analysis. He also has worked on developing alternative environmentally responsive methods and processes for producing electronic chemicals and device materials.

Mitchell has received several awards, including the Pharmacia Industrial Analytical Chemistry Award in 1978 and the PERCY LAVON JULIAN Research Award in 1981, as well as several others. He is a member of the National Academy of Engineering and he has lectured internationally about his work. He usually emphasizes in his talks that science requires a constellation of skills and commitments. Analysis and quantitative skills are necessary, he says, but so are communications skills. Also, he likes to think of doing science as needing a three-way commitment—a dedication to one's work, a dedication to the community of science colleagues, and a dedication to one's family because that's the source of emotional support.

Further Reading

Kessler, James H., J. S. Kidd, Renee A. Kidd, and Katherine A. Morin. *Distinguished African American Scientists of the 20th Century.* Phoenix, Ariz.: Oryx Press, 1996.

Milite, George A. "James W. Mitchell." Kristine Krapp, ed. Detroit: Gale Research, 1999, 234.

Morgan, Garrett Augustus
(1877–1963) *inventor*

Garrett Morgan had a talent for coming up with inventions that improved people's lives—made them safer or made something basic, such as traffic, move more smoothly. He is responsible for an improved automatic traffic signal, a gas mask, and several handy items, such as a zigzag attachment for a manual sewing machine and personal grooming products.

Garrett August Morgan was born on March 4, 1877, in Paris, Kentucky. He became part of an ever-growing family—the seventh of 11 children. His father, Sydney Morgan, was a former slave who was freed in 1863, and his mother was Elizabeth Reed Morgan. Garrett Morgan left home at age 14 and headed for Cleveland. He had only an elementary school education, but he was naturally practical, adept, and confident. Moreover, he had a talent for gadgets and mechanics and an innate understanding of what was useful. He figured out how to repair sewing machines and he worked for several companies in the Cleveland area before settling down in 1907 with his own shop for sewing machine sales and repairs. His enterprise quickly showed success, and in 1908, he married Mary Anne Hassek. Eventually, they would have three sons.

Later, Morgan opened a tailoring shop, and serendipitously came up with his first unique invention. He had noticed that sewing machine needles sometimes scorched the cloth because they got up so much speed. So he tried a liquid solution to cool the cloth to prevent this undesirable outcome when sewing fine fabrics. However, he noticed that the curly fibers in the cloth straightened out when he applied the liquid. He tried it on a dog's fur. It straightened it. When he tried it on his own hair, it straightened that, too. Morgan had found a hair straightener—so

Garrett Augustus Morgan's talent for invention led to numerous useful and successful devices, including a gas mask and a traffic signal, both of which saved many lives. *(Western Reserve Historical Society)*

he called it the G. A. Morgan Hair Refining Cream and sold it very successfully.

In 1912, Morgan came up with another idea, which he called a Safety Hood and patented as a breathing device. Ultimately, it became known as a gas mask. The Safety Hood was worn over the head. A hollow tube through which the wearer could breathe extended from the front and reached almost to the ground. At the bottom of the tube Morgan had placed a spongy material to filter air flowing through the tube. He received a patent on the device in 1914. Morgan's Safety Hood received extensive attention and several awards, not the least of which was the first Grand Prize from the Second International Exposition of Safety and Sanitation in New York City. According to Morgan's description, the intended use was "to provide a portable attachment which will enable a fireman to enter a house filled with thick suffocating gases and smoke and to breathe freely for some time therein, and thereby enable him to perform his duties of saving life and valuables without danger to himself from suffocation. The device is also efficient and useful for protection to engineers, chemists and working men who are obliged to breathe noxious fumes or dust derived from the materials in which they are obliged to work."

The Safety Hood was truly put to the test on July 24, 1916, when a tunnel exploded at the Cleveland Waterworks. Noxious fumes and smoke from the explosion filled the area, trapping workers in a tunnel under Lake Erie. Someone at the explosion site remembered seeing Morgan demonstrate his device and ran to find him. Many stories exist, but many agree that he, his brother, and two volunteers put on the breathing devices, went into the tunnel, and were able to carry out several men who otherwise would have lost their lives. For his bravery, Morgan received the Carnegie Medal and a Medal of Bravery awarded to him by the city. He also received honorary membership in the International Association of Fire Engineers. Morgan established a company to manufacture and sell the devices, and many firefighters used them. The devices saved many lives during World War I when combat troops wore an updated version of them when they were subjected to chlorine gas and other toxic fumes.

Unfortunately Morgan encountered prejudice when people discovered that the device was invented by an African American. He usually used a white salesperson to do demonstrations, especially in the South, while he masqueraded as an American Indian from Canada who was just there as a helper.

Some historians think that Morgan's second outstanding invention, an automatic traffic signal, may have saved even more lives than the breathing device. The traffic signal eliminated the need for a policeman or other traffic director to be present. The signal had arms to clearly indicate when the flow of traffic was to stop. Before Morgan worked on the problem, traffic signals had just two commands, Stop and Go. Morgan's traffic signal had a bell atop a tall pole. Two flags bearing the word *Stop* could be raised or lowered. An intermediate position meant to slow down and prepare to stop. On the other side of the flags, the word *Go* appeared. The traffic signal rotated to control traffic in all four directions. Morgan's traffic signal received a patent on November 20, 1923, and he sold the rights to General Electric for the enormous sum of $40,000.

In 1920, Morgan established the *Cleveland Call*, a newspaper that reported local and national news of interest to African Americans. He also was active in the Cleveland Association of Colored Men, the local precursor of the National Association for the Advancement of Colored People, in which he was also active after the merger. Morgan lost most of his sight late in life to glaucoma. He died on July 27, 1963.

Further Readings

Aaseng, Nathan. *Black Inventors*. New York: Facts On File, 1997, 87–99.

"Garrett Augustus Morgan," Department of Transportation. Available online. URL: http://eduction. dot.gov/aboutmorgan.html. Downloaded on June 10, 2001.

Murray, Sandra
(1947–   ) *cell biologist, educator*

A high school guidance counselor once tried to discourage Sandra Murray from pursuing a career in science, explaining that it was no career for someone who was black and female. Murray had her own ideas, though. She continued with her vision of a career in cell biology—and she succeeded, both as a researcher and as a teacher.

Born on October 7, 1947, in Chicago, Illinois, Sandra Murray was the daughter of Charles and Muggy Wise Murray, who were in the moving business. Murray's father had a knack for making toys out of found objects or fixing toasters with pieces of junk. The toys could be given to his children and the fixed toasters and other gadgets could be sold at the outdoor market. Murray became interested in how the things he made were put together. Later, she began to wonder how the parts, systems, and organs of the human body functioned and interrelated. As a girl, she had corrective surgery on her shoulder and was cooped up in the hospital, but she used the opportunity to study X rays, ask dozens of questions, and request detailed explanations from her doctors. She already had acquired one of the scientist's most valuable tools—boundless curiosity.

In high school, her capabilities and interests won her the opportunity to attend weekend classes in biomedical research at the University of Chicago, and she was fascinated. This experience

Sandra Murray's work has centered on hormone research and aspects of communication between cells, and she has received invitations to conduct research all over the world, in France, Ethiopia, and Italy, as well as the Marine Biology Laboratory at Woods Hole and Scripps Research Institute on Molecular Biology in California. *(Courtesy of Sandra Murray)*

prompted the discouraging comment from the counselor about aiming beyond her reasonably expected range of success. However, though a little shaken, she decided to keep trying. She got a job working summers and vacations in the anatomy laboratory of the University of Illinois School of Medicine, and this no doubt built her confidence. One of the scientists there, Lucille Wentworth, showed Murray how to prepare tissue samples for observation through high-powered microscopes. Seeing the tiny structures of the tissues and cells through the microscope opened up an entirely new world.

Murray enrolled for classes at the University of Illinois at Chicago Circle in Chicago in 1966, and as soon as she took her first biology course she knew she was traveling the right path—the subject matter was fascinating and she soaked it up easily and thirstily.

While completing her undergraduate degree, she had to work to support herself and pay her expenses at the same time she was attending classes and studying. She received her bachelor's degree from Illinois in 1970 and enrolled in the graduate biology program at Texas Southern University in Houston, where she had a teaching assistantship. She received her master's degree in 1973. Murray then entered the University of Iowa for her doctoral studies, this time supported by a Ford Foundation fellowship. Her area of research was glandular hormones and how they affect the growth of cancer cells in the same gland that produces the hormone. She received her Ph.D. in 1980. The University of California at Riverside offered her a postdoctoral research position with William Fletcher, and she was able to pursue further research on hormones, especially the effects of adrenocorticotropin and gap junction-mediated cell-cell communication on the glands that produce hormones.

Murray received an appointment at the medical school at the University of Pittsburgh, where she taught first- and second-year medical students courses in human anatomy, cell biology, and endocrinology. At the same time she was able to continue her research on cell biology and glandular cancer. She was promoted from the rank of assistant professor in 1987 and then to full professor in 1999 in the department of cell biology and physiology in the medical school.

She has also had research appointments and opportunities at the Marine Biological Laboratory at Woods Hole, Massachusetts (summers, 1986–90) and at the Scripps Research Institute on Molecular Biology at La Jolla, California (1992); Communications Cellulaires et Différenciation, Hôpital Debrousse (INSERM-INRA U 418), Lyon, France (1995); Minister of Defense Health Officer's Institute, Addis Ababa, Ethiopia (1996); and the Department of Reproductive Biology, University of Siena, Siena, Italy (2001).

In recent years, Murray has scheduled visits to schools having high minority student populations to encourage minority students to enter careers in the sciences. Her enthusiasm and her presence give students evidence of both the possibilities and the rewards. In this way, she can advance the spread of knowledge and enthusiasm for science in three ways—through her teaching, through her research, and through her example.

Further Reading

"ASCB Profile: Sandra Murray." American Society for Cell Biology newsletter. Available online. URL: http://www.ascb.org/news/vol20no6/profile.html. Downloaded on August 6, 2002.

Kessler, James H., J. S. Kidd, Renee A. Kidd, and Katherine A. Morin. *Distinguished African American Scientists of the 20th Century.* Phoenix, Ariz.: Oryx Press, 1996.

"Sandra Murray, Ph.D." Department of Cell Biology and Physiology, University of Pittsburgh School of Medicine. Available online. URL: http://www.cbp.pitt.edu/gradprog/progfaculty/pages/murray.html. Downloaded on May 5, 2002.

"Sandra Murray, Ph.D., Professor. Research Interests." Department of Cell Biology and Physiology, University of Pittsburgh School of Medicine. Available online. URL: http://www.cbp.pitt.edu/faculty/murray.htm. Downloaded on May 5, 2002.

N

Nabrit, Samuel Milton
(1905–) *biologist*

Trained as an biologist, in 1932 Samuel Nabrit was the first African American to receive a Ph.D. from Brown University in Providence, Rhode Island. The accomplishment was only one of many firsts. Nabrit would later become nationally influential in science policy. He was a member of President Dwight Eisenhower's National Science Board and he was also the first African American to serve on the Atomic Energy Commission, appointed by President Lyndon Baines Johnson in June 1966. The following year, he became the first African-American trustee at Brown University.

Born on February 21, 1905, in Macon Georgia, Samuel Milton Nabrit was the son of James M. Nabrit, a Baptist minister and teacher, and Augusta Gertrude West Nabrit. Samuel Nabrit received his bachelor's degree from Morehouse College in Atlanta, Georgia, in 1925. When he applied to enter graduate studies at Brown University initially, his application was denied, and efforts were made to discourage him even after he arrived. However, Nabrit was not so easily defeated. He completed his master's degree by 1928 and his doctorate in just three years, entering the program in 1929 and completing his Ph.D. in biology in 1932.

Nabrit originally planned to go into medicine, but at Brown he realized he really wanted to teach, and he juggled teaching biology at Morehouse College from 1925 to 1932 with his studies at Brown. "It's exciting in a way to see youngsters respond in the mastery of something which they never thought they could master," Nabrit said in a 1999 interview.

He also completed research at the Marine Biological Laboratory at Woods Hole in Massachusetts during the summers of those years. He was studying the ability of fish to regenerate tail fins. He found a link between the size of fin rays on the fins and the rate at which they regenerated. His work was published in *Biological Bulletin* and was still being cited as recently as the 1980s.

After receiving his degree at Brown, Nabrit joined the faculty at Atlanta University in 1932, where he served as chair of the biology department until 1947, when he became dean of the graduate school of arts and sciences. From there, he accepted the presidency of Texas Southern University.

When Nabrit was president of Texas Southern University in Houston—from 1955 to 1966, at the height of civil rights activities—he announced that no student would ever be expelled for participation in civil rights activities, despite wishes to the contrary by members of the community. He never backed down on his commitment and he always publicly supported the movement (although he did remove the movement headquarters from campus property). Nabrit himself was active in the peaceful desegregation of Houston. "All that we tried to do was do what we thought was right and ask that all the barriers to our participation be eliminated," he later remarked. "There was no fighting, no quarrels." He coordinated an across-the-board desegregation of movie theaters in Houston so individual theater owners would not lose money for being in the vanguard.

In addition to his appointments to the National Science Board and the Atomic Energy Commission, Nabrit was a founding member of Upward Bound, a program designed to encourage students to stay in college for more than one year. He also served as director of the Southern Fellowships Fund until his retirement in 1981. This pioneer affirmative-action program helped hundreds of African-American students earn their doctorates.

Nabrit also served as trustee of Brown University from 1967 until 1972. In recognition of his many achievements, Brown University honored him by establishing the Nabrit Fellowship in 1985, actually five four-year fellowships to be awarded to minority students in his name. He also received an honorary degree from Brown in 1962. As a further tribute to his accomplishments and his service to Brown University, the university had a portrait in oil done of Nabrit and hung it ceremoniously in a university building.

Further Reading

Coleman, Judy. "Nabrit remembers struggle to receive doctorate," Over Coffee With, Heraldsphere News, browndailyherald.com. Available online.

Samuel Milton Nabrit's early research on fish fin regeneration received citations in scientific journals for nearly 50 years, but he is best known for his roles in shaping national science policy as a member of the National Science Board and later the Atomic Energy Commission. *(AP/Wide World Photos)*

URL: http://www.browndailyherald.com/stories. cfm?S=0&ID=179. Posted on September 30, 1999.

Kessler, James H., J. S. Kidd, Renee A. Kidd, and Katherine A. Morin. *Distinguished African American Scientists of the 20th Century.* Phoenix, Ariz.: Oryx Press, 1996.

Ohles, Frederik, Shirley M. Ohles, and John G. Ramsay. *Biographical Dictionary of Modern American Educators.* Westport, Conn.: Greenwood Press, 1997, 235–236.

Okikiolu, Kathleen Adebola
(Kate Okikiolu)
(1965–) *mathematician*

For both her mathematical work and her work with inner-city children, Kathleen Adebola Okikiolu has received prestigious recognition from both her peers and national-level organizations. She has received particular recognition for her work with elliptical differential operators, which her colleagues consider a major contribution.

Mathematical genius runs in Kate Okikiolu's family, and she is true to her birthright. Her father, George Okikiolu, is a renowned Nigerian mathematician living in London, who has published three books and nearly 200 papers—making him the most published black mathematician on record. Her mother teaches high school mathematics. Kathleen was born in England in 1965.

Okikiolu completed her predoctoral work at Cambridge University, in England, earning her B.A. in mathematics in 1987. She earned her Ph.D. in mathematics from the University of California at Los Angeles in 1991. Her thesis topic was *The Analogue of the Strong Szego Limit Theorem on the Torus and the 3-Sphere.*

After receiving her doctorate, Okikiolu taught at Princeton University as an instructor and then as assistant professor from 1993 to

Okikiolu's award-winning, innovative research on geometric analysis and elliptical differential operators forms the backbone of her rapidly solidifying career in mathematics. Her approachable style and interest in math education have also helped her reach inner-city children with intriguing introductions to mathematical thinking. *(Courtesy of Kathleen Okikiolu)*

1995, followed by an appointment as visiting assistant professor at the Massachusetts Institute of Technology (MIT) from 1995 to 1997. Meanwhile, she joined the mathematics faculty at the University of California at San Diego in 1995, becoming associate professor there as well.

Okikiolu is active in professional organizations in her field, and she is often an invited speaker at their meetings. In 1996, she was an invited speaker at the 25th anniversary meeting of the Association of Women in Mathematics, and in 2002 she delivered the Claytor-Woodard lecture at the conference of the National Association of Mathematics, an organization for African-American mathematicians.

The recipient of numerous awards, Okikiolu became the first black to win a Sloan Research Fellowship in 1997. Later that same year, she won the Presidential Early Career Awards for Scientists and Engineers for "Innovative research in geometric analysis, particularly the determinant of the Laplacian under smooth perturbations, and developing student workshops and mathematics curricula for inner-city children." The award, which carries a prize of $500,000, is made to only 60 scientists and engineers in the United States each year.

Further Reading

San Diego Metropolitan Magazine, Daily Business Report. Available online. URL: http://www.sandiegometro.com/1997/nov/dailyupdt.html. Posted on November 18, 1997.

Williams, Scott W. "Kate Okikiolu," Mathematicians of the African Diaspora. Available online. URL: http://www.math.buffalo.edu/mad/okikiolu.html. Downloaded on August 1, 2002.

———. "Who Are the Greatest Black Mathematicians? The Masters," Mathematicians of the African Diaspora. Available online. URL: http://www.math.buffalo.edu/mad/madgreatest.html. Updated on July 24, 2001.

Owens, Joan Murrell
(1933–) *paleontologist, marine biologist*

Joan Murrell Owens was the first African-American woman to earn a doctorate in geology. Having grown up near the ocean, Owens naturally developed an early plan for a career in marine biology. However, that career did not happen easily.

Born on June 30, 1933, in Miami, Florida, Joan Murrell is the daughter of William H. Murrell, a dentist, and Leola Peterson Murrell, a former teacher. As a child, Murrell loved the ocean and her favorite book was Jacques Cousteau's *Silent World.* She dreamed of exploring that world as her lifework.

In 1950, she began her undergraduate studies at Fisk University in Nashville, Tennessee, only to find out that no one encouraged either women or African Americans in marine biology. Discouraged, she followed her mother's advice and prepared for a teaching career. When she graduated in 1954, she had a major in fine art, along with a double minor in mathematics and psychology. She went on to graduate school at the University of Michigan in Ann Arbor, enrolled in the master's program in commercial art in the School of Architecture. Dissatisfied, she changed to education, receiving her M.A. in 1956. She tried working with disturbed children and then taught college-level English. She could never get her original career plans out of her mind, though, and she never felt comfortable with the alternatives she came up with. By this time, she had married Frank A. Owens, a programming analyst for the U.S. Postal Service.

By 1970, Owens decided to start fresh and re-enrolled at the undergraduate level at George Washington University in Washington, D.C. She decided on a major in geology and a minor in zoology. Upon graduation in 1973, she immediately began to work on a master's in paleontology in the geology department, receiving her degree in 1976. She went on to pursue a doctorate in geology. In search of a dissertation topic, she talked to Stephen Cairns at the Smithsonian Institution, who suggested a group of deep-sea corals known as "button corals." Little was known about them and they might be interesting to study, he thought. She finally finished her degree in 1984—and had already been teaching in Howard University's geology and geography department for the past eight years. She continued teaching there, moving to the biology department when the geology department was discontinued. Somehow, she had arrived at marine biology by the back door. Her research produced a large amount of information on the sea corals she investigated. She developed insights that enabled her to redefine their classification. She even found new organisms. (She named one

Letepsammia franki in honor of her husband.) Finally, she had the satisfaction she had looked for. She found students gratifying—always excited when they found they could grapple with something they thought was beyond them. Joan Owens retired from teaching in 1995.

Further Reading

Kessler, James H., J. S. Kidd, Renee A. Kidd, and Katherine A. Morin. *Distinguished African American Scientists of the 20th Century.* Phoenix, Ariz.: Oryx Press, 1996.

Warren, Wini. *Black Women Scientists in the United States.* Bloomington: Indiana University Press, 1999, 206–218.

P

Parker, John P.
(1827–1900) *inventor*

John P. Parker, who began life as a slave, succeeded in purchasing his freedom, helped free many other slaves, and became an entrepreneur and an inventor with several patents to his name.

John P. Parker was born in 1827 in Norfolk, Virginia. He was the son of a black slave mother and a white father, and he was sold away from his mother when he was eight years old. The slave caravan to which he was sold took him to Mobile, Alabama, where he was purchased by a physician. While in the employ of the physician as a household servant, Parker learned to read and write. When he was 16, in 1843, he traveled north with the physician's sons, who were going to college. However, the physician apparently became nervous he would make a break for freedom in the North and had him come back to Mobile. He was apprenticed to various craftsmen, including an iron molder. Ultimately, after serving an apprenticeship at several foundries, he saved $1,800 and was able to purchase his freedom.

Finally free, he headed for Indiana. There he worked with abolitionists and helped with the Underground Railroad, rescuing people who were fleeing from slavery in the South. He risked being caught many times as he smuggled people out. He married Miranda Boulden of Cincinnati in 1848, and then two years later he moved his family to Ripley, Ohio, where he is said to have ferried more than a thousand slaves to freedom.

In Ripley he established his own foundry, the Ripley Foundry and Machine Company. In 1863, he became a recruiter for a black unit of the Union Army for combat in the Civil War, and his foundry also made casings for the military. Also at the foundry, he invented the devices for which he obtained his patents. In 1884, he recorded a patent for a "Follower-Screw for Tobacco Presses" and another, similar device for a tobacco press in 1885. Later he patented a type of harrow to break up dirt clods while farming—which became known as the "Parker Pulverizer."

John P. Parker is one of the few African-American inventors on record to have obtained patents during this period. Parker died on January 30, 1900, but his foundry kept on working until 1918.

Further Reading

"His Promised Land: The Autobiography of John P. Parker, Former Slave and Conductor on the Underground Railroad" (book review), *Publishers Weekly* 243, no. 37 (September 9, 1996): 71.

"John P. Parker," *World of Invention*, 2nd ed. Detroit: Gale Group, 1999.

Parker, John P. *The Autobiography of John P. Parker, Former Slave and Conductor on the Underground Railroad,* Stuart Seely Sprague, ed. New York: Norton, 1996.

Trachtman, Paul, "His Promised Land (Review)," *Smithsonian* 28 no. 3 (June 1997): 152.

Peery, Benjamin Franklin

(1922–   ) *astronomer, physicist*

An authority on stellar atmospheres, Benjamin Franklin Peery was one of the first African Americans to enter the field of astronomy—and there still is only a handful of African-American astronomers. Successful as both researcher and teacher, and featured on a Public Broadcasting Service (PBS) television show, *The Astronomers,* he has attracted many minority students to the study of astronomy.

Born on March 4, 1922, in St. Joseph, Minnesota, Peery grew up in Minnesota, where his father worked for the railroad and the night-time skies were broad and open. He became fascinated early with the stars and their mysteries—and even more absorbed by the answers he found in astronomy books. He also built and flew model airplanes, and that interest dominated some of his early decisions about his career. In the meantime, though, the United States was on the verge of entering World War II when he graduated from high school in 1940, and he served in the U.S. Army from 1942 to 1945.

After his discharge, Peery entered the University of Minnesota with a major in aeronautical engineering, but midway through his undergraduate studies he realized he liked theoretical science better than applied science. So, he completed his bachelor's degree in physics in 1949.

He took time out to teach at the Agricultural and Technical College of North Carolina from 1951 to 1953 and then completed his M.A.

in 1955 at Fisk University in Nashville, Tennessee. Finally, he entered the graduate program in astrophysics at the University of Michigan, where he served as instructor in 1958, and he completed his Ph.D. in 1962, while teaching at Indiana University.

Peery spent almost two decades, from 1959 to 1976, teaching astronomy at Indiana University. His research during this period centered on the interiors of stars and stellar energy generation. His approach to these areas of investigation was to examine stars in binary star systems in which the proximity of the two stars causes them to affect each other. Numerous scientific articles by Peery have appeared in the *Astrophysical Journal.*

In 1976, Peery became professor of astronomy at Howard University in Washington, D.C., and began to shift some of his emphasis from research to education. Because Howard's students are primarily African American, this location helps bring focus to the presence of African Americans in astronomy. When Peery was interviewed on the PBS series *The Astronomers,* many viewers were both stunned and elated to see an African-American presence in astronomy. Peery is especially committed to developing programs that ensure that young children learn about astronomy. Through a grant from the National Science Foundation, he headed a team that provided future teachers with skills in working with elementary school students.

From 1974 to 1978, Peery was a member of the Astronomy Advisory Panel of the National Science Foundation. He is also a member of the American Association for the Advancement of Science, the American Astronomical Society, and the Astronomical Society of the Pacific, and he has served as a trustee of Adler Planetarium in Chicago.

Now retired, he still loves the stars and all the fascinating processes that take place in the vast universe of stellar objects.

Further Reading

Goldsmith, Donald. *The Astronomers*. New York: St. Martin's Press, 1991.

Henderson, Ashyia N. ed. *Who's Who Among African Americans*, 14th ed. Detroit: Gale Group, 2001, 1,016.

Person, Waverly

(1927–   ) *geophysicist*

Waverly Person has headed the U.S. Geological Survey's National Earthquake Information Center in Golden, Colorado, since 1977. Person and his staff locate between 45 and 50 earthquakes daily as they monitor worldwide seismic activity.

Waverly Person was born in Blackridge, Virginia, on May 1, 1927. He is the son of Bessie Butts Person and Santee Person. He grew up in Lawrenceville, Virginia, where he attended St. Paul's College, receiving his bachelor's degree in 1949, with major areas of study in industrial education and general science.

After completing his undergraduate work, Person joined the army, serving combat duty during the Korean conflict. He left the army in 1952 with the rank of first sergeant and received Good Conduct and Asian Pacific medals. For several years, Person worked at odd jobs until he was offered a position with the U.S. Department of Commerce. His job was to maintain the recording drums and the rolls of records of seismic measurements at the National Earthquake Information Center, part of the Department of Commerce at that time. The squiggly lines on the records aroused his curiosity and he set out to find out what they were all about. It has been a passion with him ever since.

Person recognized that he had hit a limit as a technician—not a lot of room for advancement was available without further training. So, while he continued his work for the National Earthquake Information Center, he began to pursue graduate studies. He took courses from American University and George Washington University for 11 years, from 1962 to 1973, while working at the Information Center. Aware of his interest and aptitude, his supervisors kept giving him more challenging and interesting work. He became a qualified geophysicist, transferring to the U.S. Geological Survey's National Earthquake Information Center in Colorado. He was named director in 1977.

Person has received numerous awards for his work, including an honorary doctorate from his alma mater, St. Paul's College, in 1988 and the Outstanding Government Communicator Award, also in 1988. He is the author of many publications on earthquakes in scientific journals and has contributed to a number of textbooks in the earth sciences. He has earned the respect and appreciation of his colleagues, and people have stopped asking him why an African American would want to be a geologist. He says doing something new raises questions, but when people realize you are good at your job, "people don't see your color anymore."

Person finds his work fascinating, challenging, and never boring because, he says, "No two earthquakes are alike."

Further Reading

Collier, Aldore. "If your problem is earthshaking, call Waverly Person," *Ebony*, September 1987, 134ff.

Henderson, Ashyia N. ed. *Who's Who Among African Americans*, 14th ed. Detroit: Gale Group, 2001, 1,025.

Kessler, James H., J. S. Kidd, Renee A. Kidd, and Katherine A. Morin. *Distinguished African American Scientists of the 20th Century*. Phoenix, Ariz.: Oryx Press, 1996.

Q

Quarterman, Lloyd Albert
(1918–1982) *chemist*

Lloyd Quarterman had the distinction to be one of the select few scientists—and one of only six African-American scientists—who worked on the Manhattan Project, the top-secret U.S. research project that led to the building of a nuclear bomb. In the process, he had the opportunity during World War II to work with Albert Einstein at Columbia University. He also worked with Enrico Fermi after the war on quantum mechanics at the Argonne National Laboratory. Additionally he was a respected researcher in fluoride chemistry, inventing a "diamond window" for the study of compounds using corrosive hydrogen fluoride gas.

Born on May 31, 1918, in Philadelphia, Pennsylvania, Lloyd Albert Quarterman was interested in chemistry from early childhood. He attended St. Augustine's College in Raleigh, North Carolina, where he earned his bachelor's degree in 1943. Immediately after that, the War Department hired him to help work on the Manhattan Project, which was the code name for the secret building of an atomic bomb during World War II. His title at the outset was junior chemist, and he spent time at two locations of the project, Columbia University in New York and the secret underground laboratory at the University of Chicago that later was called the Argonne National Laboratory. In addition to these locations of the project, there were others, which were spread out in different parts of the country, including the famous site at Los Alamos, New Mexico.

The group at Columbia University was the group that initially split the atom, and to do that, the scientists had to isolate the isotope of uranium (U 238) necessary for the fission process. Quarterman was one of the scientists assigned to this task. After the war, Quarterman received a certificate of recognition for "work essential to the production of the Atomic Bomb, thereby contributing to the successful conclusion of World War II."

After the war, Quarterman became primarily a fluoride and nuclear chemist. He used fluoride solutions to create new chemical compounds and new molecules. His colleagues said he was good at purifying hydrogen fluoride, the highly corrosive gas that gave interesting results when combined with other compounds. He succeeded in creating a xenon compound using this technique, which was a surprise at the time, since xenon was one of the "inert" gases—supposed not to combine at all with other atoms.

After having such intense on-the-job training on the Manhattan Project and later at the

Argonne National Laboratory, Quarterman finally returned to school to obtain a master of science degree from Northwestern University in 1952. In addition to his work with fluoride, Quarterman studied interactions between radiation and matter using spectroscopy. He developed the diamond window because he needed to dissolve his compounds in hydrogen fluoride and then shine an electromagnetic beam through the solution to see the vibrations of the molecules and study the X-ray, ultraviolet, and Raman spectra. His window was truly made of diamonds—two of them—which cost $1,000 each.

Later in his career, Quarterman began to work on "synthetic blood." However, he was not able to complete the project before he died in Chicago, Illinois, in the summer of 1982.

Further Reading

Kessler, James H., J. S. Kidd, Renee A. Kidd, and Katherine A. Morin. *Distinguished African American Scientists of the 20th Century.* Phoenix, Ariz.: Oryx Press, 1996.

McMurray, Emily, ed. *Notable Twentieth Century Scientists.* Detroit: Gale Research, 1995, 1,628–1,629.

R

Rillieux, Norbert
(1806–1894) *chemist, inventor*

Before Norbert Rillieux automated the process of refining sugarcane into sugar, sugar making was a labor-intensive, crude, and difficult process, often resulting in poor-quality and expensive sugar.

The son of a wealthy plantation owner, Albert Rillieux was born on a New Orleans, Louisiana, plantation on March 17, 1806. His father, Vincent Rillieux, was a French engineer and his mother, Constant Vivant, was a free mulatto who had previously worked on the plantation as a slave.

Brought up in the luxury of his father's plantation, young Rillieux soon showed that he had a quick and agile mind as well as an interest in machinery. Like many other well-to-do quadroons at the time, as soon as Rillieux was old enough, he was sent by his family to France to further his education. ("Quadroon" was a term popularly used at the time to designate anyone who was more than half white.)

In 1830, Rillieux began his studies at the École Centrale in Paris. An exceptional student, at age 24 he became an instructor in applied mechanics at that same school, and in 1830 he published a series of articles on the newly developing field of steam mechanics.

When he returned to New Orleans in 1833, Rillieux brought with him some new ideas about sugar refining that he had been working on while studying and teaching steam mechanics in Paris.

The technique used to refine sugar at the time was known as the "Jamaica Train." It was a backbreaking and dangerous procedure that involved slaves pouring hot sugarcane back and forth from one large kettle to another until the thick liquid evaporated enough to produce a finished product that looked not unlike lumpy molasses. Not only was the technique slow and inefficient but the slaves handling the large kettles were more often than not badly burned during the process.

Rillieux knew that part of the answer was the use of an evaporating pan. Others had experimented with the pan to refine sugar from the cane but without much success. Basically, the vacuum pan was a mechanical process utilizing a container placed inside a larger container from which the air had been evacuated. Under such conditions liquids boiled under lower temperatures. This system, though faster, safer, and more economical, had more than its share of problems however and had never successfully worked. Controlling the heat was one of its many problems. Too little heat and the sugar failed to refine; too much and the sugar caramelized.

Rillieux's idea was an improvement on the basic system using a more complex arrangement of condensing coils in vacuum chambers in which the steam released in the first step of evaporation could be utilized in heating the sugary substance in a second step, thus giving greater control over each step in the process. It took a long series of trials and errors, but Rillieux finally had a working system for which he was able to obtain a patent in 1843. After adding improvements to the system, he received a second patent in 1846.

Suddenly, with scores of sugar refiners switching over to Rillieux's patented process, he was both a wealthy and a famous man. Wealth and fame, however, did not guarantee happiness. He was still a black man at a time and place where prejudice and injustice held sway with a heavy hand.

Even as one of wealthiest and most famous citizens in New Orleans, he could not walk the streets without fear and restrictions. When he was called in as a consultant to help firms switch over to his process, he was given special housing, away from whites. He was never invited to social events or professional meetings, and no professional engineering journal would read, much less publish, his work.

Finally, when a law was passed in New Orleans requiring that even free blacks carry a pass with them at all times on the city streets, Rillieux had had enough. In 1854, he moved back to Paris. Apparently frustrated when the French showed little interest in his work, he turned surprisingly to a new activity. For the next 10 years he devoted all of his time to the study of Egyptology and hieroglyphics.

In the 1880s, though, he once again returned to sugar refining, and he patented an innovation on his original system in 1881. The innovation cut in half the costs for fuel used in refining sugar in the French beet sugar houses.

Norbert Rillieux died in Paris on October 8, 1894.

Further Reading

Aaseng, Nathan. *Black Inventors*. New York: Facts On File, 1997.

"Additional Biographical Material about Norbert Rillieux: Sugar Chemist and Inventor," Faces of Science: African Americans in the Sciences. Available online. URL: http://www.princeton.edu/~mcbrown/display/rillieux_biography.html. Updated on June 4, 2000.

Milite, George A. "Norbert Rillieux," *Notable Black American Scientists*. Kristine Krapp, ed. Detroit: Gale Research, 1999, 263–264.

"Norbert Rillieux," Inventors Assistance League. Available online. URL: http://www.inventions.org/culture/african/rillieux.html. Updated in 1999.

"Norbert Rillieux: Sugar Chemist and Inventor," Faces of Science: African Americans in the Sciences. Available online. URL: http://www.princeton.edu/~mcbrown/display/rillieux.html. Updated on June 4, 2000.

Smyth, Elaine. "Sugar at LSU: Archiving the Past, Researching the Future," Louisiana State University Library site. Available online. URL: http://www.lib.lsu.edu/special/exhibits/sugar/intro.html. Updated on November 22, 1996.

Sullivan, Otha Richard. *African American Inventors*. Black Stars series, Jim Haskins, ed. New York: John Wiley & Sons, 1998.

Roberts, Louis Wright
(1913–1995) *physicist, mathematician, inventor*

A physicist, mathematician, and inventor, Louis Wright Roberts served for several years as director of Energy and Environment at the Transportation System Center of the U.S. Department of Transportation in Cambridge, Massachusetts. He also served as chief of the Optic and Microwave Laboratory at the National Aeronautics and Space Administration (NASA). Roberts was the author of 15 journal articles and some 120 company, university, and government reports published on the subjects of microwaves, optics, and electromagnetism. He also was editor and author of *Handbook of Microwave Measurements* and the holder of nine patents.

Louis Wright Roberts was born in Jamestown, New York, on September 1, 1913, the son of Dora Catherine Wright Roberts and Louis Lorenzo Roberts. Roberts received his A.B. from Fisk University in Nashville, Tennessee, in 1935, earning his M.S. the following year from the University of Michigan.

He joined the faculty as an instructor at St. Augustine's College in Raleigh, North Carolina, in 1937, receiving a promotion to associate professor of physics and mathematics during the 1941–42 academic year. He moved on to Howard University the following year, where he served as associate professor of physics, for the 1943–44 year.

Roberts began his career in industry in 1944 when he joined the firm of Sylvania Electric Products Inc., as manager of the tube division, where he continued from 1944 to 1950. He joined the Massachusetts Institute of Technology (MIT) Research Laboratory for Electronics as a tube consultant from 1950 to 1951.

Also an entrepreneur, he founded his own firm, Microwave Associates, Inc., and served as president from 1950 to 1955. He developed and helped found Bomac Laboratories, Inc., in Beverly, Massachusetts, where he also worked as an engineering specialist and consultant from 1955 to 1959. Roberts founded a third company, METCOM, Inc., in Salem, Massachusetts, and served as vice president and director from 1959 to 1967. During that period he also helped found and served as president of Elcon Laboratories, in Peabody, Massachusetts, from 1962 to 1966.

Roberts became chief of the microwave laboratory at the NASA Electronics Research Cen-

ter from 1967 to 1968, later becoming chief of the optics and microwave laboratory from 1968 to 1970.

From NASA, Roberts moved on to work for the U.S. Department of Transportation, Transportation System Center. He remained there for the rest of his career, nearly 20 years, serving as deputy director, office of technology, 1970–1972; director, office of technology, 1972; director, office of energy and environment, 1977–79; deputy director, 1979; director, office of data systems and technology, 1980–82; director, office of administration, 1982–83; associate director, office of operations engineering, 1983–84; acting deputy director, 1984; acting director, 1984–85; and finally, director, 1985–89. During that time, Roberts also served as visiting senior lecturer at MIT for the 1979–80 academic year.

Roberts helped guide policy on several key boards and committees. From 1969, he served as a member of the Marine Electronics Committee Panel of the U.S.–Japan Natural Resources Commission. He was a member of the advisory board of the College of Engineering of the University of Massachusetts, beginning in 1972; a member of the board of trustees of the University Hospital at Boston University beginning in 1973; and he was a member of the President's Advisory Board of Bentley College from 1974 to 1990.

Roberts received many awards, including a doctor of laws degree from Fisk University, 1985; the University of Massachusetts Order of the Engineer Award, 1980; a Letter of Appreciation from AGARD/NATO in 1979; an Outstanding Achievement Award, University of Michigan, 1978; election in 1964 as Life Fellow, Institute of Electrical and Electronic Engineers; and the Apollo Achievement Award from NASA.

Louis W. Roberts died on November 3, 1995.

Further Reading

Brown, Mitchell C. "Louis W. Roberts." Faces of Science: African Americans in the Sciences. Available online. URL: http://www.princeton.edu/~mcbrown/display/roberts.html. Updated on June 4, 2000.

Henderson, Ashyia N. ed. *Who's Who Among African Americans,* 14th ed. Gale Group, 2001, 1103–04.

Rouse, Carl Albert

(1926–) *astrophysicist*

In describing astrophysicist Carl Rouse, colleagues tend to use terms such as "controversial," "maverick," and "pioneering." He has been quietly challenging assumptions about the structure of the Sun for some 40 years—sometimes provoking the solar physics community with his "nonstandard" ideas. These questions and theories, however, are issues he has tackled on his own time, as he worked on applied research for such prestigious institutions as the Lawrence Livermore National Laboratory, and the Naval Research Laboratory in Washington, D.C.

Born on July 14, 1926, in Youngstown, Ohio, Carl Albert Rouse grew up as part of a large extended family that included nine children—two cousins, four younger sisters, and two older brothers. His father was an excellent mechanic and the owner-operator of his own auto shop.

As a boy, Rouse was active and learned about science from his hobbies, which were photography and model plane building and flying. Practical engineering experience came from helping out in his father's auto shop. As a student in high school, he excelled, making superior grades, and his chemistry teacher encouraged him to go into science. He graduated a semester early, in February 1944, at a time when the United States was deep in war. However, the army recognized that Rouse had intellectual tal-

ents that were useful to the country and sent him, not into combat, but to engineering school at Howard University in Washington, D.C., Pennsylvania State College (now University), and New York University. The plan called for about two years and six months of course work and by that time the war was over. Rouse received his discharge in July 1946.

Rouse spent a year in Ohio as an engineering draftsman and then resolved to return to college, this time to study physics. He enrolled in nearby Case Institute of Technology (now Case Western University), located in Cleveland. The course work he had done for the army did not transfer, unfortunately, but he did well and his teachers began encouraging him to go on to graduate school. He received his bachelor's degree in 1951. He had also received election to two national honor societies, Sigma Xi and Tau Beta Pi, and was awarded a Physics Prize in recognition of his achievements.

Rouse's scholastic record at Case provided entrance for him to the master's program in physics at the prestigious California Institute of Technology (Caltech), where he received a one-year fellowship. Combined with money for his education from the GI Bill and his earnings from drafting, the available funds made graduate school possible. In his second year at Caltech, Rouse became research assistant to Carl D. Anderson, who had won the Nobel Prize in physics in 1932 for his discovery of a subatomic particle called a positron. Tiny—in fact similar to an electron in size—a positron has a positive charge instead of a negative charge (as the electron does).

Meanwhile, Rouse's own research was guided by his adviser, Eugene W. Cowan. Rouse's project was to design a new instrument for detecting subatomic particles. Because of their extremely small size, subatomic particles present a major challenge for detection. When a particle reacts with another material in a particle detector, however, scientists can detect its presence by observing the disturbances, or "tracks," it makes, imprinted on a glass plate. Once the pattern of tracks is photographed, physicists can study the patterns and learn details about the nature of the particle by observing how much energy it released when it reacted with the other material. The machine that Carl Rouse helped design was able to reveal different patterns of tracks that are characteristic "signatures" of different types of particles. This became the topic of his Ph.D. dissertation.

Rouse obtained his doctorate in particle physics at the California Institute of Technology in 1956. A researcher's researcher, Rouse would much rather research than teach. He worked for the Lawrence Livermore National Laboratory, one of the two national laboratories managed by the University of California at Berkeley. There, Rouse studied the effects of the extremely high temperatures caused by an atomic bomb detonation.

This project led to his interest in the behavior of very hot gases of the Sun and other stars. He concluded that other physicists and astrophysicists were wrong about the structure of the stars (and the Sun). However, the questions he asked stirred up a controversy. He branched out into astrophysics and in his lectures and writings, and he challenged the assumptions made about the intensely hot gases that constitute the sun and stars. Livermore did not provide much support for his ideas, though.

From Livermore, Rouse went to the General Atomic Laboratory in San Diego in 1968. There, he worked on practical applications of atomic energy. His work there went well, and he received a patent for his improvement of a material used to provide protective shielding in nuclear power plants.

Meanwhile, he continued to work on his own questions about the structure of the stars. In 1986, he was able to arrange to make use of the supercomputer at General Atomic Labora-

tory for his project. He continues to write and give lectures on the subject of the Sun's structure. In 1992, he founded his own consulting company, Rouse Research, Inc., in Del Mar, California. He hopes through his efforts to answer some of the mysteries he has explored.

Further Reading

Kessler, James H.; J. S. Kidd; Renee A. Kidd; and Katherine A. Morin. *Distinguished African American Scientists of the 20th Century.* Phoenix, Ariz.: Oryx Press, 1996.

"A Quiet Maverick Sees a Different Sun," NP&D Online. National Partnership for Advanced Computational Infrastructure. Available online. URL: http://www.npaci.edu/online/v5.7/rouse.html. Updated on April 4, 2001.

Russell, Edwin Roberts
(1913–) *inventor, chemist*

During World War II, chemist and inventor Edwin Russell was one of six African-American scientists who worked on the Manhattan Project, the top-secret drive to produce an atomic bomb and bring the war to an end. He went on to work with atomic energy and its processes for most of his life and holds 11 patents relevant to those subjects. Russell has explored areas of research relating to various modes of testing within his research interests, including bioassay and radioactive tracers (both frequently used for testing in medicine) and basic nuclear chemistry topics such as gas absorption, ion exchange absorption, and monomolecular films. He also worked with environmental issues such as treatment of radioactive waste.

Edwin Roberts Russell was born in Columbia, South Carolina, on June 19, 1913. In 1935, he earned his bachelor of arts degree from Benedict College in his hometown of Columbia, obtaining his master of science degree from Howard University in Washington, D.C., two years later. While working on his master's degree at Howard, he served as an assistant and instructor in chemistry from 1936 to 1937, then continuing in that employment after receiving his degree until 1942. At that point, he became assistant research chemist at the Metallurgical Laboratories for the University of Chicago, where he worked from 1942 to 1947. During this time, Russell also worked on the Manhattan Project at its University of Chicago labs (later known as the Argonne National Laboratory). Several famous physicists were involved in this top-secret project, including Italian-American physicist Enrico Fermi.

During the years 1947 to 1953, Russell returned to his hometown of Columbia, South Carolina, to serve as chair of the division of science at Allen University, a small, historically black liberal arts institution. He also served as a consultant in chemistry at Allen from 1947 to 1949.

Russell left academia in 1953 to become a research chemist for the firm of E. I. DuPont de Nemours and Company, Inc., at the company's Savannah River Laboratory in Aiken, South Carolina, southwest of Columbia near the Georgia border. There he earned 11 patents, while pursuing research relating to atomic energy processes. He spent the rest of his career in these research pursuits.

Russell is a member of the American Association for the Advancement of Science (AAAS) and the American Chemical Society. He received an honorary doctorate of science from his alma mater, Benedict College, in 1974, and he received a Special Service Award from the Manpower Commission. He also has served as a trustee for Friendship Junior College in Rock Hill, South Carolina. Edwin Russell is retired.

Further Reading

American Men and Women of Science, 13th ed. New York: R. R. Bowker, 1976, 3,823.

"Edwin Roberts Russell: Chemist, Inventor," *Faces of Science: African Americans in the Sciences.* Available online. URL: http://www.princeton.edu/~mcbrown/display/russell.html. Updated on June 4, 2000.

The Negro in Science. Julius Taylor, ed. Baltimore, Md.: Morgan State College Press, 1955, 185.

S

Shaw, Earl D.
(1937–) *physicist, inventor*

Sometimes called the "Henry Ford of free electron laser technology," Earl D. Shaw is coinventor of a device known as a spin-flip tunable laser. That is, it is a laser that the user can adjust, much like using a dimmer switch on a light. This capability is highly useful for complex or delicate procedures, especially in materials science and biology.

Born on November 26, 1937, in Clarksdale, Mississippi, Earl Shaw faced tragedy at the young age of six when his father was shot to death. His mother, Augusta, raised him alone. They lived on a plantation and he attended a three-room school. The small school may actually have worked to his advantage, since he was exposed to more advanced material at an early age.

Shaw and his mother moved to Chicago when he was 12 years old. They lived in a poor, gang-oriented neighborhood, but Shaw focused on excelling at Crane Technical High School, which he attended. His strong scholastic record gained him entrance to the University of Illinois, and he earned his B.S. in physics in 1960. He entered graduate school at Dartmouth College in Hanover, New Hampshire, completing his master's degree in 1964. For his doctoral

studies he attended the University of California at Berkeley, where he studied magnetic systems using pulsed magnetic resonance techniques. He earned his Ph.D. in physics in 1969.

From Berkeley, Shaw went to work for Bell Laboratories in Murray Hill, New Jersey, and there, with colleague Chandra K. N. Patel, he developed the spin-flip tunable laser. Shaw and Patel in part made use of the work of Indian physicist Sir C. V. Raman, who had experimented with wavelengths of light in the 1920s. As a result, they have named one type of spin-flip tunable laser the "Raman laser."

Their laser's value to experimental scientists lies in the adjustability that derives from the design. An experimenter can back the laser intensity down just enough to achieve results without destroying the material being examined. The spin-flip tunable laser was patented in 1971.

While continuing his work at Bell Labs, in 1991 Shaw accepted a position simultaneously teaching physics at Rutgers University. He later received an appointment as head of the Rutgers-New Jersey Institute of Technology program in Newark. Recently, he has been working on a new laser technology—a far-infrared free electron laser. When completed, this laser is intended to generate short, tunable far-infrared light pulses. Shaw expects this technology to be

During his 19 years as a research scientist at Bell Laboratories, Earl Shaw coinvented the "spin-flip tunable laser," highly useful for scientific research that requires "dimmer-switch" fine tuning in the use of a laser. *(Lucent Technologies, Inc./Bell Labs)*

useful for enhancing biochemical activity with far-infrared radiation.

Earl Shaw is a member of the National Society of Black Physicists.

Further Reading

Sammons, Vivian O. *Blacks in Science and Medicine.* Hemisphere Publishing, 1990.

"Earl D. Shaw—professional activities," Rutgers University Department of Physics and Astronomy. Available online. URL: http://ww.physics.rutgers.edu/people/pdps/Shaw.html. Downloaded on April 23, 2002.

Slaughter, John Brooks

(1934–) *electrical engineer, physicist, administrator*

John Brooks Slaughter has a long reputation in the education, engineering, and scientific communities. He is a former director of the National Science Foundation, president of Occidental College in Los Angeles, and chancellor at the University of Maryland, College Park. In 1993, Slaughter was named to the American Society for Engineering Education Hall of Fame.

John Brooks Slaughter was born on March 16, 1934, in Topeka, Kansas. He was the oldest of three children. His father sold used furniture and worked as a janitor in the well-known Menninger Clinic in Topeka. Young John always wanted to become an engineer—the idea of designing and building things appealed to him—and his parents encouraged him. In high school, though, teachers and coaches tried to steer him toward vocational courses, so he did not get the math and science courses he needed. However, he had a great capacity to learn on his own, and he taught himself much of what he needed to know, such as principles of electronics and how to relate theory to the process of solving practical problems. He set up his own radio repair business, which helped him finance the education he wanted. After graduation from high school, he attended Washburn University in Topeka, so he could live at home while going to school. To obtain the courses in engineering he wanted, though, he had to transfer after two years to Kansas State University in Manhattan, Kansas, a school with a strong engineering reputation. Slaughter received his degree in 1956.

Slaughter began his career as an electronics engineer at General Dynamics in San Diego, California, an aerospace firm. There he worked on many different projects, but had little choice in choosing them. So he took night courses from the University of California at Los Angeles extension division so he could get a better job, receiving his master's degree in 1961. In the meantime, he heard of an opening at the Naval Electronics Laboratory in San Diego. Since Slaughter had developed an interest through his coursework in electronics and control systems, he was of great interest to the navy. While working for the Naval Lab, Slaughter had a chance to work on several interesting projects involving electronic control systems, such as automatic pilots on multiengine military and commercial aircraft. Slaughter did a great deal of work on this subject.

Later, he worked on his Ph.D. in engineering science from the University of California at San Diego, which he completed in 1971. His experience working on his doctorate piqued his interest in two facts about higher education. First he became aware of some of the difficulties involved with managing institutions that offer higher education. Second, he noticed how few African Americans were actively involved in either science or engineering at any level, but especially at the advanced-degree level.

That laid the groundwork for Slaughter's work as an administrator. He went on to become professor of Electrical Engineering at the University of Washington and then academic vice president and provost at Washington State University.

Most recently, he has served as the Irving R. Melbo Professor of Leadership in Education at the University of Southern California. Slaughter is also president and CEO of the National Action Council for Minorities in Engineering.

John Brooks Slaughter is an elected fellow of the National Academy of Engineering, where he has served on the Committee on Minorities in Engineering and chairs its Action Forum on Engineering Workforce Diversity. He is also a fellow of the American Association for the Advancement of Science, the Institute of Electrical and Electronic Engineers (IEEE), the American Academy of Arts and Sciences, and the Tau Beta Pi Honorary Engineering Society. In 1993, he was inducted into the American society for Engineering Education Hall of Fame. He also holds honorary degrees from more than 20 institutions.

Further Reading

"John Brooks Slaughter," The National Action Council for Minorities in Engineering. Available online. URL: http://www.nacme.org/abou/officers/slaughter.html. Updated on March 18, 2002.

Kessler, James H., J. S. Kidd, Renee A. Kidd, and Katherine A. Morin. *Distinguished African American Scientists of the 20th Century.* Phoenix, Ariz.: Oryx Press, 1996.

PRESTON RIDGE LIBRARY
COLLIN COLLEGE
FRISCO, TX 75035

T

Taylor, Welton Ivan
(1919–   ) *microbiologist*

Welton I. Taylor's innovations in detection of bacteria that cause food-borne infections made breakthroughs that rendered foods much safer today than they were just a half-century ago.

Welton Ivan Taylor was born in Birmingham, Alabama, on November 12, 1919. However, his parents, Cora Lee Brewer Taylor, and Frederick Enslen Taylor, moved the family to Chicago soon after his birth. By 1930, because of the stock market crash of 1929 and the ensuing depression, the Taylors moved from Chicago to Peoria, where jobs were less scarce. In this less urban area, young Taylor found he was surrounded by living things. He became fascinated with the snakes, caterpillars, and other creatures he found. Back in Chicago by 1936, Taylor graduated from high school at the top of his class. His school record caught the attention of a wealthy African-American family who offered to send him to college. Taylor still had to work while he was in school, but the pressure of finances was not nearly as great. He graduated with a B.S. in bacteriology in 1941, just as the United States was entering World War II, and because he was in the Army Reserve, he was ordered to active military duty immediately. Despite poor (but correctable) eyesight, he became a spotter pilot as part of the first all-black division in combat in the war. During off-duty hours, he studied insects in the jungles of the South Pacific.

After the war, Taylor used the GI Bill to obtain his master's degree at the University of Illinois in 1948 and his doctorate in 1949. During his doctorate research, he became interested in the study of bacteria that cause food-borne diseases, especially botulism, a deadly form of food poisoning.

He joined the faculty of the University of Chicago as an instructor in bacteriology in 1948. By 1950, he was an assistant professor. During this period he worked on new treatments for tetanus and gangrene, two forms of blood poisoning. His approaches to these infections combined new antibiotics and pain medication with conventional treatments such as hot soaks.

His work with food-borne bacteria attracted the interest of the meatpacking firm of Swift and Company, which offered Taylor a job as microbiologist to set up programs for ensuring that Swift foods would be safe for human consumption. He worked for Swift for five years, later returning to academics, teaching at the Children's Memorial Hospital in Chicago, Northwestern University's School of Medicine, the World Health Organization, the Pasteur Institute in France, and the Colindale Central Public Health Laboratories in England.

In 1965, back at the University of Illinois, Taylor made a breakthrough in detection of certain bacteria that are responsible for food-borne illnesses. By the 1970s, the standards set down by Taylor became the regimen for Food and Drug Administration food inspections. By the early 21st century, they had become standard worldwide.

Taylor's expertise placed him in demand for consulting on issues surrounding microbiological and bacteriological investigations. He is a member of many professional associations, including the American Association of Bioanalysts and the Chicago Medical Mycological Society. In 1985, in honor of Taylor's contributions to the field of bacteriology, a new species of bacterium received the name *Enterobacter taylorae.*

Further Reading

Kessler, James H., J. S. Kidd, Renee A. Kidd, and Katherine A. Morin. *Distinguished African American Scientists of the 20th Century.* Phoenix, Ariz.: Oryx Press, 1996.

Phelps, Shirelle. *Who's Who Among African Americans,* 1998–99. Detroit: Gale Research, 1998.

Temple, Lewis, Sr.

(1800–1854) *inventor*

Lewis Temple's invention of an improved harpoon for whaling revolutionized the whaling industry and brought profit to its inventor, even though he never took out a patent on his work.

Lewis Temple was born a slave in 1800 in Virginia. Little is known about him until he arrived in New Bedford, Massachusetts, sometime in the 1820s. By 1829, he was free and he had married Mary Clark. The couple had three children, Lewis, Jr., Nancy, and Mary. New Bedford was a whaling town on the southern coast of Massachusetts, and Temple, who was a blacksmith and a metalsmith, was reasonably successful, even before he invented his harpoon. Initially

he worked at a blacksmith shop owned by someone else, but by 1845, he had his own shop.

No one had made any real improvement to the harpoon in several centuries, so Temple's innovation was truly a revolution. Prior to Temple's invention, harpoons were like big spears with a line attached. A sharp triangular head pierced the skin of the whale. However, because the sharp edges could cut on their way out as well, a harpoon often slipped back out, especially if the whale gave a good tug. Barbs on the point were added to prevent the back cutting, but the whole head could still cut in the reverse direction. Many whales were lost in this way.

In 1848, Lewis Temple added a toggle to the harpoon head. The toggle worked something like a toggle bolt does in sheet rock. The harpoon head slipped neatly through the whale's skin because the toggle was pulled back against the harpoon's shaft. Once the head had penetrated the whale's skin, the lines to the harpoon could be pulled and the head would swivel inside the skin to form a secure T, with the wings of the T flat against the skin. The cutting edge was then turned away from the skin, and the harpoon was much less likely to cut its way back out and far fewer whales were lost.

The new toggle head was enormously popular, and even though Temple never did patent the invention, he still profited. Still, he had to scramble to keep ahead of his competitors. By 1849, they were hawking his invention with great success. One of them manufactured and sold 13,000 of Temple's toggle-head design.

In 1853, Temple had the misfortune of tripping on a board in a New Bedford street. He sued the city and received a promise of recompense of $2,000. With such a promise in hand, he began building a new shop, but he died in May 1854 from complications stemming from his fall. The city did not come through with the promised recompense for his family, either. However, a statue in honor of Temple now stands outside the New Bedford Public Library.

Further Reading

Aaseng, Nathan. *Black Inventors*. New York: Facts On File, 1997, 1–8.

Hayden, Robert. *Nine African-American Inventors*. Frederick, Md.: Twenty-first Century Books, 1992.

Tolbert, Margaret Ellen Mayo

(1943–) *analytical chemist, administrator*

Margaret Tolbert is director of the New Brunswick Laboratory of the Department of Energy (DOE). She is the first African American and the first female to serve as director of a DOE laboratory. The responsibilities of the New Brunswick Laboratory include prevention of the spread of nuclear materials, preparation and certification of nuclear reference materials for use in the standardization of instruments, and evaluation of nuclear material in samples from around the world.

Born on November 24, 1943, in Suffolk, Virginia, Margaret Ellen Mayo was the third of six children. Her father was J. Clifton Mayo, who served in the army during the war and later worked as a landscape gardener. Her mother, Martha Artis Mayo, was a domestic worker. Her parents separated when Margaret was young and her mother died soon afterward, so the neighbors took care of the children until her paternal grandmother took them in. Later, when her grandmother became ill and unable to take care of the children, Margaret did what she could working as a domestic and doing odd jobs to help put food on the table. One of the families for which she worked took her in when she was a teenager and encouraged her to plan to go to college. She took advanced placement courses in math and science.

Mayo entered Tuskegee Institute (now University) in Tuskegee, Alabama. There, she studied chemistry, graduating in 1967. She had had an opportunity to help as a research assistant on a research project involving the ability of different chemicals to conduct electricity in water under varying degrees of resistance. She had also had the opportunity to attend summer seminars at Central State College in Durham, North Carolina, and Argonne National Laboratories in Illinois. She attended graduate school at Wayne State University in Detroit, Michigan, where she completed her master's degree in analytical chemistry by 1968. Then she returned to Tuskegee, where she supervised research projects and taught mathematics.

In 1970, she set off for Brown University at Providence, Rhode Island, where she began her doctoral work. The Southern Scholarship Fund provided partial funding for her doctoral re-

In 1996, Margaret E. M. Tolbert became director of the New Brunswick Laboratory, U.S. Department of Energy, in Argonne, Illinois. She was both the first African American and the first woman to serve in this capacity. *(Photograph by ANL Media Service—Courtesy of the New Brunswick Laboratory/U.S. Department of Energy)*

search, which dealt with biochemical reactions in liver cells. She also taught math and science to adults at the Opportunities Industrialization Center in Providence. In 1973, she accepted a teaching position as assistant professor of chemistry at Tuskegee, receiving her doctorate the following year, in 1974. At Tuskegee, she was able to continue research on liver cells at the Carver Research Foundation laboratories. In 1977, she became associate professor at the College of Pharmacy and Pharmaceutical Sciences at Florida A&M University. Within two years she was associate dean of the school of pharmacy. (Tolbert and her husband divorced in 1978.)

In 1979, Tolbert had the opportunity to spend five months in Brussels, Belgium, at the International Institute of Cellular and Molecular Pathology researching how different drugs are metabolized in rat liver cells, for which she received funding from the National Institute of General Medical Sciences. After continuing the studies at Brown University, back in the United States, she produced two reports on the biochemistry of the liver.

Before taking charge of the New Brunswick Laboratory, Tolbert had already chalked up an impressive list of firsts. They began in 1979 with the Carver Foundation when Tolbert became the first female director of the Carver Research Foundation of Tuskegee University. She later became the first African-American female to serve as director of the Division of Educational Programs at Argonne National Laboratory. She was the first African American to serve as special assistant to the vice chairs of the Presidential Committee on Education and Technology of the Federal Coordinating Council for Science, Engineering and Technology. She was also the first director of the Research Improvement in Minority Institutions Program of the National Science Foundation.

In 1998, Tolbert was elected a fellow of the American Association for the Advancement of Science. She is also a member of the Sigma Xi honorary society, the American Chemical Society, the Organization of Black Scientists, and the American Association of University Women. She has also served on the advisory committee for training in nuclear power and nuclear safety of the International Atomic Energy Agency in Vienna, Austria, and has served as team leader for tours to Liberia, Senegal, Ghana, South Africa, Libya, and Sudan. Margaret Tolbert has not only done solid original research as a chemist, she has exhibited outstanding qualities as a manager and wisdom as a policy maker.

Further Reading

Kessler, James H., J. S. Kidd, Renee A. Kidd, and Katherine A. Morin. *Distinguished African American Scientists of the 20th Century.* Phoenix, Ariz.: Oryx Press, 1996.

Warren, Wini. *Black Women Scientists in the United States.* Bloomington: Indiana University Press, 1999, 253–254.

Turner, Charles Henry

(1867–1923) *zoologist, entomologist*

Charles Henry Turner garnered an international reputation as a researcher in animal behavior. His primary interest was insects, mainly bees and ants, but his expertise extended to biology, neurology, psychology, and chemistry. Turner was a delegate to the Seventh International Zoological Congress in 1912, and he became one of the few African Americans elected to membership in the Academy of Sciences of St. Louis at that time. He served on the faculty of the University of Cincinnati and headed the science department at Clark University in Atlanta, Georgia.

Born on February 3, 1867, in Cincinnati, Ohio, Charles Henry Turner began life just two years after the end of the Civil War. Thomas Turner, his father, was a custodian of a local church. Turner's father had not ever been a slave, since he was from Canada, where slavery had not ever existed. His mother was a practical nurse and a freed woman from Kentucky.

Turner's father, an avid reader, had a library of several hundred books, and young Turner was fascinated. After graduating from high school, Turner enrolled at the University of Cincinnati, graduating in 1891. He remained to pursue a graduate degree, and he received his master of science degree in 1892. After working briefly as an instructor in a science laboratory at the university, he then taught biology from 1893 to 1895 at Clark College in Atlanta. He taught at several schools from 1896 to 1908, including a high school in Indiana and another in Cincinnati. He briefly served as principal at a high school in Cleveland and taught in a couple of normal schools, which provided education for teachers.

During these years of teaching, he also conducted experiments on insects, reporting his findings in the scientific literature. He soon became recognized as an expert on insects. This original research helped gain him entrance into the University of Chicago doctoral program. Not only were doctorates very scarce in the general population, but most colleges and universities discriminated against African-American students. It was an enormous feat for Turner to obtain his Ph.D., which he did in 1907 from the University of Chicago.

The following year, Turner traveled to St. Louis, Missouri, where he took a position teaching biology at Sumner High School, where he continued teaching for the rest of his life.

Turner's research centered on questions of how ants find their way back to an ant colony, whether insects can hear, and similar questions. He devised carefully conceived experiments to find the answers, demonstrating that insects can hear and distinguish pitch and that roaches can learn by trial and error. He published 49 papers on invertebrates.

Charles Henry Turner's international reputation as a zoologist and entomologist stemmed from his 49 publications in scientific journals, primarily on his studies of insects. An elected member of the St. Louis Academy of Sciences, he earned his Ph.D. in 1907. *(From the archives of the Academy of Science at the Saint Louis Science Center)*

Charles Turner continued to teach at Sumner until 1922. He died in Chicago on February 18, 1923.

Further Reading

Hayden, Robert C. *Seven African-American Scientists.* Brookfield, Conn.: Twenty-First Century Books, 1992, 34–57.

McMurray, Emily, ed. *Notable Twentieth Century Scientists.* Detroit: Gale Research, 1995, 2,056–2,057.

Tyson, Neil de Grasse
(1959–   ) *astronomer, astrophysicist*

Author, astrophysicist, and director of the Hayden Planetarium, American Museum of Natural History, Neil de Grasse Tyson is an urbane and outspoken champion of science as well as an active debunker of many of the current popular pseudoscience crazes.

Born in 1959 in New York City, Tyson was raised in the tough streets of the Bronx. Viewing the stars through a pair of binoculars from a Bronx rooftop, Tyson knew at an early age that

Neil de Grasse Tyson brings his scientific expertise as an astrophysicist and his talent as a communicator to his position as director of the Hayden Planetarium, American Museum of Natural History. *(Photograph by Patrick Queen,* Columbia Magazine*)*

he wanted to study space science. In a neighborhood where athletic ability was admired much more than brains, it wasn't an easy decision. In his neighborhood being smart was "not on the list of things that gets you respect," he recalled. Fortunately Tyson was also an exceptional athlete and mixed his rooftop star sessions with an active participation in school sports. He was lucky also in finding a few close friends who shared his more cerebral interests such as chess and mathematical puzzles. He bought his first telescope at age 14 with money he had earned walking dogs for busy neighborhood adults. Fortunately, too, his parents actively supported his interest in astronomy. His mother was an "astromom" he remembers. "If I ever needed a lens or a book, she would work to insure that I got it."

Others, too, noted young Tyson's determined fascination with astronomy. His sixth-grade science teacher, for example, showed him an advertisement for a special Hayden Planetarium evening course called Astronomy for Young People. He was younger than most of the other students who attended, but he quickly proved himself one of the brightest of the participants. "It opened my eyes to the study of the universe as an academic pursuit rather than as a weekend curiosity," Tyson says. Other special classes at the Hayden followed. Soon he became a member of the Amateur Astronomers Association and editor of the *Physical Science Journal* while attending the Bronx High School of Science, where he specialized in astrophysics. While in high school he also began to actively observe the career paths of astronomers and scientists by reading biographies and articles in popular science magazines. Determined to become a professional scientist, he made a careful study of just "what kind of people they were," he notes, "and where they got their degrees." Even at an early age he was showing the kind of cool determination that would mark his later scientific work.

While working for his bachelor's degree in physics at Harvard University, Tyson also managed to keep up his athletic pursuits, becoming a member of the Harvard wrestling team and rowing on the crew team. After receiving his master's degree from the University of Texas at Austin, he returned to New York, where he completed his doctoral work in astrophysics at Columbia University.

Always a lucid communicator and staunch advocate of science, in addition to dozens of professional publications Tyson has written numerous books on astronomy and astrophysics for the general public. He is the author of a well-received memoir, *The Sky Is Not the Limit: Adventures of an Urban Astrophysicist,* and he has also written articles for many magazines, including a regular series of monthly essays for *Natural History.*

Returning to his beloved childhood hangout, Tyson became staff astronomer at the Hayden Planetarium in 1994. He became its acting director in 1995, and in 1996 assumed the planetarium's newly created position as Frederick P. Rose Director.

Today, as the youngest-ever director of the Hayden and visiting research scientist in astrophysics at Princeton University (where he also teaches), Tyson continues to pursue not only his science but an ever-widening range of communication channels in his attempt to reach out and instruct the public in the values of science and science education. A frequent and popular guest on television shows, he is also a fellow of the Committee for the Scientific Investigation of the Paranormal (CSICOP), an international organization devoted to science education and investigation of claims of the paranormal. The present fascination of much of the public with pseudoscience and the paranormal, as well as the growing anti-rational and anti-science stance of many educators and academics, is deeply troubling to Tyson. "Science literacy has an importance like never before," he says. "I try to carry with me a cosmic perspective and share the breadth and depth of the Universe."

Further Reading

Heckert, Paul A. *Notable Black American Scientists.* Kristine Krapp, ed. Detroit: Gale Research, 1999, 304–305.

Tyson, Neil de Grasse. "Interview with Neil de Grasse Tyson," Interviews, Rose Center for Earth and Space. Available online. URL: http://www.amnh.org/rose/interviews.html. Downloaded on April 13, 2002.

———. *Just Visiting This Planet.* New York: Doubleday, 1998.

———. *Merlin's Tour of the Universe.* New York: Columbia University Press, 1989.

———. *The Sky Is Not the Limit: Adventures of an Urban Astrophysicist.* New York: Doubleday, 2000.

———. *Universe Down to Earth.* New York: Columbia University Press, 1994.

Tyson, Neil de Grasse, Charles Liu, and Robert Irion. *One Universe: At Home in the Cosmos.* Washington, D.C.: Joseph Henry Press, 2000.

W

Walker, Arthur Bertram Cuthbert, II
(Art Walker)
(1936–2001) physicist

Art Walker was a pioneering African-American physicist who collaborated with other scientists to send multilayer mirrors into space to study the Sun. The technology he developed gave scientists and the public a spectacular new view of the Sun never before seen and is now widely used in National Aeronautics and Space Administration (NASA) satellites.

Born in Cleveland, Ohio, on August 24, 1936, Arthur Bertram Cuthbert Walker, II, was born into a family rooted in both intellectual strength and compassion. His father was a lawyer and his mother, Hilda, was a social worker and Sunday school teacher. His maternal grandfather, who came to the United States from Barbados, had settled in Cleveland and founded a black newspaper, *The Advocate*, in the early 1900s.

At about age five, Arthur Walker moved with his family to New York. He entered elementary school there, in the Sugar Hill district of Harlem. However, his mother became disappointed in the quality of education he was receiving and moved him to another district. Later, she supported his early interest in science by encouraging him to apply to the Bronx High School of Science. He passed the entrance exam and stoked his growing enthusiasm for physics with the excellent learning environment he found there. Some of his teachers painted a dismal picture of a black scientist's future in the United States—suggesting he might meet with more success in Cuba. His mother came again to his support by visiting the school and telling his teachers he would study whatever he pleased and pursue his career wherever he wanted to. He received his bachelor's degree in physics with honors in 1957 from the Case Institute of Technology (now Case Western University) in Cleveland. He earned his master's degree in 1958 and his doctorate in 1962, both from the University of Illinois. For his dissertation he wrote on the use of radiation to produce the particles that bind protons and neutrons together in the atomic nucleus.

In 1962, Walker joined the U.S. Air Force with the rank of first lieutenant. He received assignment to the Air Force Weapons Laboratory, where he developed instrumentation for the experiment that was to be launched by rocket and carried into orbit aboard a satellite to measure the Van Allen belt radiation in Earth's magnetic field.

Once his military duty was fulfilled, Walker joined the Space Physics Laboratory of the Aerospace Corporation, where he conducted pioneering physics experiments over a span of

Solar physicist Arthur B. C. Walker works in his home office, preparing for a lecture at Stanford University, where he taught for 27 years. *(Courtesy of Victoria T. Walker)*

nine years to study the Sun and upper atmosphere of the Earth.

Walker joined the faculty at Stanford University at Stanford, California, as professor of physics and applied physics in 1974. There he directed the student observatory and taught astronomy courses including two popular classes for non-physics majors, Applied Physics 15, "The Nature of the Universe," and Physics 50, "Observational Astronomy."

In the 1980s, Troy Barbee, a senior research associate at Stanford's Center for Materials Research, created multilayered thin films that could capture images produced by extremely hot solar gas. Barbee once pointed out, "One of the things I have learned over the years as a materials scientist is that materials don't *do* anything; people do things with materials. Art [Walker] has taken those things which I was able to put on the table and use them to demonstrate new science and develop new technologies." In 1987, Walker used these materials to develop telescopes and complex instrumentation. He then mounted the telescopes on rockets and launched them into space to capture the first detailed pictures of the Sun's outermost atmosphere, or corona. His pictures were the first "soft X-ray" images of the Sun. Bob Byer, chair of the department of applied physics at Stanford later recalled, "The images showed spectacular surface details of the Sun, including flares, bubbles, and gas jets. Art was just thrilled with these images. I will never forget his face when he showed us the first images." Images taken during the first flight of Walker's solar telescope became such hot news in the scientific world that they made the cover of the September 30, 1988, issue of *Science* magazine.

Walker was the only African American named in 1986 to the 10-member presidential board investigating the cause of the *Challenger* space shuttle disaster. He supervised the doctoral research of Sally K. Ride, who was the first American woman in space and was also a member of the presidential panel.

Walker was also a leader in the community of African-American physicists, an active advocate for diversifying academic institutions, and a role model for many.

Arthur Walker died of cancer in his home in Stanford, California, on April 29, 2001.

Further Reading

"Black solar physicist on Space Shuttle Commission," *Jet*, February 24, 1986, p. 4.

Glanz, James. "Arthur Walker, 64, Scientist and Mentor, Dies." *New York Times*, May 9, 2001, p. B8.

Levy, Dawn. "Art Walker: 'favorite sun' of solar physics." *Stanford Report*. Available online. URL: http://www.stanford.edu/dept/news/report/news/october4/walkerprofile-104.html. Updated on October 4, 2000.

The New York Times Biographical Service vol. 32, no. 5 May 2001, pp. 831–832.

Williams, Scott. "Arthur Bertram Cuthbert Walker, Jr.," Physicists of the African Diaspora. Available online. URL: http://www.math.buffalo.edu/mad/physics/walker_arthurbc.html. Updated in April 2002.

Walker, Sarah Breedlove McWilliams (Madam C. J. Walker)
(1867–1919) *inventor, entrepreneur*

Sarah Breedlove McWilliams Walker, who preferred to be called Madam C. J. Walker, was one of the most successful African-American entrepreneurs of her time—a woman who had considerable ingenuity and business know-how. In fact, she was the first self-made woman millionaire in the country. Most of her success came from the sales of products she invented and, as with GARRETT AUGUSTUS MORGAN, she had a knack for knowing what people wanted and would buy.

Sarah Breedlove was born on December 23, 1867, to Owen and Minerva Breedlove in Louisiana, just across the river from Vicksburg, Mississippi. She was the first of her parents' three children to be born free. Her parents both died seven years later, in a yellow fever epidemic. She and her older sister tried to manage by taking in laundry, but finally Sarah tried to escape her predicament by marrying Moses McWilliams when she was 14. The couple had a daughter, Lelia (later known as A'Lelia), in 1885. Then just two years later, McWilliams was killed in an automobile accident. Sarah was down on her luck again, this time with a daughter to feed. She decided to head north, took in laundry, and sent her daughter to public schools. The stress of her situation plus other factors began to make her hair fall out, and she tried to find an ointment that would stop the hair loss. She even tried selling one that was on the market, but it didn't work for her, so it was difficult to sound very convincing. She was desperate until one day she had a dream that, she said, supplied the secret formula for a hair loss treatment that would work. She tried her formula and it worked for her, so she shared it with friends. She began to realize that most hair treatments and pomades were designed for white women, who had completely different concerns—more interested in curling their hair than straightening it. She began by selling her hair ointment to friends and acquaintances. In 1905, she heard that her brother had died in Denver, Colorado. His wife and two daughters were in need, and Sarah devised a plan that involved going to Denver, which she did, arriving with no more than two dollars in her pocket. Her two products were the hair ointment and a hot steel comb with wide teeth that worked well on African Americans' thick, wiry hair. An acquaintance, C. J. Walker, advised her to place some ads in black newspapers, which she did. She and C. J. married in 1906 and he helped set up the new business, which flourished. However, they had different goals. Sarah was willing to risk everything on trying to make big money; C. J. liked to play it safe. They divorced in 1912, but she kept her moniker, "Madam C. J." and he continued to sell product for her company. Walker had brought her daughter Lelia into the business in 1906, and by 1910, they had moved the company headquarters to Indianapolis.

Walker preceded Mary Kay Cosmetics by several years with the concept of hiring and training salespeople to demonstrate and sell the products door to door. By 1917, the Madam C. J. Walker Manufacturing Company was a multimillion-dollar success story. It was, in fact, the largest black-owned business in the country.

That same year, Walker made one of her greatest statements of success by building an impressive 20-room dwelling in Irvington, New York, on the Hudson River. Always committed to supporting black enterprise, Walker chose a black architect. She named the place Villa Lewaro and furnished it opulently, including a gilded piano.

Eager to add to her achievements, she continued to travel tirelessly, pouring her energy into making her business ever bigger and even more successful. Finally, in 1919 on a trip to St. Louis, Walker collapsed. She was hurried home by private railroad car. On May 25, 1919, her kidneys failed due to high blood pressure, and Madam C. J. Walker died.

At a time when women were considered to have no practical or mechanical abilities and no business sense, the idea of a female inventor-entrepreneur went against the grain. So, where black male inventors such as Garrett Morgan could not sell their own products, it is easy to imagine what kinds of obstacles a female African-American inventor faced. Sarah Breedlove

Madam C. J. Walker, as Sarah Walker liked to be called, was both a creative inventor of hair treatments for African Americans and an innovative and successful entrepreneur. *(Madam C. J. Walker Collection, Indiana Historical Society, C2140)*

McWilliams Walker was fully up to the challenge, however.

Further Reading

Aaseng, Nathan. *Black Inventors*. New York: Facts On File, 1997.

Notable Black American Women, Vol. 1, Jessie Carney Smith, ed. Detroit: Gale Research, 1996, 1,184–1,188.

Washington, Warren Morton

(1936–) *physicist, meteorologist*

In the 1960s, Warren Washington was among the first to develop atmospheric computer models at the National Center for Atmospheric Research (NCAR) in Boulder, Colorado. The complexity of these equations makes them almost impossible to complete manually. The book *An Introduction to Three-Dimensional Climate Modeling*, coauthored by Washington and Claire Parkinson, has become a standard text in the field.

On August 28, 1936, Warren Morton Washington was born in Portland, Oregon. In 1958, he earned his B.S. in physics from Oregon State University in Corvallis. He received a master of science degree in meteorology in 1960 and a Ph.D. in 1964 from Pennsylvania State University. For the next two years, he worked at Pennsylvania State as a research assistant in the department of meteorology. Then from 1963 to 1969, he joined NCAR as a scientist. From 1969 to 1971, he taught in the department of meteorology and oceanography at the University of Michigan. From 1975 to 1978, he served on the Government Science Advisory Committee, State of Colorado, and from 1978 to 1984, he served on the President's National Advisory Committee on Oceans and Atmosphere, returning to NCAR in 1987 as senior scientist. Washington became climate division director for NCAR in 1993.

At NCAR, Washington and others have followed up his groundbreaking work in atmo-spheric computer modeling with more complex models. Washington has worked with others on incorporating ocean and sea ice physics as part of climate models. Contemporary models, as of 2002, usually involve atmospheric ocean, sea ice, surface hydrology, and vegetation components.

Washington is a member of the National Science Board, the Secretary of Energy's Advisory Board, and the Secretary of Energy's Biological and Environmental Research Committee (BERAC) and is chair for Global Change for BERAC. He is also a member of the National Centers for Environment Prediction Advisory Committee and the National Oceanic and Atmospheric Agency Science Advisory Board. He belongs to several professional organizations, including the National Academy of Sciences, the National Science Foundation, the American Association for the Advancement of Science (AAAS), and Minorities in Science.

Further Reading

Hawkins, Walter L. *African American Biographies, 2*. Jefferson, N.C.: McFarland & Co., 1994.

Who's Who Among African Americans, 14th ed. Detroit: Gale Group, 2001.

West, Harold Dadford

(1904–1974) *biochemist, educator*

The science center at Meharry Medical College in Nashville, Tennessee, is named for Harold Dadford West and there is good reason. West devoted nearly his entire career—47 years of biochemical research and teaching, 13 of them serving as president of Meharry—to that institution.

Harold Dadford West was born on July 16, 1904, in Flemington, New Jersey. He was the son of George H. West and Mary Ann Toney West. He received his bachelor's degree from the University of Illinois in 1925, becoming associate professor and head of the science department at Morris Brown College in Atlanta from 1925 to 1927.

Then in 1927, he went to Meharry Medical College as an associate professor of physiological chemistry. While on the Meharry faculty, West continued with the graduate studies he had not yet completed. With the help of a Julius Rosenwald fellowship, he was able to attend the University of Illinois to obtain his master's degree in 1930. Then, as a Rockefeller Foundation Fellow, he pursued his doctorate degree at Illinois, completing it in 1937. His dissertation title was "The Chemistry and Nutritive Value of Essential Amino Acids." The following year, West became professor of biochemistry and chair of the department.

West left an enormous legacy in biochemical research. His work was supported by grants from the John and Mary R. Markle Foundation, the Nutrition Foundation, the National Institutes of Health, and the American Medical Association. Several professional journals published his research reports, including the *American Journal of Physiology, Southern Medical Journal,* and *Journal of Biological Chemistry.*

As a biochemical researcher, educator, and administrator, Harold Dadford West worked tirelessly to contribute to the growth of his field, his students, and his school, Meharry Medical College, of which he became the first African-American president in 1952. *(AP/Wide World Photos)*

In his work with amino acids, he succeeded in synthesizing threonine. He studied tuberculosis and other bacilli. He investigated the antibiotic biocerin, and he studied aromatic hydrocarbons. The *Journal of the National Medical Association* published this additional list of his studies: "the role of sulfur in biological detoxification mechanisms; blood serum calcium levels in the Negro in relation to possible significance in tuberculosis; relation of B-vitamins, especially pantothenic acid, to detoxification of sulfa-drugs and susceptibility to bacillary disease."

West became the first African-American president of Meharry Medical College in 1952. He was also the first African American to serve on the State Board of Education, a distinction he earned in 1963. West retired from the presidency in 1965, returning to teaching until his retirement in 1973. He then became a trustee of the college.

West received an honorary doctor of laws from Morris Brown College in 1955, and in 1970, Meharry Medical College also bestowed an honorary doctor of science degree on him. He also belonged to several honorary and professional societies. Harold Dadford West died on March 5, 1974.

Further Reading

Cobb, W. M., and C. C. Sampson. *"Harold Dadford West." Journal of the National Medical Association* 66, no. 5 (September 1974): 448–449.

Sammons, Vivian Ovelton. *Blacks in Science and Medicine.* New York: Hemisphere Publishing, 1990.

Wilkins, J. Ernest, Jr.

(1923–)   *mathematical physicist*

J. Ernest Wilkins, Jr., is a respected applied mathematician and nuclear engineer whose career has included the governmental, industrial, and academic spheres. Early in his career he contributed to the Manhattan Project, the top-secret U.S. project to build a nuclear bomb during World War II. He also pioneered in nuclear reactor design. During his career, he has contributed to optical instruments in space, as well as the mathematical theory of Bessel functions, differential and integral equations, and the calculus of variations.

J. Ernest Wilkins, Jr., was born in Chicago, Illinois, on November 27, 1923. His father, J. Ernest Wilkins, was a prominent lawyer and served as assistant secretary of labor during the Dwight D. Eisenhower administration. His mother, Lucile Beatrice Robinson Wilkins, had a master's degree and taught school. Wilkins had two brothers, both of whom became lawyers, but Wilkins preferred mathematics. He entered the University of Chicago at age 13—becoming the youngest student ever admitted there. He earned his doctorate by the time he was 19, in 1942. For postgraduate studies, he earned a Rosenwald scholarship to the Institute for Advanced Study in Princeton, New Jersey, for a year, followed by teaching at the Tuskegee Institute for the 1943–44 academic year. From 1944 to 1946 he worked in the Metallurgical Laboratory on the Manhattan Project at the University of Chicago.

From 1946 to 1960, Wilkins worked in industry for various firms and a variety of projects. He started with the American Optical Company in Buffalo, New York, as a mathematician. In 1950, he went to the Nuclear Development Corporation of America (NDA), which later became United Nuclear Corporation, in White Plains, New York, starting as senior mathematician, filling various managerial positions in research and development. During this period he earned a bachelor of mechanical engineering (1957) and master's of mechanical engineering (1960) from New York University.

Wilkins served as president of the American Nuclear Society during 1974 and 1975, as well as several other offices in the 1960s and 1970s. He also moved west to work for the General

Atomic Division of General Dynamics Corporation in San Diego, where he remained until 1970. Then he returned to the East Coast, joining the faculty of Howard University in Washington, D.C., for seven years as Distinguished Professor of Applied Mathematical Physics.

In 1977, EG&G Idaho in Idaho Falls hired Wilkins to serve as associate general manager and later deputy general manager. From there, Wilkins returned to Chicago to become an Argonne Fellow at Argonne National Laboratory from 1984 to 1985, when he retired. Since then, he has continued to work as a consultant, and in 1990 he accepted the appointment of Distinguished Professor of Applied Mathematics and Mathematical Physics at Clark Atlanta University in Georgia.

Further Reading

Agwu, Nkechi, and Asamoah Nkwanta. "Dr. J. Ernest Wilkins, Jr.: The Man and His Works." *African Americans in Mathematics*, DIMAZS, vol. 34 Providence, R.I.: American Mathematics Society, 1997.

Houston, Johnny L. "J. Ernest Wilkins, Jr." MAA online, The Mathematical Association of America. Available online. URL: http://www.maa.org/summa/archive/WilkinsJ.htm. Originally published fall 1994 NAM Newsletter. Last update in fall 1994.

Kessler, James H., J. S. Kidd, Renee A. Kidd, and Katherine A. Morin. *Distinguished African American Scientists of the 20th Century*. Phoenix, Ariz.: Oryx Press, 1996.

Tubbs, Vincent. "Adjustment of a Genius," *Ebony*, February 1958, 60–67.

Williams, Daniel Hale
(1856–1931) *surgeon, hospital administrator*

Daniel Hale Williams was the first surgeon to operate successfully on a patient's heart. He founded the first interracial hospital in the United States and the first training school for black nurses.

Daniel Williams, Jr., and Sarah Price Williams, the parents of Daniel Hale Williams, were free blacks of mixed white, black, and Indian ancestry. Williams was born on January 18, 1856, in Hollidaysburg, Pennsylvania. He was one of seven children. His father, a barber by profession, died when Daniel was 11. Unable to support the seven children by herself, his mother separated the family and sent them to various relatives and boarding schools. Williams was apprenticed out to a shoemaker who was a friend of the family.

Not caring much for the shoemaking trade, Williams soon left that position and began seeking other odd jobs to support himself. After a few years of wandering, he settled down with an older sister in Janesville, Wisconsin. There Williams took up his father's trade, working for a local barber, Charles Anderson. Anderson took a liking to the young man who was so quick and agile with his hands, and he encouraged Williams to pick up his schooling again in his off-hours. With this encouragement Williams made up for lost time and graduated in 1877.

While working in the barbershop, Williams made the acquaintance of a local doctor, Henry Palmer. Like Anderson, Dr. Palmer was quick to recognize Williams's keen mind and agile hands. Intrigued by Dr. Palmer's discussions of medicine from the barber chair, Williams became interested in the medical profession. It was common practice at the time for young men to begin their medical training by working with a local doctor before entering medical school, so Palmer took the bright young man on as his assistant.

In 1880, with money he had managed to save and a financial helping hand from Anderson, Williams joined two other apprentices of Palmer's as they left the doctor's employment to attend the Chicago Medical College. Williams received his medical degree in 1883 and after serving a short internship at Mercy Hospital began private practice in Chicago's South Side in 1884.

Williams had demonstrated a talent for surgery while in medical school and it soon became his area of specialization in private practice. As was common then, he often performed surgery in the patient's home under less-than-ideal circumstances, with a dining room table substituting for an operating table. Williams was a strong proponent of the then-controversial ideas of English surgeon Joseph Lister, who insisted that antiseptic and sterile conditions be observed in the operating room. So Williams made certain that the same conditions were applied during his at-home surgeries. He had the walls and floors scrubbed down, fresh linen laid out on the table, and water kept boiling on the kitchen stove for the sterilization of instruments.

"Dr. Dan," as he was called by his patients, was soon one of Chicago's busiest physicians. In addition to his own busy practice, he began serving as a surgeon at the South Side Dispensary in 1884, as well as attending physician at the Protestant Orphan Asylum. In 1885 he took over as an instructor of anatomy at the Chicago Medical College and also served as a surgeon for the City Railroad Company. In 1889, he was appointed a member of the Illinois State Board of Health.

In 1891, Williams saw a long-held dream come true with the opening of Provident Hospital. It was a project he had spent years fighting for—the foundation of an interracial hospital that would admit patients of all colors and be staffed by both black and white doctors. Equally important, the hospital would house a school for black nurses where they could receive top instruction, which was sorely needed at the time since few opportunities were open for black nurses to study their profession.

By cajoling friends, convincing authorities, and setting up committees and fund-raising events, Williams succeeded in opening up his hospital in a three-story building with only 12 beds, but it soon became one of the city's most active and respected hospitals and training facilities.

It was at Provident in 1893 that Williams made medical history by performing the world's first successful heart surgery. The patient, a young black man named James Cornish, had been stabbed in a barroom fight. The wound at first appeared superficial but Williams, then chief surgeon at Provident, observed the patient's quickly deteriorating condition and quickly surmised that the man was suffering from internal bleeding. He realized the knife that had stabbed through the young man's chest had most probably hit a blood vessel, or worse yet, the heart itself.

Opening the chest was a difficult and risky operation in the 1890s and few physicians attempted it. Most of the world's leading surgeons advised against it. Williams, however, knew that in this particular case the usual treatment of cold packs, painkillers, and rest would be of little use. With his patient near death he decided the only way to save the man's life was to operate.

With blood transfusions and X rays unknown at the time, Williams had to work carefully but quickly. By cutting a small "trap door" in the ribs, he was able to see inside the chest cavity. The knife blade had nicked a blood vessel, and worse yet, the pericardium, the sac surrounding the heart, had also been damaged, showing a tear an inch and a quarter long. Williams quickly tied off the vessel to stop its bleeding and then proceeded to sew up the wound in the pericardium. It was tricky work, with the sac moving in time to the heartbeat as Williams managed to hold the tear closed tightly and stitch it up with a catgut suture. Fifty-one days later, Cornish left the hospital, a well man. He lived for another 20 years.

When news of the operation got out, "Dr. Dan" suddenly became famous. Williams, though, was too busy with his medical and supervisory duties to write up the operation for

Hospital founder and surgeon Daniel Hale Williams pioneered in the field of open heart surgery and founded the first training school for African-American nurses and the first hospital in the United States where black doctors could practice. *(Moorland-Spingarn Research Center)*

medical journals until three years later. Williams's fame and prestige grew even greater in 1894 when President Grover Cleveland appointed him surgeon-in-chief of Freedmen's General Hospital in Washington, D.C. Freedmen's had been established after the Civil War to provide medical care for newly freed slaves. By the time Williams took over the administrative duties of the facility, however, the hospital had deteriorated into a collection of ill-equipped and ill-kept buildings housing a disorganized and poorly trained staff. Under Williams's guidance, Freedmen's was reorganized and staffed with both black and white doctors. It also opened up

a new training program for nurses patterned after the program at Provident. Within a year of Williams's appointment, Freedmen's was showing a marked improvement as its death rate dropped and its reputation climbed.

During his stay at Freedmen's, Williams also helped to found the National Medical Association, a medical society for black doctors. At the time the American Medical Association (AMA), the nation's best-known medical association, refused to admit black physicians.

Feeling that he had done all that he could at Freedmen's and, discouraged by political clashes within the institution, Williams left

Washington to return to Chicago in 1897. Returning to Provident Hospital, Williams continued his busy career both as practicing physician and administrator. He also traveled around the country as adviser and visiting professor, lending his expertise and organizational abilities to such schools as the Meharry Medical College in Nashville, Tennessee, where he began holding surgery clinics in 1900.

In 1913, his association with St. Luke's Hospital in Chicago, a white hospital where he served as an associate-attending surgeon, caused friction with members of the staff at Provident. Williams regretfully decided to leave Provident shortly thereafter. Having helped to establish 40 hospitals across 20 states, Williams returned to private practice until his health began to fail. He suffered a stroke in 1926, two years after the death of his wife, Alice, whom he had married in 1898. Daniel Hale Williams died in Idlewild, Michigan, on August 4, 1931.

In 1970, a bill in the U.S. Congress issued a commemorative stamp in his honor.

Further Reading

Brown, Mitchell C. "Dr. Daniel Hale Williams," Faces of Science: African Americans in Science. Available online. http://www.princeton.edu/~mcbown/display/williams.html. Updated on June 4, 2000.

Hayden, Robert. *Eleven African-American Doctors*, rev. ed. New York: Twenty-First Century Books, 1992, 186–203.

Sullivan, Otha Richard. *African American Inventors*. Black Stars series, Jim Haskins, ed. New York: John Wiley & Sons, 1998.

Yount, Lisa. *Black Scientists*. New York: Facts On File, 1991, 1–13.

Woods, Geraldine Pittman
(1921–1999) *embryologist, science educator*

Geraldine Pittman Woods earned her doctorate in embryology at one of the best schools in the country—and later, as a science education consultant, she used that experience to conceive programs for increasing opportunities for minority students in the sciences and improving science teaching in minority colleges and universities.

Born on January 29, 1921, in West Palm Beach, Florida, Geraldine Pittman was the daughter of Susie King Pittman and Oscar Pittman. Her parents had established themselves comfortably with a farm, lumber mill, and real estate in central Florida, so young Jerry, as she was called, grew up feeling reasonably secure financially. She started school in an Episcopal private school but later transferred to the public high school. She showed no particular brilliance as a teenager—in fact she needed tutoring to keep her grades from falling. She liked science, but no one in her family really encouraged her interest because it seemed an unlikely career for an African-American young woman at the time. Her teenage years were filled with friends, church events, playing the piano, and reading—sobered, though, by the death of her father.

After graduating from high school in 1938, she entered college at Talladega College in Talladega, Alabama. In 1940 her mother was hospitalized in Johns Hopkins Hospital due to serious illness. Pittman transferred to Howard University in Washington, D.C., to be nearby. She also began to get much better grades. The Howard University faculty was supportive, and they encouraged her interest in science—and they helped her apply for graduate school. Pittman graduated with a bachelor of science degree in 1942.

When her mother was out of the hospital and on her way to recovery, Pittman moved to Cambridge, Massachusetts, for the challenges that lay ahead: graduate school in one of the toughest programs in the country, Radcliffe College (a women's college) and its associated institution, Harvard University (where most of the graduate classes were held). However, despite stiff competition from some of the best students in the country, she completed her M.S. degree in one year, obtaining that from Radcliffe in 1943. Two years later, in 1945, she had completed her Ph.D. in embryology from Harvard. She was also elected to the honorary society Phi Beta Kappa.

Pittman's doctoral research focused on the differentiation process that occurs in the spinal cord between the early stages of embryonic formation, when nerve cells are almost indistinguishable from other cells, and later stages, when nerve cells begin to become message carriers. Pittman wanted to find out whether this differentiation was controlled genetically or by stimulation from surrounding cells. Working with embryo chicks, she was able to show that the answer was that both are influential. And she also showed that the more muscle cells that were present, the more nerve cells became dedicated as muscle activators.

Pittman took a position as instructor at Howard University. However, she had taught for only one semester when she married Robert Woods, who was studying dentistry at Meharry Medical School in Nashville, Tennessee. They commuted between Nashville and Washington until Robert finished his degree. Then, they moved to California, where he planned to set up his practice with the help of friends, and Geraldine Pittman Woods took time out to raise a family.

The second chapter of Geraldine Woods's career began after her three children were teenagers. At first she did volunteer work for community organizations and civil rights groups around Los Angeles and later became involved in activities at the statewide level. She was a persuasive advocate for minority interests, and her capabilities were soon recognized on a national level. In 1965, she received an invitation to the White House from the first lady, Lady Bird Johnson. As a result, Woods helped organize Project Head Start, a federal program established to help preschool children from low-income families gain experiences with basic concepts—such as color, shape, and numbers—before starting school.

In 1969, Woods joined the National Institutes of Health as an educational consultant. There, she helped develop two programs, the Minority Biomedical Research Support (MBRS) and the Minority Access to Research Careers (MARC) programs. The MBRS program was a simple but effective concept. With clearer understanding of methods for writing effective grant applications, minority institutions would compete more successfully for government and philanthropic grants. Woods herself taught seminars all over the country as a part of this program. The MARC program established scholarships and funded visiting scholars programs. This gave faculty members at minority colleges and universities opportunities to teach and research at other institutions and allow a cross-flow of information and techniques.

Geraldine Pittman Woods and her husband retired to Aliso Viejo, California, in 1991. However, her efforts on behalf of minority science students continued to make a difference in many students' lives. Woods died on December 27, 1999, in Los Angeles.

Further Reading

Henderson, Ashyia N., ed. *Who's Who Among African Americans,* 14th ed. Gale Group, 2001, 1,478.

Kessler, James H., J. S. Kidd, Renee A. Kidd, and Katherine A. Morin. *Distinguished African American Scientists of the 20th Century.* Phoenix, Ariz.: Oryx Press, 1996.

Warren, Wini. *Black Women Scientists in the United States.* Bloomington: Indiana University Press, 1999, 193–195.

Woods, Granville T.

(1856–1910) *inventor*

Because Granville Woods invented a telegraph system that could compete with the one invented by contemporary Thomas Alva Edison,

Woods was often referred to as the "Black Edison." He also invented the "third rail" used in subway systems worldwide, as well as the trolley system, and he improved the automatic air brake.

Granville T. Woods was born on April 23, 1856, in Columbus, Ohio. Some sources say his parents came to the United States from Australia. Little else is known about his family and early life except that he had a brother and a sister and he left school at age 10. For the most part, he was self-taught. At age 16, he went to Missouri and landed a job as an engineer on the Danville and Southern Railroad. This early exposure to the railroad no doubt set his mind thinking about related devices that could be useful. He landed other odd jobs, including working in a rolling mill and aboard a British steamer.

Back in Ohio in 1881, he began to percolate some of the ideas he had come up with along the way. He designed and patented a better steam-boiler furnace in 1884. He also patented a telephone transmitter the same year, an improvement over Alexander Graham Bell's transmitter, invented about 10 years earlier.

In 1885, he conceived of a cross between a telephone and a telegraph—an invention that Bell's company bought from Woods.

In 1887, Woods came up with a telegraphic device for transmitting messages between moving trains. However, Edison challenged with a similar device he had designed. A court ruled that the design by Woods deserved the patent. With that victory to his credit, Woods secured the funding in the 1890s to form his own company, The Electrical Company, to market his inventions, including air brakes and an egg-hatching machine.

Woods took a major role in train electrification, overhead conducting systems for trolleys and trains, invented in 1888. He also invented the third rail, which carries the electricity and uses electromagnetic switches to move the train along.

Like GARRETT AUGUSTUS MORGAN, Woods encountered prejudice because he was African American. He circulated a story in *Cosmopolitan* magazine stating that he was descended from full-blooded savage Australian aborigines. Woods apparently believed that his inventions would not be accepted if it were known that he was an African American.

Woods's health began to fail when he was in his 50s, and he died in Harlem Hospital in New York on January 30, 1910. He was 53.

Further Reading

Aaseng, Nathan. *Black Inventors*. New York: Facts On File, 1997, 63–73.

"African-American Inventors and Inventions:/ Granville T. Woods." Available online. URL: http:/www.inventions.org/culture/african/gtwoods. html. Downloaded on February 19, 2001.

"Granville T. Woods," Inventors Online Museum. Available online. URL: http://www.inventorsmuseum. com/woods.htm. Downloaded on February 7, 2002.

Wright, Jane Cooke
(1919–   )   *cancer researcher*

At a time when surgery and radiotherapy were considered to be the only viable treatment choices for cancer, the Cancer Research Foundation—founded by LOUIS TOMPKINS WRIGHT and directed by his daughter Jane Cooke Wright—studied medicines and their effectiveness in treating cancer. Their work was the antecedent of today's chemotherapy.

On November 30, 1919, Jane Cooke Wright was born in New York City into a family of physicians. Her father, Louis Tompkins Wright, had been the first African-American physician to serve on the staff of any New York hospital, and he was the first black doctor to head a public interracial hospital. He was also a member of the American College of Surgeons, the first African American to have that honor since William Hale had helped to establish it.

Jane Wright attended high school in New York and then traveled north to Smith College, in Northampton, Massachusetts. For a time she considered painting as a career, but becoming a physician was a natural step. In fact, not only did she become a physician, but so did her younger sister Barbara. Jane Wright received her M.D. with honors in 1945 from New York Medical College, and she did her internship and residency at Bellevue. She would later credit her family's supportiveness for her success as a physician. She said in 1992, at her college reunion, "I am grateful that my family supported me in all my activities, counteracting the prevailing attitudes of gender and racial discriminations." She met and married David D. Jones, a lawyer, in 1947. (He died of a heart attack in 1976.)

In 1948, Louis Wright founded the Cancer Research Foundation at Harlem Hospital. The following year, he asked his daughter Jane to join him in his research. She accepted and became interested in his concepts of chemotherapy. The two worked side by side for several years until he died in 1952. At that point, she took his place as director of the foundation and moved the foundation to New York University Medical School.

During the course of her research, she and her colleagues at the foundation studied the effects of drugs on tumors and other abnormal growths. Among the drugs they tested were triethyene melamine, thriethylene phosphoramide, puromycin, adrenocorticotropic hormone (ACTH), and folic acid antagonists. Their efforts shed a new light on chemotherapy and its possibilities for positive results.

In 1964, Wright became one of the founding members of the American Society of Clinical Oncology. In 1967, she became professor and associate dean at New York Medical College, the highest post that had ever been attained by an African-American woman in medical administration. In 1975, when her deanship ended, she continued as professor of surgery at New York

Medical College. She also served as attending surgeon and consultant at various hospitals in the New York area until she retired in 1987.

Jane Wright has been recognized by many awards and honors. Her contributions to clinical cancer chemotherapy were recognized in 1975 by the American Association for Cancer Research. She was also included in a Smithsonian Institution exhibit, "Black Women Achievements Against the Odds," which was on display in 1983.

Wright served on the editorial board of the *Journal of the National Medical Association* and as a trustee of Smith College, as well as the New York City division of the American Cancer Association.

As director of the Cancer Research Foundation at Harlem Hospital and later at New York University Medical School, pioneer researcher Jane Cooke Wright led early investigations of chemotherapy and its possibilities for treating cancer. *(Smith College Archives, Smith College)*

Further Reading

"Wright, Jane C." *Current Biography,* New York: H. W. Wilson, 1968.

Warren, Wini. *Black Women Scientists in the United States.* Bloomington: Indiana University Press, 1999, 277–284.

Yount, Lisa. *Black Scientists.* New York: Facts On File, 1991, 67–79.

Wright, Louis Tompkins

(1891–1952) *surgeon, cancer researcher*

Louis Tompkins Wright—one of the first African Americans to graduate from Harvard Medical School, the first black physician on the medical staff of a New York City hospital, and the first black police surgeon—became an early pioneer in cancer chemotherapy. He went on to become head of surgery and president of Harlem Hospital's medical board, the first African-American physician to head a public interracial hospital. He was also a tireless activist with the National Association for the Advancement of Colored People (NAACP) in the campaign for equal health care for African Americans, and he served for 18 years as chair of that organization's board of directors.

Wright's father, Ceah Ketcham Wright, was a medical doctor who also became a minister in the Methodist Episcopal Church. Lula Tompkins, Louis's mother, had met Ceah when he visited St. Mary, Georgia, on church business. The two married when Ceah was 38 and Lula 17, and they had two boys, Carl (who died at the age of 10) and Louis, who was born in La Grange, Georgia, on July 23, 1891.

Louis barely had time to know his father. Ceah died of cancer when Louis was only three. At the time of his death, Ceah had become district superintendent of the Methodist Episcopal Church in Atlanta, Georgia, where he and Lula had a home. Forced to support herself and her two toddlers after Ceah's death, Lula accepted a job supervising and teaching sewing at a girls' dormitory at Clark University, where elementary, high school, and college-level classes were taught. It was a fortunate decision. The staff of teachers at Clark immediately took to young Louis, allowing him to enter first grade at the age of four while tutoring him on the side. This arrangement solved Lula's childcare problems during the day and gave Louis a solid start on his education. The family's financial security also improved in 1899, when his mother met and married William Fletcher Penn, a distinguished physician and the first African American to graduate from Yale Medical School. Valuing education and taking to Louis as his own son, Penn encouraged young Wright to pursue excellence in his studies. He also encouraged Louis to join him on many of his medical rounds. It was during these rounds in the family car that Louis first experienced the angry hatred of white racists. Dr. Penn's shiny Cadillac was the first automobile to be owned by a black man in the city of Atlanta and when his rounds took him through white neighborhoods, he and young Wright were often stoned by angry, bigoted whites. During the Atlanta Riots of 1907, while still a teenager, Wright was forced to defend his family's home with a loaded rifle as white citizens threatened to attack. He and his family escaped lynching by hiding in a friendly white neighbor's home.

Following in both his father and stepfather's footsteps, Wright became a brilliant student. He earned his undergraduate degree at the top of his class at Clark in 1911 and enrolled in Harvard Medical in Massachusetts in 1915. Although he made some close friends at Harvard, he also became aware of racial prejudices in the north, both in school and out. During his third year at Harvard, he helped form a picket line to protest the showing of the movie *The Birth of a Nation* in the city of Boston. Claiming to be an American epic, this early silent film glorified the efforts of the Ku Klux Klan and portrayed African Americans as ignorant, barbaric, and violent.

After graduating from Harvard in 1915, he served a two-year internship at Freedmen's Hospital in Washington, D.C., and then returned briefly to Atlanta to join his stepfather's practice.

In 1917, as World War I raged, Wright joined the U.S. Army Medical Corps. He married Corinne Cooke of New York City in 1918, one month before he left for France, where he served in a field hospital. During a gas assault under enemy attack, he sustained lung damage that troubled him for the rest of his life. Awarded the Purple Heart, he was discharged from the army in 1919.

Like many American veterans returning from the war Wright was anxious to return to normal life. He and Corinne settled in New York City where Wright took a position at Harlem Hospital. At that time, Harlem's population was primarily white, and Wright became the hospital's first African-American physician. There Wright began to specialize in surgery. Struggling against the doubts of many of his white colleagues, he proved himself an outstanding surgeon, and he was invited to join the prestigious American College of Surgeons in 1934—the only black surgeon to become a charter member. Concurrent with his work at the hospital and beginning in 1929, Wright also took an appointment as police surgeon for the New York City Police Department, the first black surgeon to hold such a post. He served in that position for more than 20 years.

In the early 1940s; Wright began researching treatments for cancer, and in 1948, partially under a grant from the National Cancer Institute, he founded the Harlem Hospital Cancer Research Foundation. There, he began his research into the use of chemotherapy (the use of chemical agents to treat or control disease) to fight the growth of cancerous cells. Writing more than 100 published peer-reviewed scientific papers during his distinguished career, Louis T. Wright pioneered the concept of chemotherapy at a time when many in the medical community questioned its efficacy. Up until the 1940s, many cancer treatments involved removing tumors by applying corrosive acids, arsenic paste, or even pulverized toads. Doses of hormones had sometimes succeeded in treating cancer, and surgical removal also had been used. But little use had been made of administering drugs to attack tumors.

During this time, Wright also campaigned for improved quality in medical care for African Americans. He consistently attacked discrimination and fought against the convention of segregated hospitals for whites and blacks. In 1937, under his leadership, the NAACP established a national program to end discrimination in health care, and within two years chapters nationwide had made significant strides to implement the program. In 1940, Wright received the Spingarn Medal for his work in this arena.

Despite his active professional life, Wright also found time to encourage his two daughters in their academic pursuits. Joining the family line of distinguished physicians, one of his daughters, JANE COOKE WRIGHT, joined him at the Cancer Research Foundation in 1949 and continued his research after his death. His other daughter, Barbara Penn Wright, also became a physician.

On October 8, 1952, Louis Wright died of a heart attack. He was 61. Both the Louis T. Wright Memorial Library and the Louis T. Wright Surgical Building at Harlem Hospital are dedicated to his memory.

Further Reading

"Louis T. Wright" *Contemporary Black Biography*, Vol. 4. Detroit: Gale Research, 1993.

Cook, Jane Stewart. "Louis T. Wright," *Notable Black American Scientists*. Kristine, Krapp, ed. Detroit: Gale Research, 1999, 328–329.

"Louis T. Wright," (obituary). *New York Times*, October 9, 1952, 31.

Reynolds, P. Preston. "Dr. Louis T. Wright and the NAACP: Pioneers in Hospital Racial Integration." *American Journal of Public Health* 90, no. 6 (June 2000): 883–892.

Y

Young, Roger Arliner
(1889–1964) *zoologist*

The first African-American woman to earn a doctorate in zoology, Roger Arliner Young was also the first black woman to publish research in that field. Working with biologist ERNEST EVERETT JUST, she investigated the structures controlling salt concentration in *Paramecium*. She also experimented with direct and indirect radiation on sea urchin eggs and published those results.

Roger Arliner Young was born in Clifton Forge, Virginia, in 1889. She grew up in Burgettstown, Pennsylvania, and in 1916, she enrolled at Howard University in Washington, D.C. The first science course she took at Howard was taught by the distinguished biologist Ernest Everett Just, who was head of the biology department. Just became her mentor, overseeing her recovery from poor grades she received in her early coursework. Young earned her B.S. from Howard in 1923, and she accepted a position on the faculty at Howard as assistant professor of zoology. The following year she entered graduate school at the University of Chicago, where she became a part-time student, with the aid of funding that Just helped her secure. By now, her grades were greatly improved, and her first published article had already appeared, "On the Excretory Apparatus in *Paramecium*," published in *Science* in September 1924. In 1926, she completed her master's degree in zoology and received the distinction of being elected to Sigma Xi, the science honorary society.

She was able to spend summers from 1927 to 1936 conducting research at the Marine Biological Laboratories in Woods Hole, Massachusetts, the prestigious laboratory where Just also did summer research for many years. She spent several summers working with him on his experiments with marine organism fertilization processes. Additionally, she performed some work on dehydration and hydration in living cells. Her skills and insights grew keener, and Just remarked that she was "a real genius in zoology."

By early 1929, though, Just began to take leaves of absence from Howard to pursue research opportunities in Europe. While he was gone, Young took his place temporarily as department chair. In the fall of 1929, Young went to the University of Chicago to begin work on her Ph.D. Frank Lillie, an embryologist who had mentored Just at Woods Hole years before, was to be her adviser. However, she failed her qualifying examinations in early 1930. She was crushed and embarrassed and broke. She disappeared for a time. Finally, she turned up again at Howard and continued teaching. She also continued going to Woods Hole to conduct research in the summers, but the relationship with Just was not the same.

By 1933, rumors of romance between Just and Young began to make the situation uncomfortable, and finally they had a blowout confrontation in 1935. She was fired from her position at Howard University the following year. The stated reason: too many missed classes and mistreatment of laboratory equipment.

However, Young succeeded in continuing her research without Howard University and without Just. Between 1935 and 1938, she published four papers. She also returned to graduate school, studying for her doctorate at the University of Pennsylvania under L. V. Heilbrunn, whom she had met at Woods Hole. In 1940, she received her Ph.D., becoming the first African-American woman to do so in her field. Her dissertation title was *The Indirect Effects of Roentgen Rays on Certain Marine Eggs*.

Young secured various teaching positions in the 1940s and 1950s. From 1940 to 1947, she taught at North Carolina College for Negroes and at Shaw University in Raleigh, North Carolina, moving on to black colleges in Texas, Louisiana, and Mississippi in the later years.

In the late 1950s, in Mississippi, she entered the State Mental Asylum. Finally, in 1962, she was able to leave the hospital and she went to teach at Southern University in New Orleans. Roger Arliner Young died on November 9, 1964.

Further Reading

Hammond, Evelynn M. "Young, Roger Arliner," *Facts On File Encyclopedia of Black Women in America: Science, Health, and Medicine*, by Darlene Clark Hine, ed. New York: Facts On File, 1997, 132.

Warren, Wini. *Black Women Scientists in the United States*. Bloomington: Indiana University Press, 1999, 287–295.

Young, R. A. "On the Excretory Apparatus in *Paramecium*," *Science* (September 12, 1924): 244.

BIBLIOGRAPHY AND RECOMMENDED SOURCES

Aaseng, Nathan. *Black Inventors.* New York: Facts On File, 1997.

American Men and Women of Science, 1998–99. 20th ed. New Providence, N.J.: R. R. Bowker, 1999.

Blacks, Science, and American Education, edited by Willie Pearson, Jr., and H. Kenneth Bechtel. New Brunswick, N.J.: Rutgers University Press, 1989.

Brodie, James Michael. *Created Equal: The Lives and Ideas of Black American Innovators.* New York: William Morrow, 1993.

Brown, Mitchell C. Faces of Science: African Americans in the Sciences. Available online. URL: http://www.princeton.edu/~mcbrown/ display/faces.html.

Burns, Khephra, and Miles, William. *Black Stars in Orbit: NASA's African-American Astronauts.* San Diego: Harcourt Brace, 1995.

Contemporary Black Biography. Detroit: Gale Research, 1993.

Goldsmith, Donald. *The Astronomers.* New York: St. Martin's Press, 1991.

Hawkins, Walter L. *African American Biographies: Profiles of 558 Current Men and Women.* Jefferson, N.C.: McFarland & Co., 1992.

———. *African American Biographies, 2: Profiles of 332 Current Men and Women.* Jefferson, N.C.: McFarland & Co., 1994.

Hayden, Robert. *Eleven African-American Doctors,* revised edition. New York: Twenty-First Century Books, 1992.

———. *Nine African-American Inventors.* New York: Twenty-First Century Books, 1992.

———. *Seven African-American Scientists.* Brookfield, Conn.: Twenty-First Century Books, 1992.

Henrion, Claudia. "Double Jeopardy: Gender and Race," *Women in Mathematics: The Addition of Difference.* Bloomington: Indiana University Press, 1997.

Hine, Darlene C. *Facts On File Encyclopedia of Black Women in America: Science, Health, and Medicine.* New York: Facts On File, 1997.

Hubbard, Philip G. *New Dawns: A 150-Year Look at Human Rights at the University of Iowa.* Iowa City: University of Iowa Press, 1996.

Inventors Assistance League. Available online. URL: http://www.inventions.org/culture/ african/ matzeliger.html.

Inventors Museum, 1999. Available online. URL: http://www.inventorsmuseum.com.

Kessler, James H., J. S. Kidd, Renee A. Kidd, and Katherine A. Morin. *Distinguished African American Scientists of the 20th Century.* Phoenix, Ariz.: Oryx Press, 1996.

Krapp, Kristine, ed. *Notable Black American Scientists.* Detroit: Gale Research, 1990.

Manning, Kenneth R. *Black Apollo of Science: The Life of Ernest Everett Just.* New York: Oxford University Press, 1983.

Pearson, Willie. *Black Scientists, White Society, and Colorless Science: A Study of Universalism in American Science.* Millwood, N.Y.: Associated Faculty Press, 1985.

Sammons, Vivian O. *Blacks in Science and Education.* Washington, D.C.: Hemisphere Publishers, 1989.

————. *Blacks in Science and Medicine.* New York: Hemisphere Publishing, 1990.

Sullivan, Otha Richard. *African American Inventors.* Black Stars series, Jim Haskins, ed. New York: John Wiley & Sons, 1998.

U.S. Department of Energy. *Black Contributors to Science and Energy Technology.* DOE/OPA-0035. Washington, D.C.: Office of Public Affairs, 1979.

Warren, Wini. *Black Women Scientists in the United States.* Bloomington: Indiana University Press, 1999.

Who's Who Among African Americans, 14th ed. Detroit: Gale Group, 2001.

Williams, Scott W. Astronomers of the African Diaspora. Available online. URL: http://www.math.buffalo.edu/mad/physics/astronomy-peeps.html.

————. Computer Scientists of the African Diaspora. Available online. URL: http://www.math.buffalo.edu/mad/computer-science/computer_science.html.

————. Mathematicians of the African Diaspora. The Mathematics Department of the State University of New York at Buffalo. Available online. URL: http://www.math.buffalo.edu/mad/.

————. Physicists of the African Diaspora. Available online. URL: http://www.math.buffalo.edu/mad/physics/physics.html.

Yount, Lisa. *A to Z of Women in Science and Math.* New York: Facts On File, 1999.

————. *Black Scientists.* New York: Facts On File, 1991.

Entries by Area of Activity

AEROSPACE ENGINEERING
Darden, Christine Mann
Gillam, Isaac Thomas, IV
Harris, Wesley Leroy

AGRICULTURAL RESEARCH
Carver, George Washington

AGRONOMY
Hill, Walter Andrew

ANALYTICAL CHEMISTRY
Macklin, John W.
Mitchell, James Winfield
Tolbert, Margaret Ellen
    Mayo

ANATOMY
Cobb, William Montague
Lloyd, Ruth Smith
McKinney, Roscoe Lewis

ASTRONAUTICS
Bolden, Charles Frank, Jr.
Gregory, Frederick Drew
Harris, Bernard Anthony, Jr.
Jemison, Mae Carol
McNair, Ronald Erwin

ASTRONOMY
Banneker, Benjamin

Peery, Benjamin Franklin
Tyson, Neil de Grasse

ASTROPHYSICS
Carruthers, George Robert
McAfee, Walter Samuel
Rouse, Carl Albert
Tyson, Neil de Grasse

ATMOSPHERIC SCIENCE
Francisco, Joseph
    Salvadore, Jr.

BACTERIOLOGY
Buggs, Charles Wesley

BIOCHEMISTRY
Carver, George Washington
Chappelle, Emmett
Daly, Marie Maynard
Harris, Don Navarro
West, Harold Dadford

BIOLOGY
Craft, Thomas, Sr.
Harris, Bernard
    Anthony, Jr.
Haynes, John Kermit
Just, Ernest Everett
Nabrit, Samuel Milton
Young, Roger Arliner

BOTANY
Henderson, James Henry
    Meriwether

CANCER RESEARCH
Wright, Jane Cooke
Wright, Louis Tompkins

CELL BIOLOGY
Cobb, Jewel Plummer
Langford, George Malcolm
Murray, Sandra

CELL PHYSIOLOGY
Cobb, Jewel Plummer

CHEMICAL ENGINEERING
Green, Harry James, Jr.
Hawkins, Walter Lincoln

CHEMISTRY
Anderson, Gloria Long
Bramwell, Fitzgerald Burton
Branson, Herman
Ferguson, Lloyd Noel
Harris, James Andrew
Hill, Henry Aaron
Hill, Mary Elliott
Hunter, John McNeile
King, Reatha Belle Clark
Knox, William Jacob, Jr.

Lu Valle, James Ellis
McBay, Henry Ransom Cecil
Milligan, Dolphus Edward
Quarterman, Lloyd Albert
Rillieux, Norbert
Russell, Edwin Roberts

**COMMUNICATIONS
    ENGINEERING**
Cannon, Thomas Calvin, Jr.

COMPUTER SCIENCE
Dean, Mark
Easley, Annie
Emeagwali, Philip
Gourdine, Meredith Charles

ELECTRICAL ENGINEERING
Hubbard, Philip Gamaliel
Slaughter, John Brooks

EMBRYOLOGY
Woods, Geraldine Pittman

ENDOCRINOLOGY
Henry, Walter Lester, Jr.

ENGINEERING
Bluford, Guion Stewart, Jr.
Crosthwait, David
    Nelson, Jr.
Davis, Stephen Smith
Gregory, Frederick Drew

ENGINEERING PHYSICS
Kornegay, Wade M.

ENTOMOLOGY
Chambers, Vivian Murray
Turner, Charles Henry

FOOD CHEMISTRY
Hall, Lloyd Augustus

GENETICS
Harris, Mary Styles

GEOLOGY AND GEOPHYSICS
Bromery, Randolph Wilson
Person, Waverly

IMMUNOLOGY
Amos, Harold

INDUSTRIAL CHEMISTRY
Cooke, Lloyd Miller

INVENTION
Alcorn, George Edward, Jr.
Barnes, William Harry
Beard, Andrew Jackson
Blair, Henry
Boykin, Otis Frank
Bradley, Benjamin
Carruthers, George Robert
Croslin, Michael
Dean, Mark
Gourdine, Meredith Charles
Gregory, Frederick Drew
Hall, Lloyd Augustus
Henry, Warren Elliott
Jones, Frederick McKinney
Latimer, Lewis Howard
Logan, Joseph Granville, Jr.
Matzeliger, Jan Ernst
McCoy, Elijah
Morgan, Garrett Augustus
Parker, John P.
Rillieux, Norbert
Roberts, Louis Wright
Russell, Edwin Roberts
Shaw, Earl D.
Temple, Lewis, Sr.
Walker, Sarah Breedlove
    McWilliams
Woods, Granville T.

MARINE BIOLOGY
Jearld, Ambrose, Jr.
Owens, Joan Murrell

MATHEMATICS
Banneker, Benjamin
Bharucha-Reid, Albert Turner
Blackwell, David Harold
Browne, Marjorie Lee
Cox, Elbert Frank
Darden, Christine Mann
Deconge-Watson, Mary
    Lovinia
Falconer, Etta Zuber
Granville, Evelyn Boyd Collins
Johnson, Katherine G.
Jones, Eleanor Green Dawley
Mayes, Vivienne Lucille
    Malone
Mishoe, Luna Isaac
Okikiolu, Kathleen Adebola
Roberts, Louis Wright
Wilkins, J. Ernest, Jr.

MEDICAL RESEARCH
Ferguson, Angella Dorothea
Harris, Bernard Anthony, Jr.
Hinton, William Augustus
Kountz, Samuel Lee, Jr.
Leevy, Carroll Moton
Leffall, LaSalle D., Jr.

MEDICINE
Calloway, Nathaniel Oglesby
Elders, Joycelyn
Jemison, Mae Carol
Leevy, Carroll Moton
Wright, Louis Tompkins

METEOROLOGY
Bacon-Bercey, June
Washington, Warren Morton

MICROBIOLOGY
Amos, Harold
Brooks, Carolyn Branch
Brown, Russell Wilfred
Fuller, Almyra Oveta
Jay, James Monroe
Taylor, Welton Ivan

MOLECULAR PHYSICS
Coleman, John William

NEUROLOGY
Fuller, Solomon Carter

NEUROPHARMACOLOGY
Hudson, Roy Davage

NUTRITION
Edwards, Cecile Hoover
Kittrell, Flemmie Pansy

OCEANOGRAPHY
Forde, Evan B.

ORGANIC CHEMISTRY
Barnes, Robert Percy
Calloway, Nathaniel Oglesby
Dorman, Linneaus Cuthbert
Evans, Slayton Alvin, Jr.
Gillyard, Cornelia Denson
Julian, Percy Lavon
Massie, Samuel Proctor

PALEONTOLOGY
Owens, Joan Murrell

PARASITOLOGY
Eure, Herman

PATHOLOGY
Lewis, Julian Herman

PHARMACOLOGY
Maloney, Arnold Hamilton

PHYSICAL CHEMISTRY
Henry, Warren Elliott
King, James, Jr.

PHYSICAL SCIENCE
Francisco, Joseph Salvadore, Jr.

PHYSICS
Alcorn, George Edward, Jr.
Bouchet, Edward Alexander
Bragg, Robert Henry
Branson, Herman
Henry, Warren Elliott
Hunter, John McNeile
Imes, Elmer Samuel
Jackson, Shirley Ann
Johnson, Katherine G.
Lawson, James Raymond
Logan, Joseph Granville, Jr.
Massey, Walter Eugene
McNair, Ronald Erwin
Mickens, Ronald Elbert
Peery, Benjamin Franklin
Roberts, Louis Wright
Shaw, Earl D.
Slaughter, John Brooks
Washington, Warren Morton

PHYSIOLOGY
Dunbar, Joseph Chatman, Jr.
Franklin, Renty Benjamin
Just, Ernest Everett
Lewis, Julian Herman

PLANT PHYSIOLOGY
Henderson, James Henry
      Meriwether

RADIATION PHYSICS
Earls, Julian Manly

RESEARCH MATHEMATICS
Hunt, Fern Y.

SCIENCE ADMINISTRATION
Earls, Julian Manly
Elders, Joycelyn
Gillam, Isaac Thomas, IV
King, Reatha Belle Clark
Massey, Walter Eugene
Slaughter, John Brooks
Tolbert, Margaret Ellen
      Mayo

SCIENCE EDUCATION
Bramwell, Fitzgerald Burton
Branson, Herman
Brooks, Carolyn
      Branch
Cobb, Jewel Plummer
Davis, Stephen Smith
Falconer, Etta Zuber
Haynes, John Kermit
Henry, Warren Elliott
Hubbard, Philip Gamaliel
Hunter, John McNeile
Jones, Eleanor Green
      Dawley
Kittrell, Flemmie Pansy
Lawson, James Raymond
Massie, Samuel Proctor
Murray, Sandra
Walker, Arthur Bertram
      Cuthbert, Jr.
West, Harold Dadford
Woods, Geraldine Pittman

SOLAR PHYSICS
Walker, Arthur Bertram
      Cuthbert, Jr.

STRUCTURAL GEOLOGY
Gipson, Mack, Jr.

SURGERY
Barnes, William Harry
Drew, Charles Richard
Kountz, Samuel Lee, Jr.
Leffall, LaSalle D., Jr.

Williams, Daniel Hale

THEORETICAL PHYSICS
Lewis, Harold Ralph

ZOOLOGY
Just, Ernest Everett
Turner, Charles Henry
Young, Roger Arliner

PRESTON RIDGE LIBRARY
COLLIN COLLEGE
FRISCO, TX 75035

Entries by Year of Birth

1700–1799
Banneker, Benjamin

1800–1849
Beard, Andrew Jackson
Blair, Henry
Bradley, Benjamin
Latimer, Lewis Howard
McCoy, Elijah
Parker, John P.
Rillieux, Norbert
Temple, Lewis

1850–1859
Bouchet, Edward
    Alexander
Matzeliger, Jan Ernst
Williams, Daniel Hale
Woods, Granville T.

1860–1869
Carver, George Washington
Turner, Charles Henry
Walker, Sarah Breedlove
    McWilliams

1870–1879
Fuller, Solomon Carter
Morgan, Garrett Augustus

1880–1889
Barnes, William Harry
Hinton, William Augustus
Imes, Elmer Samuel
Just, Ernest Everett
Maloney, Arnold Hamilton
Young, Roger Arliner

1890–1899
Barnes, Robert Percy
Cox, Elbert Frank
Crosthwait, David Nelson, Jr.
Hall, Lloyd Augustus
Jones, Frederick McKinney
Julian, Percy Lavon
Lewis, Julian Herman
Wright, Louis Tompkins

1900–1904
Chambers, Vivian Murray
Cobb, William Montague
Drew, Charles Richard
Hunter, John McNeile
Kittrell, Flemmie Pansy
Knox, William Jacob, Jr.
McKinney, Roscoe Lewis
West, Harold Dadford

1905–1909
Brown, Russell Wilfred
Buggs, Charles Wesley

Calloway, Nathaniel Oglesby
Henry, Warren Elliott
Hill, Mary Elliott
Nabrit, Samuel Milton

1910–1914
Branson, Herman
Browne, Marjorie Lee
Davis, Stephen Smith
Green, Harry James, Jr.
Hawkins, Walter Lincoln
Lu Valle, James Ellis
McAfee, Walter Samuel
McBay, Henry Ransom Cecil
Roberts, Louis Wright
Russell, Edwin Roberts

1915–1919
Amos, Harold
Blackwell, David Harold
Bragg, Robert Henry
Cooke, Lloyd Miller
Ferguson, Lloyd Noel
Henderson, James Henry
    Meriwether
Henry, Walter Lester, Jr.
Hill, Henry Aaron
Johnson, Katherine G.
Lawson, James Raymond
Lloyd, Ruth Smith
Massie, Samuel Proctor

Mishoe, Luna Isaac
Quarterman, Lloyd Albert
Taylor, Welton Ivan
Wright, Jane Cooke

1920–1924
Boykin, Otis Frank
Cobb, Jewel Plummer
Craft, Thomas, Sr.
Daly, Marie Maynard
Granville, Evelyn Boyd Collins
Hubbard, Philip Gamaliel
Leevy, Carroll Moton
Logan, Joseph Granville, Jr.
Peery, Benjamin Franklin
Wilkins, J. Ernest, Jr.
Woods, Geraldine Pittman

1925–1929
Bharucha-Reid, Albert Turner
Bromery, Randolph Wilson
Chappelle, Emmett
Coleman, John William
Edwards, Cecile Hoover
Ferguson, Angella Dorothea
Gourdine, Meredith Charles
Harris, Don Navarro
Jay, James Monroe
Jones, Eleanor Green Dawley
Milligan, Dolphus Edward
Person, Waverly
Rouse, Carl Albert

1930–1934
Bacon-Bercey, June
Croslin, Michael
Deconge-Watson, Mary Lovinia

Easley, Annie
Elders, Joycelyn
Falconer, Etta Zuber
Gillam, Isaac Thomas, IV
Gipson, Mack, Jr.
Harris, James Andrew
Hudson, Roy Davage
King, James, Jr.
Kornegay, Wade M.
Kountz, Samuel Lee, Jr.
Leffall, LaSalle D., Jr.
Lewis, Harold Ralph
Mayes, Vivienne Lucille
    Malone
Owens, Joan Murrell
Slaughter, John Brooks

1935–1939
Anderson, Gloria Long
Carruthers, George Robert
Dorman, Linneaus Cuthbert
King, Reatha Belle Clark
Macklin, John W.
Massey, Walter Eugene
Shaw, Earl D.
Walker, Arthur Bertram
    Cuthbert, Jr.
Washington, Warren Morton

1940–1944
Alcorn, George Edward, Jr.
Bluford, Guion Stewart, Jr.
Cannon, Thomas Calvin, Jr.
Darden, Christine Mann
Dunbar, Joseph Chatman, Jr.
Earls, Julian Manly
Evans, Slayton Alvin, Jr.

Gillyard, Cornelia Denson
Gregory, Frederick Drew
Harris, Wesley Leroy
Haynes, John Kermit
Jearld, Ambrose, Jr.
Langford, George Malcolm
Mickens, Ronald Elbert
Mitchell, James Winfield
Tolbert, Margaret Ellen
    Mayo

1945–1949
Bolden, Charles Frank, Jr.
Bramwell, Fitzgerald Burton
Brooks, Carolyn Branch
Eure, Herman
Franklin, Renty Benjamin
Harris, Mary Styles
Hill, Walter Andrew
Hunt, Fern Y.
Jackson, Shirley Ann
Murray, Sandra

1950–1959
Dean, Mark
Emeagwali, Philip
Forde, Evan B.
Francisco, Joseph
    Salvadore, Jr.
Fuller, Almyra Oveta
Harris, Bernard Anthony, Jr.
Jemison, Mae Carol
McNair, Ronald Erwin
Tyson, Neil de Grasse

1960–1969
Okikiolu, Kathleen Adebola

Boldface locators indicate main entries. *Italic* locators indicate photographs.

COLLIN COUNTY COMMUNITY COLLEGE

3 1702 00258 8733

Learning Resources Center
Collin County Community College District
PRESTON RIDGE CAMPUS
Frisco, Texas 75035

Q
141
S6285
2003

Spangenburg, Ray,
1939-

African Americans in
science, math, and
tion.

$45.00